FIELDS OF FIRE:
THE CANADIANS IN NORMANDY

Second Edition

With *Fields of Fire*, Terry Copp challenges the conventional view that the Canadian contribution to the Battle of Normandy was a 'failure' – that the allies won only through the use of brute force, and that the Canadian soldiers and commanding officers were essentially incompetent. His detailed and impeccably researched analysis of what actually happened on the battlefield portrays a flexible, innovative army that made a major, and successful, contribution to the defeat of the German forces in just seventy-six days.

Challenging both existing interpretations of the campaign and current approaches to military history, Copp examines the Battle of Normandy, tracking the soldiers over the battlefield terrain and providing an account of each operation carried out by the Canadian army. In so doing, he illustrates the valour, skill, and commitment of the Allied citizen-soldier in the face of a well-entrenched and well-equipped enemy army.

This edition of Copp's best-selling, award-winning history includes a new introduction that examines the strategic background of the Battle of Normandy.

(The Joanne Goodman Lectures)

TERRY COPP is a professor emeritus of history at Wilfrid Laurier University and co-director of the Laurier Centre for Military Strategic and Disarmament Studies. The author of a number of books on the Canadian role in the Second World War, including *Cinderella Army*, he was the chief researcher and on-camera historian for the television series *No Price Too High* and wrote the book of the san

FIELDS OF FIRE

The Canadians in Normandy

Second Edition

The 1998 Joanne Goodman Lectures

TERRY COPP

UNIVERSITY OF TORONTO PRESS
Toronto Buffalo London

© University of Toronto Press 2014
Toronto Buffalo London
www.utppublishing.com

First edition published in 2003 (hardcover).
First edition reprinted in paperback in 2004 (Jul), (Dec), 2005, 2006, 2007, 2010

Printed in the U.S.A.

ISBN 978-1-4426-2655-3

Printed on acid-free paper

Library and Archives Canada Cataloguing in Publication

Copp, Terry, 1938–, author
Fields of fire : the Canadians in Normandy / Terry Copp. – Second edition.

(The 1998 Joanne Goodman lectures)
Includes new introduction.
Includes bibliographical references and index.
ISBN 978-1-4426-2655-3 (pbk.)

1. Canada. Canadian Army – History – World War, 1939–1945.
2. World War, 1939–1945 – Campaigns – France – Normandy.   I. Title.
II. Series: Joanne Goodman lectures ; 1998

D756.5.N6C657 2014   940.54'21421   C2014-901501-1

University of Toronto Press acknowledges the financial assistance to its
publishing program of the Canada Council for the Arts and the Ontario
Arts Council.

 Canada Council   Conseil des Arts
for the Arts   du Canada

ONTARIO ARTS COUNCIL
CONSEIL DES ARTS DE L'ONTARIO
50 YEARS OF ONTARIO GOVERNMENT SUPPORT OF THE ARTS
50 ANS DE SOUTIEN DU GOUVERNEMENT DE L'ONTARIO AUX ARTS

University of Toronto Press acknowledges the financial support of the
Government of Canada through the Canada Book Fund for its publishing
activities.

The Joanne Goodman Lecture Series

has been established by Joanne's family

and friends to perpetuate the memory of her

blithe spirit, her quest for knowledge, and

the rewarding years she spent at the

University of Western Ontario.

Contents

Illustrations follow page 154

Maps

Introduction to the Second Edition

The first edition of *Fields of Fire* and its sequel, *Cinderella Army*, offered a new interpretation of the Canadian role in the liberation of Normandy and Northwest Europe. The argument – that 'the achievement of the Allied and especially the Canadian armies ... has been greatly underrated while the effectiveness of the German army was greatly exaggerated' – has had some impact on subsequent research contributing modestly to a less theoretical, evidence-based approach to military history.[1] Concentrating on Canadian operations and tactics left little room for a discussion of the ways in which strategic decisions influenced the campaign and the Canadian experience. This prologue to the second edition, published for the 70th anniversary of D-Day, is intended to fill that gap.

The best way of approaching the broader strategic issues is to focus on the question: Why were the Allies able to defeat two German armies – more than half a million combat troops – in just seventy-six days? No one who attended the pre-invasion briefing at St. Paul's School in London[2] would have predicated a victory so rapid and complete that it would force the enemy to abandon the occupation of France and Belgium as well as Normandy in less than four months.

The sudden collapse of German resistance surprised Allied commanders who had begun to worry that the stalemate, imposed by the enemy, was creating an Allied manpower crisis particularly in the British and Canadian armies. Their various sources of intelligence, including Ultra, failed to provide evidence of the far graver crisis confronting the Germans who had received few replacements and insufficient reinforcements.

Historians often find it difficult to decide where to begin their accounts, but if we wish to analyse the impact of strategic planning on the Allied victory in Normandy we can start in January 1943 at the Casablanca Conference.[3] The conference, code-named 'Symbol,' was the first of five attempts to coordinate the strategy of the American, British, and Soviet governments in 1943. While it can be argued that it was not until the meeting with Stalin in Teheran, 28 November 1943, that final agreement was reached, the essential elements of pre-Overlord strategy were decided at Casablanca.

After Hitler declared war on the United States in December 1941, the American Chiefs of Staff were confronted with a dilemma. Public and congressional opinion demanded action against Japan but the military planners knew that a German victory in Europe – not the temporary success of the Japanese forces in the Pacific – was the more serious threat to American interests. On 6 March 1942, the U.S. Chiefs of Staff outlined a 'Europe First' strategy in a document known as the Marshall Memorandum because it expressed the views of General George C. Marshall, the U.S. Army's Chief of Staff and President Roosevelt's senior military adviser. The memorandum called for the rapid build-up of American and British Commonwealth forces in the United Kingdom in preparation for the invasion of France in 1943 known as Operation Roundup.[4]

Initially, the British prime minister and his military advisers appeared to agree but in June 1942 Winston Churchill arrived in Washington with a plan to launch other operations in 1942. He proposed the invasion of French North Africa and if possible an attack on Norway. North Africa, Churchill argued, was the true Second Front of 1942.[5] This operation, originally known as Gymnast but carried out as Torch, appealed to President Roosevelt who wished to get American troops into action against Germany in 1942 – preferably before the mid-term congressional elections in early November. The final plan was a compromise between those who sought to build a firm base in Morocco and Algeria and those who argued for the early capture of Tunisia to prevent the Axis powers from sending reinforcements to North Africa.[6]

When Churchill, Roosevelt, and their military advisers met at Casablanca, the consequences of the decision for Torch had become clear. The Allies had failed to reach Tunis before substantial Italian and German reinforcements had arrived and a combination of enemy resistance and winter rains had created a temporary stalemate. There no longer seemed to be any realistic possibility of invading France in 1943 and discussion focussed on alternate strategies.[7]

The British chiefs of staff and prime minister came to Casablanca energized by their victory at El Alamein, with a coherent strategic plan that sought 'to concentrate on the defeat of Germany, diverting only the minimum force necessary to contain Japan.' This was to be accomplished by: giving priority to the defeat of the U-boats, which, in the winter of 1942–3, threatened the Atlantic lifeline as never before; expanding the Anglo-American bomber offensive; increasing lend-lease supplies to Russia; and continuing operations in the Mediterranean to knock Italy out of the war and persuade Turkey to join the Allies.[8]

Churchill insisted that the build-up for Roundup should continue but when the conference adopted the British proposals and agreed to the invasion of Sicily in 1943, the Americans shifted resources to the Pacific theatre, abandoning the possibility of invading France in 1943. We therefore need to ask if the success of Overlord in 1944 was largely due to the endurance and growing offensive capacity of the Soviet armies, culminating in the great offensive of June 1944, Operation Bagration. Certainly this is the view of many prominent historians including Richard Overy who argues that 'the great paradox of the Second World War is that democracy was saved by the exertions of communism.'[9]

We can clarify the issue by quantifying the degree to which the Germany army and air force were committed to the Eastern Front in 1943 and 1944. On the eve of Operation Citadel, the last German offensive in the east, July 1943, 193 or 70 per cent of German field divisions were committed to the defeat of the Soviet Union. This percentage of German divisions in the east declined to between 60 and 65 per cent by the end of the year and by April 1944 just over half, 53 per cent, of the army was deployed on the Eastern Front.[10] The German air force, the Luftwaffe, was less heavily involved in the east for reasons we will shortly explore. Perhaps 40 per cent of the Luftwaffe front line strength was committed to the campaign in Russia through the summer of 1943 but subsequently the number declined to 30 to 35 per cent.[11]

Casualties are another quantitative measure and while there are different ways of calculating both absolute numbers and rates, there is no doubt that between June 1941 and the end of the war at least two-thirds of all losses suffered by the German land forces were incurred on the Eastern Front.[12] Despite heavy losses approaching one million men in 1943, the German army ended the year with 185 Divisions in the east, 22 in Italy, 26 in the Balkans, 16 in Norway, and 53 in France and the Low Countries in addition to large numbers undergoing training in the Replacement Army.[13]

The German army was still a formidable force in 1944. Equipped with Panther and Tiger tanks as well as powerful self-propelled assault and anti-tank guns, as yet it showed little evidence of a decline in morale or combat effectiveness. Some observers have suggested that President Roosevelt's 'unconditional surrender' announcement at Casablanca strengthened German resolve and limited support for those who sought to overthrow Hitler. This is not an easy argument to prove given the various attempts to assassinate Hitler culminating in the plot of 20 July 1944. At Casablanca, Roosevelt and Churchill agreed that there could be no compromise with Hitler or Mussolini, no 'escape clause' such as Woodrow Wilson's Fourteen Points, and no armistice that allowed Germany, Japan, or Italy to avoid final defeat and occupation. The announcement also reassured the Soviet Union that there would be no separate peace with Germany.[14]

The first priority, post-Casablanca, was to solve the problem of U-boat warfare. The Allies began to commit significant new resources to the Battle of the Atlantic, including long-range aircraft, Bogue-class aircraft carriers, and additional escorts. This commitment proved sufficient to counter the expansion of U-boat production organized by Admiral Karl Donitz in 1943–4. The Donitz program, which included the design and construction of the new Type XXI U-boats, became a high priority project absorbing close to 10 per cent of German war production in 1943 and 1944.[15] Despite this effort, the Allies controlled the seas by the end of 1943 and were able to safely transport the men and material for Overlord.

The second crucial decision was to continue operations in the Mediterranean. The Casablanca Directive declared that the reasons for occupying Sicily were to: secure the lines of communication through the Mediterranean; divert German pressure from the Eastern Front; intensify pressure on Italy to surrender; and encourage Turkey to enter the war as an active ally. Plans for the invasion of France were now confined to maintaining a small mobile force in the United Kingdom that, in the words of the Casablanca Directive, was to be 'in constant readiness to re-enter the continent as soon as German resistance is weakened to the required extent.' The context for this was the catastrophe overtaking the German army at Stalingrad and the possibility of an end to the war in 1943.

Operation Husky, the Allied invasion of Sicily, began on 10 July and ended on 17 August. Historians disagree over the nature of the Allied achievement in Husky,[16] but for our purposes, what matters is that the relatively rapid conquest of the island meant that when the Allied leaders met in Quebec City during August 1943 they authorized: the elimination of Italy as a belligerent; the establishment of air bases on the Italian mainland to bomb southern Germany and the Romanian oil fields; unremitting pressure on German Forces in Northern Italy to assist the Allied campaign in Northwest Europe now scheduled for 1944. Operation Overlord was to be the primary ground and air effort against the Axis powers in 1944.[17]

Formal agreement on priorities for 1943 and 1944 was confirmed at the Teheran Conference when pressure from Stalin helped to ensure that the British and Americans agreed on the timing of Overlord (May 1944) and a commitment to Anvil, the invasion of the south of France.[18] The apparent agreement between the "Big Three" masked basic differences of opinion about the value of the Italian campaign. Throughout 1943 and 1944, the British saw opportunities in Italy and Balkans which the Americans resisted as threats to the primary focus on Overlord. After the Italian surrender and the Allied occupation of Southern Italy, American strategists preferred air bases on the Fogia plain and continuous pressure on the German forces defending central and northern Italy, but unrelenting pressure from Churchill and the British chiefs of staff led to a series of major operations that continued into 1945.[19]

The war in the Mediterranean added to the proportion of war production, air power, and manpower directed against the western Allies from 1943 to the end of the war. In simple numerical terms, the Germans sacrificed 125,000 men in Tunisia and had committed 195,000 men to the defence of Italy *before* Operation Husky begun in July 1943. That number rose steadily. On 1 April 1944, the German total was close to 400,000 men, a year later in April 1945, Army Group C was 599,000strong. These totals are exclusive of German forces committed to Greece and the Balkans, a proportion of whom were present to forestall or defeat an Allied crossing of the Adriatic.[20]

One reason that Germany was willing to maintain such large forces in the Mediterranean after 1943 was the role Northern Italy played in the German war economy. The industries of Turin and Milan together with the agriculture of the lowland plain became more important assets with the shrinking of German economic space in the east. This, together with Hitler's irrational commitment to Mussolini, his oldest ally, is the basic reality of any overview of the situation in Italy. The Luftwaffe also committed significant resources to the Mediterranean. As Williamson Murray has shown, German aircraft losses in July 1943 when the Wehrmacht was engaged in the battle of Kursk-Orel were 40 per cent higher in the Mediterranean than on the Eastern Front.[21]

The key question for students of grand strategy is how much Allied effort was actually required to hold a significant level of Axis forces in Italy. Major-General Sir William Jackson, the British official historian, uses divisional comparisons to argue that the Italian campaign succeeded as a holding action because after August 1944 the Germans committed more divisions to Italy than the Allies.[22] The Canadian official historian, Col. G.W.L. Nicholson, accepts this ratio of divisions but adds that 'throughout 1944 the total strength of Allied forces in Italy continued to exceed one and a half million.'[23] So who was fighting the holding action? The figure of 1.5 million is only part of the story. The total commitment of Allied forces, men, and women to the Mediterranean theatre in 1944 was over 2 million. All of them had to be fed and clothed using resources shipped from North America or Great Britain. Many of them had to be armed. Very large numbers were hospitalized at some point during 1944, due largely to diseases such as malaria.[24]

Neuro-psychiatric casualties, battle exhaustion, or combat fatigue as the Americans called it, also raise some interesting questions. As always, caution should be employed in citing numbers because so much depends, as it does today with Post-Traumatic Stress Disorder, on who is making the diagnosis. Nevertheless, there is strong evidence that the toll of such casualties was much higher in Italy than in Northwest Europe; the figure for the British army, thirty per thousand, is double the number when we annualize 1944 figures for NWE. American numbers show a similar pattern and it appears that the incidence of disabling psychiatric illness continued to plague soldiers in Italy, in and out of combat, until the last days of the war.[25]

The related problem of absence without leave and desertion also needs to be integrated into accounts of the campaign. Always a serious problem in Italy, it reached crisis proportions in the winter of 1944–5 when deserters and absentees in the British army averaged one thousand men a month. More than five thousand British soldiers were serving sentences for desertion in 1944 and the numbers for 5th U.S. Army were similar. Most such offenses occurred 'in anticipation of action against the enemy,' meaning soldiers took off after they learned their formation would be returning to the front lines.[26]

A total of 92,257 Canadians served in Italy. Of these, 5,399 lost their lives and 19,486 were wounded. A further 1002 became prisoners of war and 365 died from 'causes other than war.'[27] Expressed as a percentage, almost one third of the Canadians who served in Italy became casualties of war, not counting those who were evacuated for battle exhaustion. The number of Canadians labeled as neuro-psychiatric casualties in Italy was exceptionally high with 5020 individuals so designated during the seventeen months of the campaign. This means that one in five non-fatal casualties was evacuated for 'battle exhaustion' with much higher rates in periods of intense combat.[28] If a case is to be made for the view that the Italian campaign was Normandy's long right flank diverting significant German resources and combat troops that might have been used to strengthen German defences in the west, the diversion of Allies resources, especially the manpower of Britain and Canada, must also be considered.

The Casablanca Directive included instructions to RAF Bomber Command to achieve 'the progressive destruction and dislocation of the German military, industrial, and economic system, and the undermining of the morale of the German people to a point where their capacity for armed resistance is totally weakened.' This statement was followed by a list of priority targets and a specific instruction to the United States 8th Air Force 'to impose heavy losses on the German day fighter force containing German fighter strength away from the Russian and Mediterranean theaters of war.'

The area bombing of German cities began in earnest in March 1943 with a series of attacks on the Ruhr. Adam Toose persuasively argues that 'there can be no doubt that the Battle of the Ruhr marked a turning point in the history of the German war economy ... the disruption in the Ruhr manifested itself across the Germany economy.' Armaments production, which had been increasing dramatically, levelled off with zero growth from May 1943 to February 1944.[29]

The 8th Air Force's attempts to penetrate deep into Germany, attacking priority targets such as the ball-bearing factories at Schweinfurt, proved that losses to unescorted B17 and B24 bombers were too heavy to allow for sustained operations. After December 1943, long-range fighter escorts, especially the P51 Mustang with auxiliary fuel tanks, provided effective protection but their most important contribution was the attrition of the Luftwaffe's day fighter force, which by March of 1944 was no longer able to maintain air-superiority over its own territory.[30] By May 1944, the Luftwaffe was a shadow of its former self, having lost 99 per cent of the day fighter pilots available at the beginning of the year.[31] Their replacements lacked experience in the air, never mind combat. This extraordinary Allied victory was won at considerable cost. In the two months before D-Day alone, 2000 aircraft and more than 12,000 men were casualties of the combined air offensive.[32] The air plan for D-Day illustrated the new reality. The Allied committed 11,000 aircraft of all types, including 3700 fighter and fighter bombers to battle.[33] The Luftwaffe, with less than a thousand aircraft of all types in the west, could not penetrate the battle space giving rise to the comment attributed to German soldiers: if it is black it is British, silver, American, and if you cannot see it, it is the Luftwaffe.

Professor Phillips O'Brien, writing in the *Journal of Strategic Studies*, has argued that the major contribution of strategic bombing was its impact on the overall German war effort. He notes that by mid-1943, more than 41 per cent of German weapons production was devoted to aircraft largely for the defence of Germany, while armoured vehicles, tanks, and self-propelled guns absorbed just 6.27 per cent of the war budget. Anti-aircraft weapons and ammunition grew as a percentage of the German war effort until it reached close to 25 per cent of all production.[34] By January 1944, two thirds of all such weapons and 70 per cent of the famous 88mm guns were defending Germany from air attack.[35]

There are qualitative as well as quantitative issues involved in this question. The Germans allocated enormous resources to the V1 and V2 rocket programs, which were developed as revenge weapons against bombing.[36] When radar and other scientific research supporting the German night fighter program are added, it is evident that the cutting edge of Germany's war machine was focused on the defence of the Reich and not the Eastern Front. The enormous effort expended to defend Germany from air attack raises the question of whether or not the true second front was created in the skies over Germany in 1943.[37] Whatever your answer, it is apparent that the Combined Bomber Offensive diverted significant human and material resources away from the Eastern Front and other theatres from 1943 to the end of the war.

Hitler waited until the fall of 1943 before turning his attention to the challenge posed by the Allied build up in England and the unmistakable signs that an invasion of France was imminent. On 3 November 1943, he issued Directive No. 51, which noted that 'the vast extent of conquered territories in the east makes it possible for us to lose ground, even on a large scale, without a fatal blow being dealt to the nervous system of Germany. No such option exists in the west and therefore, the western forces must be built up to withstand a landing and if the landing succeeds, to launch a decisive counter attack.'[38] The most challenging problem facing the German Supreme Command (OKW) and OB West was the same issue that had bedeviled the Poles in 1939, France in 1940, and the Soviets in 1941, how to defend an extended perimeter when you have no way of knowing when and where the enemy will attack. The Atlantic Wall, from the Scheldt Estuary to the Spanish border, a distance of more than 1000 kilometers, seemed to offer a number of possible landing areas all of which needed to be defended.

Much emphasis is usually placed on the debate between Field Marshall Erwin Rommel, who argued that the Allies had to be stopped on the beaches thus requiring the forward commitment of all available troops including the armoured divisions, and the advocates of maintaining mobile reserves to counter-attack an Allied beachhead once the main thrust had been identified.[39] Rommel commanded Army Group

B, an operational headquarters interposed between Field Marshal Gerd Von Rundstedt's OB West and the two armies, the 15th and 7th, responsible for the most likely invasion areas. Rommel believed that his experience in Africa had taught him that armoured divisions were incapable of proper movement in the face of Allied air superiority. He objected even to a second line of defence in Normandy, a line which Runstedt had laboriously built up along the Channel coast.[40]

When Rommel's headquarters became operational on 1 January 1944, he threw himself with characteristic energy into the job of making the beaches impregnable. Rommel travelled up and down the French coast exhorting men to build obstacles on the beaches, inventing devices which would damage and sink landing craft, and planting stakes on flat fields to prevent gliders from landing. He obtained large quantities of captured French ammunition used in explosives that were fastened to the obstacles and he advocated the laying of huge minefields along the coast. He assumed the Allies would land at high tide and so most of these were located on the beach. The Allies did not oblige. Finally he wanted to obtain control of the armoured divisions in order to place them close enough to the front so that they could intervene during the first actual landing of the enemy.[41]

The last demand created a serious problem because Runstedt believed that it would be necessary to fight a more mobile battle if the Allies succeeded in establishing a bridgehead in France. With this in mind, he had set up a headquarters (Panzer Group West) to train and command all mobile divisions. This training function was necessary because these divisions were either in the process of forming or had been returned from the east for rest and refitting. Runstedt wanted Panzer Group West to direct a properly coordinated counter-offensive. General Geyr von Schweppenburg, the commander of Panzer Group West, agreed with Rundstedt on the proper role of Panzer divisions, and the experience of the German army's Anzio beachhead counter-offensive (January-February 1944) seemed to support his reservations by illustrating the difficulties of counter-attacking within the range of naval gunfire.[42]

The whole matter was debated at a Fuehrer conference in March 1944. Rommel demanded an extension of his authority to include all of the mobile reserves in effect making him a Second C. in C. West. Hitler at first agreed but OKW, in working out the details, partly reversed the decision. The result was a compromise. Rommel obtained command of three Panzer divisions, Army Group G in the south of France retained three, while OKW controlled the movement of the remaining four. The compromise created a situation in which no single headquarters had control over all the mobile reserves.

The problem of perimeter defence, which plagued German decision-makers in the months before D-Day, was complicated by the German belief that the Allied landings would take place north of the River Somme, most likely in the Pas de Calais region closest to the English coast. To the professional soldiers of the German army, the Pas de Calais offered so many advantages to the Allies that it seemed unlikely that they would attack anywhere else. Opposite Boulogne and Calais the coast of England was little more than thirty kilometres away, maximizing the effectiveness of Allied aircraft during the landings and allowing for the rapid turn around of the ships and landing craft of the naval assault force. Once ashore, the invaders could exploit a dense road and rail network, advancing the short distance to the German border. German divisions in Normandy, Brittany, and Southern France would be cut off, harassed by Allied air power and unable to come to the assistance of 15th Army during the first week of the bridgehead battle.[43]

The Calvados coast of Normandy seemed an unlikely alternative. It was much further from Germany and as a peninsula could be sealed off if a bridgehead was established. Offshore reefs in the ocean north of Caen were thought to limit possible landing areas and the terrain to the west with its marshes and bocage, small fields surrounded by hedgerows, would slow any advance inland. Brittany seemed equally unlikely as a landing area and except for the two large ports – Cherbourg and Brest, which were heavily fortified – the rest of the Atlantic Wall in the two peninsulas consisted of isolated strongpoints and resistance nests that were not always mutually supporting.[44] The importance attached to the region north of the Seine was further enhanced when construction of the V-1 launching sites began. Hitler's Directive No. 51 had announced his intention to reinforce 'particularly those places from which the long-range bombardment of England will begin. For it is here the enemy must and will attack and it is here unless all indications are misleading that the decisive battle against the landing forces will be fought.'[45]

When Rommel assumed command of Army group B in January 1944, he focused his energies on strengthening the defences along the Channel Coast. This is evident in the Weekly Reports sent to Army Group B by 15th and 7th Armies. As late as May 1944 32,000 civilian and 27,000 military were working in the 15th Army Sector to build additional defensive positions and minefields. By late May, 70 per cent of the construction program in the Pas de Calais was complete whereas 7th Army was only beginning to employ large numbers of civilians and soldiers, reporting that just 14 per cent of the summer program had been completed.[46] The disposition of troops reflected the focus on the 15th Army and the Pas de Calais where eight static divisions defended the coast with six mobile infantry as well as two Panzer Divisions in immediate reserve. Normandy, west of the Orne, had three static divisions, two mobile infantry divisions, and one armoured division.[47]

To what degree was the strategic failure due to the British 'Double Cross' system, which used German agents controlled by British Intelligence to provide carefully scripted information exaggerating the numbers of Allied divisions available for the invasion while pointing to an assault from south-east England to the Pas de Calais? The broad deception scheme, code-named 'Fortitude South,' seems to have been effective because it reinforced everything the German high command believed. Allied attempts to persuade the German decision makers that the invasion would not take place until late in the summer, and the scheme called 'Fortitude North,' designed to stimulate preparations for an attack on Norway, were rejected by German intelligence and their senior commanders as obvious attempts to disguise the real invasion plans.[48]

The Allies were able to monitor German preparations to meet the invasion through signals intelligence, including Ultra reports from the code-breakers at Bletchley Park who were able to provide detailed information about the German order of battle, especially with regard to the location and strength of the panzer divisions. Ultra also revealed that by April 1944, the German High Command was certain that an invasion was imminent and that Allied attacks on the bridges spanning the river Seine were focusing more attention on Normandy.[49] However, Hitler, Rundstedt, Rommel, and other senior commanders were convinced that if Normandy were invaded, it would not be the main attack. That, they thought, was bound to come later, establishing the real Second Front in the Pas de Calais.[50]

Despite this, 7th Army was a formidable force on D-Day. The corps responsible for the defence of the Calvados coast deployed six divisions, more than 50,000 soldiers, in the beach defences or close proximity. During the next two days, 12SS Panzer Division, Panzer Lehr, and two infantry divisions – 243rd from the west side of the Cherbourg peninsula and 346th from 15th Army north of the Seine – added a further 30,000 and the beachhead established on 6 June was soon sealed off.[51]

There were important differences in the quality of German divisions and much has been made of the lack of mobility and age profile of the three static coastal divisions in the invasion area, however, the majority of German units were well-equipped and close to full strength. By 31 May 1944, there were more than 2,200 armoured fighting vehicles (AFVs) in France and the Low Countries including 138 'Tiger' tanks, 650 MK V 'Panthers,' 897 MK IVs, 470 self-propelled assault guns (Sturmgeschütz III), and 60 self-propelled anti-tank guns (Jagdpanzers IV and Jagdpanthers). Given the marked inferiority of the under gunned and highly vulnerable Allied armour, this was a formidable array of mobile firepower. By 9 June over 400 German AFV's were in action in Normandy. By 13 June, the accumulated AFV strength was 653.[52]

As the Allied build-up continued, Hitler and the German High Command continued to believe that Normandy was a diversion and that the real landings would soon take place in the Pas de Calais. Despite this, 2nd Panzer Division and the 101 Heavy (Tiger) Tank Battalion from 15th Army were sent to Normandy, the former to backstop the defences at Caumont, the latter to serve with I SS Panzer Corps in the British-Canadian sector. The next arrivals were 9 and 10 SS Panzer Divisions and the headquarters of II SS Panzer Corps. They crossed most of Europe from Poland to Normandy between the 11th and 28th of June. The corp's combat troops were immediately committed to battle to block a British advance, Operation Epsom. The 276th Infantry Division from the south of France and I SS Panzer Division training near Antwerp also arrived in Normandy over a two week period in late June. Both were employed in the vital Caen-Caumont sector.[53] By the third week of July Panzer Group West, defending the high ground south of Caen, constituted one of the most formidable concentrations of military force ever assembled. Between the rivers Odon and Dives, a distance of less than thirty-two kilometres, five panzer Divisions and three infantry divisions were deployed with two further Panzer Divisions in close reserve. The total number of AFVs available can only be estimated but it was not less than four hundred – six times the number in 7th Army.[54]

The most detailed analysis of the manpower in Army Group B suggests that while Panzer Group West and 7th Army deployed roughly the same number of infantry battalions, almost half of those in 7th Army were well understrength and rated as weak or combat ineffective. At midnight on 24 July, the eve of Operation Cobra, only one armoured division, Panzer Lehr with just 31 combat ready tanks, was in the Saint-Lô sector. The other Panzer division in 7th Army, 2SS, avoided encirclement and was able to withdraw largely intact. It later participated in the Mortain counterattack.[55]

When the American breakout began Panzer Group West was ordered to transfer divisions to 7th Army for a proposed counterattack as well as to meet the British thrust, Operation Bluecoat, south of Caumont. By 5 August, ISS Panzer Corps, defending the Caen-Falaise sector, deployed just three infantry divisions and the two surviving battlegroups of 12SS Panzer Division. Unfortunately, Montgomery's decision to transfer the three British armoured divisions and much else to the American flank left First Canadian Army scrambling for resources to mount an advance towards Falaise. By borrowing 51st Highland Division from I British Corps and employing two, newly arrived and inexperienced armoured divisions, 1 Polish and 4th Canadian, Lieutenant-General Guy Simonds was, for the first time, able to plan an operation with a favourable force ratio.

After the partial success of Operation Totalize, Simonds launched a second set-piece attack, Tractable, against an enemy strengthened by the addition of a fresh infantry division and various battlegroups ordered to defend the north shoulder of the shrinking Falaise Pocket. No reinforcements reached the Canadians and 51st Highland Division resumed its role holding the left flank. As a consequence, Canadian and Polish casualties mounted and as Montgomery reported in his memoirs between 6 June and 30 September 'the 3rd Canadian Division had more casualties (9,263) than any other division in 21 Army Group and 2nd Canadian Division (8,211) was next.'[56] This was the 'consequence of having spent more days involved in "intense combat" than any British division.'[57]

An eventual Allied victory in Normandy was probably inevitable given the challenges confronted by Hitler's Germany: attrition on the Eastern Front, the diversion of forces to secondary theatres, especially in Italy and the Balkans; and the continuous interruption of road and rail traffic by the Allied airforces.[58] A victory in less than three months was another matter. The failure of intelligence and imagination that kept powerful formations north of the Seine until late July was particularly damaging to 7th Army as most of the reinforcements that did arrive were committed to the vital Caen sector. On 25 July, while the Canadian Corps fought its most costly battle of the campaign against great odds, the thin grey line around Saint-Lô broke. The powerful battle-hardened American army proved irresistible and the fate of Hitler's Germany was sealed.

Notes

1 See for example John Buckley (ed), *Monty's Men: The British Army and the Liberation of Europe* (New Haven, 2013).

2 Carlo D'Este, *Decision in Normandy* (Collins; London, 1983), 75–104.

3 United States Department of State, *Foreign Relations of the United States: The Conferences at Washington, 1941–42 and Casablanca 1943*, 485–849. http:// digital.library.wisc.edu/1711/d/FRUS.FRUS194143

4 Maurice Matloff and Edwin M. Snell, *Strategic Planning for Coalition Warfare* (Washington, 1953), 181–7.

5 Winston Churchill, *The Hinge of Fate* (Boston, 1950), 181–7.

6 Michael Howard, *Grand Strategy*, vol. 4, August 1942-September 1943, London, 1972, 119–21.

7 Rick Atkinson, *An Army at Dawn: The War in North Africa* (New York, 2002) is the most recent account.

8 United States Department of State, *Foreign Relations of the United States: The Conferences at Washington, 1941–42 and Casablanca 1943*, 485–849. http:// digital.library.wisc.edu/1711/d/FRUS.FRUS194143

9 Richard Overy, *Why The Allies Won* (London, 1996), 3.

10 Horst Boog, Gerhard Krebs, and Detlef Vogel, *Germany and the Second World War*, vol 7 (Oxford, 2006), 497, note 6.

11 Phillips O'Brien, 'East Versus West in the Defeat of Nazi Germany,' *Journal of Strategic Studies*, vol 23, no 2, 96–97.

12 'German Casualties in World War II,' *Wikipedia*. This entry offers a well-researched review of the question.

13 L. F. Ellis, *Victory in the West*, vol 1 (London 1962), 59. The Replacement Army, including those recovering from wounds, soldiers in training, and the personnel of various military establishments accounted for 2.5 million men in 1944. The Dupuy Institute, *German and Soviet Replacement Systems in World War II*, 18. www.wehrmachtberitch.com

14 Howard, *Grand Strategy*, 281–285.

15 Ministry of Defence (Navy), *The U-Boat War in the Atlantic, 1939–1945* (London, 1984), 83–6.

16 For a critical view of the Allied achievement see Carlo D'Este, *Bitter Victory: The Battle for Sicily 1945* (New York, 1998). A more balanced picture placing the Canadian effort within the contest of a successful campaign is offered in Lee Windsor, 'The Eyes of All Fixed on Sicily: Canada's Unexpected Victory 1943,' *Canadian Military History*, vol. 22, no. 3 (Summer 2013), 4–32.

17 Howard, 'Final Report to the President and Prime Minister: 25 August 1943,' *Grand Strategy*, vol 4, appendix, 682–91.

18 John Ehrman, *Grand Strategy*, vol. 5, *August 1943-September 1944*, London HMSO 1956, 173–83.

19 The most recent of the many critiques of Churchill's 'soft underbelly' strategy is Christopher Catherwood, *Winston Churchill: The Flawed Genius of World War II* (New York, 2009).

20 G.W.L. Nicholson, *The Canadians in Normandy* (Ottawa, 1958), 629.

21 Williamson Murray, *Luftwaffe* (Baltimore, 1985), 144.

22 William Jackson, *The Mediterranean and Middle East*, vol 6, part 3 (London, 1987), 351–2.

23 Nicholson, 680.

24 W. F. Mellor, *Casualties and Medical Statistics* (London, 1932), 226, 241. The annual rate of admissions per 1,000 troops was 525 in Italy, 116 in Northwest Europe.

25 Terry Copp and Bill McAndrew, *Battle Exhaustion: Soldiers and Psychiatrists in the Canadian Army 1939–1945* (Montreal, 1991), 106–7 and E.F. Fighter, *From Cassino to the Alps* (Washington, 1993), 222–3.

26 British Historical Section Central Mediterranean, Administrative Monographs 1946, 'the Problem of Desertion,' LCMSDS Archive.

27 Nicholson, 642.

28 Copp and McAndrew, 107.

29 Adam Toose, *The Wages of Destruction* (London, 2000), 598–660.

30 Murray, *Luftwaffe*, 232.

31 Ibid.

32 Ellis, *Victory*, 72.

33 Ibid., 112.

34 O'Brien, 89–113.

35 Horst Boog et al, *Germany and the Second World War*, vol 7 (Oxford, 2006), 322.

36 Boog, 'The V Weapons Offensive,' *Germany and the Second World War*, 420–58. Boog concludes that the program, 'tied up a workforce of some 200,000 about one-tenth of the total employed in aerial armaments.' 454.

37 Boog et al, *Germany and the Second World War*, vol 7, part 1 offers the most detailed account of the impact of the Combined Bomber Offensive in Germany. See also Richard Overy, *Bomber Command 1939–1945: Reaping the Whirlwind* (London, 1996) and Adam Toose, *The Wages of Destruction* (London, 2006).

38 Hugh Trevor-Roper, *Hitler's War Directives* (Edinburgh 1964). The directive is also reproduced on World War II Database, www.ww2db.com.

39 Dieter Ose, 'Rommel and Rundstedt: The 1944 Panzer Controversy,' *Military Affairs* 50, no. 2 (1986) 7–11.

40 See Boog, 513 for a diagrammatic example of coastal defence in depth north of the Seine.

41 See the extracts from interviews with Admiral F. Ruge at www.history .navy.mil/library/online/rommel

42 Interview, Geyr Von Schweppenburg, Ethnet Manuscript B466, LCMSDS Archives.

43 Boog, 516–520.

44 Alan J. Wilt, *The Atlantic Wall: Hitler's Defences in the West* (Ames, Iowa, 1975).

45 Trevor-Roper, *Hitler's War Directives* and www.ww2db.com.

46 James A. Wood (ed), *Army of the West: The Weekly Reports of German Army Group B from Normandy to the West Wall* (Mechanisburg, 2007).

47 Ellis, 117.

48 Michael Howard, *British Intelligence in the Second World War*, vol 5: *Strategic Deception* (London, 1987) 185. See also Boog, 503–8.

49 F. H. Hinsley, *British Intelligence in the Second World War*, vol 3, part 2 (London, 1988), Appendix 10, 798–824.

50 Boog, P 567. See also Mary Kathern Barbier, 'Deception and the Planning of D-Day' in John Buckley (ed), *The Normandy Campaign 1944* (Milton Park, UK, 2006), 179.

51 Robert Vogel, 'Tactical Air Power in Normandy: Thoughts on the Interdiction Plan,' *Canadian Military History*, vol. 3, no. 1 (1984), 41–2.

52 Niklas Zetterling, 'Arrival of Panzer Units in Normandy,' Appendix 5 in *Normandy 1944: German Military Organization, Combat Power, and Organizational Effectiveness* (Winnipeg, 2000), 412–17.

53 Zetterling, 'Arrival of Units in Normandy,' Appendix 1, 396–400.

54 Estimates derived from Zetterling, 'German Combat Formations,' 117–392.

55 Between 6 June and 23 July, Army Group B suffered 116,863 casualties but only 10,048 replacements had arrived. Wood, 126. The greater combat power of many battalions in Panzer group West was a consequence of their later arrival in Normandy. Zetterling, part 2, 'German Combat Formations,' 117–395. For Panzer Lehr, Zetterling, 348–92; for 2nd SS Panzer Division, 318–27.

56 Bernard Law Montgomery, *The Memoirs of Field Marshal Montgomery* (New York, 1959), 277.

57 Terry Copp, 'To The Last Canadian? Casualties in 21 Army Group,' *Canadian Military History*, vol. 18, no. 1 (2009), 6.

58 Russell Hart, 'Feeding Mars: The Role of Logistics in the German Defeat in Normandy, 1944,' *War in History* vol. 3, no.4 (1996), 423, emphasizes the role of airpower in limiting supplies to 7th Army particularly after the destruction of the Tours bridges on 15 July.

Preface

The invitation to deliver the 1998 Joanne Goodman lectures at the University of Western Ontario provided a welcome opportunity to develop the case for a fundamental change in our approach to a familiar subject – the achievements of the Canadian army in the Battle of Normandy. The first lecture, 'Military History without Clausewitz,' challenged both existing interpretations of the campaign and current approaches to military history. I then outlined a new paradigm that emphasized the valour, skill, and commitment required by the Allied citizen-soldiers to attack a well-entrenched and well-equipped enemy – attacks not unlike those of the Canadian Corps in the First World War. The lectures were presented to a largely undergraduate audience that had been sensitized to the subject by the recent release of Steven Spielberg's film *Saving Private Ryan*, so we began, as Canadians so often do, with an American frame of reference. The introduction and chapter 1 are based on that first lecture. Subsequent chapters include a discussion of Operations Spring and Totalize – the subjects of the second and third lectures. This material is now integrated into an overall analysis of the Normandy campaign and the Canadian contribution to victory.

I began to study the experience of the Canadian army in the Second World War without benefit of training or extensive reading in military history. My army experience consists of two summers spent in the Canadian Officers Training Corps, the first at the Infantry School, Camp Borden, and the second in the Ordnance Corps. This arrangement allowed me to attend classes in Montreal and complete my BA in time to begin my first appointment as a lecturer in history. I did not return for a third phase of training, thus retaining that lowest of army ranks, second lieutenant. Even so, my army experience was important, for I left with a high opinion of the character and competence of the NCOs and officers and considerable respect for the ethos of the organization.

Over the next fifteen years my teaching and research focused on political, economic, and especially social history, culminating in the publication of *The Anatomy of Poverty: The Condition of the Working Class in Montreal, 1897–1929* (1974). After I left Montreal and joined Wilfrid Laurier University, I shifted my focus to labour history; then, in 1980, I entered into a partnership with my mentor and friend, the late Robert Vogel.

Bob Vogel was born in Vienna. His father, a veteran of the flying corps of the Austro-Hungarian army, fled Austria after the *Anschluss*, and Bob spent the war years in Wales. Fluent in German, trained as a diplomatic and military historian, Bob wanted to start a new research project after two terms as Dean of the Faculty of Arts at McGill University. We agreed to collaborate on a study of the campaign in Northwest Europe. Bob would examine the German sources and handle the strategic debate between Eisenhower and Montgomery while I studied the Canadian army at the tactical and operational levels.

Bob Vogel's reputation as an outstanding teacher was based on his ability to involve his students in the historian's quest for knowledge. His 'Plato to NATO' survey, held in McGill's largest lecture hall, was a *tour de force* that was audited by graduate students and faculty. Bob rarely made definitive statements; instead, he required you to think through problems with him. It was the same in a seminar or in conversation. As we began to plan our work, Bob introduced me to Clausewitz and other military writers; but in the course of our discussions we decided that a social historian, escaping a world dominated by Marxists, was entitled to be suspicious of yet another nineteenth-century authority figure. We agreed that history at the divisional, brigade, and battalion levels might best be understood by a new reading of the primary sources, including interviews with veterans and a careful study of the ground over which the battles had been fought. As one who never got over reading R.G. Collingwood's *The Idea of History*, I was certain that if I really learned what had happened I would know why it had happened that way. If Clausewitz – or any other theorist – had influenced the decision makers, it would be reflected in the source material.

We spent the next six years researching and writing the five volumes of the *Maple Leaf Route* series. There was remarkably little interest in a new history of the battles to liberate Europe, and though McClelland & Stewart agreed to publish the work, they insisted on a conventional format, and said no to the heavily illustrated, document-rich books we wanted to produce. So we published the series ourselves, shipping the volumes to book stores from the Copp farmhouse in Wellington County. The series was a critical and eventually a commercial success, and the books provided the basic narrative foundation on which all subsequent work was built.

Throughout the research, Bob and I had debated many issues. Perhaps the most difficult to resolve was the role of air power in the campaign. Most historians described air power – especially tactical air support of the armies – as the 'decisive' factor in the Allied victory, but the evidence from the primary sources provided little support for this view. We embarked on an ambitious plan to examine the contemporary German and Allied records, ignoring the postwar accounts of German generals and air force publicists. This project led us to accumulate vast amounts of research material and introduced us to military operational research, but the proposed book was never written. Instead, Bob refocused his energies on the university he loved, and I concentrated on the research that led to *Battle Exhaustion: Soldiers and Psychiatrists in the Canadian Army, 1939–1945* (1990) written with Bill McAndrew, and *The Brigade: The Fifth Canadian Infantry, Brigade 1939–1945* (1992).

While studying tactical air power at the Public Record Office (PRO), we began to explore WO 291, a newly released record group containing the reports of various army operational research (OR) sections. Following the practice I used in studying both soldiers and psychiatrists, I immediately set out to interview as many of the OR scientists as I could find. The opportunity to discuss a wide range of operational and tactical issues with the men who had observed and reported on the training and battlefield experience of the Anglo-Canadian armies was invaluable. David Hill, David Bayley Pike, Tony Sargeaunt, Omand

Solandt, and Michael Swann were especially helpful, providing personal papers and answering questions over a period of several years. While engaged in this research, I met Professor Ronnie Shephard, who had joined the Army Operational Research Group in 1942 and who had amassed a large collection of OR material, including correspondence and reports not available in the PRO. Shephard's archives are now at the Laurier Centre for Military Strategic and Disarmament Studies.

Interviews with Canadian and British veterans continued to absorb my time and to force me to reconsider established ideas. I would have liked to acknowledge all of those who helped me better understand the battlefield, but too often, conversations at unit reunions or other social events resulted in notebook jottings rather than tapes and written transcripts. Formal acknowledgments are therefore limited to those whom I interviewed in some depth.

It would be difficult to write about this or any other military campaign without a detailed knowledge of the ground. For more than a decade now, my wife and I have travelled each year to the Canadian battlefields. These trips include study tours with the Canadian Battle of Normandy Foundation. Introducing Canadian university students to the battlefields has been an especially rewarding experience, and I have learned much from their questions and insights.

My colleagues and students at the Laurier Centre for Military Strategic and Disarmament Studies and the Canadian Battle of Normandy Foundation have contributed both directly and indirectly to this work, and I am grateful for their support. David Barnhill, Mike Bechthold, the late Shaun Brown, Sean Bennett, Robert Cotey, Paul Dickson, Serge Durflinger, Christopher Evans, Kate Fitzpatrick, John Gipson, Oliver Haller, Geoff Hayes, Kathleen Hynes, Andrew Iarocci, David Lenarcic, Dave Macri, Ian Miller, David Patterson, Jody Perrun, Brian Rawding, Scott Sheffield, Allan Thurott, Jock Vance, Randy Wakelam, and Lee Windsor will all find some of their ideas reflected in this work. The manuscript was read in whole or in part by Mike Bechthold, Lt.-Col. A. Caravaggio, Jack Granatstein, Jack Hyatt, Roman Jarymowycz, Chris Madsen, Marc Milner, David Patterson, Shelagh Whitaker, and two anonymous reviewers for the University of Toronto Press. Their comments have helped me improve the manuscript, though they share no responsibility for errors, omissions, and interpretations of events, which are mine alone. I have benefited from the opportunity to discuss the Normandy campaign with John A. English, Roman Jarymowycz, and the late Robert Vogel. Roman Jarymowycz has been especially kind in helping me think through interpretive problems.

It is more difficult to single out veterans, but I must at a minimum acknowledge the assistance of W.A.B. Anderson, Gordon Brown, Leslie Chater, Douglas Copp, Ernest Coté, D.G. Cunningham, Reg Dixon, Ed Ford, Charlie Forbes, Tony Foulds, Trevor Hart Dyke, Dalt Heyland, James Hill, Richard Hillborn, Don Learment, W.J. Megill, Stewart Moore, Joe Nixon, Jacques Ostiguy, George Pangman, S. Radley-Walters, Gordon Sellar, and Denis Whitaker. I must also pay tribute to the work of Jean Portugal. Her interviews with veterans of the 3rd Canadian Infantry Division and 2nd Canadian Armoured Brigade were published as *We Were There* (Toronto, 1998).

Wilfrid Laurier University provided a small research grant, as well as that most valuable of commodities, time, through a course release grant. Allan Thurott and Karen Priestman prepared successive versions of the manuscript from my penciled drafts. Mike Bechthold prepared the maps and offered assistance in many other ways. I wish to thank the University of Western Ontario and Eddie Goodman for making the series and the book possible. I dedicate it to Mr Goodman and all his comrades.

FIELDS OF FIRE:
THE CANADIANS IN NORMANDY

1

Introduction: Military History without Clausewitz

When *Saving Private Ryan* was filling the theatres in the summer of 1998, a Canadian journalist commented that if the film had been made in this country, 'the Allies would never have got off the beach. Private Ryan himself would have been flattened by a German Tiger tank and the rescue squad dead to the last man.'[1] This approach, which is usually associated with the Vietnam War generation and the CBC, has in fact been dominant in Canadian universities and military colleges since 1962, the year C.P. Stacey published *The Victory Campaign*. Stacey's volume of the official history was strongly influenced by British military writers, especially Liddell Hart and Chester Wilmott, who had established an interpretative framework contrasting the 'superior generalship' of Lt.-Gen. Bernard Montgomery with the constant interference from Hitler that paralysed the German Command. Liddell Hart drew an equally sharp contrast between the Allied soldiers – American, British, and Canadian – and their German counterparts, arguing that the performance of the latter was greatly superior. The old cliché 'lions led by donkeys' might, he argued, need to be reversed when the 'poor performance' of the Allied troops in Normandy was considered.[2]

Stacey concurred with these views, attributing the Allies' success to 'numerical and material superiority,' the paralysing effects of Allied air power, and superior generalship – especially that of Montgomery, whose 'grip of the operations was firm and effective.' Overall victory was won despite failure on the battlefield. The Canadians, he wrote, 'had probably not got as much out of our long training as we might have.' The army also 'suffered from possessing a proportion of regimental officers whose attitude towards training was casual and haphazard.' This resulted in 'occasions in the Normandy campaign when Canadian formations failed to make the most of their opportunities.' In particular, 'the capture of Falaise was long delayed and it was necessary to mount not one but two set-piece operations.' The trials of 2nd Division in the fighting for Verrières Ridge were also highlighted. Stacey quoted Maj.-Gen. Charles Foulkes's comment that his own division was 'no match for the battle-experienced German troops encountered in Normandy.' Canadian shortcomings were contrasted with the performance of the German troops who 'gave a very good account of themselves' because they got 'more out of their training than we did.'[3]

British and American historians as well as a generation of Canadians accepted Stacey's critique as definitive until John A. English wrote his penetrating study of the development of the Canadian army and its performance in Normandy, first published in 1991. English agreed with Stacey that the key question was how to explain the failure of the Canadian army, especially in relation to Verrières Ridge and the Falaise Gap; but he insisted that the chief causes were to be found in the shortcomings of the Canadian High Command, which seriously impaired Canadian fighting performance by failing to develop appropriate leadership, training, or doctrine.[4] English's book quickly became the new standard interpretation of the Canadian army's experience in the Second World War. At a 1996 conference at the University of Edinburgh, it was evident that most of those in the audience – except veterans of 51st Highland Division, who had fought as part of the Canadian Corps – 'knew' that the Canadian army had been an especially ineffective part of the Allied forces, which had relied on 'brute force' to overcome the highly skilled German army. British graduate students working on aspects of 21 Army Group's history expressed complete agreement with this approach.[5]

English's work developed out of a very different context than Stacey's. A serving officer in Canada's regular army and the author of the internationally recognized study *On Infantry* (1981), English chose to study the Canadian role in the Normandy campaign for his doctoral dissertation. 'The intention,' he wrote, was 'neither to attack nor defend the Canadian record, but to subject it to critical analysis, which, to employ the wisdom of Carl von Clausewitz, involves the application of theoretical truths to actual events.' But English had decided before he began his research that Canadian performance in Normandy was 'lackluster,' and he quoted with approval the views of historians and military writers who had simply echoed Stacey's criticisms.[6]

English had served in a variety of army postings, including Chief of Tactics at the Canadian Combat Training Centre and War Plans Officer in NATO's Central Army Group Headquarters. He seems to have shared assumptions about the comparative combat effectiveness of the German and Allied armies that were commonly held in NATO training and doctrinal circles. The origins of these assumptions are worth tracing. When the Second World War ended in the bombing of

Hiroshima and Nagasaki, the operational and tactical lessons of the war seemed to belong to a remote prenuclear age of slight relevance to modern armies. The Korean War was treated as an aberration and did not shake the general view that nuclear weapons had transformed the art of war. In a classified study dating from the early 1950s, British operational researchers studied the consequences of using tactical nuclear weapons on the battlefields of 1944. They concluded that the use of weapons in the one kiloton range would have changed everything to such a degree that the historical events were of little interest. If you nuke Verrières Ridge, your problem then becomes how to avoid it, not capture it.[7]

Nevertheless, the Cold War in Europe and the expansion of NATO ground forces in the 1950s led the military to selectively re-examine the battles of the Second World War. Since NATO forces were bound to be on the defensive if Soviet armoured vehicles advanced across the north European plain, it made sense to study how the German army had slowed down the Soviet and Anglo-American armies in 1944–5. Kurt Meyer, who commanded the 12th SS in Normandy and was convicted of the murder of Canadian soldiers, left his prison cell in Dorchester, New Brunswick, to explain how he had stymied the Canadians in August.[8]

The superiority of the German army and especially the SS became an article of faith among NATO armies, and attempts were made to explain this 'astounding battlefield success' in terms that would be palatable in democratic societies. The key was to ignore ideology, indoctrination, the murderous discipline that led to the execution of thousands of German soldiers, the kith-and-kin proclamations that promised death to the family members of a soldier who surrendered, and the evidence of what actually happened on the battlefield. Instead, military theorists insisted that the Germans won battles due to better morale, tactics, doctrine, and leadership. Impressive-sounding German words were employed to lend an air of professionalism to this task. The favourite is *Auftragstaktik*, translated as 'mission command,' said to be the foundation of current NATO army doctrine.

The development of NATO doctrine at first had little impact on military history, largely because universities ignored the subject. The Vietnam War changed that situation, as it changed so much else. In

Vietnam the United States found itself entangled in a war in which nuclear weapons were irrelevant and the military seemed incapable of winning against an apparently inferior enemy. Suddenly questions about how conventional wars were fought and won seemed urgent and important, and military history was revived as an important field of study.

In 1976, Peter Paret and Michael Howard published a new edition of Clausewitz's *On War*. Together with Paret's study of Clausewitzian thought, published in the same year, the books set off an explosion of interest in the classical approach to military history. Clausewitz writes about war as an idealized construct, 'an act of force to compel our enemy to do our will.' When Clausewitz writes about the actual battlefield, it is to describe the sources of 'friction' that limit the effectiveness of the well-trained army following the well-conceived plan. 'A battalion,' he writes, 'is made up of individuals, the least important of whom may chance to delay things or somehow make them go wrong.'[9] Through better selection and training, a well-led army will minimize or even eliminate the human component of friction. The appeal of Clausewitzian analysis to those concerned with training an all-volunteer army is obvious. In the post-Vietnam context, the study of combat effectiveness became a growth industry.

The only armies that seemed to come close to the Clausewitzian ideal of unity between state, army, and people with a commitment to total war were the German army and perhaps the Soviet army after 1942. Given the limited access to Soviet sources, military historians studied and celebrated the military excellence of the Wehrmacht and the SS. The work of Col. Trevor Dupuy – especially his books *A Genius for War* (1977) and *Numbers Predictions and War* (1979) – provided an apparently objective quantified statement of German superiority. The Israeli scholar Martin Van Creveld then prepared a study for the Pentagon, *Fighting Power: German and U.S. Army Performance, 1939–1945* (1983), which sought to further explain the superior combat performance of the German army.

Van Creveld's study attributed the prowess of the German army to its organization and training. He admitted that 'to some extent, indoctrination with national socialist ideas, the exalted social status of the military and even some odd quirks of national character may have contributed to the results.' That said, Van Creveld insisted, the German soldier fought superbly because 'he felt himself a member of a well-integrated, well led team whose structure, administration and functioning were perceived to be ... equitable and just.'[10] *Fighting Power* is the basic text for what may be called the 'combat effectiveness' approach to military history. But Van Creveld, who had a well-deserved reputation for his previous work on foreign policy and military logistics, did not bother to study actual military operations. Instead, he used Dupuy's numerical analysis as hard evidence that 'the Wehrmacht fought equally well in defeat and victory,' whereas the American army 'with its less than mediocre officer corps'[11] failed to develop adequate fighting power. But Dupuy's numbers are derived from unproven assumptions about the effects of weapons, terrain, and the 'posture' of the troops engaged in combat; change the assumptions and the scores that are said to measure effectiveness also change. Dupuy developed his model from a detailed analysis of 78 engagements involving American, British, and German troops. However, since none of these engagements occurred in Normandy, no detailed critique of his method will be offered here.[12]

Clausewitz and his disciples did not have the field of military history to themselves. In 1976 the Sandhurst historian John Keegan published *The Face of Battle*, a book that did more to revive military history as a respectable academic discipline than any other. Keegan was one of the keynote speakers at the 1996 Conference on the Soldiers' Experience of War in Edinburgh, Scotland. In his paper, he recalled his motivation for writing *The Face of Battle*.

> The military history I had been taught at Oxford, Clausewitz and the rest of it – simply did not coincide with what veterans told me about the battlefield. The warrior in Clausewitz was a sort of a cypher – a being subject to fear and fatigue and capable of bravery but faceless, unindividualistic and asocial. Friendship with soldiers, immersion in their company told me that someone must be wrong; either Clausewitz and conventional military historians or soldiers with experience of war.

Keegan decided that 'it was not the soldiers who were misinforming me.' He then set out on a quest to understand what actually happened on the battlefield. He began with the assumption that 'a rational army would run away and a rational soldier would refuse to fight,' and from this developed a theory of combat motivation built on those concepts, inducement, coercion, and narcosis:

> Men fought partly because they were forced to do so (conscription) and partly because there were rewards for fighting – which might be material (loot) but could be symbolic (medals) or emotional, the emotional including self-esteem or the esteem of close comrades, friends, family, state, nation – and they suppressed the reflex antipathy to the risks involved, when necessary with alcohol or drugs.[13]

In Edinburgh, Keegan revised his triad by adding the concept of 'the big man,' the individual soldier of extraordinary ability and personality who exerts influence both through leadership and through the mimicry of his behaviour by other soldiers. He also suggested that historians need to understand the cruelty, frenzy, and fantasy that combat arouses. Stephen Spielberg took this suggestion to heart in his Omaha Beach scenes.

These two approaches to military history – the study of combat effectiveness and the study of combat motivation – were just beginning to flourish at the time when English and his American and British counterparts were beginning to write about the Normandy campaign. The influential American historian Russell Weigley was first into the field with *Eisenhower's Lieutenants* (1981). Weigley, previously a practitioner of the 'new' military history, now proposed 'to carry his studies from the political and social' to the test of war. 'A day's trial by battle,' he wrote, 'often reveals more of the essential nature of an army than a generation of peace.' Weigley chose to write a history of 'the American army's greatest campaign, told from the perspective of its commanders.'[14]

Weigley began his discussion with a brief overview of the American and German armies. He based his critique of the American infantry on S.L.A. Marshall's statement that 'only 15 percent of the riflemen ever fired a shot at the enemy.' Weigley provided his own gloss on Marshall's opinion, adding that in the absence of a sergeant 'watching closely as he had in earlier wars ... most soldiers could not bring themselves to fire.'[15] Weigley had some trouble in sticking to these ideas when examining actual battles but for the most part his analysis of command floated on a sea of untested assumptions about what happened on the battlefield. He drew an equally theoretical picture of the German army, which he insisted 'still could claim to be qualitatively the best army in the world' in 1944. This qualitative advantage, he believed, 'lay in firepower enhanced by superior professional skill among the officers and superior combat savvy and unexcelled courage among the ranks.' This was, he insisted, 'due to the ability of German officers to transform individual soldiers into cohesive units' at the company level instead of the squad or platoon, as was the case for the Americans. He concluded: 'It is not dedication to a cause but unit consciousness and solidarity that makes an army an effective fighting force.'[16] Weigley did not trouble to document any of this, by the 1980s such views, backed by the 'social science' of Martin Van Creveld and Trevor Dupuy, were as widely accepted as Marshall's 'ratio of fire.'

Carlo D'Este's *Decision in Normandy*, published in 1983, strengthened the image of hesitant, unaggressive Allied soldiers confronting bold, resolute Panzer grenadiers. D'Este, a retired American army officer with a gift for clean writing and enormous energy for research, set out to examine what he called 'the unwritten story of Montgomery and the Allied Campaign.' Like Weigley, he was essentially interested in strategy and was determined to prove that Montgomery never followed his famous 'masterplan.' In seeking to explain Montgomery's actions, D'Este emphasized a number of contemporary accounts of the problems encountered by British and Canadian troops in Normandy. He was especially impressed by Brigadier James Hargest, a New Zealand officer attached to British 50th Division as an observer. Hargest's harsh criticisms of 'the English soldier,' who 'differs from soldiers in the dominions,'[17] require more detailed analysis than can be offered here. His comments are specific to one British division during a period of frustration and stalemate and should be considered in that light.[18] D'Este generalized from such evidence to argue that the Anglo-Canadian armies lacked both leadership and combat effectiveness. According to D'Este, Montgomery's operations were, like the battle for Caen, 'too little, too late.'[19]

This approach was also evident in Max Hastings's bestseller *Over-*

lord: D-Day and the Battle for Normandy, published on the fortieth anniversary of D-Day. Hastings believed that past accounts of Normandy
had been 'full of chauvinistic post-war platitudes,' and quoted Liddell
Hart's view that 'there has been too much glorification of the campaign
and too little objective investigation.'[20] In a chapter titled 'Soldiers,'
Hastings wrote of 'the glory of German arms in Normandy'[21] and cited
Trevor Dupuy's numerical analysis as proof of German superiority.

The scholarly and journalistic consensus on the performance of the
Allied armies did not go unchallenged. When Harold Leinbaugh and
John Campbell began their research for *The Men of Company K* (1985),
they were astounded to discover that historians like Weigley and Keegan believed Marshall's story that 'not more than 15 percent' of combat
soldiers actually fired at the enemy. As combat veterans, they knew
this was nonsense, and they persuaded Roger Spiller, founder of the
Combat Studies Institute at Fort Leavenworth, Kansas, to review Marshall's evidence. Spiller discovered that the mass interviews of men
fresh from combat – interviews that were said to be the basis of the
'ratio of fire' – had never taken place. Also, the interviews recorded in
Marshall's notebooks made no reference to questions about how many
men fired their weapons. In other words, Marshall had made it all
up![22]

Other American historians, including Stephen Ambrose and Michael
Doubler, began to challenge the consensus. However, no similar
debate developed in Britain, where the scholarly and popular consensus about the failure of the British army has been maintained by a new
generation. The distinguished military historian John Gooch, writing
as the co-editor of a series on military history and policy, introduced a
study of the training of the army with this statement: 'The combat performance of the British Army in North West Europe ... has been measured against that of the German army and found to be wanting in
almost every respect, saved from the embarrassment of its own inadequacies chiefly by the combined weight of Allied superiority in the air
and the support of high volumes of artillery fire.'[23]

The book's author, Timothy Harrison Place, hesitates to fully en-
dorse this view. Even so, his examination of military training in Britain
is premised on the idea that British and Canadian troops were
ineffective. This approach was further developed by Russell Hart in a

comparative examination of British, Canadian, and American combat performance in Normandy. Hart concluded that the American army 'demonstrated an ability to learn quickly'[24] whereas the British and (especially) Canadian armies were poorly trained, badly led, and slow to learn.

The first faint signs of revisionism appeared with the publication of David French's *Raising Churchill's Army* (2000). This thoughtful and carefully researched book suggested that though traditional 'explanations of the limitations of the British army's combat capability are not wrong, they are in some respects superficial, incomplete and based on a limited analysis of the available evidence.' French promised 'a fuller and better documented account of why the British army fought the war against Germany in the way that it did.'[25] To accomplish this, he analysed material on doctrine, morale, weapons, and training; however, he provided no direct examination of specific military operations. A second 'revisionist' work, Stephen A. Hart's *Montgomery and 'Colossal Cracks': 21st Army Group in Normandy, 1944–45*, defended Montgomery and his two army commanders while accepting assumptions about the 'limited capabilities' of the Anglo-Canadian soldiers.[26] No attempt to re-examine what happened on the battlefield was undertaken.

My account of the Canadian experience in the Battle of Normandy is based on the best available evidence of what actually happened in combat. The basic sources are the Message Logs (which recorded the signals exchanged between units), the War Diaries, the Historical Officer interviews conducted within days of the battle, the written orders issued in the field, operational research reports, air photos and maps, and an intimate knowledge of the ground.

The argument of this study is that the evidence demonstrates that the achievement of the Allied and especially the Canadian armies in Normandy has been greatly underrated while the effectiveness of the German army has been greatly exaggerated. The defeat and near destruction of two German armies in just seventy-six days was one of the most remarkable military victories of the Second World War. It was a victory won primarily by Allied soldiers employing flexible and innovative operational and tactical solutions to the challenges confronting them. The Canadians played a role in this victory all out of proportion to the number of troops engaged. Their performance at both the tactical and operational level was far from perfect but it compares favourably with that of any other army in Normandy.

The evidence shows that in both the Allied and German armies, combat motivation and combat effectiveness varied across time for individuals and units. Motivation is an especially difficult theme to generalize about. In Normandy, the great majority of soldiers on both sides waged war with the general belief in the legitimacy and necessity of what they were doing. Most of them coupled this with an equally strong belief in what Leonard V. Smith has called 'proportionality.' Smith's study of the French 5th Infantry Division in the First World War led him to conclude that for the soldier of the Third Republic, the key issue was 'whether and under what circumstances they considered the level of violence expected of them relevant to the goal they shared of winning the war.'[27] For the soldiers fighting in Normandy, from generals to privates, combat was subject to the same sort of rational analysis. Orders were negotiated, amended, or ignored as individual decision makers engaged in calculations of risk versus gain. Units that were brave and effective in one situation could be cautious and wholly ineffective in another. Leadership could falter as men were killed, wounded, or simply worn out. Leadership could be restored as new men, in new situations, created or re-created unit cohesion or as veteran combat leaders were re-energized.

Chance played a significant role in the development of unit morale and effectiveness. If a battalion was selected for what turned out to be an impossible task while a sister battalion waited in reserve, the consequences long outlasted the day's fighting. Early success in a winnable battle had equally far-reaching effects, though a good reputation was likely to lead to more 'opportunities' to demonstrate prowess. As units gained experience, good morale and leadership might increase the chances of success on the battlefield but success to a platoon, company, or battalion commander could mean survival as much as the capture of a designated objective.

All the armies that fought in Normandy entered the battle trained to employ explicit operational and tactical doctrines. These doctrines were helpful in some situations, positively dangerous in others. Doctrines were amended, abused, or ignored as the situations confronting the combat troops changed. The Germans continued to believe in immediate counterattack until experience convinced front-line commanders that such predictability played to Allied strengths. The Allies learned that their version of fire and movement – artillery fire neutralizing the enemy while infantry advanced to the objective – rarely worked the way it was supposed to due to the inaccuracy of predicted fire. Both sides learned that survival on a battlefield dominated by mortars and artillery meant digging in and remaining out of sight until a carefully co-ordinated advance or withdrawal was ordered. A great deal of learning took place between D-Day and the end of August 1944.

Before examining life and death on the battlefields of Normandy, we need to know more about the Canadians who fought there. In the spring of 1944 the Canadian army consisted of 405,834 men and women who had volunteered for 'General Service,' meaning that they had agreed to serve wherever required. A further 72,971 were enlisted under the terms of the National Resources Mobilization Act (NRMA), which limited their service to Canada.[28] A relatively small part of that very large force, around 100,000 men, were on the strength of First Canadian Army preparing for Operation Overlord, the invasion of France.[29] Less than one-third of these would be involved in close combat. It is the experience of this group that will be investigated.

The first thing to note about them is that the volunteers were very young. Two-thirds were between eighteen and twenty-five, and most of the rest, including company and battalion commanders, were not much older. The great dividing line between officers and men was formal education.[30] An officer without a high school diploma was a rarity, but in the ranks around one-third had not completed primary school and another third had ended their education with grade seven. Only one in eight had finished high school. The view that unemployment was the crucial factor in enlistment is quite wrong. A survey of the occupational histories of 347,000 men who had joined the armed forces in the first three years of the war reported that 89 per cent had left jobs to enlist. The figures would be different for 1939 and 1st Division, but not as dramatically different as folklore has suggested.[31]

A large number of volunteers had been rejected due to bad teeth, poor eyesight, or flat feet, not to mention tuberculosis, but even after the most obvious cases were weeded out, the army recruited large numbers of men who today would seem to be poor physical specimens. The average soldier was 5'7" and weighed less than 160 pounds, and this average includes many who were considerably smaller in stature.[32] Years of plentiful food and rigorous physical training would transform these recruits into men who could spend a day on a long route march and still have plenty of energy to use on an overnight pass.

The army at first resisted any form of personnel selection on the grounds that training would sort out the recruits more effectively. But social scientists, determined to establish their professional claims, persuaded National Defence Headquarters to institute 'intelligence tests' and psychiatric screening.[33] We therefore have personnel records in Ottawa that provide a great deal of information about the attitudes and values of the middle-class university graduates who conducted the interviews, and even a bit of useful information about the men they studied. By 1944 most soldiers had taken the M-Test and undergone some form of personnel selection interview that included questions related to motivation. A review of hundreds of these files suggests that Canadian soldiers understood the war and their part in it in simple but clear terms: Hitler's Germany was a threat to their world and their values. Their world often included a close and sentimental relationship with Great Britain. This has led many to perceive that they were not quite authentically Canadian – a presentist view that they would have found very strange.

As Jonathan Vance has demonstrated, Canadians shared a collective memory of the Great War that included graphic images of trench warfare and heavy casualties but also involved a deeply held belief that the sacrifices had been necessary and meaningful.[34] Everyone who volunteered in 1939 was aware that war might turn out to be hell. Those who volunteered after June 1940 also knew that the war would last a very long time. Few doubted the need for action. Unfortunately, the Canadian army was not in a position to make the most of its keen young volunteers. The militia regiments, which were to be the foundation of the active service force, had been starved of money and equipment for so long that they could offer little in the way of training for modern war. The War Diaries of the units mobilized in 1939 and 1940 present an extraordinary picture of an army without enough weapons, boots, or warm clothes. After 1st Division left for England, taking what little was available, the regiments assigned to 2nd Division concentrated on physical conditioning through route marches and team sports. We need to study the role of organized sport in the making of the army and perhaps much else in Canadian society. The hockey rink, the gymnasium floor, and the football field provided the platoon, the company, and the battalion with the opportunity to forge the kind of spirit and teamwork necessary in combat. Many junior NCOs, the vital combat leaders of 1944, first came to notice on the playing field. In Britain, games continued to be a vital part of training. For the first two years of the war the Canadians were committed to a static role that allowed for little more than individual, platoon and company training based on concepts employed in the Great War. Early attempts to deploy large motorized units on the narrow roads of Sussex produced chaos and did little to build confidence that the army had mastered the art of mobile warfare.

Two years is a very long time in the life of a young man, so we should not be surprised that routine training and barrack life in an all-male environment did not fully engage the hearts and minds of all the soldiers all the time. British beer, especially in its weak wartime guise, compared poorly with the real Canadian stuff, but it was still possible to consume it in large quantities. English girls presented fewer adaptation problems and were eagerly sought after. The focus of everyone's life was leave – a trip to London, a longer journey to Scotland, a reunion with a friend posted to another unit. Inevitably the numbers absent without leave skyrocketed. Those few soldiers who survived the years in England without an AWL blackmark on their records probably owe it to a sympathetic orderly officer.[35]

In the fall of 1941 the Canadian army was jolted out of its coastal defence routine by the introduction of 'battle drill,' a method of practising small unit tactics that transformed attitudes toward training. Battle drill was developed by a British divisional commander, and reached the Canadians through the missionary efforts of Lt.-Col. Fred Scott and his Calgary Highlanders. Battle drill began with simple rules for fire and movement, which soldiers were to learn like athletes practising team sports. The elements could be taught on a parade square. The whole idea might have quickly degenerated if the Calgaries had not constructed a training area that simulated a battlefield.[36]

Battle drill fever spread like wildfire, transforming section, platoon, and company training as well as raising morale. Senior officers responded to this grass roots movement with mixed feelings, but by early 1942 battle drill schools had been formed in England and Canada. Battle drill helped invigorate the training cycle, but as the desert battles and the Dieppe raid were to demonstrate, the British army had not yet learned how to wage war against the German army at the operational level.

Lessons were learned on 19 August, but long after Dieppe the Commonwealth forces, preparing for the invasion of France, were few in number and were accorded the lowest priority as equipment was upgraded. It is hard to argue with an allocation of scarce resources that favoured the air force, the navy, and units engaged in North Africa and Italy, but it is surely remarkable that the divisions allotted to 21 Army Group for Overlord did not receive many of the basic weapons they would fight with until the second half of 1943 or early 1944. The delivery of the 6-pounder antitank gun, the PIAT, the 17-pounder, the Sherman tank, and the M10 self-propelled antitank gun constituted a virtual revolution in the combat capability of the British and Canadian divisions, yet little attention has been paid to the transformation.

The 'new' infantry battalion was still based on four rifle companies, each of three platoons, but both company and battalion headquarters could draw on the specialized platoons of a 200-man-strong Support Company. The antitank platoon with its six carrier-towed 6-pounders provided immediate tank-killing power to infantry consolidating on an objective. The gun's low profile and stopping power at ranges of 500 to 800 yards meant the battalion no longer depended on the divisional antitank regiment.[37] The mortar platoon of 1944 was equipped with a vastly improved version of the 3-inch mortar. This weapon, which had long compared badly to its German counterpart, the 81 mm mortar, had been refined through the introduction of smokeless powder, changes in bomb design, and dramatic improvements in range. Comparative tests at the infantry school in Yorkshire suggested that the modified British mortar was now the superior weapon.[38] The mortar platoon deployed six of these weapons, which allowed for heavy concentrations during enemy attacks. The carrier platoon could employ its thirteen Bren gun carriers in a support role, providing firepower and mobility. In the right hands the carrier platoon could operate as light armour. The pioneer platoon dealt with enemy mines and sowed battalion minefields; it also provided light engineering assistance.

In a 1944 infantry division, the nine rifle battalions accounted for fewer than 8,000 of the 18,000 serving officers and men. The three field artillery regiments – a fourth was added for the D-Day assault – and the antitank regiment added 2,400 to the total. The 1944 order of battle also included a machine gun and mortar battalion, which employed the 4.2-inch mortar and the venerable but still very effective Vickers medium machine gun. These battalions provided companies of platoons to serve with the rifle battalions, adding enormous weight to their firepower. Each infantry division also included a reconnaissance regiment that provided contact detachments on D-Day and an effective mobile reserve during the bridgehead battles.[39]

All of these changes required a good deal of retraining. But this was done, and by May 1944, 21 Army Group was ready for battle, provided a number of conditions were met. First, the Soviets would have to continue to engage the energies of two-thirds of the German army. Nothing was more vital to the success of Overlord than a Soviet summer offensive. Second, the elaborate deception scheme code-named Fortitude, designed to reinforce the German army's belief that the real invasion would take place in the Pas de Calais, had to work. Third, complete air and naval superiority had to be established. Within this strategic framework, British leaders, ever mindful of the sacrifices of the Great War, proposed to wage a campaign that would minimize casualties in 21 Army Group and especially the Second British Army. Montgomery shared this approach, especially after the War Office warned that if the fighting became intensive and prolonged, at least two divisions and several separate brigades might have to be disbanded for lack of reinforcements.[40]

This led British commanders to plan a campaign that would proceed in a series of managed phases. After the invading troops were ashore they were to establish and defend a bridgehead, defeating the German counterattacks with naval, air, and artillery fire. The bridgehead was, if possible, to include the city of Caen, the centre of the road and rail network in Normandy. If Caen could not be captured before German reinforcements arrived, the city was to be masked until the buildup of Allied forces was sufficient for a set piece attack.[41] The capture of Caen and the high ground south of the city was of particular importance to tactical air force officers, who wanted sites for their airfields, but everyone agreed that the city and the bridges across the Orne had to be taken as quickly as possible.

South of Caen, the country was open, with good roads leading to the Seine and Paris. The planners assumed that the enemy would defend this area in strength, as a breakthrough here would cut off German forces in the west and bring a quick conclusion to the Battle of Normandy. If the enemy behaved rationally, there would be a fighting withdrawal to a new defensive line at the Seine, with the Caen sector held as a pivot. The plan called for the American army to capture Cherbourg and then fight its way south, turning west into Brittany to capture Brest and create a new port at Quiberon Bay. With the Brittany ports and Cherbourg available, the Allied forces would complete the buildup necessary to liberate France by the autumn of 1944.[42] All of this was the basis of Montgomery's 'master plan,' a broad strategic concept that proved to have little operational significance except that it focused attention on Brittany.

If 21 Army Group could be maintained at full strength, there would be ten infantry and five armoured divisions available to wage war against the German forces on the eastern flank. Even with five additional armoured brigades available to support the infantry divisions, the prospects of achieving the force ratios necessary to overcome the enemy in this vital sector were bleak. The presence of three or four German armoured divisions and a like number of infantry divisions would make it impossible to achieve the 3:1 ratio thought to be necessary for successful attacks on well-defended positions.

The planners hoped to compensate for this weakness by fighting on Allied, not German, terms. This meant employing the largest possible amount of artillery in the bridgehead. Each corps was to be supported by an Army Group Royal Artillery (AGRA) with 4.5- or 5.5-inch medium guns. Air observation pilots flying light aircraft were to direct this fire, and there were to be abundant allotments of ammunition for both the medium and field artillery. Fully 18 per cent of the men in 21 Army Group were gunners; just 15 per cent were to be wearing infantry flashes.[43]

This approach to war required commanders to emphasize logistics, elaborate fire plans, and centralized command and control. If shells were to be substituted for men's lives, they had to be delivered to the right places at the right times. Little attention has been paid to the pre-Normandy investment in survey regiments, air photo interpretation, meteorological reports, sound ranging, flash spotting, and other elements of the gunner's war,[44] but these efforts were an essential part of the preparations for a victory at a blood price the Allies could afford.

The British attitude to war in 1944 was influenced by growing concerns about the future. The great successes of the Red Army in 1943 had raised the spectre of a Europe dominated by the Soviet Union; also, the growth of American military power in the Pacific pointed to a future in which Britain might be marginalized in Asia. Churchill had, in his own words, 'not become His Majesty's First Minister to preside over the liquidation of the British Empire,' and he was anxious to ensure that when war ended there would be sufficient British forces available to secure western Europe and the Mediterranean and to reconquer Southeast Asia. When the British soldiers of 21 Army Group were told that they were to be called the British Liberation Army, they ruefully noted that the initials BLA also stood for 'Burma Looms Ahead.'[45]

Canadian leaders approached the coming invasion from a somewhat different perspective. Prime Minister William Lyon Mackenzie King deliberately avoided involvement in broader strategic questions, hoping that the war would end before casualties to Canadian troops again raised the spectre of conscription. But King had little influence on his Minister of National Defence, J.L. Ralston, who understood that English-speaking Canadians regarded themselves as one of the principal Allied nations and that they wished to play a large and visible role in the war. As much as Churchill and Brooke were influenced by the memory of the Somme, Ralston and his senior army commanders saw themselves as carrying on the traditions of those men who had triumphed at Vimy Ridge and led the way to victory in August 1918 at Amiens. Canada's generals were eager for battle and anxious to demonstrate that they and their men were worthy successors to Arthur Currie and the Canadian Corps. The transfer of a Canadian division to 1 British Corps for the assault phase of Overlord was a product of both British and Canadian attitudes. Ralston had insisted on sending Canadian troops to Italy in 1943 because he feared that the war might end before the Canadian army got into action.[46] He and his generals were determined to have a Canadian presence on D-Day, and the British were more than willing to share what everyone feared might be a bloodbath on the beaches of Normandy.

With 1st Division in Italy and 2nd recovering from Dieppe, 3rd Canadian Infantry Division was the only possible choice for the assault on Fortress Europe. The division had been formed in the summer of 1940 in response to the invasion of France. The need to give all regions of the country representation delayed final decisions on the order of battle until late 1940, but it scarcely mattered, as little was available in the way of equipment. The division concentrated itself in the Maritime provinces at camps in Sussex, New Brunswick, and Debert, Nova Scotia. Debert was under construction and could offer little more than drafty H-Huts and improvised parade squares. The rifle range at nearby Truro was 'unused and overgrown,' and a new range took months to construct.

Small-town Nova Scotia, with its restrictive liquor laws, offered few temptations, and it took the authorities months to open a wet canteen. The people of Truro were friendly, and the winter was spent in elementary training, route marches, and sports. By the summer of 1941 the patience of many of the young men, numbed by the boring routines of army life, was wearing thin. A dollar and thirty cents a day was not much compensation for a year in rural Nova Scotia and a life that seemed only vaguely related to waging war against Hitler. Requests to transfer to the RCAF, RCN, or any army unit going overseas were routinely refused, and discipline began to sag. August was marked by some pitched battles in the streets of Truro. The order to move to Halifax to board ships for Britain was a welcome relief both to the soldiers and to the people of Nova Scotia.[47]

The division trained intensively throughout 1942, participating in a series of exercises designed to school officers in the command and control of large formations. These exercises were simply bewildering to the men who were essentially present to march long distances and demonstrate that traffic jams would occur when large numbers were concentrated in the narrow streets of English villages. In May 1942 the division was sharply criticized for its performance in Exercise Beaver IV. Lt.-Gen. Montgomery, the area commander, condemned Maj.-Gen. Basil Price as a complete amateur, totally unable to train his division, 'though a very delightful person.'[48] A month later, the report on Exercise Tiger, a simulation of an 'encounter battle,' required some units to march 250 miles in eleven days. The troops lived hard under conditions approximating active service, and even Montgomery was impressed. This did not save Price, who was replaced by Maj.-Gen. R.F.L. 'Rod' Keller, a hard-living, tough-talking, permanent force infantry officer, who would lead the division into action. Keller was to be severely criticized during the Normandy battles, but in the eighteen months before D-Day he and his 'Bay Street' staff officers transformed the division into a fully trained formation.[49] The army's severest critics have never questioned the professionalism of the divisional CRE (Commander Royal Engineers), Brig. R.J. Cassidy, or the CRS (Commander Royal Signals), Brig. G.O. Gamble. Both Col. J.D. Mingay, the GSO1 (General Staff Officer), and Lt.-Col. E.A. Coté, the AA&QMG (Assistant Adjutant and Quartermaster General), were recognized as outstanding organizers who made sure that 3rd Division functioned with smooth efficiency.

The division was especially fortunate to have Brig. Stanley Todd as its CRA (Commander Royal Artillery). Todd, a tall, imposing, and energetic leader, was to become a legend in the army. Known as 'Uncle Stanley,' he trained the field regiments in every aspect of their craft, and demanded endless repetition of the drills, to ensure that when the fighting began they would be able to place accurate, concentrated fire in the shortest possible time. Todd made sure each regiment selected the best possible men as forward observation officers (FOOs). These men would provide the link between the rifle company and the guns. The FOO was often the key to success in battle, and company commanders sometimes described their job as escorting the FOO across Europe.

The 3rd Division was also fortunate in the quality of its battlefield commanders. Harry Foster, a permanent force officer with a temperament and style similar to Keller's, commanded 7th 'Western' Brigade. Foster was no military genius, but he had been to Staff College and knew the basics. He also knew when to leave matters in the hands of his battalion commanders, who were simply outstanding. The Canadian Scottish Regiment commanded by F.N. Cabeldu, the Royal Winnipeg Rifles' J.M. Meldram, and the Regina Rifles' F.M. Matheson had worked hard to train junior leaders and maintain high morale. The Canscots and Reginas were to prove to be two of the most effective battalions involved in the Normandy campaign in any army. The miseries of the Winnipegs were, as we shall see, beyond their control.

Eighth Brigade was commanded by Ken Blackader, a Black Watch militia officer from Montreal whom many, including Montgomery, had tagged as a future divisional commander.[50] His brigade included the Queen's Own Rifles, one of Canada's oldest and most famous militia regiments. Lt.-Col. J.G. Spragge and his men would need all their skill to survive D-Day and continue to function, but this they undoubtedly did. The North Shore (New Brunswick) Regiment could not compete with the prestige of the Queen's Own, but Lt.-Col. D.B. Buell and his battalion had been rated highly in every pre-invasion scheme. The English and French speaking Canadians had easily jelled, and morale was never a problem. The Régiment de la Chaudière, the only French-Canadian battalion in 3rd Division, was a question mark because the army overseas was desperately short of French-speaking infantry. In the weeks before the invasion, other battalions had been combed for French-speaking personnel to post to the reinforcement unit so that the Chaudières could continue to function after the first shock of combat. Lt.-Col. J.E. Mathieu had worked hard to train his battalion, but Blackader knew it would have to be used with care.

The 9th Highland Brigade presented a completely reassuring picture. The Highland Light Infantry of Canada from Waterloo County and the North Nova Scotia Highlanders had all the characteristics of good, locally recruited militia regiments. Each was commanded by men from outside the regimental family selected on the basis of performance. F.M. Griffiths, an RMC graduate who had maintained a militia connection while practising law, took over the HLI in January 1944. He liked what he saw but warned the 'big happy family' that promotion would be by merit and that everyone would have to prove themselves.

By June, 'Smokey' Griffiths and his battalion were deeply devoted to one another. Charles Petch, Black Watch and RMC, took over the North Novas in a similar situation and established good rapport with everyone despite a shakedown of the unit. The Stormont Dundas and Glengarry Highlanders, one of the most consistently effective units, found their battlefield commander from among the officers who joined in 1940. Lt.-Col. G.H. Christiansen, who developed the battalion battle school, impressed everyone with his calm, confident manner.

The division began the campaign with the 2nd Canadian Armoured Brigade under command. Brig. R.A. Wyman was brought back down from Italy to lead the brigade, but as regiments were assigned to work with infantry brigades and squadrons with battalions, the armoured brigadier's role in combat was chiefly administrative. The Fort Garry Horse and the First Hussars equipped two of their three squadrons with duplex-drive (DD) amphibious tanks and spent the months before D-Day re-equipping and learning to 'swim' their tanks ashore. The Sherbrooke Fusiliers, assigned to the reserve infantry brigade for the advance inland from the beachhead, worked closely with the North Nova Scotia Highlanders, who were to lead the brigade to their D-Day objective – Carpiquet.[51] Critics of Allied planning and doctrine have often questioned whether battalions and armoured regiments received enough combined arms training, but in the preparatory period, 3rd Division focussed on what everyone thought would be the main job – getting ashore and staying there. These tasks were thoroughly rehearsed, and there were no problems with infantry–tank co-operation either in the assault phase or during the advance inland.

All of the evidence from training reports in the six months before D-Day indicates that everyone who reviewed the performance of 3rd Division and 2nd Armoured Brigade believed that they were ready for action. When Dr Robert Gregory arrived to take up his appointment as divisional psychiatrist in March 1944, he met with regimental medical officers and padres as well as combat officers. He reported that 'general morale throughout the division is excellent. The troops are relaxed and in the highest spirits. Some of the officers and practically all of the other ranks feel that our troops will go twenty-five miles in one day ... there seems to be no talk of hazard.' Gregory was asked to screen the division and remove doubtful individuals who might not be able to withstand the shock of combat. In three months, he found just 127 men who required reclassification. He noted, however, that the situation was different in the reinforcement units, where training was inadequate and morale doubtful.[52] The Allied system of keeping replacements in a holding unit to be sent forward as individuals offered maximum flexibility, but many wondered if there would be a price to pay for managerial efficiency.

While 3rd Division prepared for the assault on Fortress Europe, 2 Canadian Corps, under its new commander Lt.-Gen. Guy Granville Simonds, trained for operations beyond the beachhead, to 'attack, wear down and destroy' German troops 'who would fight a series of defensive battles' on ground of their own choosing. There was broad agreement on how this was to be accomplished, but Simonds knew that most of his subordinate commanders had not been in action, and he was determined to ensure that they understood how the battles were to be fought. On 17 February 1944 he issued a directive on 'Operational Policy' that outlined clearly the doctrine the British and Canadian armies would employ in Normandy.[53] (The full directive is reproduced in Appendix A and should be read in conjunction with chapters 6 to 10.)

Simonds sent copies to Lt.-Gen. M.C. Dempsey, the officer commanding Second British Army, who replied that he was 'very glad to see you and I left Italy with the very same view ... I agree with everything you say,' and to Montgomery, who read it 'with complete agreement.'[54] Simonds's version of Allied operational doctrine called for centralized control of virtually every aspect of the battle. The enemy, he believed, could only be overcome by attacks that were 'carefully organized and strongly supported by all available artillery.' The Germans, he noted, established forward defences that 'are not thickly held in terms of men, but are strong in automatic weapons and well supported by mortars sited up to three of four thousand yards' behind forward lines. The essence of the German system of defence was the counterattack, and 'as long as fresh reserves are available the Germans will counterattack continuously, supported by self-propelled guns brought up to close-range.'

Simonds knew from his experience in Sicily that 'the success of the offensive battle hinges on the defeat of the German counterattacks,' and he was determined to train his corps to deal with this reality. His solution was to stage divisional attacks 'on a single thrust line, disposed in depth on a one-brigade front.' Brigades would be passed through one another to maintain momentum, with the frontage of the attack 'limited to that on which really heavy support can be given.' Simonds did not discount the possibility of manoeuvre, noting that when the enemy concentrated its strength across the thrust line, a reserve brigade could be 'thrown wide of the leading brigade' to dissipate the enemy's strength. Even so, 'the weight of artillery support must not be divided.'

Simonds saw the infantry division, always and only when supported by the artillery, as the 'sledge hammer' in the attack. The armoured division was to be 'the weapon of opportunity,' capable of dealing with enemy rearguard positions and developing a breakout, but he insisted it was too weak in infantry to carry out an attack in depth. Everything Simonds had seen in Italy persuaded him that Allied armour could not be used successfully against prepared German positions with their carefully sited and well-camouflaged anti-tank guns.

Simonds did not outline the tactics to be employed in carrying out his 'operational policy,' partly because such training was carried out in divisional battle schools and partly because his operational doctrine left little room for traditional platoon or section tactics. By 1944, experienced Allied commanders knew that the one certain way of defeating the Germans was to find, fix, and then neutralize the enemy with overwhelming firepower. This would allow the infantry to assault and occupy vital ground, which the enemy would then counterattack. This 'bite and hold' doctrine depended on the development of centrally controlled, indirect artillery fire capable of focusing the guns of a regiment, division, or corps on a specific area.[55] This technique provided the best possible answer to the enemy's doctrinal commitment to immediate and continuous counterattacks and German technical superiority in infantry weapons and armoured vehicles.

An artillery-based battle doctrine required the infantry to move forward at a steady pace, leaning into the barrage, so as to be on the objective before the enemy could engage the attackers. Rifle companies, supported by tanks, would clear and consolidate, bring the antitank guns forward, and dig in to meet counterattacks from enemy infantry, who would be advancing behind tanks or self-propelled assault guns. Success depended largely on the ability of FOOs to direct the fire of the field and medium regiments at observed targets. The infantry companies and their antitank platoons dealt with any enemy who had survived the artillery concentrations. Battalion mortars, and the divisional mortars and medium machine guns allotted to assault battalions, thickened the defensive fire.

This procedure, rehearsed in countless exercises, did not require the infantry to practise the fire-and-movement skills learned in battle schools. It did, however, raise questions about other aspects of infantry training. These issues were widely debated within the army, and on 20 April 1944 a four-day conference was held at the School of Infantry to exchange ideas and information. The format called for demonstrations of currently approved tactics followed by question-and-answer sessions. The 'Record of Discussions,'[56] distributed by the school on 15 May 1944, suggests that though there was broad agreement on operational policy, the implications of the approved doctrine for tactical training had not been fully worked out.

One of the most contentious questions was raised by a staff officer representing 2nd British Army, who noted that present teaching placed too much emphasis on the use of infantry weapons in the attack, especially the Bren. Experience had shown that the ammunition problem was acute in the counterattack phase. Ammunition fired in the attack was seldom aimed and was therefore wasted. The same officer insisted that though the rifleman used his weapon in defending a position, in the attack he was 'mostly employed as an ammunition carrier for the Bren.' This realistic view of the impact of operational doctrine on tactics directly challenged the traditional emphasis on teaching the infantry to fight their way forward, with their own weapons, by fire and movement. It also raised questions about what would actually happen in battle when the attack plan called for soldiers to fight through the enemy's forward positions onto a reverse slope.[57]

The Infantry School, like the rest of the army, had devoted considerable effort to analysing German defensive doctrine, which was based on lightly held forward positions and strong reverse slope defences.[58]

The spokesman for the School of Artillery suggested that an optional pause in the fire plan, which allowed time for the infantry commander, through his FOO, to direct fire on the reverse slope, worked well in exercises; however, there was no agreement that this was a workable solution.[59] Everyone understood the logic of bite and hold, but no one was willing to argue for such a conservative approach to be embedded in doctrine. This uncertainty was evident in a discussion of the implications of the decision that all troops should carry a shovel and a pick into battle. Obviously, the additional weight would limit the ability of the soldier to fight his way forward; yet without entrenching tools, no position could be held against enemy counterattacks and mortar fire.[60]

The critics of 21 Army Group's preinvasion training are quite right when they argue that the army's leadership 'failed to enforce a coherent and effective tactical doctrine.'[61] But was this a weakness or a strength? There was agreement on operational doctrine, and a flexible approach to tactical problems encouraged officers to seek solutions based on specific battlefield conditions, especially analysis of the terrain using air photographs. A problem-solving approach to combat has little appeal to military theorists, but it proved to be an effective method of dealing with the enemy.

The discussions at the Infantry School barely touched on the role of the armoured regiments assigned to work with infantry battalions. This was the result of an earlier decision that the armoured commander, at the regimental, squadron, or troop level, 'is the sole arbitrator of how he can best employ his resources.'[62] During training this meant that the armoured commander decided how to employ his tanks in support of an infantry attack, which was itself largely determined by the artillery fire plan created at division or corps. Although 'the primary role' of tanks cooperating with infantry was 'to close with the enemy,' armoured doctrine permitted indirect support 'on account of the unsuitability of the ground' or for other reasons. Armoured officers were also reminded that 'everyone, and particularly the infantry, should understand that the tank is designed with the primary object of destroying or neutralizing enemy unarmoured troops.' In other words, it was up to the infantry to protect themselves against enemy armoured attack.[63]

Again, it is clear that those who criticize the Commonwealth forces for failing to develop the kind of integrated tank–infantry battlegroup doctrine successfully practised by the German army are correct: British doctrine, as outlined in May 1944, allowed everything and forbade nothing. It was up to individual commanders to develop methods of employing their tanks effectively. Given the vulnerability of the Sherman and Churchill tanks to enemy fire, such flexibility, when constant improvisation would be required on the battlefield, was an appropriate approach to pre-invasion training.

A similar state of uncertainty affected the preparation of 21 Army Group's five armoured divisions, only one of which had battle experience. All armoured commanders were familiar with the 1943 War Office Military Training Pamphlets that outlined 'the tactical handling of the armoured division and its components,' but each commander drew on his own experience and interpretations of the 'lessons learned' in North Africa and Italy to develop a distinct approach to battle.[64] The Guards Armoured Division favoured set piece attacks with the armour providing indirect fire support for the infantry brigade, whereas 11th Armoured practised infantry-tank cooperation in mobile battlegroups.[65] The 'Desert Rats,' 7th Armoured Division, scheduled to land on D+1 and break out of the bridgehead, trained to employ the armoured brigade as a separate force plunging deep into the enemy's rear areas. The infantry brigade was to follow and secure the ground seized by the armour.[66] The Polish Armoured Division, organized on the same two-brigade basis as the other formations, was a world unto itself. Maj.-Gen. S. Maczek was a serious student of armoured warfare and hoped to employ tank-infantry battle groups in mobile warfare.[67] Unfortunately, the language problem was just one of the sources of mutual incomprehension, which made 21 Army Group reluctant to send the Poles into action.[68]

For most of the training period, 4th Canadian Armoured Division was commanded by Maj.-Gen. F.F. Worthington, the 'father' of the Canadian armoured corps. Worthington, at fifty-four, was declared too old to command in action and was replaced in February 1944 by a veteran of the Italian campaign, George Kitching.[69] The decision to promote Kitching, an infantry brigadier who sported a handlebar mustache to go with his British accent, was a mystery to all who served under him. Two other veteran officers, Brig. J.C. Jefferson and Brig.

E.L. Booth, were brought from Italy to command the 10th Infantry and 4th Armoured Brigades. Both the CRA and CRE were also replaced.[70] The new team had little opportunity to impart whatever operational ideas they had developed in Italy because, when the division completed re-equipping with Shermans, there was no possibility of repeating the large-scale exercises carried out in 1943. Intensive training did take place, but the infantry and armoured brigades rehearsed their roles separately. The armoured brigade's main experience in working with infantry came in April, when each armoured regiment provided a squadron for a period of two weeks to give 2nd Division's infantry 'experience in working with tanks.' The following month, new emphasis was placed on 'infantry and tanks marrying up' within the division.[71] One of the last large-scale tactical exercises without troops (TEWTs), Exercise Iroquois, was specifically designed to familiarize officers 'down to and including squadron leaders' in the use of battle groups designed to defeat the enemy by 'superiority in numbers and equipment, offensive spirit, initiative and most important of all – the closest possible co-operation between the varied arms of the group.'[72] Iroquois closely approximated the organization the division employed in its first battle, Operation Totalize, but a TEWT is not a full-scale exercise.

The Canadian components of 21 Army Group – three divisions, an armoured brigade, a parachute battalion, and No. 2 Army Group Royal Canadian Artillery – were to play a major role in the Battle of Normandy. Earlier accounts of the pre-invasion training period and previous discussions of Anglo-Canadian battle doctrine were based on assumptions about inadequate performance in Normandy. Since the argument of this book is that the Canadians and the rest of 21 Army Group fought a highly successful campaign that required flexibility and improvisation, it seems logical to suggest that both officers and men must have learned the essentials of their trade before they entered battle.

2

D-Day

The best place to begin an inquiry into the D-Day landings is at Dieppe, where the ill-fated 1942 raid took place. The Canadian Battle of Normandy Foundation Study Tour brings university students there each year to walk the ground, analyse the events of 1942, and provoke a discussion of the lessons the Allies ought to have learned from this experience. The students have no difficulty developing a wish list for the assault troops. They want more firepower in all possible forms and a landing site that does not offer the enemy the advantage of clifftop positions overlooking the landing beaches. Their subsequent visit to Omaha Beach invariably reminds them of Dieppe, and they want to know why, if lessons were learned, such terrain was selected for an assault in 1944. The answer – that Omaha was the only beach between Gold and Utah – helps bring home the reality that besides best and least-bad solutions there are sometimes 'no other options available.'[1]

Seeing the terrain in the Anglo-Canadian assault area provides reassurance; here, surely, the overwhelming firepower developed for D-Day made a rapid breakthrough possible. With RAF Bomber Command and U.S. 8th Army Air Force in action and a vast tactical air force available, air power alone must have had the capacity to overwhelm the defenders. And instead of the six small destroyers deployed at Dieppe, the navy provided battleships, cruisers, and a host of smaller support vessels, including landing craft with rockets to launch at the beaches. The division's own field artillery added support, firing over the heads of the infantry during the final thousand yards.[2]

Dieppe had also helped dramatize the need for armoured fighting vehicles to lead the assault. By 1944 there were duplex-drive tanks, which were to 'swim' ashore, arriving ahead of the infantry, and a variety of specialized armour to clear minefields, build bridges, protect combat engineers, and bust concrete bunkers.[3] The planners were determined to avoid a repetition of the slaughter that took place in 1942, and they tried to think of every contingency.

What lessons had the enemy learned? The orders to begin construction of the extensive fortifications that would become known as the Atlantic Wall were issued in March 1942, but as C.P. Stacey argues, 'Dieppe strengthened Hitler's resolution and confirmed him in the belief that the Atlantic Wall idea was sound.'[4] On 25 August 1942, less than a week after the raid, Field Marshal Gerd von Rundstedt issued the following directive:

> The Fuhrer has ordered: During the winter of 1942–43 the coastal defences ... are to be strengthened by using all forces and all means for the construction of permanent fortifications according to the principles employed in the West Wall. This is to be done in a manner as to make any attack from the air, sea or land seem hopeless, and to create a fortress which cannot be taken either frontally or from the rear. Towards this end 15,000 fortifications of a permanent nature are to be built.[5]

Work started immediately, and by July 1943 some 8000 installations had been completed or were under construction. They ranged from small concrete shelters known as 'Tobruks' to elaborate fortified gun positions. Since Hitler and all senior German officers were convinced that the Allies would have to launch their main assault in the Pas de Calais, most of the work of the Todt organization was concentrated there. Though the Calvados coast of Normandy was mentioned as an alternative site, none of the senior officers believed the main invasion would be on a peninsula remote from the German border and easily sealed off from the interior of France.[6]

Even so, the Germans did not neglect Normandy. The Calvados coast offered wide beaches, several small harbours, and proximity to the port of Cherbourg, so it could not be ignored. The eighteen miles between the Orne and the cliffs at Arromanches was an obvious possibility, though the rocky ledges offshore led many to discount the chances of a large-scale landing. Two strongpoints, Franceville and Riva Bella, were constructed at the mouth of the Orne. The Merville battery, with four 75 mm guns set in steel-doored concrete emplacements six feet thick, and a battery of 155 mm guns south of Ouistreham provided additional firepower. Between Riva Bella and Strongpoint Courseulles, a distance of eight miles, nine 'resistance nests' were sited along the dunes and seawall. Each position was somewhat different, but most were built around a gun casement protected from air or naval assault by six feet of concrete on the seaward side and four feet on the roof. The gun, as a consequence, could only fire along the beach in enfilade. Each resistance nest also included pillboxes housing machine guns, as well as mortar positions and Tobruk-type concrete pits for machine guns and their crews. Large concrete bunkers and underground installations offered protection against bombardment.[7] No continuous secondary line of defence was created; instead, field and antitank guns were dug in two to four miles behind the coast. These positions, and the reserve companies quartered in inland villages, were intended to contain anyone who broke through the coastal crust until help arrived in the form of mobile reserves.

Since the spring of 1942, 716th Infantry Division had been responsible for the area. Lt.-Gen. Wilhelm Richter commanded two infantry regiments and a considerable number of artillery and antitank units – roughly 8,000 men. Two 'East' battalions, recruited from Soviet prisoners of war, supplemented his ration strength and labour force, though neither proved willing to fight when the time came.

In March 1944 the 352nd, a first-class mobile infantry division, arrived to strengthen the defences, assuming control of the western part of the Calvados coast. Two battalions of the 716th remained in their original positions, leaving Richter with four regular and two East battalions to cover eight miles of coast. This situation changed dramatically in May 1944, when 21st Panzer Division was moved to the Caen area. Two panzer grenadier battalions and an antitank battalion were placed under Richter's control to provide defence in depth.

According to von Runstedt, the German commander-in-chief in the west, the 716th was well trained and 'completely fit for defence.'[8] The addition of elements of 21st Panzer Division and the extensive program of mine laying and construction of beach obstacles, which Field Marshal Erwin Rommel inspired, added greatly to the strength of the Juno portion of the Atlantic Wall. If Hitler and his generals could agree on a coherent reaction to an invasion, Operation Overlord might prove to be a costly enterprise.

It was perhaps fortunate that Allied battlefield commanders did not learn about the presence of the 21st Panzer and 352nd divisions in the weeks before D-Day.[9] The task before them seemed difficult enough without factoring in substantial enemy reinforcements. The decision to postpone the assault because of the weather was especially trying, as it meant an extra twenty-four hours crammed aboard ship. When the order to go came there was a sense of relief mixed with trepidation. Force J, headed for Juno, passed out of the lee of the Isle of Wight shortly after 0900 on 5 June. The wind was westerly at 16 to 20 miles an hour, producing a 'moderate sea and a slight swell.' This was of little consequence to a destroyer, but it severely affected those on the heavily laden landing ships. The weather moderated toward nightfall, and the mine-sweeping flotillas were able to finish clearing two lanes for each of the assault forces. At midnight, Admiral Bertram Ramsay informed General Dwight Eisenhower that despite problems with the smaller craft, the assault forces were in position and on time.[10] The Supreme Commander was also told that the airborne landings had begun.

When historians really immerse themselves in the world inhabited by the men who planned the invasion of France, two things quickly become apparent: everyone expressed confidence that the operation would succeed, and everyone feared it might fail. Nightmares of 'the Channel running red with blood' and the dread of another Dunkirk-like evacuation persuaded the generals to use three of their highly trained airborne divisions, not to exploit success but to guard against failure.

The decision to create an Allied Airborne Army of five divisions and to commit enormous resources to gliders, special equipment, and a fleet of transport aircraft was always controversial. Ever since the conquest of Crete in May 1941, when German airborne forces lost 30 per cent of their strength, with more killed and wounded than in the entire Balkan campaign, the role of lightly armed airborne units had been questioned. Allied experience in the Mediterranean did little to silence the critics. In Operation Husky, the Sicilian invasion, 1st British Airborne had suffered heavy losses and both parachute and glider troops had been too widely scattered to be effective.[11] A week before D-Day, Leigh-Mallory, the air commander, seriously argued that the entire airborne operation should be cancelled as the projected losses in men and aircraft were too great. The drop zone for 82nd U.S. Airborne was moved twelve miles to avert a disaster on the right flank, but 6th British Airborne's drop zones and landing zones for gliders could not be changed, even though Ultra had by then reported that 21st Panzer Division had been transferred to the Caen sector.[12]

Studies of the feasibility of landing on the coast of Normandy suggested that the left flank of the beachhead was the most vulnerable point in the whole operation. A counterattack there might roll up the entire invasion force. Planners suggested deploying 6th British Airborne to meet this threat by seizing the bridges across the Orne and holding the high ground east of the river. Many of the other original elements of Overlord were changed in the months that followed, but no one could come up with a better solution for securing the left flank.[13]

The men of 1st Canadian Parachute Battalion knew nothing of these debates when they arrived in Britain in August 1943. Recruited from volunteers under thirty-two 'with a history of participation in rugged sports or in a civilian occupation or hobby demanding sustained exertion,' the battalion had learned to jump out of airplanes at Fort Benning, Georgia, and Camp Shilo, Manitoba. At their new home in Bulford on the Salisbury Plain, they measured themselves against the men of their new sister regiments, 8th and 9th Parachute Battalions and 3rd Parachute Brigade. They also met the man who would forge them into combat soldiers and lead them in battle, Brig. James Hill, DSO.[14]

Hill has become a legend among Canadian and British veterans of the airborne division. In 1943 he was thirty-two years old, a tall, rugged-looking professional soldier who had fought in the Battle of France and had caught the last destroyer out of Dunkirk. He volunteered to join the original paratroop force, and by early 1942 was commanding 1st Paratroop Battalion in its first action in North Africa. Wounded while capturing three enemy tanks, he recovered in England and was posted to command the only mixed British and Canadian brigade formed during the war.

Hill could do anything he asked his men to do and still function as a commander conducting a wide-ranging battle. He needed these skills and all the power of his personality to succeed in Normandy. As he later remembered:

Each battalion had a personality of its own ... The 8th were rugged, relentless in achieving an objective, very tough, and not too fussy about detail. This was the opposite of the 9th who were masters of detail, tackling an assignment only after intensive preparation and approaching all problems with precision and professionalism. The Canadian battalion displayed all the characteristics of a troop of cavalry ...[15]

When they joined the brigade, the Canadians were neither well disciplined nor adequately trained. Hill 'kept a tight rein' on his Canadians, for however much he admired their spirit, he had no wish to command a battalion of dead heroes.

It is impossible not to be impressed by the intensity of the training that the parachute battalions passed through. Hill insisted on the highest standards of weapons training and physical fitness. Nicknamed 'Speedy' because of his own rapid pace, he maintained that a paratrooper had to move across country twice as fast as anybody else – ten miles in two hours with a sixty-pound pack and personal weapon. The Canadians adapted quickly. Some, like Maj. Jeff Nicklin, a football and lacrosse star, and Fraser Eadie, a noted hockey player, ate it up and asked for more. Others fell by the wayside. By the time the battalion was briefed for its part in the Normandy invasion, the men, whose average age was just twenty-two, were ready for anything.

The importance of the airborne landings in the plans for D-Day was brought home to everyone when the senior officers met on D–1. Adm. Bertram Ramsay, the Allied Naval Commander, recorded the discussion in his diary:

Sunday 4 June: Commanders met at 0415 to hear latest weather report which was bad. The low cloud predicted would prohibit use of airborne troops, prohibit majority of air action, including air spotting. The sea conditions were unpromising but not prohibitive.

Eisenhower decided to postpone the assault for twenty-four hours. Then, trusting in a weather forecast that promised minimally acceptable cloud and sea conditions, he gave the order to go. Adm. Ramsay wrote:

Monday 5 June: Held a final meeting at 0415 ... Thus has been made the vital and critical decision to stage this great enterprise which will, I hope, be the immediate means of bringing about the downfall of Germany's fighting power and Nazi oppression. I am under no delusions as to the risks involved in this most difficult of all operations ... We shall require all the help that God can give us and I cannot believe that this will not be forthcoming.

Tuesday 6 June: I was called at 0500 which meant that nothing bad had happened ... The sky was clear thank God ... Surprise seemed to be achieved up to the time the paratroops had been dropped ... Only 29 transport aircraft were lost out of 1300. H.Q. 6 Airborne Division report themselves established.[16]

The airborne commanders had not dared to sleep. The night of 5–6 June was moonless, with patchy cloud and winds gusting up to 20 miles an hour. The odds of placing the paratroop companies in the right places were not great. Maj. John Howard's *coup de main* glider assault on Pegasus bridge was able to land on target, but high winds and flak over the coast meant that the parachutists were widely scattered. Maj. Dick Hilborn recalls what happened to one stick of Canadians:

As we crossed the coast of France the red light went on for preparing to drop. We were in the process of hooking up when the plane took violent evasive action ... five of us ended up at the back of the plane ... We got out okay and after wandering about for a bit I picked up three others of my stick. It took us three hours and the assistance of a local French farmer to find out where we were ... one and a half miles north of the drop zone.[17]

Despite the winds, flak, and almost total failure of the radar beacons[18] carried by the Pathfinders of 22nd Independent Parachute Company, the men of the two parachute brigades were able to capture or secure all of their objectives. For 1st Canadian Battalion this meant that only a fraction of C Company, which dropped first to secure the drop zone (DZ) and eliminate the enemy at Varaville, was available, but it all went like clockwork. 'A' Company was assigned to protect the flank of 9th Battalion as it advanced to capture the Merville Battery, whose guns might hamper the landings on Sword and Juno beaches. B Company had to blow a bridge at Robehomme on the Dives and then join the rest of the battalion at the le Mesnil crossroads. Having done this, everyone quickly dug in to await a German attempt to regain the high ground and break through to the Orne bridges.[19]

In their last briefing, Brig. Hill had warned his men: 'In spite of your excellent training and orders, do not be daunted if chaos reigns. It undoubtedly will.' He was right – chaos was everywhere. But small groups of well-trained men went about their tasks, knowing their comrades depended on them. Hill and his headquarters landed miles away from the DZ in a flooded area, from which it took them four hours to reach dry land. While leading the forced march, Hill was wounded by shrapnel, which took a chunk out of his backside. More than two dozen of his men were killed in this incident, a result of 'friendly fire' from fighter-bombers.

Hill used a borrowed bicycle pushed by one of his men to reach his objective. For the next forty-eight hours he issued orders sitting on 'one cheek' some distance from his men 'because his wound smelled so bad.' When asked why he refused evacuation to get immediate treatment, he replied somewhat sharply that he 'hadn't trained his Brigade for ten months to let someone else command it in action.'[20]

While 6th Airborne was completing its tasks, the bombardment of the French coast intensified. The assault troops were roused from sea-sickness and sleep at 0315 and offered a cold breakfast and a shot of navy rum. Then everyone moved to their assigned positions and began climbing down into the swaying, tossing LCAs (assault landing craft). The men were quiet, speaking softly to their friends, offering words of encouragement and attempts at humour. It was impossible to avoid fear, but it could be dealt with when you were with friends.

Force J had made the crossing on time and apparently without the enemy's knowledge. As the midget submarines surfaced, they flashed coloured lights[21] to confirm the accuracy of the navy's navigators. By this time RAF Bomber Command, including 6 Group (RCAF), was completing its attack on the coastal batteries. As the LCAs were forming up, the aircraft of the U.S. 8th Army Air Force were on their approach routes to begin bombing the coastal positions. The planners well knew that even the most accurate bombing would produce few direct hits on the beach defences and isolated batteries, but they hoped that the sheer weight of the attack would result in some destruction and help neutralize the defenders by cutting communication links and reducing morale.

Unfortunately, the weather, which contributed to the safe crossing of the Allied invasion fleet and to the achievement of operational surprise, bedevilled the bombing program. When 8th Air Force arrived over the coast, cloud conditions were 10/10ths, requiring the use of H2X, the American version of airborne radar. H2X operators had been instructed to use 5 to 30 second delays, and the consequence was that 'most bombs fell some distance back from the beaches' and only 'slight' damage was observed at any point in the beach defences. The report of the Air Force Field Party maintained that 'since bombs fell in many towns and villages adjacent to the beaches ... [bombing] helped to demoralize enemy reserves,' but admitted that at Omaha no enemy positions were hit by heavy bombers. The same was true at Juno and the British beaches.[22] Typhoon squadrons assigned to attack beach targets found the winds and overcast skies a serious challenge and refrained from exaggerated claims. Operational research investigators could find no evidence that fighter-bomber air attack played any role in the destruction of the Atlantic Wall. Bomb craters and especially the shallow elongated marks left by rocket projectiles could easily be identified, and none could be found at the strongpoints and resistance nests in the Anglo-Canadian or American sectors.[23]

For those familiar with the limitations of air power, the failure of the first part of the Allied plan was disappointing but not surprising. The real difficulty was in understanding why the attack from the sea was only marginally more effective. Maj. John Fairlie, a Canadian artillery officer attached to 21 Army Group's Operational Research Section, conducted an exhaustive investigation of the Juno sector and concluded that naval fire had done 'no serious damage to the defences.' Examination of the physical evidence coupled with cross-checked testimony revealed that the enemy's concrete emplacements were 'overcome by D.D. tanks, engineer and infantry assault.' Fairlie noted that the neutralizing effect claimed for naval fire was

difficult to assess because of the German method of siting guns to enfilade the beach area only. As few guns could fire seaward it is difficult to say whether the delay of the enemy in opening fire was due to neutraliza-

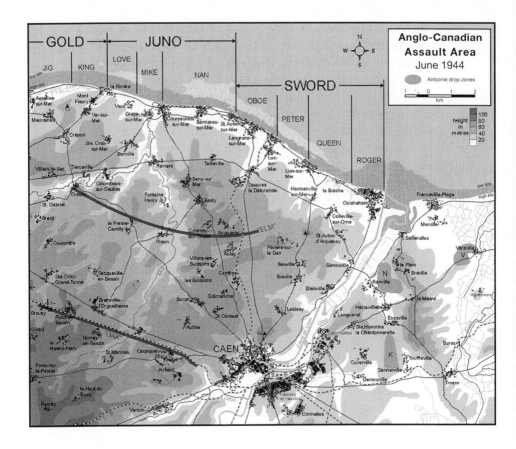

tion or the fact that the guns could not bear. In any event the defences were substantially intact when the infantry touched down and the enemy were able to deliver lethal fire in great quantity against our troops.[24]

The Royal Navy's report on Overlord had much to say about neutralization but agreed that the pattern of the coastal defences 'allowed [the enemy] to present a solid front of concrete to seaward of his pillboxes against which naval gunfire had no destructive effect. On the straight Normandy coastline, with shallow water off shore, ships could not be berthed so as to enfilade these pillboxes.' The report concluded that such positions were not 'a legitimate naval target.'[25]

The plan also called for the artillery field regiments to add weight to the attack by firing during the run-in. The 105 mm self-propelled guns were lashed to the decks of the landing craft to provide 'concentrations or barrages lasting up to 40 minutes and delivering up to 150 rounds per gun with reasonable accuracy upon pre-arranged area targets among beach defence localities.' Unfortunately, reasonable accuracy could not be obtained from the pitching decks of LCTs (tank landing craft) even when correction, through the dust and smoke of battle, was possible. At Courseulles, 13th Field Regiment's concentrations fell 100 to 200 yards 'plus' of the target. No measurable damage and little neutralization occurred. The 50 per cent zone of 14th Field at Bernières was centred well to the left of the fortified area, while at St-Aubin, 19th Field was unable to bring concentrated fire on the main strongpoint or the fortified houses.[26]

What all this means is that Charlie Martin's description of the Queen's Own Rifles' assault on Nan White Beach, Bernières-sur-Mer, where he found 'no sign of any bombardment,' is hauntingly accurate:

> As we moved further from the mother ship and closer to the shore, it came as a shock to realize that the assault fleet just behind us had disappeared from view. Suddenly there was just us and an awful lot of ocean ... Ten boats stretched out over fifteen hundred yards is not really a whole lot of assault force. The boats began to look even tinier as the gaps widened, with more than the length of a football field between each.[27]

When the order 'down ramp' came at Nan White Beach, there was nothing to do but race for the sea wall, enduring the heavy machine gun and mortar fire. There was no sign of the DD tanks, which had not been launched because of sea conditions. Instead, the LCTs beached shortly after the infantry, and the armour was only able to offer fire support during the final stages of the struggle to subdue the Bernières resistance nest.[28]

This position, some three hundred yards long, comprised a beach gun and four concrete pillboxes housing machine guns set along the sea wall. The QORs were supposed to land well to the right of this position and take it from the flank, but the landing craft were pushed downwind, and Baker company landed directly in front of the resistance nest. Half the company were killed or wounded in the first minutes of the battle, and only the extraordinary valour of the men who attacked the pillboxes with hand grenades stopped the slaughter.

Three men from Baker Company, Lt. W.G. Herbert, Lance-Cpl. René Tessier, and Rifleman William Chicoski, took out one pillbox with 'grenades and Sten gun fire,' but the battle was by no means over.[29] One hundred yards to the east, the lead company of the Royal Berkshire Regiment, which formed the core of No. 8 Beach Group, landed shortly after the QORs and immediately came under intense crossfire. Lt. C.I. Spackman with two NCOs crawled forward past 'the remnants of a Canadian platoon scattered in the sand,' and after both his men were wounded charged the position single-handed. Spackman then cleared an 'intricate network of underground defences,' capturing twenty-six prisoners.[30]

The intense battle in front of the resistance nest permitted most of Able Company, landing well to the west, to get off the beach without heavy casualties. Once over the seawall they were pinned down by accurate mortar fire and it was up to individuals and small groups to work their way forward. One of Maj. H.E. Dalton's platoons, landing on the battalion's open right flank, was confronted by a gun position missed by photo reconnaissance. Two-thirds of the platoon were killed or wounded before the enemy was overcome.[31]

The reserve companies landed at 0830, just twenty-five minutes behind the assault companies. By the time Maj. J.N. Gordon's Dog Company landed without difficulty, only one machine gun was left to defend the sea wall. According to Gordon, the Germans encountered by his company were 'mere boys' and 'very frightened' and 'ran away.' The company was clear of the beach in four minutes and moving on toward its final objective, the southern outskirts of Bernières-sur-Mer.[32] Charlie Company, Maj. O.N. Nickson, and battalion headquarters suffered losses when half the LCAs struck mines, but all but a few of the men swam or waded ashore.'[33] By 0845 both reserve companies were moving toward the forward edge of the town and the reserve battalion, Le Régiment de la Chaudière, had landed. The QORs had cracked through the Atlantic Wall in less than one hour. The cost of sixty-one killed and seventy-six wounded was the highest price paid by any Canadian battalion on D-Day.[34]

The situation at Nan Red Beach was similar in intensity though different in detail. In 1944 there was only a scattering of houses on the beach at Bernières, but at St-Aubin, seaside villas stretched along the sea wall. Two and three storey houses, many of which survive to the present, provided direct observation of the beach. The planners assumed that these houses would be ideal defensive positions and proposed to avoid the area. Air photographs had revealed the existence of a resistance nest, and this became a primary target for both air and naval bombardment.

The North Shores landed two companies up with Baker Company assigned to secure the resistance nest by advancing south to the main road and then attacking from the rear. Intelligence reports suggested that the position was manned by 'a garrison of 40 all ranks' classified as 'poor troops.'[35] Able Company, landing to the west, was to clear the beach, capture a gap designated as a main vehicle exit, and link up with the QORs. The two reserve companies, avoiding the battle for the coastal defences, were to clear the western half of the village and advance to Tailleville, where a second resistance nest was reported. If all went well the battalion would then assault the heavily fortified radar station at Douvres-la-Déliverande.

At H+45 minutes 48 Royal Marine Commando was scheduled to land behind the North Shores. They were to cross the Channel in Landing Craft Infantry (small), whose wooden construction and sharply pitched bow ramps made them deathtraps in an opposed landing, so the planners must have assumed that the battle for St-Aubin would be over in less than forty-five minutes. Perhaps it would have been if any of the elaborate methods of air or seaborne bombardment had worked, but it was quickly evident that the fortified area had not been touched by bombs or shells.[36]

The North Shores were able to land both assault companies with far fewer casualties than the QORs, but the resistance nest, with its 50 mm antitank gun, mortars, and machine guns, was still completely intact and delivering continuous and accurate fire. The company assigned to clear the position found that all approaches were covered by machine guns and by snipers who could move underground as well as from house to house. Without armour this was a tough proposition, but a battalion 6-pounder antitank gun was brought forward and one pillbox was put out of action by two direct hits. The 2-inch mortars were also used effectively before the first armour – an AVRE mounting a Petard, and the Fort Garry tanks – arrived to complete the work.[37]

The Fort Garry DD squadron was not launched at sea because 'the waves were smashing above the doors of the LCT.' The naval commander brought his LCTs close to shore. The DDs moved ashore in what the Garries recall as a 'wet wade.' The 50 mm antitank gun in the strongpoint, which according to operational researchers used more than seventy rounds on D-Day, had a clear field of fire and sank one LCT and damaged another. The landing was chaotic, but everyone knew what they were supposed to do, including Sgt. J. Martin and his crew, who, when their tank was hit, backed it into deep water to put out the fire and then used their main gun and machine gun to engage the enemy until the rising tide forced them to wade to shore.[38]

The struggle to subdue the resistance nest had barely started when 48 Royal Marine Commando began its run-in. Lt.-Col. J.R. Moulton, the commanding officer, tried to obtain information from the Beach Control vessel, but none was forthcoming and the order to increase speed and advance line abreast was given. The rising tide that had caused the North Shore reserve companies trouble now covered many of the beach obstacles, and two of the five craft were hung up well out from shore. Moulton's own vessel was fouled, but the waves carried it forward. Mortar and machine gun fire cut through the plywood, inflicting heavy casualties. Many of those who tried to swim ashore were drowned, caught by the undertow. Those who made it to shore – less than half the original strength of the five-hundred-man commando, made contact with the North Shores and continued clearing the village. Their advance east did not begin until the next morning.[39]

On every anniversary of D-Day, the people of the towns and villages along the Normandy coast gather to pay tribute to their liberators. At five-year intervals, larger crowds and delegations of veterans and politicians arrive to observe or participate in the ceremonies. But each year, veterans of 48 Royal Marine Commando journey to St-Aubin to lay wreaths upon the water in memory of their comrades.

The enemy's defence of the resistance nest continued long after the main 50 mm gun was put out of action.[40] Eventually, four officers and seventy-five ORs were taken prisoner, 'and another 50 killed or wounded'; once the fighting ended, it took two hours to search, carefully, the gun position and underground tunnels.[41] Baker Company's battle could not be allowed to interfere with other tasks, and while Dog Company cleared the village as far east as the railway station, Charlie Company with two troops of Fort Garry tanks assembled for the advance inland. The company commander, Maj. R.H. Doughney, took a bicycle and began a reconnaissance of the route forward. It was 1000 hours.[42]

The 7th Canadian Infantry Brigade and the tanks of the First Hussars were to land on the beaches at Courseulles-sur-Mer to capture a strongpoint that contained one 88 mm gun, one 75 mm gun, and two 50s. Two additional 75s were positioned on the town's flanks to cover the approaches. Twelve machine gun pillboxes, fortified mortar emplacements, and large protective shelters added to the defences, making Courseulles one of the most heavily fortified positions attacked by anyone on D-Day.[43] Air reconnaissance had revealed that several batteries could fire out to sea, and this prompted the decision to order a frontal assault to take out the guns as quickly as possible.

The Royal Winnipeg Rifles, when they landed on the west side of the River Seulles, found the enemy defences untouched by the bombardment. Their War Diary entry reads:

> 0749 hrs. In spite of air bombardment failing to neutralize, RN bombardment spotty, the rockets falling short and the AVREs and DDs being late C Company Canadian Scottish Regiment and RWR companies landed all within seven minutes. The bombardment having failed to kill a single German soldier or silence one weapon these companies had to storm their positions cold and did so without hesitation ... Not one man flinched from his task.[44]

Baker Company, landing in front of the strongpoint, faced an unbelievable task. There were four large casements and twelve machine gun positions to overcome, and this could not be done by infantry. 'A' Squadron of the Hussars had launched their DD tanks at 1500 yards while under fire. The first tanks arrived shortly after the infantry and were able to bring direct fire on a 75 mm gun position that was well defended. By the time the strongpoint was clear, Baker Company consisted of one officer, Capt. P.E. Gower, and twenty-six men. The assault party of 6th Field Regiment RCE attached to the company had twenty-six casualties – two-thirds of its strength.[45]

To the right Dog Company jumped off into waist-deep water and struggled ashore. The Germans had relied on barbed wire, minefields, and scattered weapons piles to supplement the gun intended to fire in enfilade from the fortified area. Under direct attack, the Germans in the strongpoint could not interfere with Dog Company, and with the assistance of 5 DD tanks, Maj. Lockie Fulton and his men quickly captured the German positions along the sand dunes. In accordance with the carefully rehearsed plan, Dog Company pressed forward to Graye-sur-Mer. Behind them, the battle for the strongpoint and the island formed by the bend in the River Seulles continued. Charlie Company was committed to the island, while Able moved to Ste-Croix-sur-Mer, which was strongly defended until the tanks appeared and 'with cool disregard for mines and atk [antitank] guns beat down the M.G. positions and permitted Able company to mop up.'[46]

The Canscot company, added to the assault to attack a pillbox 1,000 yards to the west, found the position was unoccupied. Their only opposition came from isolated infantry and mortars. Their second objective, the Chateau Vaux, was the site of a field gun battery protected by wire and machine guns. This position was quickly overrun, and the chateau was captured. The Canscots reported that the battle drill they had so carefully practised worked smoothly with everyone confident of what to do.[47]

East of the river, the Regina Rifles' experience paralleled that of their sister regiment from Winnipeg. Able Company, on the right, had to assault the main part of the strongpoint, initially without any assistance. No damage had been done to any of the defences, and there was no apparent neutralization as the Reginas came under fire before touchdown. As with the Winnipegs, the intense battle in front of the strongpoint focused the enemy's attention and allowed the second assault company, Baker, to cross the beach virtually unscathed. They quickly set about clearing the town, joined by DD tanks, AVREs, and

Royal Marine Centaurs, all of which had come ashore well to the east of the strongpoint. Able Company was finally able to outflank the resistance nest, and for a time it appeared to be under control, but when the diminished force moved on to its second objective, enemy soldiers reappeared from underground and began directing fire on the beach. The company was forced to return to the strongpoint with additional armoured support. The position was finally secured at 1400 hours.[48]

By the time the Reginas' reserve battalions arrived, the incoming tide had covered many of the beach obstacles. Charlie Company landed without mishap, but the LCAs carrying Dog Company struck mines, and only forty-nine men were able to move inland. Their objective was the bridge at Reviers, and they moved inland quickly to take it. At 1035, 7th Canadian Infantry Brigade reported 'Yew,' the codeword for the capture of the first set of objectives.[49] The Western Brigade had torn a large hole in the German defences.

No one who examines the events of the first hours of D-Day can fail to be impressed by the accomplishments of the assault battalions. Most of the elaborate fire-support plan failed, leaving the infantry, combat engineers, and armoured troopers to overcome the enemy by direct fire. It took incredible courage just to keep going; words cannot do justice to the individuals who rose to the challenge and led assaults on deadly enemy positions. Canada's official historian, Col. C.P. Stacey, recognized this, declaring that 'the D-Day achievement was magnificent. In one morning's work, on most sections of the front, the Atlantic Wall was breached and the way opened for a final victorious campaign.' But Stacey also joined the chorus of postwar critics who insisted that British and Canadian troops had missed the opportunity to seize Caen and the original D-Day objectives. According to Stacey, the successful assault was not followed up aggressively, and as a consequence we failed to seize ground 'which we later had to purchase by many weeks of bloody fighting.'[50] Before examining this view, we need to determine exactly what happened in the Canadian sector during the late morning and afternoon of D-Day. Unless otherwise indicated, the timings and wireless messages quoted in the following paragraphs are from 3rd Canadian Infantry Division's Message Log, the record of radio messages received and sent by divisional headquarters.[51]

As the assault battalions strove to complete their initial tasks, the divisional commander, Maj.-Gen. Rod Keller, was trying to make sense of the conflicting reports reaching HMS *Hillary*, the command ship. For Keller, the crucial decision was when and where to land the reserve brigade that was to pass through the beachhead and advance to the high ground around Carpiquet airport. The preferred plan was to land 9th Brigade at both Bernières and St-Aubin; the scheduled timing was between H+4 and H+6 hours. The alternate plan was to pass the brigade through the Courseulles beaches.[52]

Before Keller's decision a steady stream of messages from 8th Brigade units had painted a very optimistic picture. As late as 1050 the Chaudières were said to be 'making progress slowly,' and the North Shores had reported 'proceeding according to plan.' Keller did not know that the navy had closed Nan Red Beach at St-Aubin, which would force the entire brigade to land at Bernières. News from the 7th Brigade was sparse, and the signal 'troops in Banville and Ste-Croix' was logged at 1050 as the landing order was issued. It was not until 1215 that 8th Brigade finally admitted, 'Progress slow after Yew [the road inland from the beach]. Trying to engage 88 battery. Naval support requested.'[53]

The reserve brigade was, therefore, committed to land on a narrow beach whose exits were already packed with the vehicles of 8th Brigade. No one who was at Bernières that day will ever forget the confusion as vehicles and men milled about. A massive traffic jam had developed in the narrow streets of the village. Drivers took the opportunity to dewaterproof their vehicles, which further immobilized the procession. 'Into this mess the 9 Brigade began landing ... the roads were plugged with zealous soldiers impatient to get on. Fortunately, the Germans did not shell the town.'[54] Fortunate indeed. Ross Munro, the Canadian Press correspondent, who had been at the Dieppe and Sicily landings, took one look and got as far away as he could! At 1245 Keller went ashore to discover that no one was moving forward. Blackader, Cunningham, and their officers were desperately trying to sort out the situation as Keller charged furiously into the confusion, demanding action.[55]

The chaos in Bernières was largely the result of an incident on the southern edge of the village. The brigade's reserve battalion, le Régiment de la Chaudière[56] had begun to move to its assembly area shortly after 1000 hours, but the traffic jam slowed the progress of the tanks and self-propelled guns of 14th Field Regiment. At 1150 hours, two troops of the field regiment arrived to take up their gun position in the open field south of Bernières. Three M8s of E Troop, which were towing ammunition sledges, were promptly shelled, and a series of explosions that killed and wounded a number of gunners and Chaudières rocked the area for more than an hour.[57] There are conflicting reports as to whether the damage was done by a German field battery or an 88 mm gun reported to be in a small wood. The battery had been on the pre-invasion target list and was apparently silenced by *HMS Diadem* at 0700, but it came to life, as did the 88 that fired airbursts at various targets.[58]

From the south edge of Bernières, the countryside is open and flat. The ground rises slowly to 60 metres at Beny-sur-Mer, and the roads – little more than narrow tracks in 1944 – were at field level. There is no *bocage*, not even stone walls to obscure vision or sight lines. When part of a squadron of Fort Garry tanks arrived to join the 'Chauds,' the squadron leader 'was loath to leave cover and advance up a grassy field' until the enemy guns had been dealt with.[59] Brig. Blackader, who was trying to untangle the traffic jam and exercise control of all three battalions, tried to get HMS *Diadem* to 'engage 88 mm battery at 993829' without success. Finally, at 1440, the advance began, with 14th Field and the Vickers machine guns of the Camerons of Ottawa providing suppressing fire.

While leading his platoon toward the enemy position, Lt. W. Moisan was struck by a bullet that ignited one of his smoke grenades, setting his battle dress on fire. He continued to press the attack, which overran the enemy.[60] The 'Chauds' also captured the field battery, which yielded fifty-five prisoners, and went on to secure Beny-sur-Mer before advancing to Basly, which they reached at 1815. The way was now clear for the reserve brigade to begin the advance to Carpiquet.

A thousand metres to the east, the North Shores faced a different situation. Maj. Daughney returned from his bicycle recce and got his tank–infantry group moving. Lt.-Col. Buell, who with his battalion HQ group followed Charlie Company at a 500-yard interval, watched as 'Daughney and his company put in a good attack' on Tailleville, using the 2-inch mortars for high explosive and smoke.[61] The chateau at Tailleville was the headquarters of the 2nd Bn, 736th Panzer Grenadier Regiment, which had transformed the area into a series of interlocking defences with underground connections. Charlie Company reported Tailleville as under attack at 1205 and 'practically secure' at 1325. But snipers kept appearing, and the CO was nearly killed when a machine gun began firing from a 'cleverly imitated manhole.'[62]

The North Shores kept discovering new dug-outs, and Capt. J.E. Leblanc began using a 'lifebuoy' portable flame thrower. 'The flame followed the contours of the passage and seared everything inside, even setting fire to the timbers. Those who were not killed emerged yelling.'[63] Tailleville was reported clear at 1450, but the struggle to control the rabbit warren defences flared up again, and at 1645 Buell reported that it 'may take another 45 minutes to overcome' the enemy. More than eighty prisoners were taken during the battle for Tailleville; forty more were rounded up that night.[64] The prolonged battle ended any realistic possibility of launching an attack on the final objective, the fortified radar station, and even plans to clear a small woods south of Tailleville were overruled by brigade. Buell was ordered 'to consolidate in his present dispositions.'[65]

The 7th Brigade faced less serious opposition. The Canscots assault company became involved in the fighting at Ste-Croix, and Lt.-Col. Cabeldu sent Able Company to assist them. He ordered the rest of his battalion to bypass the area and move inland to seize crossings of the Seulles. By 1400 the battalion carriers had arrived, and the advance to the intermediate objective continued. At 1630, four miles in from the beaches, the Canscots reported 'Elm.' The advance continued, with the lead troops flushing out many enemy stragglers. At Camilly a German artillery battery came to life; after a brief battle, at 1715, success was signalled to brigade. The battalion was now six miles inland, well beyond 'Elm.' The War Diary of the Canadian Scottish Regiment notes that at 1830 hours, Lt.-Col. Cabeldu 'wanted to push on to the battalion's final objective but permission was not granted.' Instead, Brig. Foster ordered the Canscots to consolidate at Pierrepoint, their intermediate objective. Cabeldu interpreted this order loosely, selecting better defensive ground some 1,400 yards farther south.[66]

After securing the bridge at Reviers, the Reginas followed the winding road along the Mue River to Fontaine-Henry, where mortar fire inflicted casualties and antitank guns slowed the advance.[67] Brig. Foster reported that the lead elements of all three battalions were on the intermediate objective 'Elm' at 1555. An hour later the brigade reported opposition 'from mortar and isolated MG and antitank' as slight; even so, no one except a reconnaissance troop of the First Hussars continued the advance.[68]

The advance of 9th Brigade was well underway when Brig. Cunningham was ordered to halt. By 1900 the brigade vanguard, made up of the North Nova Scotia Highlanders and Sherbrooke Fusiliers, was clear of the Bernières traffic jam and ready to advance to Carpiquet. At 2013 the vanguard ran into its first serious resistance at Villons-les-Buissons.[69] This was overcome, and the advance resumed. Under British double summertime there were still several hours of daylight left and there was little doubt that the 9th Brigade could reach Carpiquet, but the army commander, Lt.-Gen. Miles Dempsey, ordered his three assault divisions to stop on their intermediate objectives.[70]

Dempsey's decision was based on the situation confronting 3rd British Division. Shortly after 1600 a scout troop of the Staffordshire Yeomanry reported that 'enemy tanks were advancing from Caen.' The 21st Panzer Division battlegroup consisted of fifty Mk IV tanks and a battalion of infantry. When their initial thrust down the D17 was stopped cold by 185th Brigade, they swung west into the gap between the British and Canadian beaches.[71]

The divisional commander, Maj.-Gen. T.G. Rennie, ordered a battalion of 9th British Brigade to hold at Perriers-le-Dan and ensure that the Sword bridgehead could not be rolled up from the west. Their antitank guns were in position in time to turn back an attack by the German tanks, which then moved north to within sight of the coast. By early evening the German battlegroup had lost about one-third of its tank strength but was still a formidable force. With other German troops holding out in Lion-sur-Mer and the radar station at Douves-la-Délivérande, the threat to both Sword and Juno was very real. Then, the arrival of hundreds of aircraft bringing reinforcements to the 6th Airborne spooked the German corps commander, who ordered 21st Panzers to withdraw to their start line.[72] Before this withdrawal became evident, General Dempsey had concluded that more armoured counterattacks could be expected. So he ordered all three assault divisions to dig in at their intermediate objectives. This decision was relayed to subordinate commanders sometime after 1900. General Keller's headquarters confirmed the order at 2115.

The extraordinary achievements of the Allied soldiers, who won the battles for the beachhead despite the failure of the preparatory bombardment 'to kill a single German soldier or silence one weapon,' have failed to impress most military historians, who emphasize the failure to reach final objectives. Chester Wilmott, the Australian war correspondent who was closely associated with Montgomery, thought the Canadians had done well. On the other hand, he was sharply critical of the 3rd British Division, which, he insisted, had 'dropped the momentum of the attack.' Wilmott argued that the 3rd had not been spurred on either by the divisional commander or by the brigadier commanding the assault battalions, 'who was ill-cast for the role of pursuit.'[73]

C.P. Stacey extended this critique to the Canadians when he wrote:

> Reviewing the day as a whole ... one may be permitted to enquire whether we could have accomplished even more on the 6th of June. Was it really impossible to reach the inland objectives? Could not a more sustained effort in the later phases have produced deeper penetration ...? It is worth noting that more than one reserve brigade did not come into full action on D-Day. We shall see in this volume that the British and Canadian forces – and the same is probably true of those of the United States – were usually better at deceiving the enemy and achieving initial success in the assault than they were at exploiting surprise and success once achieved. Perhaps they were too easily satisfied.[74]

For most Allied soldiers, seasick and deprived of sleep, D-Day passed in a blur. The men interviewed in the following days could rarely recall even approximate timings. All of them had studied the air photos and rehearsed their actions, but no training could have prepared them for the noise and confusion of combat. The sight of comrades face down in the water or sprawled lifeless on the sands registered, but in the rush of events there was no time to mourn. Gordon Brown, who landed with the Reginas as the transport officer, helped some of his wounded comrades and then got on with the job of landing the battalion's vehicles. Later in the day he learned that his best friend, Lt. Glen Dickin, who had survived the beach assault, had been killed by mortar fire at Fontaine-Henry. Brown was stunned by the news but carried on with his assigned duties, just the way thousands of other young men did.[75]

During the advance inland the British and Canadians fought the way they had been trained, moving forward to designated objectives in controlled bounds and digging in at the first sign of a counterattack. Given the uncertainties surrounding the whole invasion project, this was a sensible if cautious approach to battle. One Canadian officer, Lt.-Col. F.N. Cabeldu, commenting on the rumours that swept through the ranks that day, recalled that 'we were green soldiers in a strange land' and that everything was new.[76] Lt. Bill McCormick, who led his Hussars troop well beyond the infantry advance, met Cabeldu's battalion as it was approaching Secqueville. McCormick's report that he had just come through the undefended village was ignored.[77] No chances were to be taken; Cabeldu mounted a proper attack. There is no doubt that 7th Brigade, which met little more than snipers and stragglers, could have reached its final objectives on D-Day. It did so with ease the next morning. The 9th Brigade was also within striking distance of Carpiquet when Dempsey and his corps commanders decided to stop the advance. To Dempsey it made little sense to let the Canadians continue advancing south, further extending their flank in an area known to be occupied by enemy armoured units. Far better to wait until first light and hope that both the British brigades could overcome the strong resistance they were facing and join the Canadians in a concerted drive to Caen, Carpiquet, and the railway line.

This reasonable if cautious decision has been criticized, on the assumption that if the Canadians had reached their objectives they would not have been overwhelmed by the kind of counterattack mounted by 12th SS on D+1. But if 9th Brigade had reached Carpiquet and dug in, with the artillery in position to offer support, the commander of the 26th Panzer Grenadier Regiment might have followed orders and waited until a coordinated counterattack with other panzer divisions had been organized. Such an attack might well have done far more damage to the Allied beachhead than the hastily improvised operation actually carried out. Though we will never know what the consequences of an alternative strategy might have been, there is no reason to assume that a different decision would have produced better results.

3

The Bridgehead

An assault landing on a defended shore is perhaps the most dangerous military operation in modern war, but by midnight on 6 June it was clear that the Allies had pulled it off. The landings at Omaha beach had run into serious difficulties, but elsewhere the battle had gone far better than anyone could have expected. Much was owed to the weather, which had won surprise, but the Allies were also assisted by the confusion that enveloped all levels of the German command.

At the strategic level, the German decision makers held to the view that a landing anywhere south of the Seine was bound to be a diversion. On the evening of 6 June, the situation report issued by the German High Command in the West flatly declared: 'The enemy command plans a further large-scale undertaking in the Channel area.'[1] This fixation on a landing in 'the Channel area' was partly due to the efforts of the 'double cross' system, which used German agents who had been captured and turned by British Intelligence to provide carefully scripted information exaggerating the numbers of Allied divisions available and pointing to an assault on the Pas de Calais coast.[2] This broad deception scheme, codenamed 'Fortitude,' was effective because it told the German generals what they wanted to believe. Their own estimate of the enormous challenges confronting the Allies pointed to an invasion in the narrow Channel area because of the short range of Allied fighter aircraft, rapid turnaround time for landing ships, and proximity to Germany. This massive failure of both intelligence and imagination must be recognized as the essential background to the uncertainty and indecision that marked all aspects of the German response to the D-Day landings.[3]

The confusion was especially pronounced in the British-Canadian sector where 84th Corps controlled 716th coastal defence division but not 21st Panzer Division, which was under Rommel's Army Group B. The two other armoured divisions, stationed within a day's march of the Calvados coast, Panzer Lehr and 12th SS, were in OKW reserve under Hitler's control so that they would not be hastily committed in response to a feint attack. Once it was clear that a major landing – if not the major attack – had taken place, Panzer Lehr and 12th SS were released to 7th Army and together with 21st Panzer assigned to 1st SS Panzer Corps commanded by Sepp Dietrich. However, during the morning 21st Panzer had been subordinated to 84th Corps and begun counterattacking 3rd British Division, thus entangling itself in a series of disjointed actions. The 12th SS Hitler Youth Division was ready to move by 0300 on 6 June, and scouting parties reached the invasion area, sending full reports to division headquarters by mid-morning. Orders to move to the Caen area were finally issued at 1740. The division's march was therefore carried out after the heavy overcast of the morning had broken up. By late afternoon there were only scattered clouds and Allied fighter-bombers repeatedly attacked the long, strung-out columns. Losses were not severe – eighty-three casualties and a small number of soft-skinned vehicles – but the advance was slowed preventing any possible intervention against the landings on D-Day.[4]

On the morning of 7 June the situation in the Caen sector was so uncertain that higher command could play no role in the day's events. Dietrich's headquarters ordered 12th SS and 21st Panzer to launch a simultaneous counterattack to break through to the beaches, but only one SS Panzer Grenadier regiment with some tanks and artillery had reached the area west of Caen.[5] As for 21st Panzer, it could be placed under Dietrich's command but it could not be disengaged from its battle with 3rd British Division. There would be no major counterattack on 7 June. The best that could be hoped for was a coordinated advance by two regiments, one from each panzer division.

The Allied troops in the Caen sector spent their first night ashore collapsed in sleep interrupted by brief firefights as German stragglers blundered into their positions. Brigades held orders group before dawn so that battalion commanders could brief their men in time for an advance at first light. There was no need for a new plan – everyone knew what had to be done. The 185th Brigade would try to overcome the enemy defences at Lebisey woods and drive through to Caen; 9th Canadian Brigade would resume its march to Carpiquet. Neither could afford to wait for 9th British Brigade to catch up, but if all went well it would fill the gap, advancing from Périers to Cambes, St-Contest, and St-Germain. On the right, 7th Canadian Infantry Brigade was responsible for a much larger area and would continue to move two battalions up. When Montgomery met his army commanders early in the morning of 7 June, he reiterated the need to reach the D-Day objectives. Both Dempsey and Bradley assured him that operations to fulfil his orders were already underway.[6]

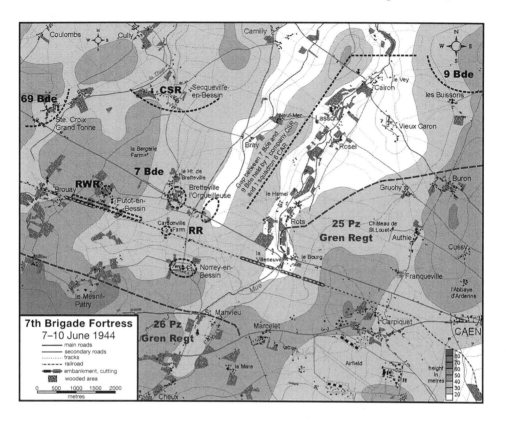

The advance began at first light, but 185th Brigade could not penetrate the defences on the wooded ridge at Lebisey. The guns of three field regiments and a cruiser were employed, but 21st Panzer Division committed all available resources to holding this vital ground. The 9th British Brigade also met sharp resistance and was unable to reach Cambes until mid-afternoon.[7] As a result, 9th Canadian Brigade advanced toward Carpiquet with an open left flank. Both the divisional commander Rod Keller and the brigade commander Ben Cunningham understood the situation, but there was little they could do – it was vital to get inland and stake out ground. No one considered ignoring orders because of uncertainty about the success of flanking formations.[8]

The battlegroup that led 9th Canadian Brigade inland was a well-organized, balanced combat team composed of an infantry battalion, the North Nova Scotia Highlanders, an armoured regiment, the Sherbrooke Fusiliers, a battery of M10 self-propelled antitank guns, and mortar and machine gun platoons from the Camerons of Ottawa. Lt.-Col. Charles Petch, the CO of the North Novas, was in command, though in accordance with doctrine the Sherbrooke CO, Lt.-Col. Mel Gordon, was responsible for the tactical direction of his tanks.

Critics of Anglo-Canadian operational doctrine make much of the practice of allowing armoured officers to work in cooperation rather than under command. This 'flawed doctrine' is unfavourably contrasted with the Germans' system of single command of mixed battlegroups. There is no evidence that this was a problem on 7 June. The Sherbrookes and North Novas had messed together for several months and had rehearsed their plans for the advance inland. The two COs were in constant contact. The forward observation officers (FOOs) of 14th Field Regiment Royal Canadian Artillery, who were the essential component of any Allied battlegroup, were also well integrated with the subunits.[9]

Maj. Don Learment of the North Novas participated in planning the role of the vanguard he was to command. A mixed force of some three hundred men, including his own company mounted in Bren gun carriers, a medium MG platoon, a troop of M10s, and the recce squadron of the Sherbrookes, were to move rapidly to the high ground overlooking Carpiquet and make contact with the lead battalions of the British and Canadian brigades on their flanks. They were the pointed tip of a diamond-shaped formation that employed squadrons of Sherbrooke medium tanks on either flank with a third squadron in reserve. The flanking squadrons carried two other North Nova companies, with the remaining company and squadron in reserve.[10]

Surviving elements of 716th Division, with attached units from 21st Panzer, held well-camouflaged positions along the road to Buron. This forced the Canadians into a series of time-consuming engagements.[11] Buron itself was defended, and the approaches were under enemy mortar fire from the higher ground around St-Contest. Petch and Gordon reacted promptly – B Squadron broke to the left of the centre line and A to the right while the reserve squadron sent first one troop and then another forward to Buron to assist the vanguard.[12]

The Sherbrookes moved quickly, suppressing both MG and mortar fire. Buron was cleared of the enemy, and the advance pressed forward to Authie. This aggressive attempt to push through to Carpiquet was based on the belief that the enemy consisted of elements of the 716th and 21st Panzer divisions. There was no indication from air reconnaissance that an entire Panzer Grenadier regiment, with a battalion of MK IV tanks and artillery, had arrived at St-Germain and were assembling on the backslope south of the Caen–Bayeux road.[13] At 1300, Learment signalled the capture of Authie and an advance to Franqueville, but he also reported sighting 'enemy armour 800 yards east of Authie.'[14] The Sherbrooke recce troop, with its light tanks, had been joined by Shermans from C Squadron. The lead troop was 800 yards south of Authie when it came under fire from enemy armour.[15] This first exchange resulted in the destruction of three Mk IVs,[16] but in the next minutes a number of Sherbrooke tanks, advancing around Authie, were hit.[17] The German counterattack had begun.

The commander of 25th Panzer Grenadier Regiment, Standartenführer (Colonel) Kurt Meyer, had watched the approach of the Canadians from the tower of the church at the Abbaye d'Ardenne. Corps headquarters had ordered 12th SS and 21st Panzer to start their joint attack at 1700, but the arrival of the Canadians removed all possibility of surprise and threatened to outflank Meyer's regiment. The Canadians could not be permitted to reach Carpiquet and dig in. Meyer decided to attack immediately, employing two of his three infantry battalions as well as three Panzer companies of about fifty Mk IV tanks.[18]

At this stage, Learment believed that Authie could be held, so he began to organize its defences.[19] Petch ordered Able Company, advancing on the right, to dig in on the high ground behind Authie while the balance of the battalion held at Buron.[20] This was a well-practised response to the prospect of an enemy counterattack; all that was required now was timely and accurate fire support from 14th Field Regiment and the navy. Unfortunately, none was available. The Forward Observer Bombardment, a young naval officer attached from HMS Belfast, lost radio contact with the cruiser when his wireless set failed. There was no backup. However, contact was eventually regained when equipment was salvaged from knocked out tanks.[21] The problems of 14th Field Regiment were more complex. This regiment was supposed to move forward in bounds so that artillery support was always available. But as two of the batteries reached Basly they came under mortar fire from Douvres-la-Délivrande, and for two crucial hours they were unable to meet requests for fire support.[22] The North Novas and Sherbrookes were on their own.

Meyer deployed his forces across the extended Canadian flank and struck with overwhelming force. A squadron of the Sherbrookes was engaged by German tanks, and the two forward troops on the west side of Authie were forced to withdraw after losing three of their six Shermans. To the east of the village, B Squadron, with eleven Shermans, fought a close-range battle, destroying several German Mk IVs before artillery fire and a 'tank trap' forced a withdrawal. About a hundred North Novas were now cut off and forced to defend Authie relying on the one remaining Sherbrooke tank, a Firefly, to fend off the German armour. Able Company, north of Authie, was still digging in when the Germans attacked. Without artillery or armoured support, they were quickly surrounded and taken prisoner. The battle for Authie began with a heavy barrage from the 12th SS artillery followed by an infantry–tank attack. The defenders held on for more than an hour and beat back several enemy thrusts, but outnumbered and without artillery support, they were soon overcome.[23]

The battle for Buron lasted longer and resulted in heavier casualties to the attackers, because contact was re-established with the navy and 14th Field was in range. Buron was lost, recaptured, and then abandoned to the enemy as the brigade commander decided to withdraw what was left of the battlegroup to a 'brigade fortress' in Villons-les-Buisons.[24] The Canadian losses of 110 killed, 64 wounded, and 128 taken prisoner were much higher than any Anglo-Canadian unit suffered on D-Day.[25]

The violence of this brief encounter on 7 June did not end when the fighting stopped. In Authie, 'wildly excited' Hitler Youth began murdering Canadian prisoners while the battle still raged, and continued killing prisoners systematically after the fighting ceased. Today's visitor to Authie is shown the Rue des Canadiens, where the bodies of two murdered soldiers were placed in the street so that a tank could repeatedly run over them. Other murders were committed in Buron and during the German withdrawal from the village, bringing the total to at least thirty-seven men. After the war, SS Lt.-Col. Karl-Heinz Milius, the battalion CO, was indicted for war crimes, but he was never brought to justice. More Canadians were executed in cold blood in the courtyard of the Abbaye d'Ardenne.[26]

While Meyer's 2nd and 3rd battalions attacked the Canadians, the 1st battalion, on the German right, moved toward Cambes. The Royal Ulster Rifles, vanguard of 9th British Brigade, reached the village minutes before the Germans, and a fierce, close-range battle erupted. The momentum of the battle now shifted. The British withdrew to high ground north of Cambes and used artillery and mortar fire to great advantage.[27] Fritz Witt, commanding 12th SS division, ordered Meyer to break off the action. Meyer had stopped the Allied advance well short of Carpiquet and had inflicted very heavy casualties, but his regiment had lost fifteen tanks and more than three hundred men.[28] Meyer's action also resulted in the piecemeal commitment of three battalions that could not now be disengaged without giving up ground. Since 21st Panzer was involved in a similar struggle south of Caen, the chances of launching a major counterattack on the beachhead were very greatly reduced.

German senior commanders now attempted to regain control of a situation that was getting out of hand. General Leo, Baron Geyr von Schweppenburg, an experienced armoured commander who had long opposed Rommel's 'destroy them on the beaches' theories and who advocated concentrated attacks outside the range of naval guns, was to command Panzer Group West, with responsibility for the eastern sector of the bridgehead. Despite Geyr's views on the proper employment of armour, the three Panzer divisions of 1st SS Panzer Corps were ordered to mount an attack on the beaches.[29]

It seems that neither Geyr nor Dietrich understood the situation facing the 21st and 12th SS Panzer divisions, nor did they have solid information on the location of the various units of Panzer Lehr. This 'demonstration' division, like the 12th SS, was well equipped and included cadres of experienced officers and NCOs. It had begun to move from its base near Chartres, 100 miles from the invasion area, on D-Day, and reached Thury-Harcourt on the morning of 7 June. The advance continued throughout the day, moving north in three widely separated columns. Allied air attacks slowed the approach and caused some losses, but by the morning of 8 June most of the combat elements of the division had reached their designated assembly areas.[30] There was, however, considerable confusion. One of the three columns had been ordered to an area also assigned to 26th Panzer Grenadier Regiment of 12th SS. Another, including the 902nd Panzer Grenadier, was prematurely drawn into combat with 50th British Division and suffered heavy losses from naval gunfire.[31] Helmut Ritgen, who was second-in-command of one of the tank battalions and later the author of the divisional history, noted that his battalion was in position early on 8 June but then waited all day for orders that never came.[32]

While Ritgen waited, Wilhelm Mohnke, the officer commanding the 26th Panzer Grenadier Regiment of 12th SS, followed the lead of Kurt Meyer and ordered his infantry battalions into action within hours of reaching the battle zone. Mohnke faced a very different situation from the one confronting Meyer. The lead battalions of 7th Canadian Infantry Brigade had reached their objectives eight hours ahead of the enemy and were well dug in, with their antitank guns ready and supporting artillery in position and on grid.[33] The Canadians had selected their defensive positions from maps and air photos, and knew that stretches of the Caen–Bayeux railway line would serve as antitank barriers. At Putot-en-Besin, the Royal Winnipeg Rifles deployed three companies along the railway, with one company in reserve. They soon discovered that the British had not reached Brouay. The flanking battalion, the Green Howards, were finally located more than a mile north of the railway line.[34] Lt.-Col. Meldram decided to cover his open right flank with a battery of self-propelled 17-pounder antitank guns from the corps antitank regiment.[35]

The Winnipegs found themselves in a classic dilemma. They were to fight on both a divisional and corps boundary. The 69th British Brigade, part of 50th Northumbrian Division and 30 Corps, had shifted west as if pulled by the magnetic attraction of Bayeux. Their thrust southwest to Ducy-Ste-Marguerite left the Winnipeg flank up in the air.[36] The situation for the Winnipegs was not helped by Meldram's decision to deploy his entire force in a straggling village with limited observation and poor fields of fire.[37]

The Regina Rifles employed a very different approach to the defence of their sector. Lt.-Col. Foster Matheson was confident that his companies could operate independently, holding widely separated positions and relying on both direct and indirect fire to smother enemy attacks. The Reginas' operational order, dated 24 May, called for Able Company to hold Bretteville, and Baker Company Rots, with Dog Company occupying la Villeneuve and linking up with 9th Brigade while Charlie Company crossed the railway line to Norrey-en-Bessin. The high ground west of the River Mue provided an ideal location for the battalion's share of 3rd Anti-Tank Regiment's M10s and 6-pounders.[38]

When news of the counterattack against 9th Brigade reached Brig. Foster, he deployed one of his two remaining armoured squadrons and a company of the reserve battalion, the Canadian Scottish, to the high ground west of the Mue and ordered the Reginas to withdraw from la Villeneuve and Rots. Matheson was still confident that his men could fight from separate fortress positions. Baker Company dug in east of Bretteville, and Dog Company moved to Cardonville Farm, relieving a Winnipeg carrier platoon. Lt.-Col. Clifford of 13th Field Regiment was given the new coordinates. He promised that his gunners would be ready.[39]

The 26th Panzer Grenadier Regiment established its headquarters at Cheux on the evening of 7 June, and without any preliminary reconnaissance ordered an attack on Norrey and Putot. The two battalions of Panzer Grenadiers were to be supported by artillery and tanks, but these weren't yet in place when the 1st Battalion set out across the fields to Norrey at 0300 on 8 June. As the young soldiers shook out into attack formation for their first battle, the sky was illuminated by flares and 13th Field Regiment filled the air with preregistered fire. In Norrey, the Reginas joined in with mortar and Bren, crushing the attack before it got going. According to Hubert Meyer, Canadian radio interference prevented contact with their artillery. This may help explain why the operation was called off before Matheson and his headquarters in Bretteville realized this was a serious attack.[40]

The battalion slated to attack Putot was late arriving, and waited for the supporting armour and artillery before beginning a probing advance at first light. The Winnipeg company covering the railway overpass known as the Brouay crossing, assisted by the medium machine guns of the Camerons, beat back this thrust. The battalion antitank guns claimed two armoured vehicles destroyed. Some Hitler Youth did succeed in infiltrating the straggling village, and 'snipers came to life' throughout the morning.[41] The Winnipegs had lost 10 officers and 118 ORs on D-Day, and although some reinforcements arrived on the night of 6 June the rifle companies were understrength. But the real problems confronting Lt.-Col. Meldram and his men were the open right flank and an extended linear defence that could not, given the terrain, prevent infiltration. The Winnipegs felt the full weight of enemy artillery and mortars, and shortly before 1300 a battle group of armoured assault guns and infantry crossed the railway line to the west of Putot, threatening the flank. The battery of British 17-pounder antitank guns at la Bergerie farm dealt with the armour[42] but could not prevent infantry infiltration, which was also successful at other points along the perimeter. By 1330 the three forward Winnipeg companies were surrounded. All that 12th Field could do in this confusing situation was fire smoke to cover a withdrawal to positions on the left of the village held by Dog Company.[43]

German attempts to exploit this success by advancing beyond Putot to the Caen–Bayeux highway were stopped cold by tanks of 24th Lancers[44] and by fighting patrols from the Canscots, but the Canadians were not willing to concede the village. Brig. Foster ordered his reserve battalion, the Canadian Scottish, with one squadron of Hussars, to recapture Putot, and gave them two hours to prepare. In the meantime 12th Field forced the enemy in Putot to find shelter.[45]

Lt.-Col. F.N. Cabeldu's preparations were as complete as time would allow. Since his battalion was all that stood between the Germans and the beaches at Courseulles, he had to ensure that the village could be held after it was recaptured. He used smoke to mask the open right flank and asked Maj. Frank White to deploy his tanks on that flank and provide close fire support for the infantry. With the carrier platoon covering the left flank, Cabeldu hoped to shoot his companies into Putot using a 'creeping barrage ... with a lift sufficient for a 3 mile an hour advance then lifting to concentrations south of the railway line.'[46] The confidence with which everyone went about their tasks helped sustain the morale of men, but in the flat, open wheatfields, German mortar fire exacted a terrible toll. The Canscots kept going, advancing into what their War Diary calls a 'veritable wall of fire.'

Once on the objective, Maj. A.H. Plows organized the defences with 'cool, calm direction' that steadied everyone.[47] The enemy had neither tanks nor antitank guns forward, and as the Hussar tanks moved into the village the Hitler Youth withdrew, establishing a new position some 300 metres south of the railway line.

The Canscots defended Putot by establishing identifiable fortress positions. Plows, who commanded what was left of D Company as well as his own A Company, decided that the initial position at the railway bridge was too exposed and asked Cabeldu for permission to withdraw a short distance to obtain better cover and improve the field of fire. The new position, in a small orchard, was little more than 200 feet square, but it could be organized for all-round defence. When the first serious counterattack developed, concentrated small-arms fire and the support company's 3-inch mortars were enough to check the enemy. When tanks appeared, the artillery, which was ranged on the bridge approaches, persuaded the Hitler Youth to leave the village to the Canadians.[48] The battle for Putot was won at a terrible cost. The Royal Winnipeg Rifles lost 265 men, including 60 killed. The Canscots suffered 45 dead and 80 wounded. No complete record of German losses is available, though the divisional historian reports 45 killed and 48 wounded and missing, not including losses in the counterattacks of 9 and 10 June.[49]

The horror of combat with the Hitler Youth was again evident when officers of 3rd Battalion, 26th Panzer Grenadier Regiment, ordered the execution of twenty-six Canadian prisoners of war at the Chateau d'Audrieu. Other Canadian soldiers were murdered even farther from the front.[50] Some historians have tried to contextualize the war crimes committed by 12th SS in Normandy, reporting anecdotal – usually second- or third-hand – evidence of the killing of German prisoners. The reality is that there is no evidence, anecdotal or otherwise, pointing to the killing of enemy prisoners behind Allied lines in response to orders. Nor is there any indication that other German divisions committed such crimes in Normandy.[51]

Field Marshal Erwin Rommel arrived at the headquarters of Panzer Lehr just as the Canscots were retaking Putot. He was quickly briefed on the situation, and was informed of the devastating effects of naval fire, which had 'cut to pieces' units of the division, including a vital heavy weapons company. Rommel ordered Panzer Lehr to shift west and organize an attack to retake Bayeux. General Witt, the 12th SS commander, reported that his Panzer battalion was waiting for dusk to attack Bretteville and Norrey. This attack was intended to secure the start line for a full-scale divisional thrust to the coast. Rommel approved these plans and departed for his headquarters.[52]

The battlegroup preparing to attack the Reginas consisted of two companies of Panthers, a motorcycle company, and two batteries of self-propelled howitzers. Kurt Meyer was in command. His plan called for a direct attack down the main highway into the village. How tanks with few infantry were to accomplish this was quite unclear. The Panthers, 'staggered one behind each other,' came under flanking fire from 3rd Anti-Tank Regiment, which carefully waited until the lead tanks were at the edge of Bretteville. Three Panthers were destroyed before this approach was abandoned. Just before midnight, two Panthers groped their way down the main road into Bretteville. Lt.-Col. Matheson described the result:

> One came opposite battalion headquarters and was struck by a PIAT bomb, fired from behind a stone wall at 15 yards range, safe from the tank's huge gun. It halted for a moment started again and after 30 yards was hit by a second PIAT. It stopped, turned around and headed out of town. A third PIAT hit finished it off so that it slew around out of control running over a necklace of 75 grenades which blew off a track. The crew dismounted and attempted to make off but were killed by small arms fire. During this incident the second Panther had remained farther up the road. Seeing the fate of its companion it commenced to fire both 75mm and MG wildly down the street like a child in a tantrum doing no damage whatsoever except to set fire to the first Panther. Rifleman Lapointe, J.E. with great coolness and determination was instrumental in knocking out the first tank.[53]

Meyer now employed his self-propelled artillery and one company of Panthers as a fire base, shelling the entrance to Bretteville while his second Panther Company swung left in an attempt to enter the village from the south. At Cardonville, they encountered Dog Company and were soon involved in pounding the Regina company with everything they had. But as Acting Major Gordon Brown, Dog Company's commander, noted: 'Tanks without infantry and at night made no sense. They could take ground and batter buildings, cause some casualties and generally terrorize us but without infantry they could not hold what they had captured.'[54]

Back in Bretteville, the situation was even more frustrating for the Germans. The motorcycle company had suffered heavy losses, and the Panther crews with their limited visibility found night fighting in the streets of Bretteville confusing and pointless. German veterans of the Eastern Front knew that 'the tactic of surprise, using mobile fast infantry and Panzers, even in small numerically inferior Kampfgruppen, had often been practised and proven in Russia.' But as Hubert Meyer notes in his history of the 12th SS:

> This tactic, however, had not resulted in the expected success here against a courageous and determined enemy, who was ready for the defence and well equipped. Through good battlefield observation, the enemy had recognized the outlines of the preparations for the attack and drawn his own conclusions. The deployment of D Company to Cardonville had prevented a breakthrough by 2/26 from the farm south of the rail line to Bretteville, only 1000 meters away. The antitank defences all around the village were strong enough to thwart all attempts by Panzers to by-pass the town to the south and north. The surprising use of parachute flares with glowing magnesium light blinding the Panthers and clearly outlined them to enemy Pak. The enemy was especially strong in the defence and could not be taken by surprise. He fought with determination and courage.[55]

The disastrous attack of 8–9 June, which cost 12th SS a further 152 casualties as well as six tanks, did not persuade 'Panzer' Meyer that his operational doctrine was flawed. He ordered a new assault concentrated on Norrey, which he now believed to be the key to unlocking the Canadian defences. The 3rd Panzer Company of 12th Panzer Regiment, which had not participated in the previous attack, was to cross the railway line and advance on Norrey shortly after noon on 9 June, when the skies would, it was hoped, be free of fighter-bombers. The first battalion of Mohnke's 26th Regiment was to advance simultaneously on Norrey from the south.[56]

The operation turned into a nightmare for the Hitler Youth. The infantry were quickly hammered back into their slit trenches by artillery and mortars. The Panthers drove on Norrey 'as a body at high speed without any stops' until the lead tank was hit. Then another Panther had its turret torn off. Five more were lost in the next few minutes; the remainder withdrew at full speed. A single 17-pounder Firefly of the First Hussars accounted for seven of the Panthers, which had advanced on Norrey with their vulnerable side-armour exposed.[57]

Even this costly setback did not persuade 12th SS to abandon piecemeal attacks on the Canadian positions. The next morning, the pioneer battalion tried to follow the 'heaviest possible barrage' into Norrey. Charlie Company of the Reginas used its own weapons and the divisional artillery to crush the attack. Four attempts to capture Norrey had failed at a cost of more than three hundred Hitler Youth. Their divisional historian later noted:

> This village together with Bretteville, formed a strong barrier, blocking the attack plans of the Panzerkorps. For this reason, repeated attempts were made to take these positions through a number of attacks. They failed because of insufficient forces, partly because of rushed planning caused by real or imagined time pressures. Last but not least they failed because of the courage of the defenders which was not any less than that of the attackers. It was effectively supported by well constructed positions, strong artillery, antitank weapons and by tanks.[58]

While 7th Brigade was successfully defending its sector, other units of the Second British Army were engaged in offensive operations aimed at securing their D-Day objectives. Montgomery proposed an attack on Caen, with 51st Highland Division pushing out of the Orne bridgehead and 7th Armoured advancing from Bayeux to Villers-Bocage and Evrecy. If these operations were successful, 1st British Airborne Division was to seize ground south of Caen and complete the encirclement.[59]

Panzer Lehr had received orders to attack along the same road, Tilly-sur-Seulles–Bayeux, that the 7th Armoured Division was to use, and on 10 June a series of inconclusive battles erupted along the front to the west of the Canadians. The German attack was called off before the 7th Armoured began its advance at 1830 and before the medium bombers of No. 2 Group 2 TAF, acting on an Ultra decrypt, destroyed the headquarters of Panzer Group West.[60] The Desert Rats reached Bucéels before dark and prepared to continue the advance at first light on 11 June. During the day, 69th British Brigade, providing flank protection, fought its way south to Point 103, but it was unable to advance farther.[61] Dempsey was determined to force the pace. He overruled a plan to use 2nd Canadian Armoured Brigade to clear the Mue valley and then push the Canadian front forward, scheduled for 12 June. Instead, the brigade, with one battalion of infantry, the Queen's Own Rifles, was to come to the support of 69th Brigade by forming the left-hand pincer for a renewed attack on the high ground south of Cristot.[62]

Army commanders who are determined to order operations involving different brigades in different divisions in different corps should probably avoid haste and improvisation. They should also insist on mechanisms for coordinating such attacks. Dempsey ignored these obvious prerequisites because 7th Armoured Division's attempt to break through the German defences and reach Villers-Bocage had priority and was to be supported, whatever the cost. The Queen's Own Rifles were ordered to rendezvous with the First Hussars at 1100. The two units had never trained or worked together before, and both COs listened to Brig. Wyman's instructions at the 'O' group with disbelief.[63] Wyman outlined a three-stage operation to seize the high ground two miles south of Norrey-en-Bessin at Cheux. One battlegroup was to make the first bound to le Mesnil-Patry at 1300. Both COs protested, asking for adequate time to tee up the operation, but they were told this was impossible. The 7th Armoured Division had renewed its attack on Tilly-sur-Seulles, and 50th Division was engaged in a bitter struggle to expand the eastern flank of the salient. The Canadian attack might force a German withdrawal from Cristot and help 50th Division advance south.

The operation 'conceived in sin and born in inequity'[64] began when a company of the Queen's Own, riding on the Hussar's tanks, arrived at Norrey-en-Bessin at 1400. The Reginas, who had held the village for three days, had not been consulted, and there was no time for a briefing. Maj. Stu Tubb and his men pointed out the minefield they had laid on the area designated as the forming up place (FUP), and then watched in amazement as the tanks struggled to make the turn in the narrow streets of the village crossroads. The Reginas never claimed to have cleared the flat fields with waist-high grain that stretched toward le Mesnil-Patry, and they had seen no evidence of any German withdrawal. Mortar and artillery fire struck the village as if to remind everyone of that reality.[65] The area was held by the Pioneer Battalion of 26th Panzer Grenadier Regiment, which had established well-camouflaged positions in the fields. To the south, a hidden company of Panzers waited in an ambush position, which they used to advantage in destroying the Canadian battlegroup.[66]

'B' Squadron of the First Hussars had been involved in continuous combat since D-Day, and its losses meant that many of the tanks were crewed by men who had only recently joined the regiment. 'D' Company of the Queen's Own Rifles had landed on D-Day as a reserve company, avoiding casualties on the beach and the advance inland. Maj. J.N. Gordon recalled that total losses to that morning were 'about 13 out of a total strength of 120.' By the evening of 11 June, 96 of the 105 men who went into action had been killed or wounded, along with 80 from the Hussars.[67]

The advance to le Mesnil-Patry was launched at approximately the same time two battalions of the Green Howards and the 4/7 Dragoon Guards were scheduled to attack Cristot, but their advance was delayed until long after the Hussars battlegroup had been destroyed. Dempsey continued to underestimate the strength of the German defences and their commitment to fighting for the ground they held. He agreed to Lt-Gen. Bucknell's request to sidestep 7th Armoured Division to the west and attack Villers-Bocage from that direction while 50th Division continued attacking south to focus German attention on the Tilly–Cristot front.[68] As a result of this manouevre, 7th Armoured Division suffered a major reverse and was withdrawn from Villers-Bocage. The humiliation of the 'Desert Rats,' who lost more than a score of tanks to a single German Tiger,[69] marked the postponement of further attempts to penetrate defences with armoured spearheads. A bridgehead had been established, but different methods would be required to fight an enemy employing Panzer divisions to hold ground defensively.

4

The Battles for Caen

The battles for Villers-Bocage and le Mesnil-Patry were part of Montgomery's first attempt to capture Caen. His plan for a pincer movement, with 1st British Airborne seizing ground south of the city, had failed, with both the 7th Armoured and 51st Highland running into determined resistance and powerful counterattacks. Montgomery decided to think the problem through again. He prepared a new plan that would employ the three divisions of Lt.-Gen. Richard O'Connor's 8 British Corps in the area west of Caen. Crocker's 1 British Corps, including the Canadians, was 'to practise aggressive defence' in front of the city, forcing the enemy to maintain the strongest possible forces in that sector.[1]

Operation Epsom was outlined in Montgomery's directive of 18 June. The next day, a strong channel storm wrecked the American Mulberry harbour and damaged the British Mulberry at Arromanches. 'When at last, on June the 22nd, the storm abated the whole invasion coast was strewn with wreckage. About eight hundred craft of all types were stranded, most of them heavily damaged and many entirely destroyed.'[2] The storm seriously affected the rate of build-up of Allied forces in Normandy and forced Montgomery to postpone Epsom until 25 June. This delay allowed the enemy to greatly strengthen its defenses all across the front and to speed up the arrival of three infantry divisions, which were supposed to relieve the Panzer divisions from static warfare.

Montgomery had other worries besides these. From Ultra he was receiving timely information on the build-up of Panzer formations. The 1st SS Panzer Division had left Belgium on 17 June and was expected to reach the front in the Caen sector on 21 June. News of the transfer of 2nd SS Panzer Corps with 9th and 10th SS Panzer Divisions from Poland was confirmed on 24 June, when reports of their arrival in the Paris area were received. One hundred forty trains had been required to move these divisions, and all had reached their assembly area without interference from air attack. On the eve of Epsom, 21 Army Group's intelligence summary noted: '1st SS and the van of 9th and 10th SS were in the Argentan-Dreux area concealed in the *bocage*.' The report suggested that this 'formidable reserve' might be used for the long-delayed counterattack.[3]

Despite this disturbing information, Montgomery gave every appearance of optimism informing Eisenhower that once the 'Blitz attack of 8 Corps goes in ... I will contrive the battle on the eastern flank until one of us cracks and it will not be us.' As usual, he added a reference to his master plan, which was to pull the enemy onto the British so as to assist the Americans when they attacked south, but he seemed genuinely convinced 8 Corps would be able break through to the Orne.[4]

Montgomery initially planned to attack Caen from both sides, but the narrowness of the Orne bridgehead persuaded him to concentrate on a single thrust from the west. To divert attention and attract reserves, 51st Highland Division was ordered to stage a limited attack on the eastern flank of the bridgehead. The Highland Division, veterans of North Africa and Sicily, mounted a brilliant operation, advancing at night without any preliminary artillery preparation. The enemy was taken by surprise, and the village of Ste-Honourine was quickly captured. The inevitable counterattack from 21st Panzer Division's 'Battle Group Luck' was beaten back, and thirteen German tanks were destroyed.[5]

The start line for Epsom was an 8 kilometre stretch of countryside between Norrey-en-Bessin and Tilly-sur-Seulles. On the right flank there was classic Normandy *bocage* – small, hedge-rowed fields in hilly, broken countryside. O'Connor planned to squeeze his three fresh, 'unblooded' divisions, 15th Scottish, 11th Armoured, and 43rd Wessex, through a 3 kilometre corridor on the relatively open left flank. Apart from Panzer Lehr and 12th SS, the main obstacles were the high ground north of the River Odon with its strong reverse-slope positions; the heavily wooded river valley and narrow stream; and, if these barriers were overcome, the flat-topped ridge south of the river known by its altitude as Hill 112. To extend the attack, the army commander ordered 49th West Riding Division, part of 30 Corps, to advance into the *bocage* on a wide front. This would force Panzer Lehr to defend itself instead of coming to the assistance of 12th SS. The 49th, nicknamed the 'Polar Bears,' began Operation Martlet twenty-four hours before Epsom, attacking on the divisional boundary between the Hitler Youth and Panzer Lehr. This forced both divisions to commit reserves.

Panzer Lehr had already lost 2,300 men, 75 per cent of them from its infantry battalions,[6] and while its tanks, self-propelled guns, artillery,

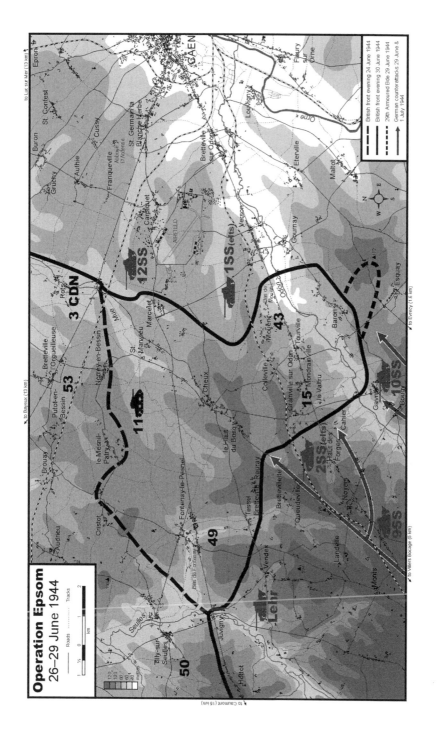

Operation Epsom
26–29 June 1944

Roads ------- Tracks

1 ½ 0 1 2 km

metres 60 90 120 150

British front evening 24 June 1944
British front evening 30 June 1944
29th Armoured Bde 29 June 1944
German counterattacks 29 June &
1 July 1944

to Luc sur Mer (13 km)
to Bayeux (13 km)
to Caumont (15 km)
to Villers Bocage (5 km)
to Évrecy (1.6 km)

CAEN

Epron
St. Contest
Cussy
Buron
Gruchy
Authie
Franqueville
Abbaye
D'Ardenne
St. Germain la
Blanche Herbe
Bretteville
Sur Odon
Verson
Eterville
Mallot
Louvigny
Fleury
sur
Orne
Orne

12SS
1SS (elts)
3 CDN
Rots
Mue
Marcelet
St.
Manvieu
Cheux
Colleville
Mouen
Bas de
Mouen
Odon
43
Gournay
Baron
Tourville
Grainville sur Odon
15
Mondrainville
le Valtru
Gavrus
Bouoy
10SS
Esquay

Bretteville
l'Orgueilleuse
Puto-en-
Bessin
Norrey-en-Bessin
53
le Mesnil-
Patry
11SS
le Haut
du Bocq
Fontenay-le-Pesnel
49
Tessel
Bretteville la
Bretteville Rauray
Queudeville
2SS (elts)
Haut des
Forges
Cahier
9SS
Noyers
Monts
Llandelle
Brouay
Cristot
Audrieu
Bas de Fontenay
Vendes
Juvigny
Tilly-sur-
Seulles
Seulles
50
Haltot

Leur

and mortars could still exact a heavy price when attacked,[7] the division was losing its capacity to act as an offensive formation. Rommel hoped to withdraw Panzer Lehr for rest and refitting as soon as 276th Infantry Division arrived. The Hitler Youth had also suffered heavy casualties before 25 June, 'estimated at 2,530 men, fifty percent of the strength of its infantry regiments.' Like Panzer Lehr, 12th SS remained a formidable defensive force, deploying fifty-eight Panzer IVs, forty-four Panthers and seventeen 88 mm antitank guns as well as its artillery and mortars across a 12 kilometre front. Since there had been ample time to dig in, place camouflage, lay mines, prepare alternative positions, clear fields of fire, and register mortars and artillery, the Hitler Youth would be difficult to overcome. To the rear of the two Panzer divisions, three regiments of 3rd Flak Corps with dual-purpose 88 and 40 mm guns had taken up position.[8] In an antitank role, 88 mm gun crews had been instructed to open fire at ranges in excess of 2000 metres.[9] This meant that the guns positioned on the slopes of Hill 112 could hit tanks crossing the crest of the ridge on the north side of the Odon.

Operation Martlet began in darkness and a thick mist at 0415, 25 June, with an assault by two brigades and a barrage of 250 army and naval guns. This was to be a classic set piece attack, and each battalion had rehearsed using cloth models. Once across the start line, the limited visibility – often restricted to five yards – meant that command and control beyond the section level was nearly impossible. Fortunately, the enemy was firing on fixed lines, and this allowed the troops to work their way forward. By 0500, with visibility now up to 60 yards, the lead elements had entered Fontenay-le-Pesnel, crossed the Caen–Caumont highway (D9), and advanced to Tessel Woods.[10]

The German response to Martlet hinted of desperation. A 3 kilometre penetration had separated the two Panzer divisions and was threatening the flanks of both. Local reserves were committed to contain the British advance, and a battle of extraordinary intensity developed. That night, orders for a concentrated counterattack were issued. Kurt Meyer arrived to orchestrate this attack, which was halted by a British advance just before Epsom began. In his memoirs, Meyer described the scene:

> The attack initially advances well, but is stalled by an English counterattack. It turns into a battle of tank against Panzer which is fought with great

determination. The broken terrain covered with hedges does not allow our Panzers to take advantage of the longer range of their guns. In particular the lack of infantry becomes noticeable. The concentrated artillery fire greatly inhibits any cooperation and later makes direct command almost impossible ... It is starting to rain. Thank God this protects us from fighter-bombers – But what is this? The ground seems to open up, to devour us all ... This is the expected major offensive ... Caen is the objective.[11]

Meyer ordered an end to the counterattack, the absolute defense of the Raury spur, and the immediate return of the Panzers to the main battle area. Martlet had accomplished its dual purpose – distraction and attrition.

The attack by 15th Scottish Division also began two brigades up. Weather conditions did not permit air support, but a massive artillery barrage (seven hundred guns) allowed the infantry with their supporting armour from the 31st Tank Brigade to breach the main defensive line. The heavily fortified villages of St-Manvieu and Cheux required house-to-house and hand-to-hand combat to clear. Enemy mortars, firing from the south side of the Odon, struck each village as soon as it was entered, causing the bulk of the hundreds of casualties sustained in the first phase. The 12th SS battlegroups arriving from Raury counterattacked St-Monrien but were beaten off by artillery. A third fortified village, le-Haut-du-Bosq, could not be cleared at any price the Scottish Division was willing to pay. Gen. O'Connor decided to push 11th Armoured Division through to the Odon, but all attempts to move south of Cheux were met with devastating fire. That evening, in a torrential rain, the reserve brigade of 15th Scottish tried without success to clear the reverse slope positions. Reserves in the form of Panzers, assault guns, and a company of Tigers were helping establish a new position. The Hitler Youth, vastly outnumbered, fought with the kind of reckless courage that has won the admiration of professional soldiers and military historians. In contrast to the citizen soldiers opposing them, these young, fervent Nazis did not hesitate to forfeit their lives in hopeless tactical situations.[12]

The first day of Epsom ended in a stalemate, with extraordinary losses on both sides. Hitler Youth casualties – 88 killed, 230 wounded, and 412 missing – were the most of any single day. The Pioneer Battalion, with 320 casualties, had practically ceased to exist, and 26th Regiment was reduced to platoon-sized companies.[13] At 0500 the relentless British attack began again. The fighting of 27 June followed the pattern established the previous day – fierce, deadly battles for each field and farmhouse. One company of 2nd Panzer Division, with seventeen Panthers, attempted to recapture Cheux, but this attempt to reverse the tide of battle failed and was quickly broken off; this suggests that some German commanders were making rational choices. Infantry of 227th Highland Brigade, supported now by the tanks of 11th Armoured Division, fought their way to the river, seized an intact bridge at Tourmauville, and reached the lower slopes of Hill 112.[14] Thus was formed the 'Scottish Corridor' – a 3 kilometre wide, 8 kilometre deep spike driven into the heart of the enemy's defences.

The next day, 28 June, the headquarters of Panzer Group West, destroyed by medium bombers on 11 June, was ready to resume operations, still under command of Geyr, the apostle of flexible defence and concentrated counterattacks. Geyr had developed a plan for his Panzer group that he described as 'an offensive method of defence against Second British Army.' This plan called for a night attack to penetrate in 'one fell swoop' the Allied line, reaching the 'heights on either side of Bayeux.'[15] Had the growing British casualty lists led Montgomery to back off, Geyr's offensive might still have been possible as 2nd SS Panzer Corps had yet to be committed. Since both Montgomery and his army commander, Dempsey, knew from Ultra that 2nd SS Corps would be ready to intervene in the next twenty-four to thirty-six hours, their decision to continue Epsom requires careful scrutiny.

The American historian Carlo D'Este, the best-informed of Montgomery's critics, is clearly puzzled by the events. D'Este's central argument is that Montgomery arrived at his 'master' plan to pull the Panzer divisions onto the eastern flank after his own attempts to break out failed. D'Este insists that the real object of Epsom had been 'to outflank Caen from the west and, like the Villers-Bocage ploy, it was a dismal failure.' Yet D'Este admits that the Germans 'suffered a sharp defeat ... in terms of men and material' and agrees that Epsom 'forestalled and spoiled the last German effort to break the Allied front.' But for D'Este, this does not count, because it was a 'fortuitous result' of an offensive that he insists failed at the tactical as well as the operational level.[16]

The evidence strongly suggests that generals, both Allied and German, were setting ambitious objectives so that in the unlikely event that all went well, momentum would not be lost. Montgomery and Dempsey hoped that Epsom would work and provided outline plans for an advance to the Orne, but no one thought of this as a single throw of the dice. The German army in Normandy had to be worn down before a breakout could occur and destroying the enemy – killing, wounding, or capturing German soldiers – was the real objective of all operations. Montgomery knew this, and decided that a continuation of Epsom would serve his primary goal of attrition and extend the policy of 'getting the enemy heavily involved on the eastern flank so that my affairs on the western flank could proceed the easier.'[17] D'Este is quite correct in arguing that Montgomery was putting the best spin on a situation created by Hitler's no-withdrawal policy, but there is a difference between pointing out a rationalization and analysing decision making.

Montgomery decided to press ahead, ordering 11th Armoured Division to expand the bridgehead over the Odon while 43rd Wessex Division won control of Marcelet and Mouen on the eastern flank. These operations convinced the enemy that the British offensive had to be stopped at all costs, because even with the help of 2nd SS Panzer Corps, the danger existed that the enemy would push through to the Orne and that Caen would fall as a result. Geyr therefore abandoned his plan and ordered 2nd SS Panzer Corps to attack the salient as soon as possible.[18]

The British had no definite information as to the timing or direction of the attack by 2nd SS Panzer Corps, but on the morning of 29 June, O'Connor's men were told to dig in and get ready! Ultra provided more detailed information in the afternoon, just as the German attack got underway.[19] 2nd SS Panzer Corps' orders were 'to take the Baron, Mouen, Cheux areas and to destroy the enemy who had crossed the Caen–Villers-Bocage road.' In other words, to eliminate the salient and 8 British Corps. Did Geyr actually expect to achieve this goal, or was he providing exactly the kind of orders that Montgomery had issued for Epsom?

The German attack made some initial progress but soon bogged down. Their axis of advance across the broken, hedgerowed Odon valley forced them into the roads and 8 Corps artillery was able to wreak havoc. By noon on 30 June, Panzer Group West reported: 'The attack is halted ... by the most intense artillery fire [including] British naval artillery.'[20] The War Diary of O.B. West reported that 'after several hours of fluctuating fighting the II SS Panzer Corps attack was smothered ... Our forces suffered grievous losses.'[21] The Germans did regain Hill 112, but the next morning, 1 July, a new attack by elements of two Panzer divisions ended in defeat. Their objective, the Raury spur, was held by 49th West Riding Division, which checked all attempts to infiltrate its position and inflicted heavy casualties.[22]

Those historians who are wedded to the view that the 'failure to gain Caen in June 1944 revealed a weakness of fighting power and tactics within the British army'[23] have dealt especially harshly with 49th Division because of the collapse of one of its nine battalions. The story of the 6th Duke of Wellington Regiment is recounted by D'Este, Max Hastings, and other critics of the British soldier. None of these historians draws conclusions based on the achievements of the other eight battalions of 49th Division or on the heroic efforts of the men of 15th Scottish Division.

By any reasonable standards, Operation Epsom was a considerable success. 8 Corps had taken the initiative away from the enemy and ended any possibility of a strong, coordinated counteroffensive. The fighting had dealt a final blow to Panzer Lehr's ability to function as an armoured division and it was withdrawn to be employed as a source of armoured battlegroups to hold the *bocage* against the Americans.[24] The Hitler Youth Division's 26th Panzer Grenadier Regiment could no longer muster enough men to form battalions, and the survivors served in ad hoc battlegroups, deadly in a defensive role but incapable of offensive action. Losses to the other Panzer divisions were also significant, and neither men nor tanks could easily be replaced. The experience of the Odon battle led Geyr to abandon plans for an offensive and to urge Rommel to draw 'clear sighted and realistic' conclusions from the battle. The enemy, he wrote, 'intends using his superiority in material to wear down the Panzer divisions.' If Caen-North was abandoned and the line of the Orne–Caen-South–Villers-Bocage held, 21st, 12th SS, and Panzer Lehr divisions could be withdrawn for recuperation. He concluded: 'A clear cut choice must be made between the inevitable tactical patchwork of static defense which leaves the initiative to the opponent, and a fluid operation drawing the initiative our way from time to time at least.'[25] On 3 July, Geyr, whose realism was no longer acceptable to Hitler, was dismissed and replaced by another Panzer expert, Gen. Heinrich Eberbach.[26]

The British paid a high price for their victory, with total casualties exceeding 5,000 men.[27] The infantry battalions of 15th Scottish and 49th West Riding, which bore the brunt of the fighting, were reduced to half-strength, and the ratio of battle exhaustion casualties to wound casualties rose, from 1:10 to 1:5. The intensity of combat was imposing an extraordinary burden on men's minds as well as on their lives. The British were already drawing on the last available pool of trained replacements and could ill afford large numbers of psychiatric casualties. Most divisions took steps to establish front-line exhaustion centres designed to quickly treat men who had broken down and return them to duty. Medical officers were confident that a high return-to-unit rate could be achieved through forward psychiatry, but no follow-up studies were done to see if it actually worked.[28]

The early capture of Caen to secure room for airfields had been such a prominent part of pre-D-Day planning assumptions[29] that Montgomery's decision to call off Epsom drew immediate criticism, especially from the three RAF air marshals who controlled the Allied air forces: Air Chief Marshal Arthur Tedder, Deputy Supreme Commander under Eisenhower; Air Chief Marshal Trafford Leigh-Mallory, Commander of the Allied Expeditionary Air Force; and Air Marshal Arthur Coningham. This was not the first time the senior air officers had criticized Montgomery, and it would not be the last.[30] Part of the problem was a personality clash, but the quarrel was also rooted in differing expectations about the role of the air force and was exacerbated by a failure to resolve these differences.[31]

To understand the part played by air power in the battle of Normandy, one must begin by reminding oneself that the RAF had been operating over western France long before D-Day, and that its leaders believed they understood the role that air power would play in the invasion. The essential task was winning and keeping air superiority over the battlefield. Once the invasion was launched, it became obvious that the Luftwaffe was largely a spent force, only capable of nuisance raids. In the months leading up to D-Day the Allied air forces had devoted enormous effort to attacks on German airfields and radar installations. But this was only one of the tasks that the Allied air forces carried out in April and May – tasks that led to the loss of 12,000 air crew and 2000 aircraft before the first soldier set foot on the shores of France.[32]

The second major priority was to disrupt the French and Belgian railway network so that German supplies and reinforcements could not take advantage of this efficient system. Known as the Transportation Plan, this operation was highly controversial: many doubted its effectiveness, and many others – including Churchill – worried about collateral damage to French civilians.[33] The third task was the almost continuous attack on the coastal batteries and strongpoints that made up the Atlantic Wall. These positions were heavily defended by anti-aircraft guns, as were the V1 launching sites known as 'Crossbow' targets. It was assumed at first that the heavy bombers would concentrate on the Transportation Plan while the medium B-24s and fighter-bombers took on the coastal defences and V1 'ski sites.'

The tactical air forces were not happy about this assignment. Their own experience with air-to-ground attacks on fortified and defended targets suggested that neither fighter-bombers nor medium bombers were likely to succeed in this role. RAF Fighter Command had begun to study air-to-ground operations before the bulk of its squadrons were transferred to Second Tactical Air Force, and early experiments with bomb and rocket equipped fighters had produced discouraging results. In January 1943 a full-scale model of a German artillery division with forty-eight mock guns and fifty-eight dummy soldiers was created. 'Every effort was made to aid the fighter-bombers in their attack but neither Mustangs strafing, nor Typhoons firing their new rockets with 60lb war heads were able to inflict more than negligible damage on the position.'[34]

Second Tactical Air Force's operational research section found that there was little improvement over the course of the year that followed, partly because of the enormous turnover in pilots, and partly because too much time was spent on operations instead of training, but largely because the problem could not be solved with the available technology. A June 1944 study by the OR section of the AEAF noted that even in the most favourable circumstances, average pilots were lucky to concentrate rocket projectiles in a circle 150 yards in diameter.

> In order to hit a small target with R.P. [Rocket Projectile] the pilot must be at the right height and dive angle, have the correct speed, have his sight on the target and make the right angular depression on his sight, make the correct wind allowances and be free from skid or 'g' ... All of these factors are important but it is difficult for the pilot to have them all right at the same time.[35]

If this was the reality faced by pilots on practice runs, what happened in actual attacks when they had to evade anti-aircraft fire? The researchers concluded that previous views on the accuracy of RP attacks and of dive bombing – which was even more subject to aiming error – must have been based on 'the performance of a few very keen and experienced pilots who can hit small objects such as tanks with RP.' Such men might be grouped in a corps d'elite to attack precision targets, but only continual training and practice would improve the accuracy of the average TAF pilot.[36]

Given this, it is not surprising that fighter-bombers were unable to inflict serious damage on the small, 50-yard ramps of V1 launching sites. By May 1944 there were 520 88 mm and 730 40 mm anti-aircraft guns in the 'ski' site belt between Dieppe and St-Omer.[37] Low-level air attacks produced crippling losses. Medium bombers suffered fewer casualties, but the probability of actually hitting vital equipment was even lower than with fighter-bombers. Both the U.S. 8th Air Force and Bomber Command were persuaded to try, but neither regarded Crossbow targets as legitimate tasks for the heavies, and most of the effort had to be made by the tactical air forces, with predictable results and very heavy pilot casualties.[38] The problem was especially serious for the British and Canadian squadrons of 2TAF, which were entirely equipped with liquid-cooled aircraft designed as fighter-interceptors. During a ground attack the cooling systems, located on the bottom of the plane, were especially vulnerable to flak. This defect was thought to account for most of the losses in ground attack operations.[39]

The RAF had encountered a different set of problems when converting fighter pilots to a ground attack role. In March 1943, Fighter Command issued a Tactical Memorandum outlining the results of controlled studies on the ability of pilots to find camouflaged targets on the basis of map references. The report concluded that fighter pilots 'given a six figure map reference were unable to spot well camouflaged guns even when the guns were actually firing.'[40] Pilots could usually find coastal batteries and the distinctive V1 launching sites, but they were quite unable to locate camouflaged defensive positions of the kind the Germans were by then constructing in Normandy.

In sum, the air forces approached the Normandy campaign with a clear understanding of their own strengths and weaknesses. This was reflected in the Initial Joint Plan for Overlord, which was completed in February 1944. It required the Allied Expeditionary Air Force first to 'attain and maintain air superiority', second 'to assist the Allied Armies ashore', and third 'to impose delay on enemy reinforcements of the bridgehead and, in particular, to prevent German Panzer divisions from massing for a counterattack during the first critical period immediately after the assaults.'[41] Winning and maintaining air superiority was expected to require an enormous effort. On 6 June, fifty-two fighter squadrons provided cover over the beaches, with six in immediate reserve. A further fifteen covered the sea lanes, while twenty-four squadrons waited in England to respond to crises or opportunities.[42] The Luftwaffe was known to be weak in France, but Overlord's planners believed that it would respond to the invasion with an all-out effort.

The second task – assisting the Allies ashore – proved difficult to plan and execute. The army wanted pinpoint attacks on beach defences and inland gun positions, which the air force was hesitant to attempt. A compromise was reached, and target lists were developed, but as we have seen, the poor weather and cloud cover limited the number of sorties attempted and helped frustrate the ones that were made. The plan to hinder German troop movements toward the beaches called for the medium bombers of No. 2 Group to attack road and rail nodal points, especially in Caen, St.-Lo, and Lisieux on the eve of D-Day. The weather severely hampered this effort, and little damage was done.[43] On D-Day, cloud conditions and the hesitant German response provided few targets until late in the day, when columns of 12th SS Division were caught on the move.

Between D-Day and D+8, when Montgomery announced his decision 'to be defensive in the Caen sector,' the tactical air forces were still based in England, from which base they carried out their mandate to 'maintain air superiority' and impose a delay on enemy reinforcements. They were wholly successful in the first task, turning back or shooting down virtually every German daylight attack on the beachhead. We must not underrate this achievement, for though it is true that the Luftwaffe lacked the capacity to challenge Allied control of the skies, it was still able to direct a series of raids at the crowded beachhead – raids that could have inflicted serious damage on the naval armada lying off the coast. For example, on 7 June, 401 Squadron RCAF intercepted a dozen Ju88s headed for the landing areas. The suadron claimed six enemy machines; none were able to deliver their bomb loads.[44]

Throughout June the air forces devoted much energy to delaying the flow of enemy forces toward the battlefront, with mixed success. Under frequent air attack, the enemy's 2nd Parachute Corps moved its divisions from Brittany to the western side of the landing area, and along with 17th SS Panzer Grenadier Regiment came into action between D+3 and D+6. On the eastern flank, 346th Division, having been released from 15th Army, crossed the Seine in daylight. Its lead elements cycled to the Orne bridgehead and came into action on D+2. Both 12th SS and Panzer Lehr were delayed for up to twenty-four hours. The order to move 2nd Panzer Division from Abbeville to lower Normandy was issued on D+3 and a full week elapsed before it could intervene in the battle. The 101st Heavy Tank Battalion (Tigers) left Beauvais, north of Paris, on 7 June and was hit hard by air attack the following night, but as 7th Armoured Division was to discover, two companies of Tigers were fighting in Normandy on 13 June at Villers-Bocage.[45] The RAF saw all this as evidence that the interdiction campaign was effective; after all, pre-invasion estimates had predicted a much more rapid buildup.[46] Sceptics have maintained that Hitler's hesitation and the success of the Fortitude deception scheme played a larger role than the air force in determining the pace of the German response.[47] At the time, the Air Marshals did not agree, and their confidence in their strategic planning was bolstered by the apparent triumph of air power. Air superiority had been established, the Allied armies were safely ashore, and German reinforcements were being delayed. What more could the army ask for?

This triumphant mood may help explain the behaviour of the senior RAF officers when they were presented with Montgomery's proposals for employing Allied air power on the battlefield. The first confrontation was over Montgomery's plan to use 1st British Airborne to help encircle Caen. This was strongly opposed by Leigh-Mallory, who instead suggested that the heavy bombers be employed to break the enemy's resistance around Caen.[48] Montgomery agreed, but when a conference to work out the details was held at the headquarters of the Second British Army, Air Marshal Coningham, as commander of the tactical air forces, insisted that all army requests for air support would have to be channelled through his headquarters. The tactical air forces, Coningham insisted, could provide all the air support Montgomery needed.[49]

As an immediate result of this clash, the use of heavy bombers in support of the land battle was postponed for three weeks. But the far more important consequence was that relations between Montgomery and Coningham continued to deteriorate. For the balance of the war, Coningham commanded 2nd Tactical Air Force as an independent entity pursuing the same objectives as the army but on a parallel course. This was in sharp contrast to the close co-operative relationship that developed between the U.S. army and its tactical air force.[50]

During the early days of the invasion, Coningham insisted that the army make known its next day's requirements for air support by 1730 hours, when the evening conference was held at 2TAF headquarters. This meant a lapse of at least twelve hours between requests and execution of what were known as Direct Support missions. The RAF recognized the need for emergency close-support missions and helped create air support signal units (ASSUs), which were located at brigade headquarters. Requests for air support were dispatched by the ASSU, and if these were accepted, a turnaround time of one hour was considered the norm.[51]

After 83 Group, which was to work with the 2nd British Army, was established in France, evening meetings to decide on the following day's operations were continued and requests for direct support of army operations were integrated into an overall plan. Impromptu support was still arranged mainly through ASSUs, but experiments with 'Cabrank' procedures began in July. Cabrank involved air force personnel in contact cars maintaining radio contact with aircraft assigned to a given rendezvous point close to the battlefield. Pilots reported in, received target instructions, and proceeded with an immediate attack. Cabrank greatly improved the effectiveness of 2TAF as far as the army was concerned, but it was a very small part of the program carried out by 83 Group in Normandy.[52]

The standard operating procedures of 2TAF required 83 Group to devote the vast majority of its effort to patrols designed to maintain air superiority. Almost 50 per cent of the sorties flown in June and 40 per cent of those flown in July were fighter-interceptor missions. These pilots often used their machine guns and cannon to strafe 'targets of opportunity' remote from the battlefield, harassing German troop and supply movements. Direct support was the second priority, accounting for 20 per cent of all sorties. 'Armed reconnaissance,' along with photo, weather, and tactical reconnaissance, accounted for the balance of sorties.[53]

The campaign carried out by 83 Group was enormously successful according to the criteria established by Coningham. The Allied armies were able to manouevre freely behind their lines and to maintain a flow of supplies that was never interrupted by enemy action. Armed reconnaissance and attacks on 'targets of opportunity' forced the German army to avoid major moves during daylight hours and to take extraordinary pains when it came to dispersing and camouflaging supply dumps. Photo reconnaissance provided the army with information vital for planning operations large and small.

Senior army officers were much less satisfied with the air effort because so little of it was directed at the German forces actually blocking the Allied advance. Once Rommel had decided that further large-scale counterattacks were unlikely to succeed, the German army began putting into practice the lessons it had learned in defensive warfare on the eastern front. The terrain in Normandy offered overwhelming advantages to the defender, and as long as the Allies could be contained between the coast and the flooded Dives valley – a distance of just 96 kilometres – the Germans could achieve a much more favourable force ratio than they had ever enjoyed on the Eastern Front.

All across Normandy, German defences were echeloned in depth, with forward outposts, a lightly manned main defensive line, and a strong reserve including tanks or self-propelled assault guns available to carry out immediate local counterattacks. This defensive zone was 700 to 1,000 yards deep and was supported by artillery, mortar, and Nebelwerfer positions hidden still farther back behind reverse slopes. Allied air superiority and the crushing power of naval guns made the assembly of large forces for a prepared counterattack nearly impossible, so emphasis was placed on dispersing armour into 'penny packets' to provide immediate tactical support. According to German reports from the battlefront, the Panzer division had become an 'anachronism.' In Normandy, 'Panzers could only be employed piecemeal in support of infantry at most in squadron strength.'[54]

From the army's perspective, the tactical air force was ideally equipped to help destroy such defences. As early as 1943, operational researchers had argued for air attacks on German positions on reverse slopes, and by 1944 this had become an obsession.[55] In Normandy it also seemed logical to ask for air strikes on smaller armoured concentrations as they moved out of cover and into position for a counterattack, but this was rarely possible. Brigade and divisional commanders were especially unhappy that they weren't able to influence the pattern of air operations in their sectors. They seldom knew whether requests for prearranged direct support would be carried out, and they never learned whether impromptu requests had been accepted until the aircraft appeared or failed to show. In late June, Lt.-Gen. Crocker took advantage of a visit by the Air Officer Commanding 83 Group, Air Vice Marshal Harry Broadhurst, to present the army's point of view. Crocker's staff had canvassed each division and developed a wish list, which began mildly enough with a request for regular information about the plans made at the evening conference for the next day. Broadhurst could handle this, but demands to know 'what percentage of total effort' was 'allotted to a particular front' were dismissed as argumentative.

Divisional commanders also wanted to know why it was so difficult to arrange air attacks on '*small* areas of woods and villages' believed to be 'tank harbours, mortar or gun areas or infantry concentrations.' They asked for assurances that such targets 'will be taken on in spite of the fact that specific details of what exactly is in the area are not given.' Anticipating Broadhurst's reply, they noted that 'before demands for air attack are submitted the possibility of engagement by RA or RN is always considered.' Broadhurst could not provide any such assurances; 2TAF reserved the right to establish priorities and select targets. All commanders emphasized the importance of close air support 'both from the point of view of damage to the enemy and the excellent morale effect of our own troops.' But without proper coordination, air support could not be integrated into the overall battle plan, and this greatly reduced its value.[56]

Although the divisional commanders did not know it, they were asking the tactical air force to attack precisely the kinds of targets it wished to avoid. Operational research had demonstrated that the low rises – which the army called hills in Normandy – could not be distinguished from the air, and small targets were difficult to identify and even harder to hit. Operations against a variety of targets were carefully examined in the weeks before D-Day, and the results confirmed past experience. It was found that Typhoon rockets hit a viaduct 500 yards long and eight yards wide only one in fifteen times. Bombs dropped from 'Bombphoons' and Spitfires struck the same target one in eighty-two times.[57] Typhoon rocket attacks on gun positions produced results varying from 110 RPs fired at a casement in Courseulles-sur-Mer with zero hits to two hits out of 127 against a similar target. None of these attacks had been against well-defended positions.[58]

To complicate matters, enemy anti-aircraft guns were invariably positioned close behind the forward defences, so low-level attacks – the only kind that had a faint hope of producing results – were extremely costly. Experience in the Mediterranean and operations in the preparatory phase of Overlord had confirmed OR studies of what could be seen and what could be hit. 2TAF doctrine insisted that 'there may be rare occasions ... when lack of cover enables fighter-bombers to take advantage of targets of opportunity in the enemy's forward areas – but as a general rule they should not be used against gun positions, strong points or fighting troops on the battlefield which can be engaged by artillery.'[59]

2TAF was not always able to maintain this stance in the face of repeated requests from the army. Typhoons were often assigned to take on gun positions, strongpoints, and even troop concentrations in close proximity to the battlefield, but few airmen thought the results justified the cost in pilots' lives. Coningham's preference for armed recce patrols well behind enemy lines coupled with a limited number of direct support missions, was based on the knowledge that 2TAF could perform these tasks much more effectively and at a lower cost than the kinds of close support operations preferred by the army. He was, however, reluctant to inform the army about problems with navigation or accuracy; instead he insisted that the tasks 2TAF intended to perform were more vital – a view that, to put it politely, the army did not share.

D.K. Hill, one of the pioneers of operational research and a member of the Army Operational Research Group, spent several months before D-Day on attachment to 2TAF ORS before leaving to join the staff of Brig. B.G. Schonland, Montgomery's scientific adviser. Hill knew a good deal about 2TAF's problems, but he also knew that every weapons system studied by operational research teams had turned out to be far less effective than the designers and practitioners claimed. Hill assumed that training would improve navigation and target destruction, but that the improvements would be marginal without further technical innovations. This had been the experience of other branches of the RAF, but 2TAF – unlike Bomber or Coastal Commands – resisted innovation related to the ground support role. It also marginalized operational research.[60]

The army in the field learned about the difficulties of target recognition through repeated air attacks on their own forward positions. This led to elaborate measures to create visible bomb lines using bulldozers or graders, white painted strips on tarmac roads, tarred strips on gravel roads, and coloured panels.[61] Casualties from friendly fire were frequent enough to make soldiers well aware of the dangers of close air support, but this did not stop them from wanting more of it. The sight of a Typhoon swooping down from the sky and releasing its rockets with an audible wooshing roar was a great morale booster when those rockets were not aimed at you. The impact of Typhoon attacks on enemy morale could not be quantified, but neither could it be doubted. One consequence of 2TAF's decision to emphasize air superiority and armed recce and to confine most direct support missions to prearranged targets was that it forced Montgomery to bypass Coningham and turn to Bomber Command and the U.S. 8th Army Air Force for direct assistance in overcoming the enemy's defences.

While air support and the use of the heavy bombers in a renewed assault on Caen were being discussed, 1st British Corps was practising 'aggressive defence' in the Caen sector. Something very like First World War conditions characterized this static battlefield. Movement on either side brought down artillery or mortar fire, and the rainy conditions prolonged a mosquito season that many regarded as a worse trial than the enemy. To survive, forward troops had to live underground in slit trenches or bunkers. Incessant demands for patrols to capture prisoners or gather intelligence were sent forward from division and brigade, and considerable ingenuity was required when it came to filling out patrol reports that would satisfy higher command.

The 9th Canadian Infantry Brigade, holding the left flank of the divisional sector was exposed to a full month of this kind of warfare. The Highland Light Infantry (HLI) in Villons-les-Buison and the Stormont Dundas and Glengarry Highlanders, 'the Glens,' in Vieux-Caron looked south toward Buron and the Abbaye d'Ardenne as the Germans thickened the crust of their defences. A commemorative memorial in Villons-les-Buissons reminds the visitor that to the men on the ground in 1944, this quiet hamlet was 'Hell's Corners.'[62]

Enemy resistance in the Caen–Carpiquet sector was especially intense because 12th SS Hitler Youth Division fought with unusual skill and determination. The 25th Panzer Grenadier Regiment defended essentially the same ground occupied on 7 June, and there had been ample time to build field fortifications, camouflage dugouts, and register artillery and mortar fire. But there was more to it than well-trained young soldiers working under experienced officers and NCOs. Most of the Hitler Youth believed in the Nazi creed and saw themselves as warriors fighting in a great cause. On 1 July 1944 their commander, Standartenführer Kurt Meyer, gave a talk on German radio that expressed the ideals of his division:

Our division was formed from young volunteers of the German breed ... and it was as political soldiers first and foremost that our young men entered the fight. Every one of them knows why he is in the west and

realizes how much depends on his delight in battle, on his will to fight ...
Be comforted, my homeland. As long as youth displays such delight in
battle, one day victory will be ours.[63]

Fortunately, such fanaticism was uncommon among German soldiers
in 1944.

While Montgomery developed plans for a frontal assault on Caen, his
army commander, responding to pressure from 8 Corps, ordered an
attack on the high ground overlooking the Odon valley from the east.
As long as the Germans held Carpiquet airport they could observe and
respond to every movement toward Hill 112. Operation Ottawa,
planned for 28 June, had been designed to capture the airfield and
village. Then it was cancelled, only to be revived in 'a more robust
form' as Operation Windsor.[64]

Dempsey gave the task to Crocker, who decided to employ a
reinforced brigade of 3rd Canadian Division in an attack scheduled for
4 July. The plan required 8th Canadian Infantry Brigade, with the
Royal Winnipeg Rifles under command, to attack 'three up' across
2 kilometres of flat, open fields. Brig. Blackader was to have support
from twenty-one regiments of artillery, HMS *Rodney*'s 16-inch guns,
two squadrons of rocket-firing Typhoons, and three squadrons of Fort
Garry tanks, plus Flails, Petards, and Crocodiles from 79th Armoured
Division.[65] Crocker believed that this would be more than adequate for
a set piece attack with limited objectives, and so decided not to incor-
porate Windsor into the major operation against Caen, now just four
days away. Blackader was assured that 43rd Division would be
launching a simultaneous advance on the right flank while a squadron
of Sherbrooke Fusiliers was to stage a diversionary attack on Franqueville, engaging the enemy on the left flank.

Despite the extraordinary efforts of the Sherbrookes, who broke
through the German minefields and shot up the defences of Chateau-
St-Louet and Gruchy before withdrawing across the River Mue,[66] the
North Shore regiment was subjected to intense fire from the left flank
as well as from the defenders of Carpiquet. Maj. J.E. Anderson, who
commanded one of the lead companies, described Carpiquet as the
graveyard of the regiment:

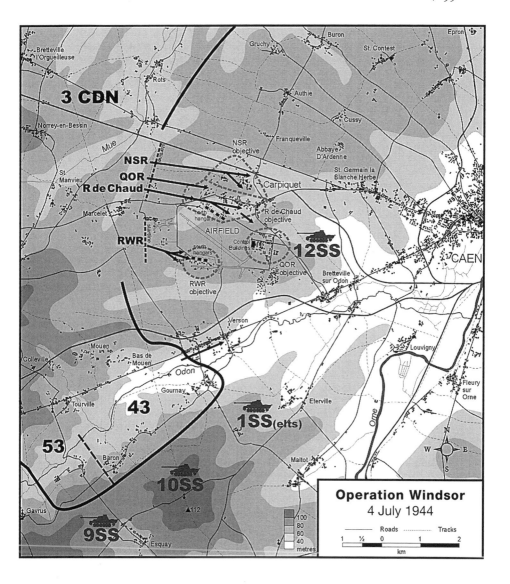

Operation Windsor
4 July 1944

> I am sure that at some time during the attack every man felt he could not go on. Men were being killed and wounded on all sides and the advance seemed pointless as well as hopeless. I never realized until the attack on Carpiquet how far discipline, pride of unit, and above all pride in oneself and family, can carry a man even when each step forward meant possible death.[67]

The Chaudières, attacking in the centre, were spared much of the fire directed at the North Shores. Their real trial came in the defence of the village after it was cleared.[68]

The Royal Winnipeg Rifles, attacking the south hangars, were exposed to fire from the south side of the Odon as well as the airport. 'The enemy,' the RWR War Diary noted, 'began to mortar us at once, which seems to be their policy to follow our own barrage with their fire.'[69] The Winnipegs advanced with only indirect fire support from tanks, as the one available squadron of the Garrys was also designated as armoured reserve. One troop was later sent forward, with several Crocodiles, to attack the bunkers, but in that open country tanks were vulnerable at long ranges, and two of the four tanks were quickly destroyed.[70]

Around 1200, Brig. Blackader ordered the Queen's Own Rifles[71] to join the Chaudières and prepare to attack the airport control buildings and barracks. The Winnipegs were told to make a new effort, with a squadron of tanks, to 'execute a sweeping attack by the lower ground around the enemy's left flank.'[72] This manouevre was based on assurances that British troops from 43rd Wessex Division had occupied Verson and could protect the Canadian flank. The British apparently did enter Verson, but as anyone who has been on the ground can see, this offered no defence against a counterattack from the southeast.[73] The Garrys' armoured sweep ran into a battlegroup of Panthers and was overwhelmed.[74] Despite growing doubts about the wisdom of immediate counterattacks, the enemy was unwilling to accept the loss of Carpiquet village and counterattacked from Francqueville shortly after midnight. The Chauds, who describe Carpiquet as 'the inferno,' beat back all attacks, and at first light, the artillery settled the issue, forcing the Germans to concede that the village could not be retaken.

The 12th SS lost 155 men, most of them in the counterattacks of 5 July.[75] The Canadians suffered 377 casualties, including 127 dead.[76]

Both sides conducted post mortems on Carpiquet. The Germans concluded that the main attack to take Caen would shortly follow and could not be won. Rommel now agreed with Geyr and wanted to get 12th SS Division out of Caen before it was completely destroyed. Hitler was of a similar mind, but only the supply and support units could be withdrawn, as 271st Division had not yet arrived. The 12th SS would have to face one more onslaught from fixed defensive positions.[77]

The Canadian response to Carpiquet was to circulate a 'lessons learned' review, which included an implicit critique of the plan for Operation Windsor. The brigade's 'lessons of war' noted that on a battlefield where a well-entrenched enemy employed a series of interlocking company defensive positions, and relied on 'large concentrations' of observed fire from mortars, 'attacks must be launched on a broad front' simultaneously so that the enemy 'cannot fire in enfilade from localities not being attacked.' Broad front attacks, the report added, would also split the enemy's defensive fire.[78]

Montgomery had come to a similar conclusion, and his plan for Operation Charnwood, the attack on Caen, employed three divisions striking a front of some 14 kilometres. The preliminary artillery program was especially elaborate, with the battleship HMS *Rodney* and the monitor *Roberts* and two cruisers employed to interdict enemy movement. Spotter aircraft were to direct the naval guns onto the enemy concentrations throughout the day. Medium artillery and the field regiments of five divisions were tasked to strike at known enemy positions.[79]

Charnwood began with the 'never to be forgotten sight'[80] of streams of Halifax and Lancaster bombers arriving over the city to bomb an area 4,000 yards long and 1,500 yards wide in the northern sections of the city. This area of 'four map squares' was well behind the fortified villages and mobile reserves that made up the defences of Caen, because Bomber Command, which had at first endorsed a plan to bomb an area 'independently of a major offensive,' insisted on a wide safety margin and a separate target area.[81]

The attack made use of 656 artillery pieces, the navy, medium and heavy bombers, and the Typhoons. Many observers then and since have suggested that with all this capacity, Charnwood ought to have produced a rapid breakthrough. Instead, all three divisions paid an enormous price, estimated at about 3,000 men killed, wounded, and

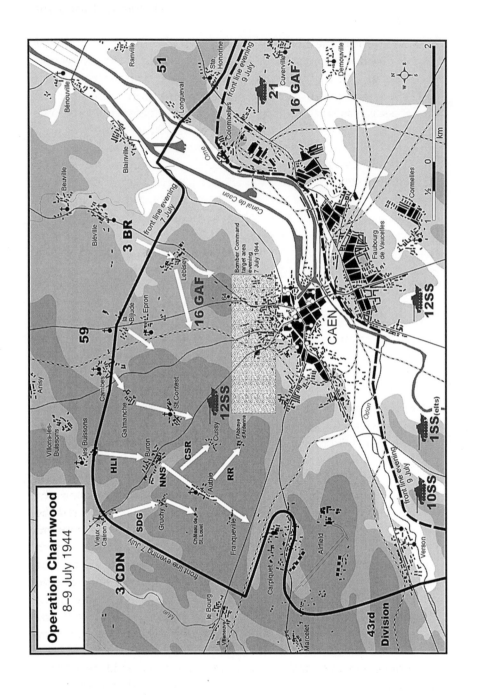

Operation Charnwood
8–9 July 1944

missing, in one of the most difficult battles of the campaign.[82] The War Diaries of 3rd Division's 9th Brigade, which attacked Lebisey Woods, make it clear that 16th GAF Division, which had replaced 21st Panzer in the line, though it lacked the resolution and direct firepower of its predecessor, was still able to inflict hundreds of casualties on the brigade through constant mortar and Nebelwerfer fire.[83]

The sector attacked by the 59th and 3rd Canadian divisions was defended by 12th SS. Its infantry battalions were at 60 per cent strength and were backed by tanks and self-propelled guns. Two Panzer battle groups, one composed of twenty-three Mk IVs and the other of seventeen Panthers, were held in reserve.[84] The plan called for 59th Division to attack at first light on a two-brigade front, advancing along the axes La Bijude–Epron and Galmanche–Malon–St-Contest. A two-brigade front translated into two battalions plus supporting armour, and while both battalions reported initial progress, neither had taken its objective when the corps commander ordered Phase II to begin at 0730. The 9th Canadian Brigade thus began its attack on Gruchy and Buron with the enemy still in full possession of the high ground to the east. The 1/7 Warwickshire Regiment, bypassing the fighting in Galmanche, began to attack St-Contest at 0930, but it did not finish capturing that village until mid-afternoon.[85]

The task of taking Buron fell to the Highland Light Infantry of Canada. Lt.-Col. Griffiths had decided to request concentrations on Buron instead of a moving barrage, and his lead companies reached the twelve-foot-wide antitank ditch in front of the village without difficulty. The infantry and tanks cleared out some machine gun posts, and twenty prisoners were taken, but the armour could not follow the infantry, who now entered a killing zone between the ditch and the edge of the village. The two assault companies lost half their strength in attacking well-camouflaged machine gun posts, few of which seemed touched by the bombardment. With the supporting armour now stuck on a minefield, Griffiths was forced to commit his reserve companies to a battle that was far from won. Finally, one troop of tanks was guided to the left flank by the battalion intelligence officer. The tanks could not make two hundred Hitler Youth surrender, but they could help ensure they were eliminated.[86]

Griffiths, while establishing his headquarters in the village, learned that his assault companies had lost two-thirds of their strength. Mortaring and shelling from the east was continuous, but orders were to push on to the high ground south of Buron. This feature, an 80 metre ring contour, was clearly marked on the 1:25,000 maps but it is not visible on the ground. One company was sent forward while the others dug in around the village. The casualty toll, which now included the CO and most of his command group, grew steadily, and the Germans decided to try to retake the village. A battle group of Mk IVs and Panthers followed an intense barrage toward Buron, but for once in a tank battle, fortune favoured the Allies. Two troops of 245th battery, 62nd Anti-Tank Regiment, Royal Artillery, had been attached to the HLI, and both were equipped with 17-pounder antitank guns. B Troop, with eight self-propelled M10 17-pounders, took up position on the edge of an orchard looking south toward the Abbaye d'Ardenne. They were ideally placed when the Panzers advanced on Buron. In the brief engagement that followed, thirteen German tanks were destroyed in one of the most successful Allied antitank engagements of the Normandy campaign.[87]

The day-long battle for Buron was in sharp contrast to the rapid capture of Gruchy, which the Stormont Dundas and Glengarry Highlanders reported clear in less than two hours. There was little sign of the fanatical resistance encountered in Buron, suggesting that not all Hitler Youth were still committed to dying for the cause. Despite this success, the whole area was drenched with mortar and artillery fire that inflicted scores of casualties while the Glens were waiting to move to their second objective, Chateau de St-Louet. The fighting in Buron delayed the advance of the North Novas to Authie, and it was 1430 hours before both attacks got underway. Authie was undefended, but the wheatfields around the chateau were manned by the remnants of a Panzer Grenadier company, who put up some resistance before surrendering. The Glens intelligence officer, Lt. Reg Dixon, reported that the twenty-five prisoners were 'boys from 17 to 18 years old' who looked 'strained, dirty, bedraggled.'[88]

The 7th Canadian Infantry Brigade was to begin Phase 3, the attack on the village of Cussy and the Abbaye d'Ardenne, as soon as Authie was clear. The long delay in clearing Buron allowed 59th Division to renew its efforts to capture St-Contest, which finally fell to the Lancashire Fusiliers just before the Regina Rifles and Canadian Scottish

Regiment crossed their start lines. Unfortunately, the enemy still held Bitot[89] and the rest of the inner ring of defences centred on the Abbaye d'Ardenne. The Canscots found their approach to the start line north of Authie contested by snipers and mortar fire. Lt.-Col. Cabeldu had sought permission to stay well back until the attack really was on. 'I could visualize many casualties while waiting close to the start line,' he later remembered. He assured Brig. Cunningham that 'we would make a forced march ... and hit it at the appointed hour.'[90] The Canscots linked up with C Squadron of the First Hussars and began their advance to Cussy at 1830. The distance is little more than a kilometre, but the flat fields of grain offered no cover, and neither the walking pace barrage nor the many counter-battery shoots seemed to diminish the volume of fire produced by the German artillery and the 83rd Werfer Regiment.[91]

The Reginas, with B Squadron, moved toward the Abbaye d'Ardenne on a parallel course. The lead companies of both battalions worked their way forward in sections. It was difficult for even platoon commanders to maintain control, so everything depended on individual initiative. The Reginas' lead company reached the 'mound,' an abandoned anti-aircraft gun position, with fewer than fifty men. The follow-up companies found that movement beyond this brought machine gun fire from the Abbaye and positions to the south. The gunners responded with stonks on the Abbaye, and the remaining Hussars tanks were able to begin providing closer support. The enemy still held Francqueville and the reverse slope to the south, so it was impossible to approach the Abbaye from that direction. Dog Company circled around to the north, penetrating the outer walls as daylight faded. It reported the capture of the Abbaye d'Ardenne shortly before midnight.[92] The situation in Cussy was equally difficult; the Canscots reported that they could not hold the village unless reinforced. Two companies of the Winnipegs were sent forward to join them in the ruins of Cussy, which were gradually cleared.[93]

However difficult the experience, 7th Brigade's success and 3rd British Division's advance into Caen from the east forced Rommel to recognize that the city was lost. At 1915 he sanctioned the withdrawal of all heavy weapons across the Orne. Kurt Meyer had already issued orders to disengage after dark and begin a staged withdrawal.[94] By dawn on 9 July only German rearguards remained north of the river. British and Canadian patrols entered the ruined city, and were greeted by stunned civilians emerging from cellars and the great churches. Caen, or what was left of it, was finally in Allied hands.

The performance of 3rd Canadian Division on 8 July did not draw any criticism from Crocker or Dempsey. The plan for Charnwood had prevented the enemy from concentrating his fire on a narrow front and had limited the possibilities of enfilade fire, since all localities were under attack at the same time. Given a reasonable chance of success, the Canadian soldier proved capable of overcoming even the most elaborate defensive positions.

The next morning, Operation Jupiter began, with 43rd Wessex Division supported by one infantry and two tank brigades renewing the struggle for Hill 112. The Germans responded by committing 1st SS Panzer Division and the Tiger tanks of 102nd SS Heavy Tank battalion. General Eberbach, Geyr's replacement as commander of Panzer Group West, insisted that '112 was the pivotal point of the whole position'[95] west of Caen and must be held. By evening on 11 July, it was evident that both sides were exhausted, and Jupiter ended in stalemate. The German forces though terribly weakened by the attritional battles of the past eighteen days, still held the high ground west and south of Caen.

5

Stalemate?

By the second week of July, the senior German officers in the west feared that their armies were on the verge of collapse. Battle casualties now totalled more than 100,000, and fewer than 9,000 replacements had arrived. The loss of 2,360 officers was especially worrying. Nine generals, seven officers of the general staff, and 137 'commanding officers' had been killed or seriously wounded between 6 June and 7 July.[1] Hitler's 'Directive for the Conduct of Operations in the West,' issued on 8 July, offered little hope. Hitler remained convinced that 'the enemy will probably attempt a second landing in the 15th Army sector ... primarily between the Somme and the Seine ... but also against Belgium and southern Holland ... surprise attacks designed to effect the capture of one of the large ports of Brittany cannot be ruled out. Similarly, an attack against the French Mediterranean Coast may also be expected.'[2] To meet these threats, Hitler required his generals to avoid 'any major offensive aimed at the destruction of the enemy in the bridgehead' and to fight a strictly defensive battle until additional forces arrived in Normandy. Since 15th Army could not be further weakened, the buildup depended on the arrival of divisions from other parts of France, but only two were due to arrive in the next ten days.[3]

Hitler had dismissed his C in C, Von Rundstedt, and both army commanders because they had advocated a phased withdrawal. Their replacements, Field Marshal von Kluge and Generals Eberbach and Hauser, at first seemed to believe that Hitler's strategy would succeed, but the attritional battles at Caen and St-Lo during their first days in command persuaded them that their predecessors had been right. If the present position had to be held, they would have to prepare a defence-in-depth and try to withdraw the armoured divisions for rest, refitting, and a possible counterattack.[4] But this depended entirely on the willingness of the Allies to suspend further offensive operations until the Germans were ready!

On 15 July, two days before he was wounded by a strafing aircraft, Rommel prepared a new 'Analysis of the Situation,' which began with this statement: 'The position on the Normandy Front ... is rapidly approaching its crisis.' Noting the heavy losses in men and equipment – '17 tanks to replace about 225' – and the weakness and inexperience of the newly arrived infantry divisions, he concluded that 'the enemy will shortly be able to break through our thinly held front, especially in the 7th Army sector ... the end of the unequal battle is in sight.'[5] SS General Paul Hauser, who had taken over 7th Army, was equally pessimistic: 'Our strength has sunk to such a low level that the local commanders can no longer guarantee their holding out against enemy large-scale attacks.'[6] The crisis confronting the German commanders in Normandy seems to have been entirely missed by their Allied counterparts. Ultra provided no information about the growing loss of confidence among the German generals. Only one part of Hitler's directive – a message to all officers demanding the defence of every square kilometre to gain time for new weapons to be deployed – was decrypted, and this, together with evidence that the Germans still believed in a second landing, was all that Allied intelligence had to go on.[7]

Lacking reliable information about the enemy, and shocked by the losses incurred in the battles of late June and July, the British and American commanders were almost as pessimistic as the Germans. After capturing Cherbourg, the First U.S. Army turned south to confront the *bocage* country. Martin Blumenson, who wrote the official history of this phase of the campaign, described what confronted the Americans:

> Through the region made for ambush when the German defenders had dug into the hedgerow banks and erected strong defences the Americans were to fight from field to field, from hedgerow to hedgerow, measuring the progress of their advance in yards. Over it all a steady rain was to pour, and the odors of the Normandy soil were to mingle with the smell of decaying flesh and become part of the war.[8]

On 5 July, Eisenhower in one of his regular letters to General George Marshall commented: 'The going is extremely tough.' He was concerned about some of his divisional commanders, especially Maj.-Gen. Eugene Landrum, a highly regarded professional soldier who had taken over 90th Infantry Division. Landrum, Eisenhower reported, 'seems quite negative.'[9] Two days later, the Supreme Commander wrote to Montgomery expressing the fear that they might be on the verge of a stalemate with the Germans, increasing their *'relative strength'* (italics in the original).[10] As late as 27 July, Eisenhower continued to believe that 'time was vital' and that advances were 'disappointing slow.'[11]

Montgomery still expressed confidence in his strategy, but he had no idea how close the enemy was to collapse. Worried that a prolonged attritional battle might weaken 21 Army Group, he sought to conserve his shrinking manpower resources. Before Overlord, the War Office had warned that the supply of reinforcements was limited. One or two infantry divisions and up to three independent brigades would have to be disbanded before the end of 1944 as a result of normal wastage. The rapid increase in the weekly casualty rates during Epsom and Charnwood and the promise of similar casualties in the weeks ahead indicated that a manpower crunch was imminent.[12]

By 9 July, casualties in 21 Army Group had exceeded 30,000 men.[13] This did not include evacuations for sickness and battle exhaustion. Before Epsom Maj. D.J. Watterson, the senior psychiatrist for the 2nd British Army, described the 'ratio of exhaustion as lower than expected, probably 10 percent [of those wounded] or a little more.' Two weeks later, what seemed to be a full-blown crisis was at hand, with some divisions reporting soaring exhaustion ratios. According to Watterson:

> The initial hopes and optimism were too high and the gradual realization that the 'walk over' to Berlin had developed into an infantry slogging match caused an unspoken but clearly recognizable increase in the incidence of psychiatric casualties arriving in a steady stream at the Exhaustion Centres and reinforced by waves of beaten and exhausted men from each of the major battles.

Writing after the crisis was over, the psychiatrist added that such 'swings of morale often tend to overshoot the mark and this happened during the first two weeks in July.'[14]

Was Montgomery among those whose 'swings of moral' overshot the mark? His difficult relations with Eisenhower and his growing irritability with anyone who questioned his strategy suggests he was. He reacted angrily to a recommendation to disband or retrain 6th Duke of Wellington Regiment, which had collapsed after a series of disastrous events in late June, insisting that the commanding officer was a 'defeatist.'[15] After this incident he seems to have lost confidence in the entire division, and the 49th (West Riding) – which overall had fought very well – was exiled to serve in a static role on the left flank.[16] The 51st Highland and 7th Armoured, which Monty had brought back from the Mediterranean for Overlord, also fell out of favour. Two major-generals, Bullen-Smith and Erskine, were soon replaced, but the division that first caught his critical eye was 3rd Canadian.

On 5 July 1944, Lt.-Gen. John Crocker wrote a formal letter to the army commander documenting his dissatisfaction with Maj.-Gen. R.F.L. Keller and the performance of the Canadians. Dempsey immediately forwarded the letter, with his own supporting comments, to Montgomery, who in turn wrote to Crerar endorsing their views. Crocker's letter, written the day after the attack on Carpiquet, suggests that the corps commander, who was also unhappy with the performance of his other divisions, was profoundly pessimistic. After acknowledging the 'great enthusiasm and considerable success' evidenced by the Canadians on D-Day, he insisted that apart from Foster's 7th Infantry Brigade, which had withstood considerable enemy pressure with great fortitude, 'the Div. became jumpy and excitable ... the state of the Div. was a reflection of the state of its commander [who was not] standing up to the strain and showed signs of fatigue and nervousness (one might almost say fright) which were patent for all to see.' According to Crocker, the division had failed to recover 'anything approaching its original offensive enthusiasm. Patroling was bad or non-existent and an atmosphere of "anything for a quiet life" seemed to pervade.' Then came the attack on Carpiquet. 'The limited success of this operation' was due, Crocker claimed, 'to a lack of control and leadership from the top.'[17] Dempsey echoed this view, insisting that 'Carpiquet proved to me quite conclusively that he [Keller] is not fitted to command a Division ... Had it been a British Division I would recommend most strongly that he be removed from command at once.'[18]

Rumours that higher command was dissatisfied with the Canadian performance reached divisional and brigade staffs,[19] but no one knew the specifics of Crocker's complaint. It was perhaps just as well, for those involved in carrying out the corp commander's orders at le Mesnil-Patry and Carpiquet would have been furious at such comments. Those Canadians, in a position to understand the role played by the corps commander, in common with their counterparts in the 3rd British and 51st Highland divisions, were highly critical of Crocker's penchant for isolated battalion or brigade attacks on strongly held enemy positions.[20]

The 3rd British Division suffered heavy casualties in several such battles, especially the struggle for Chateau-de-la-Londe. Here, on the 'bloodiest square mile in Normandy,' 8th British Infantry Brigade had attacked on a limited front, bringing the full weight of enemy fire down on its two assault battalions. The 2nd Suffolk Regiment reported 16 killed, 75 missing, and 71 wounded, while casualties to the 2nd East Yorkshires totalled 106.[21] This operation was the subject of bitter complaint in 3rd British Division war diaries.

Attitudes toward 1 Corps were equally negative in 51st Highland Division, whose divisional and brigade commanders viewed Crocker's orders to make limited attacks for limited objectives as a waste of precious manpower.[22] It was the failure of one such attack, on the factory area at Colombelles, that led Montgomery to dismiss the divisional commander and declare 51st Highland Division 'not battleworthy.' According to Montgomery, 'it does not fight with determination and has failed in every operation it has been given to do.'[23] This was simply not true and was a reflection of Montgomery's dark mood.

Though there is little doubt that the Canadians would have reacted strongly to Crocker's criticism of their performance, especially after the division's solid achievements in Operation Charnwood, it is also true that Keller was a controversial leader. Crerar described him as a 'dynamic, two-fisted commander' who might well be promoted to lead a corps.[24] The Canadian Chief of the General Staff, Ken Stuart, had a very different view, describing Keller as 'pompous, inconsiderate of others. Anything but brilliant and much over-rated ... he has not the ability to command a brigade in the field much less a division.'[25]

Both estimates, made well before D-Day, may tell us as much about the authors as the subject. Lt.-Col. E.A. Coté, who as a senior staff officer worked closely with Keller on the preinvasion planning, knew Keller as a competent and energetic leader in the preinvasion period.[26] However, Lt.-Col. J.D. Mingay, Keller's operations officer, reported that Keller did not function well under the stress of combat.[27] When Keller was shown copies of the letters from his corps and army commanders, he 'was distinctly upset' and indicated that 'in any extent he did not feel his health was good enough to stand the heavy strain and asked that he be medically boarded as he felt he would be found to be unfit.'[28]

Crocker's attempt to secure the replacement of Keller highlighted questions about the relationship between the Canadian and British armies that went well beyond the immediate issue of Keller's capacity to deal with stress. Montgomery's connection with Crerar and the Canadian army went back to the winter of 1941–2, when the three Canadian infantry divisions, grouped together as 1 Canadian Corps, were part of Southeast Command. Montgomery replaced General Claude Auchinleck and immediately began to re-examine the existing training and command arrangements. He found a willing pupil in Maj.-Gen. Harry Crerar, who had just been appointed to command the Canadian Corps. Not surprisingly, Crerar was anxious to make changes in the senior appointments and was pleased when Montgomery offered 'to visit units down to battalion level' and offer his own assessment.[29]

Crerar moved swiftly to remove those officers whom Montgomery thought were too old or too limited, and he tried to implement the advice offered on training matters. This process helped enshrine a master-pupil relationship between Montgomery and Crerar well before the First Canadian Army came under Montgomery's command for the invasion of Europe. In the interval, Montgomery concluded that Guy Simonds, who commanded 1st Canadian Infantry Division in Sicily under Montgomery's tutelage, was the best and perhaps only Canadian officer capable of commanding a corps or an army.[30]

Montgomery was also less than pleased to have to deal with Harry Crerar as the commander of one of the two armies in 21 Army Group because Crerar took his responsibilities as the senior officer in Canada's national army seriously.[31] Montgomery's attitude toward expressions of Canadian autonomy were typical of most British politicians and senior officers. Concessions to national feeling must occasionally be made, but the whole concept was painfully inconvenient and could not be allowed to interfere with existing command arrangements. By the summer of 1944, Montgomery had heard enough about Crerar's constitutional responsibility to the Government of Canada to move cautiously on the Keller matter. 'I would prefer,' he informed Crerar, 'that any official action that may be necessary should be taken by Canadian generals.' Crerar responded that the matter must be 'considered and decided by Canadians' and asked Guy Simonds to review the issues as 3rd Division was leaving Crocker's corps to serve under his command.[32]

Crocker had delivered a parting shot at the Canadians, suggesting that they had failed to press the advance into Caen on 9 July. He had gone forward to the Abbaye d'Ardenne, where he and his staff exchanged sharp words with the CO of the Reginas over their alleged failure to advance into Caen.[33] When it became clear that this task had been assigned to 9th Brigade, Crocker criticized Cunningham's cautious approach, and Keller – who was also impatient with Cunningham's deliberate rate of advance – recommended that Cunningham be replaced. Ironically, Simonds was being asked to review the future of Keller and Cunningham at the same time. After several interviews, Simonds concluded that both men should carry on in their appointments until he had had the opportunity to judge their abilities.[34] After the outstanding effort of 3rd Division in Operation Atlantic, Simonds decided that both should stay. He informed Dempsey and Montgomery that 'the individual qualities of General Keller are unimportant at the moment in comparison with the bigger problem of maintaining the morale of 3 Canadian Division.' Keller, Simonds insisted, was 'capable of commanding the division successfully,' and he was 'not prepared to recommend his removal on evidence at present available to me.'[35]

The debate over Keller led to a further deterioration in relations between Montgomery and Crerar, though, strangely enough, not between Montgomery and Simonds. When Crerar raised the question of setting a definite date for the activation of the First Canadian Army in Normandy, Montgomery was evasive. His real opinions were expressed in a letter to Brooke. Montgomery noted that all Canadian troops in Normandy were now under the command of Guy Simonds, who was 'far better than Crerar' and 'the equal of any British Corps Commander.' Crerar, Montgomery insisted, was a 'bad judge of men ... and does not know what a good soldier should be.' He was reluctant to allow a second Army HQ to operate in Normandy and commented that 'when I hand over a sector to Crerar I will certainly teach him his stuff, and I shall give him tasks within his capabilities. And I shall watch over him carefully. I have a great personal affection for him, but this must not be allowed to lead me into doing unsound things.'[36]

Most historians have accepted at face value Montgomery's criticisms of Crerar, which were seconded by Brooke. But such opinions need to be closely examined. In 21 Army Group, the function of an army commander and his headquarters was to provide administrative, technical, and logistical support to the corps serving with that army. In theory, the army commander was also responsible for coordinating the work of the tactical air force group, but in practice, the daily meeting with the air staff provided little more than an occasion to make proposals about the next day's air operations – scarcely an opportunity to exercise command.

Did Montgomery and Brooke have grounds for doubting Crerar's ability to command an effective army headquarters? In the preparatory stages of Overlord they had insisted that since one of the two corps in the First Canadian Army was to be British, half the staff officers at headquarters must also be British.[37] The Canadians were a bit startled by this pronouncement, but cheerfully accepted the newcomers, who quickly came to identify themselves with the First Canadian Army. It was soon apparent to even the most condescending British senior officer that Crerar's staff were an outstanding group of men who could hold their own with any army HQ under Eisenhower's command. Brig. Churchill Mann, Crerar's chief of staff, may have appeared too flippant to some at 21 Army Group, but everyone acknowledged that he was a brilliant and innovative officer. During the balance of the war no one even suggested that the rest of the Canadian staff were less competent than their British counterparts, and Lt.-Gen. Brian Horrocks – the most highly touted British corps commander – clearly preferred Crerar to Demspey as an army commander.[38] One must therefore conclude that Montgomery and Brooke would have been critical of any senior Canadian officer who expressed the Canadian national interest.[39] Simonds, who had no commitment to such issues, won Montgomery's support for this as well as for his skills as a corps commander.

The man Montgomery described as Canada's best general established his headquarters in Normandy on 11 July. Included in 2 Canadian Corps were the newly arrived 2nd Canadian Infantry Division as well as 2nd Canadian Army Group Royal Artillery with its medium gun regiments. Together with 3rd Division and 2nd Armoured Brigade, the corps was now a challenging mixture of veterans and green troops. Elements of 2nd Division were immediately sent forward to gain whatever benefits might be provided by the experience of being shelled and mortared in static positions, and Simonds began a series of meetings with brigade and divisional officers.

Simonds's chief of staff, Brig. N.E. Roger, wrote of Simonds:

> Never have I worked for anyone with such a precise and clear and far seeing mind – he was always working to a plan with a clear cut objective which he took care to let us know in simple and direct terms ... He reduced problems in a flash to basic facts and variables, picked out those that mattered, ignored those that were side issues and made up his mind and got on with it.[40]

Not every officer who served under Simonds would have described him in such enthusiastic terms. The general's cool, detached, analytical mind was accompanied by the appearance of total self-confidence and a degree of arrogance that could make life very difficult for those who disagreed or failed to live up to his standards. Simonds did not attempt to lead – he sought only to command.

On 16 July Simonds met with the commanding officers of all units in 3rd Division and 2nd Armoured Brigade to 'welcome' them into 2 Canadian Corps. The lengthy talk that followed left no doubt that Simonds was in charge but raised other questions. He began by quoting Montgomery's pre-D-Day remark: 'We will have the war in the bag this summer.' The enemy, according to Simonds, was 'groggy on his feet and needs but the knockout blow to finish him off.' To accomplish this, he continued, 'we must have the offensive spirit':

> The offensive spirit and the will to carry on an all-out effort is always present with the Canadian soldier, and it should not be destroyed by the flagging spirit of a commander who is tired ... If a commander finds himself up against stiff opposition he must find ways to break through the enemy. It is fatal to stop. He must never sit down. He must always be doing something.

The audience, made up of men who had been fighting a difficult and costly battle since D-Day, had heard this kind of thing before. It was the sort of pep talk that generals gave. But Simonds's second theme startled his polite listeners. 'We can't fight the Boche without incurring casualties,' he declared, 'and every soldier must know this ... For example, if the operation is worthwhile and I call it off with 50 per cent casualties incurred then I have achieved nothing but a waste of lives; if I continue, and incur a further 20 per cent casualties and bring the operation to a successful conclusion then the operation is worthwhile.'

This incredibly callous introduction to 'my policy in handling troops' must have met a mixed reception, for Simonds immediately qualified his remarks, noting that such rates were grossly exaggerated – the percentages in battles were normally 15 to 25 per cent. Abandoning this theme, Simonds concentrated on those favourite panaceas of senior commanders – aggressive patrolling and discipline, including saluting, which 'he placed great stress on.'[41] This was not on balance an auspicious start to his relationship with the men who would lead the division into battle in a few days, but how much did it really matter? A citizen-army of volunteer soldiers in a foreign country fighting for a cause most did not yet fully understand might have benefited from a leader able to engage their ideals and emotions, but the British and Canadian armies had always relied on regimental loyalties rather than brigade, division, or corps identities. Montgomery and to a certain extent Eisenhower were the overall leaders; after that came the regimental family, and the company, platoon, or section that constituted each soldier's primary group. The available evidence suggests that this system worked well; good morale was maintained throughout the battle of Normandy.

One indication of this was the determination of so many wounded men to return to their own units. For example, in mid-July Capt. Eddie Goodman and three lieutenants hitched a ride to France and rejoined the Fort Garry Horse on the eve of battle. The regimental War Diary notes: 'These four officers were offensive in the eyes of the local fuhrers because they adopted unorthodox (but faster) methods of getting from England to France.' Brought before Gen. Crerar, they were officially reprimanded, but Crerar made it clear that he understood and admired them.[42]

The Canadian army made a strong effort to survey the attitudes and opinions of its soldiers, especially by reviewing correspondence sent from the field. Two kinds of letters were examined. The ordinary ones, subject to censorship in the unit, were thought unlikely to produce reliable evidence. However, the British and Canadians had re-established a 'Green Envelope' system that allowed individual soldiers to bypass their own officers. The censors at Canadian Military Headquarters in London naturally concentrated on the 'Greens,' reviewing the contents of more than 30,000 letters written in June and July.[43] It was evident that the ordinary soldier appreciated the chance to write intimately to loved ones. 'This letter,' one soldier wrote, 'is free from prying eyes except the base censor, he does not count as far as I am concerned.'

Letters from the preinvasion period portrayed the same high morale and impatience 'to get cracking' that was evident to all observers. One surprise was the enormous enthusiasm generated when Eisenhower inspected the men before D-Day. 'Ike's' personality and manner 'immediately appeals to the men,' the censor wrote. Montgomery might have had a formidable rival for the affections of the Canadian soldier if they had seen more of him.

During the first week of action, letter writing declined somewhat, but over 5,000 'Greens' were examined. It was, the deputy chief censor reported, 'a cheerful and confidential mail ... Morale is very high, strengthened by battle experience ... Confidence in weapons, equipment, leadership and in their fellows is freely expressed ... Troops have a poor impression of the PW they have seen, but reveal a proper respect for the enemy as a fighter.'

Mail from the period 28 June to 12 July – which included the battles for Carpiquet and Caen – was equally upbeat. There are, the censor reported, 'no indications of depression ... even when weary there is no indication of desire to avoid resumption of combat ... pride in formation and unit is manifest.' One rifleman admitted that the month in action had been 'damned grim,' but added, 'I wouldn't have missed it for the world.' A private described the 'nice slit trench' he was sharing. It was 'shoulder wide at the top with a little porch at the bottom for sleeping room. We got a little straw for the bottom and feel as happy as a pair of pigs in a pen.' More mail, newspapers from England, and cigarettes were needed, and there was a steady stream of complaints about how both the BBC and the newspapers ignored the Canadians. 'Its not that I want blazing headlines about us,' one soldier wrote, 'but they could at least mention us.'

The critical attitude toward the British media did not extend to the British soldier. A Canadian corporal wrote: 'Remember how the Canadians and Limeys used to argue and fight ... That has all been forgotten now and we get along the very best.' Mail from British soldiers produced similar appreciation of the Canadians, and both had developed a new admiration for the 'Yanks.' Soldiers were also impressed by the organization and administration of the invasion, even praising the quality of the food. The medical services won repeated recognition, as did the air force. When one soldier wrote, 'We have no fear of the Luftwaffe if there is any Luftwaffe,' he was speaking for everyone in the bridgehead. Favourable references to Montgomery and Eisenhower continued. Divisional troops without regimental postings spoke of pride in the achievements of the entire formation, but for most soldiers the regiment remained the primary focus.

Official hesitancy in promoting a separate Canadian identity was evident in the army's low-key approach to what everyone in 1944 called Dominion Day. The only senior officer who seems to have thought of 1 July as the Canadian national holiday was Eisenhower. He sent a cable to his British naval, air, and army commanders for transmission 'to all Canadian units under your command.' It read:

> To you Canadian members of this Allied Force, all your team mates send you Dominion Day felicitations. We are proud of the fighting record that you are every day establishing by land, by sea and by air. On this the 77th anniversary of the Dominion's birth you are adding new glories to the name of Canada and standing true to the principles that have made her great.[44]

We know that Eisenhower sent this message to Montgomery, but it does not seem to have been widely distributed. It would be of interest to know why.

Canadian soldiers, sailors, and airmen had always taken special pride in their Canada shoulder flash, the only distinguishing feature of their British-style uniforms. Other expressions of national identity emerged slowly and spontaneously. The Red Ensign, which served as Canada's national flag, flew prominently at headquarters in the rear areas, but the common symbol of the Canadian presence on the battlefield was the stylized Maple Leaf, which appeared on vehicles and signposts wherever Canadians went. The Maple Leaf became the unifying symbol of the Canadian army long before it was adopted for the national flag.

After the capture of Caen, the army began producing a Normandy edition of *The Maple Leaf*, the weekly newspaper that had proved so popular in Italy. 'Herbie,' the marvellously drawn, sad-sack cartoon character, thus made his appearance in France. Many others got into the news business, producing regimental, brigade, and divisional newsletters. The Queen's Own Rifles began printing *The Big Two Bugle* in June. Their war correspondent, Rifleman Ike Gregory, satirized both the BBC bulletins and Montgomery's insistence on not allowing the press to print the names of the regiments in action. From a 'special cable' reporting on Operation Epsom:

> As this correspondent writes, the initial bombardment of the great new attack is fast fading ... What it can be like on Jerry's side of the bomb line is beyond conjecture. There are 8002 guns firing 7009 rounds a piece, as well as the support supplied by a famous 'Central Canadian Regiment' which has posted two men in a forward OP with Sten guns and commando knives.

The same issue included a new version of 'The Road to Mandalay':

> On the road to Carpiquet
> Where the moaning minnies play
> And the guns flare up like thunder
> From the gully across the way
> On the road to Carpiquet
> Where the moaning minnies play
> And the dusty men go marching
> Where the waiting snipers lay

All the battalion newsletters carried this sort of light-hearted writing and offered readers some of the worst jokes ever told. The most common themes were, not surprisingly, sex and officers – sometimes in combination. This exchange between 'Moe' and 'Gus' was better than most.

Moe: I saw a girl in a Café near Camilly drinking rum the other afternoon.
Gus: Jamaica?
Moe: Hell no she was with an officer.[45]

The 'trench newspapers' during the First World War have long been studied by historians seeking to understand the soldier's experience of war. A comparable examination of similar Second World War material would be of great interest, and help to document the energy and optimism of the young men who served at the front.

The generally high morale of the Canadian soldier did not immunize all men from the ravages of traumatic stress. The division had been screened for those individuals psychiatrists thought might be predisposed to anxiety neurosis and 'apt to give trouble in action,' as well as those army psychiatry categorized as 'inadequates' – men who had been found wanting 'throughout their lives both in the civilian and army sphere.' Maj. Bob Gregory, who landed on D+2, established a divisional exhaustion centre that treated approximately two hundred men in the first two weeks. The symptoms he treated included gross hysterical reactions, depression, withdrawal, sleeplessness, pronounced startle reactions to noise, and a number of other disabling behavioural patterns. After relatively brief treatment with sedated rest, some men seemed ready to return to their units, but most joined the stream of medical evacuations from the bridgehead to England. Gregory thought that the greatest number of neuro-psychiatric casualties occurred when troops were 'very tired, very static, dug-in under heavy counterattack. Fully 80 percent of the NP casualties complained bitterly of mortar and 88mm fire.'[46]

The battles for Carpiquet and Caen produced no dramatic increase in the 'NP ratio' (battle exhaustion to wounded), though there were striking differences in the recorded rates among battalions. By late July, 17 officers and 506 men from 3rd Division's infantry battalions had been diagnosed as suffering from battle exhaustion; this was rougly one-fifth of the total non-fatal casualties. This was a somewhat lower rate than was reported for most of the British divisions, which suggests that Crocker's view of the Canadians as 'not standing up to the strain' was simply wrong.[47]

On the basis of evidence from the battlefield, it is clear that the Canadians had fought with great success during the landing and the bridgehead battles, and with skill and determination at Carpiquet and Caen. The difficulties encountered in these two battles were a product of the challenges that confronted all Allied formations once the enemy switched to the defensive. Clearly, no one on the Allied side knew how to overcome these defences except through attritional battles of the kind that threatened to weaken the combat strength of the infantry divisions available to 21 Army Group. The search for tactical and operational solutions was becoming urgent.

Among the most serious problems confronting the Allies was the terrible toll that enemy mortars and rockets were inflicting. By Allied standards, the Germans were weak in artillery, unable to provide sufficient fire support to their own troops or effective counter-battery fire to suppress Allied guns. They compensated for this by using large numbers of mortars and rocket projectors. A German infantry division possessed fifty-seven of the basic 81 mm mortars and between twelve and twenty of the 120 mm type. Panzer divisions had about half this number. Nebelwerfer regiments, each unit with fifty-four projectors, were available in the Caen sector on a scale of one per division.[48] Once the German army went over to the defensive, the gently rolling terrain provided a series of reverse slopes that allowed them to dig in and conceal these weapons 1000 to 4000 metres behind the forward defended lines. A few rounds were used to register the approaches the Allied troops would use in an attack; observers on the crest of the hill could then direct observed fire. Whatever else the Germans were short of in Normandy, it wasn't mortar bombs or Nebelwerfer rockets. By July, 70 per cent of all casualties to British and Canadian troops were due to these two weapons alone.[49]

The British and thus the Canadians had left the question of counter-mortar organization to the individual divisions. In practice, counter-mortar was a poor stepsister to the well-established routines of artillery counter-battery work. This meant a skeleton staff relying on shared access to sound-ranging, flash spotting and air photograph interpretation to produce estimates of mortar locations.[50] Senior commanders from Montgomery down to his major-generals could contribute little to the solution of this problem, which was dealt with by the gunners and the soldier-scientists of No. 2 Operational Research Section (ORS).

In late June, Maj. Michael Swann of No. 2 ORS, who had studied the use of mortars and reverse slope positions while assigned to the Infantry School at Barnard Castle, began systematically studying counter-mortar activity. He first surveyed medical officers in four divisions, including 3rd Canadian, to determine the extent of casualties from enemy mortars. Then he examined the counter-mortar organization in each division. His recommendations – to expand the CMO staff, to establish separate counter-mortar observation posts, and to improve co-ordination and signals capacity – were acted on promptly and successfully at the divisional level. The 3rd Canadian Division claimed that it cut the volume of enemy mortar fire by 60 per cent by applying these methods.[51]

Experiments with radar and with four-pen recorders – miniature microphones connected to a recording machine, with the pens recording the vibrations from the microphones and deducing the locations of hostile mortars – were showing great promise.[52] Swann believed that a combination of all known methods of location plus dedicated counter-mortar fire could bring the problem under control, especially if more radar sets were made available. The creation of No. 1 Canadian Radar Battery and No. 100 British Radar Battery in August were a direct result of recommendations made by ORS and by Montgomery's scientific adviser, Brig. Schonland.[53]

The ORS was also anxious to continue the work of the Army Operational Research Group in Britain on the accuracy of predicted artillery fire. The Allies' reliance on barrages and concentrations in the attack was based on assumptions about accuracy that the OR scientists knew to be faulty. Unfortunately, other issues took precedence, and the section was unable to examine the results of predicted artillery fire until the battle for Normandy was over. When this work was completed in October 1944, it showed 'gross inaccuracies in many of the concentrations.' The gunners knew that the 50 per cent zone – the area in which half the shells fired would land – was much larger than they wanted. They also knew that 'only 5 percent of rounds fired by prediction could be expected to fall in an area 100 yards by 100 yards,' but they had no idea that the mean point of impact was so often wide for line and over or under for range. This evidence from the OR studies helped explain why predicted fire was much less successful in Normandy than everyone had assumed.[54]

Methods of countering enemy mortars and improving the accuracy of artillery fire were not the only issues requiring attention. The officers who carried out the orders issued by corps commanders needed to know how to improve their odds when attacking well-constructed and carefully camouflaged defensive positions. Everyone at the sharp end studied this problem, including 3rd Canadian Division where a staff officer, Lt.-Col. M. McLellan, began to coordinate the distribution and discussion of 'combat lessons' in mid-June.[55]

McLellan identified a number of the very specific questions that neither doctrine nor experience seemed to have solved:

(a) How is the killing of 88s to be achieved?
(b) How does the enemy hold villages by day or night?
(c) What is the best method of attacking strong points?
(d) What factors decide whether a strong point should be bypassed?
(e) What is the quickest and most effective method of eliminating local sniping?
(f) How should underground portions of strong points be cleared?

These were not easy questions, but throughout late June and July, attempts were made to share ideas and refine tactics. In the aftermath of Carpiquet, 8th Brigade prepared a detailed study, 'The Barrage in the Attack,' which recommended deception shoots and emphasized the importance of using artillery to box off the enemy. The brigade also pressed for air attacks on 'the weapons ranged against us.' This could best be achieved if a squadron was assigned to the brigade 'on call.'[56]

Brig. Foster's 7th Brigade produced detailed comments on virtually every aspect of battle experience. The Regina Rifles reported on their success with PIATS even against Panthers, and noted that the

6-pounder antitank gun using SABOT ammunition 'appears able to KO any German tank by striking at either the back or the side of the tank.' Snipers were best dealt with by detailing a party of your own snipers, but they also recommended using the 2-inch mortar to achieve air bursts against trees that might be used for snipers' nests.

The enemy, the Reginas noted, tried to make occupied villages tank-proof; weapon slits were sited outside villages. Antitank guns, machine guns, and mortars were sited to 'cover the approaches from outside the village and to a flank.' The only way to deal with this was through close coordination with the artillery observer. Strongpoints, once reached, were best dealt with by smoke and pole charges to the rear of the pillbox. Training was required to improve fire control in the attack and to prepare junior leader replacements. The Reginas confidently reported that after inoculation, reinforcements 'had been found capable of replacing casualties.'[57]

When 7th Brigade summarized the input of each battalion, a number of very practical points were emphasized including complaints about the limited time available to brief everyone after an attack was ordered. The greatest need was for more flexible use of artillery. 'No great difficulty has been experienced in getting troops onto an objective, the problem is to keep them on it against heavy mortaring and counterattacks.' The fire plan had to continue well after the position was taken, to provide 'harassing fire on the flanks and on the rear.' The overall solutions to the problems encountered in July were better isolation of the battlefield by artillery and broad-front attacks to prevent the enemy from concentrating resources on one sector. Once ground was taken, the piece that the enemy had just been knocked off should never be occupied: 'All of his positions have been registered for artillery and mortars and he is quite prepared to kill his own troops left in a position once he has decided the position is lost.' One of the most general complaints was lack of information about the overall battle:

The individual soldier spends a lot of time in his slit trench without much apparently happening around him. 'What's new?' is a query heard a hundred times a day. If it is possible to get to the soldier in the slit trench up to date news of what is happening with other attacking formations he keeps his morale up with the knowledge that someone else is doing the damage. If a 'sitrep for soldiers' is sent out frequently he will sit and take it with a smile whether it be boredom or mortaring.[58]

Ideally, the infantry also wanted much more support from tanks, but 7th Brigade was not unsympathetic to the plight of the highly vulnerable Shermans.

> The armour in this flat country cannot go flat out to an objective and survive against the well placed and well concealed enemy antitank guns. Therefore they work their way forward on a flank usually supporting the infantry by fire. The one criticism the infantry have of this procedure is that the armour is inclined to be too far back. This is because of the antitank guns which the infantry cannot get at because of MG fire.[59]

One solution was more time for reconnaissance, liaison, and planning; this would permit the preselection of hull-down positions, from which the tanks could provide closer support.

The regiments of 2nd Canadian Armoured Brigade began their response to McLellan's question about 'killing 88s' with the comment that the enemy's excellent camouflage required good recce. Very often the first indication that an 88 was in the area was when a tank was hit. The armoured squadron could then carry out its own direct or indirect shoot or call for artillery, mortar, or infantry attack. There were no pat or easy answers. The Germans concentrated on knocking out the Firefly, which had a long, distinctive, 17-pounder gun. It was therefore vital to ensure that the one Firefly per troop was safeguarded or employed only after careful recce. The 88 and 75 German tank guns could both destroy a Sherman 'at up to 2000 yards,' and the Firefly was the only weapon that could hit back at anything approaching that range. The officers recognized that the 17-pounder was in short supply but 'eventually two 17 pounders per troop were required' to maintain the capacity to engage long-range targets.

Everyone agreed that more work had to be done to improve tank–infantry cooperation. Here, the armoured brigade had some practical suggestions. An infantry officer 'should ride in the squadron commander's tank manning a wireless set on the company frequency.' Phones on the rear decks of the tanks were essential to improve communications; and better liaison before a battle was necessary. But the real problem was persuading the infantry commander to bring his antitank guns forward quickly to allow the tanks to return to their forward rally, where they could serve as a mobile reserve to deal with enemy penetrations: 'It must be remembered that tanks are primarily an anti-infantry weapon and not an antitank weapon. Infantry should be taught that even though co-operating tanks may not be in their immediate view the tanks are probably in fire positions from which when called upon they can give supporting fire.'[60]

One of the many unresolved doctrinal issues was the relationship of the divisional antitank regiment with the armour. The tank regiments, confronting an enemy with vastly superior weaponry, wanted the M10 self-propelled guns allocated to armoured squadrons to be used in the same way as the Firefly. Doctrine demanded that the M10s be held back to give depth to the defence. However, during Charnwood, British M10 17-pounders had moved into Buron quickly before the position was consolidated and had been able to destroy a German armoured counterattack that could well have overrun the village. Bringing the M10s into action very early had proven feasible in Charnwood, and 2nd Brigade thought this tactic should be 'generally adopted.'[61] No explanation of why the thinly armoured M10s should do what the Shermans tried to avoid was offered.

The problems confronting tank crews in Normandy ought not to have come as a surprise. The British and Canadian armoured corps specialists had read the reports detailing the thickness of armour on the enemy's Panthers, Tigers, and self-propelled guns. They also knew about the range and penetrating power of the enemy's antitank guns. The ORSs attached to the Armoured Fighting Vehicle School at Lulworth and the section working with the School of Artillery at Larkhill had established that the Sherman 75 was unlikely to destroy any German armour at ranges beyond 500 yards, and that even at shorter ranges no penetration of the frontal armour of anything except a Mk IV was likely. They had also established that the 17-pounder's effective range was limited to about 1000 yards.[62]

Research in England was supplemented by a survey of 'Sherman Tank Casualties Suffered between 6 June and 10 July 1944,' prepared by Maj. Tony Sargeaunt, the OR tank specialist. Sargeaunt examined forty-five tanks and determined that forty of them had been destroyed by armour-piercing shells fired by an enemy tank or an antitank gun. Most of the damage, 77 per cent, was done by 75 mm guns, just 18 per cent by 88s. Almost every shot that hit a Sherman penetrated the armour, and 73 per cent caught fire and were 'brewed up.' It was so difficult to improve the 'low resisting power' of the Sherman armour that the only realistic improvement Sargeaunt could suggest was to provide 'a better gun to make the German tanks more vulnerable' – that is, to increase the proportion of Fireflys in each squadron.[63] The contrast with those German tanks inspected was striking. Only 38 per cent of the hits from Sherman 75s or 6-pounder antitank guns penetrated German armour, and both the Panther and the Tiger often survived one or two penetrations. The sloping frontal armour of the enemy's Panthers and self-propelled guns survived 75 per cent of all direct hits.[64] The 'low resisting power' of the Sherman's armour and the inadequacy of the standard 75 mm gun raised fundamental questions about the employment of Allied tanks. The Sherman was more or less equal to the task of dealing with the enemy's Mk IV tank, but against any other tank or an antitank gun, survival depended on avoiding enemy fire.

Before the invasion, Sargeaunt had worked closely with armoured corps officers in an effort to convince commanders that armoured brigades must operate in close cooperation with the artillery. Neither Shermans nor Cromwells and Churchills could lead an advance against even hastily constructed German defences without supplementary suppressive fire. Even then, Sargeaunt insisted, advances should be made only after careful recce, with possible hull-down positions identified so that tanks could move in bounds and provide covering fire for one another. Close cooperation with infantry battalions was important in closely wooded or built-up areas. In open country, unarmoured infantry could do little to assist tanks in dealing with enemy guns firing from ranges in excess of 1,000 yards. Only artillery, mortars, or (if available) Typhoons would help.[65]

When Sargeaunt was shown the outline plan for Operation Goodwood he immediately wrote a paper arguing against an armoured attack across country 'that was flatter than the desert.' The cultivated ground lacked the kind of hull-down and turret-down positions that were common in North Africa. Sargeaunt contended that once the tanks passed beyond the range of supporting artillery, they would be outgunned and outmanoeuvred. Although some armoured corps officers agreed with his views, the forecast was suppressed. Brig. Schonland knew that Montgomery was determined to launch an 'armoured blitzkrieg,' and no report from an OR scientist was going to stop him.[66]

6

Operation Goodwood – Atlantic

As the battles for Caen and additional bridgeheads across the Orne wound down, Montgomery issued a new directive on 10 July that offered a clear and balanced plan of action. The Americans were now facing 'some seventy infantry battalions and 250 tanks,'[1] so progress in the *bocage* was bound to be slow. It was up to the 2nd British Army, Montgomery insisted, to stage operations that would 'have a direct influence on the American effort' and that would hold enemy forces on the eastern flank. This meant a new offensive west of the Orne to support the First U.S. Army's advance to St-Lo.

Montgomery decided to reorganize the 2nd Army before launching this attack. He concentrated his three armoured divisions in the 8th Corps and informed O'Connor that the corps was to be held in reserve for possible use *east* of the Orne if the major offensive west of the river was successful. 'The opportunity for the employment of this Corps may be sudden and fleeting,' he wrote, 'therefore a study of the problems involved will begin at once.'[2] Lt.-Gen. Neil Ritchie's 12th Corps was to take over the Odon and Hill 112 sector, and together with 30th Corps on its right to 'operate strongly in a southerly direction, with its left flank on the Orne.' The general objective was the line Thury-Harcourt–Mont-Pincon–le-Beny-Bocage.[3] With six infantry divisions and five armoured brigades available, such an advance might well stretch German resources beyond the breaking point and force a withdrawal of enemy forces facing the Americans.

O'Connor was reluctant to leave his balanced corps of infantry and armour for a command consisting only of armoured divisions, and he said so. Before handing over, he discussed the situation with Ritchie and described a plan to overcome German resistance on Hill 112. This plan called for the high ground at Noyers to be seized. Then a second advance would be launched to seize Evrecy, followed by a third behind Hill 112. O'Connor argued that the capture of Noyer, 'which could not be dominated by high ground on the other side of the river,' was the key to controlling the river valley, which could then be bombarded by day and hit by fighting patrols at night. 'This method,' O'Connor suggested, 'would eventually so soften the enemy ... that when we wanted to pass across the river we should have little difficulty in doing so.'[4] It is ironic that the man who recommended a carefully staged, patiently executed attack by infantry divisions and their supporting armoured brigades, with overwhelming air and artillery support, should instead be selected to command an ill-conceived armoured blitzkrieg on the other side of Caen.

The inspiration for what became Operation Goodwood apparently came from Montgomery's chief planning officer, Brig. Charles Richardson, who on 7 July presented a 'Review of the Situation at D+30.' This document, full of exaggerated fears about a possible stalemate, recommended that a major armoured operation be undertaken not because there was evidence it would work but because the large numbers of tanks available were 'sufficient to enable us to take big risks ... Unless we are prepared to fight him with our tanks it seems that no further progress on the British sector is likely for many weeks to come.'[5] According to Gen. Dempsey's postwar recollections, it was he who pressed a reluctant Montgomery to agree to the proposal and give O'Connor command.[6] After winning approval, Dempsey went to O'Connor's headquarters on 13 July accompanied by Generals Crocker and Simonds, whose troops were to play a supporting role in the operation.[7]

The debate over Montgomery's intentions with Goodwood began before the battle ended and continues to this day. Some argue that Montgomery was deliberately attracting the German armour to his front to help the Americans break out in the west; others mock this idea as a rationalization of failure.[8] Both views were developed only after the outcome of Goodwood was known.

When Montgomery issued his instructions to Dempsey on 15 July, General Omar Bradley was planning to launch his major offensive, Operation Cobra, in three days. Goodwood was to start the day before. Inclement weather and slow progress in the battle for St-Lo led to a revised timetable: Goodwood on the 18 July and Cobra three days later.[9] Montgomery also issued orders for Operation Greenline, which required 12th Corps to capture Evrecy and exploit to Thury-Harcourt.[10] Greenline was to be carried out by 15th Scottish Division while 43rd Wessex 'dominated' the enemy on Hill 112. A brigade of 53rd Welsh Division was committed to supporting the Scottish attack, which was to begin in full darkness with the aid of 'movement light' created by searchlights.[11]

These largely forgotten operations directed against the German

276th and 277th infantry divisions forced Eberbach to bring the 9th and 10th SS Panzer divisions back to the Odon battlefield to prevent a breakthrough. They checked the British advance and inflicted more than 3,000 casualties. This was Normandy at it most brutal. When German losses of around 2,000 are added, the second battle of the Odon ranks as one of the bloodiest encounters of the campaign.[12]

Montgomery was orchestrating a series of blows, any one of which might succeed, and he had to plan for all contingencies. His real intentions were spelled out in a directive in which he described the ultimate purpose of all these operations as follows: 'We must engage the enemy in battle unceasingly; we must "write off" his troops; and generally we must kill Germans.'[13] Normandy had become a battle of attrition, and Montgomery was doing his best to ensure that it was the enemy who collapsed first.

The outline plan for Goodwood required the full co-operation of the tactical air forces, RAF Bomber Command, and the U.S. 8th Air Force to provide heavy bombing of enemy positions on the corps' flanks and fragmentation bombing in the path of the armoured divisions. Everyone agreed that the plan was too risky without such assistance. Air Marshall Harris complained briefly about this improper use of his strategic air force, but he and his American counterpart, Gen. Hap Arnold, co-operated fully, integrating their bombers with the complex artillery fire plan.[14]

Final preparations for Goodwood began on the night of 16–17 July, when the armoured divisions began moving into the Orne bridgehead. At 0545 on 18 July, 1,056 Lancasters and Halifaxes began bombing the woods and villages on the eastern flank of the advance as well as the factory areas to the west, which were 3rd Canadian Division's objectives. The enemy was anticipating a major offensive with thrusts both east and west of Caen, and prepared as best it could, placing infantry divisions in the forward areas and concentrating the Panzer divisions in reserve.[15] The low hills south of Caen, known as Bourgebus Ridge to the British and as Verrières Ridge to the Canadians, provided reverse-slope protection to the artillery. They also provided long-range killing zones for a flak regiment, which had seventy-eight 88 mm guns positioned on the high ground.

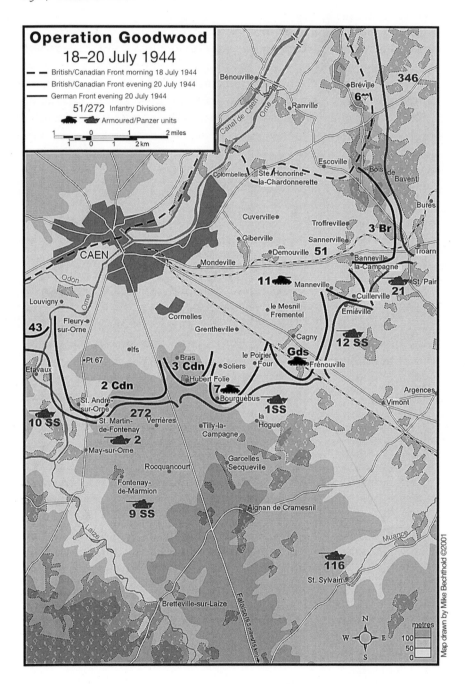

Operation Goodwood
18–20 July 1944

— — British/Canadian Front morning 18 July 1944
—— British/Canadian Front evening 20 July 1944
—— German Front evening 20 July 1944

51/272 Infantry Divisions

Armoured/Panzer units

1   0   1   2 miles
1   0   1   2 km

When the second wave of bombing ceased at 0745, eight field regiments fired a rolling barrage to assist 11th Armoured Division forward while two field, six medium, and two heavy regiments supported the infantry on the flanks. The first enemy met were too dazed from the bombing to offer significant resistance, but by the time the leading armoured regiments reached the Caen–Vimont railway line with its 3 metre embankment, the enemy had begun to recover and move reinforcements into the bombed areas. The village of Cagny, which had been ringed but not hit by bombs, contained a battery of 88s, and these blocked efforts to take or bypass the village.[16] By noon the armoured regiments had advanced 12 kilometres from their start line. They could go no further. Enemy tanks and antitank guns, posted on commanding ground with good fields of fire, systematically destroyed 128 tanks from 11th Armoured and 63 tanks from the Guards Armoured Division, which had followed 11th into the killing zone.[17] The inevitable traffic jam, which was exacerbated by the resistance at Cagny, and the caution of veteran commanders, who had little confidence in the plan, saved 7th Armoured Division from a similar fate.[18] By day's end the British had lost 224 tanks.[19]

The Canadian part in Goodwood, known as Atlantic, began at H+45 minutes with 8th Brigade making use of its own rolling barrage. The Queen's Own Rifles, on the left flank, reported no serious opposition from the stunned conscripts of the Luftwaffe's 16th Field Division. Machine gun fire from the factory buildings on the right flank was temporarily neutralized by the attached troops of Hussars tanks, which worked closely with the lead companies, destroying several enemy self-propelled guns and supporting the QORs into the outskirts of Giberville.[20] The village had been identified as a primary target for both the medium bombers and the barrage, but no bombs fell on Giberville and the barrage stopped short.[21] Giberville was held by a half-battalion of 16th Luftwaffe supported by a battle group from 21st Panzer Division.[22] A number of houses in the village had been fortified, and approaches had been cleared to provide good fields of fire. The enemy was determined to hold the village as a thorn in the side of the British advance and to complicate Canadian attempts to clear Colombelles.

The most serious problem for the QORs was an ammunition shortage – the carrier platoon could not get forward through the chaos in the crowded bridgehead. Captured German weapons were used in what turned into a day-long battle, which was followed at 2100 by a strong effort by the enemy to retake the village. The QORs fought this off and took another large batch of prisoners. At 2230 hours the battalion reported that it was 'solid in Giberville' and would soon finish clearing the village.[23] Much has been made of the setback experienced by the QOR and First Hussars at le-Mesnil-Patry, but no similar attention has been paid to the achievements of these two regiments at Giberville. A close examination of this very successful battle suggests a high level of tank–infantry cooperation, especially during the period when radio communication with the artillery had broken down and the riflemen and troopers were on their own.

Le Régiment de la Chaudière ran into similar opposition in the chateau and woods north of Colombelles. This area had not been bombed, and the barrage had passed over it quickly, leaving the enemy strongpoints intact.[24] The Chauds had no tank support[25] and the artillery was committed to other tasks, so little progress could be made. The reserve battalion, the North Shores, were held up, and behind them the lead battalion of 9th Brigade, the Glens, were brought to a standstill. The Glens' War Diary noted: 'The battalion and the HLI behind us are in one long column, and a lovely target should Gerry decide to attack.'[26]

The Glens, impatient with the delay, worked their way forward. By mid-day they were clearing the 'very close country' around the chateau. A troop of Hussars tanks assigned to 9th Brigade bypassed the cratered area and were borrowed by Lt.-Col. Mathieu of the Chaudières 'for support in cleaning up some M.G. nests,' which the infantry were then able to clear, taking thirty prisoners. The troop was ordered back to support the Glens in attacking another strongpoint at a 'heavy stone wall with the position dug-in at the base.' Five minutes of fire from both the main gun firing high explosive (HE) and 'the co-ax' – a machine gun mounted to fire on the same axis as the 75 mm – helped the infantry take the position.[27]

Brig. Blackader decided to employ the medium artillery regiments, which became available on call late in the morning, to 'stonc' the chateau. He ordered the Chauds and the North Shores to pull back a safe distance, but he did not know that the Glens had got themselves involved in 8th Brigade's battle. They had less than five minutes' warning to withdraw and take cover. One company lost three officers and twelve other ranks to this friendly fire, which the Chauds used to break into the chateau and mop up the enemy.[28] The decision to send 8th Brigade into battle with limited armoured support was based on the estimate that their route forward would be heavily cratered and mostly impassable to tanks. This proved to be an accurate forecast, though one Hussars troop had managed to circle around the worst-hit areas and reach the Chauds. Those who maintain that Allied infantry were not sufficiently aggressive and failed to advance using their own weapons will no doubt cite the delay at Colombelles as an excellent illustration of their case. Should these citizen-soldiers have pressed the attack, whatever the cost? Or should they have made the rational calculation that support was required and would be forthcoming?

The battles for Giberville and Colombelles disrupted the timetable that Simonds had proposed for Atlantic, and he turned to the alternative plan outlined before the operation began. Brig. Foster's 7th Brigade was holding the centre of Caen, and Simonds had warned him that it might be necessary to put the brigade across the river directly into Vaucelles so that the vital bridging sites could be secured before dark. The Regina Rifles' scout platoon, led by Lt. Lorenzo Bergeron, a young Montrealer serving with the 'Johns,' had enlisted the help of members of the French resistance who were familiar with the area. Bergeron was able to enter Vaucelles and pinpoint enemy positions for the artillery before the battalion moved its rifle companies forward. Most of the men waded or swam across the river. Within a few hours they had consolidated the bridgehead.[29]

The relative ease with which the Reginas crossed the Orne, cleared parts of Vaucelles, and made it possible for the engineers to begin bridging demonstrated the difference that a detailed knowledge of exact enemy locations could make. The bombing and barrages that preceded the main attack reached an extraordinary pitch of intensity, but even very large amounts of high explosive are not very effective if they are spread out over a very large area. The chateau at Colombelles, like Giberville, had not been bombed, and the field regiments' rolling barrage had on average placed one 25-pounder shell on every 100 square yards – nowhere near enough to stun, never mind injure, dug-in troops.[30] Yet a single concentration of medium artillery, corrected by the forward observation officer, quickly ended all resistance.

After Colombelles was cleared, 9th Brigade fought its way into Vaucelles from the east while the North Shore Regiment attacked the steel mills, 'sweeping through the bombed ruins like beaters.'[31] By dawn on 19 July, all of 3rd Division's objectives had been secured. The cost, 386 casualties of which 89 were fatal,[32] was, however tragic for individuals and their families, exceptionally low for an operation that had made such important gains and confirmed Simonds's judgment that the veteran division continued to be a highly effective force.

Phase II of Atlantic required the 2nd Canadian Infantry Division to secure the area south of Vaucelles and then assist 8 Corps by seizing the high ground along the Orne. The division was commanded by Maj.-Gen. Charles Foulkes, a Permanent Force infantry officer who had served in staff positions and in command of 3rd Infantry Brigade. Foulkes was a man of intelligence and ability who would serve effectively as a postwar Chief of Staff,[33] but he had no experience of combat and a poor reputation as a trainer or leader of troops.[34] Foulkes seems to have been appointed because he was an infantry officer in an army dominated by gunners. Gen. Crerar, himself a distinguished artillery officer, was determined to change the perception that gunners ruled, and he went out of his way to promote infantry brigadiers to command divisions.[35]

By the time Foulkes took over in January 1944, 2nd Division had left the Dieppe disaster behind, trained hard for its new role in a corps that was tasked to lead a breakout from an established bridgehead. During the months under Foulkes's command, much time and energy was spent on refresher training for the rifle battalions and on river crossing studies for the staff and engineers. This latter endeavour evolved from planning for Operation Axehead, an assault across the estuary of the Seine, which the planners assumed the Germans would defend after being pushed out of lower Normandy.[36]

Foulkes made no real attempt to impress his personality on the division; instead, he worked to create an efficient staff. The CRA, R.H. Keefler, a future divisional commander, made sure the 4th, 5th, and 6th Field Regiments were thoroughly trained. Foulkes brought in Lt.-Col. C.R. Archibald as his GSO I and Lt.-Col. L.A. Deziel as his AA and QM. Both appeared to be first-rate staff officers. Foulkes also insisted on replacing all three brigadiers and appointing younger men.[37] The new brigadiers, appointed on 27 February, had to concentrate on getting to know their battalions and especially the commanding officers. Brig. Sherwood Lett had been highly rated by Montgomery in 1942, and in 1944 was identified as a future divisional commander. His 4th Brigade seemed to be in very good shape. John Rockingham, CO of the Royal Hamilton Light Infantry, was already marked for promotion, and the second-in-command (2IC), Maj. Denis Whitaker, DSO, was one of the best-known and most popular officers in the army for his exploits on the football field and on the beach at Dieppe. The Essex Scottish were commanded by Bruce McDonald, a militia officer and lawyer who had established a strong reputation during the training period. The Royal Regiment of Canada was considered solid, with doubts about the CO tempered by confidence in the company commanders and 2IC.[38]

The leadership of 5th Brigade's battalions was more problematic. Brig. Bill Megill's background was in the signal corps and in staff work. A graduate of the staff college at Quetta, he had hoped to command a battalion in action before taking on responsibility for a brigade.[39] Stuart Cantlie, the CO of the Black Watch, was outstanding as were his officers. The Régiment de Maisoneuve was a bit of a puzzle. The CO, Lt.-Col. Lefort Biss]alon, seemed competent but lacked any obvious qualities of dynamic leadership. However, his 2IC, Maj. Julien Bibeau, was another kind of character entirely, and Megill thought that Bibeau, along with some very youthful and energetic company commanders, would make the Maisies work. Megill had reservations about Lt.-Col. Donald MacLaughlan, the CO of the Calgary Highlanders, who had a reputation as a high-strung disciplinarian. However, Maj. Vern Stott, the 2IC, was a soldier's soldier and a natural leader, so if the test of battle required changes, both regiments would be well served.[40]

As for 6th Brigade, Brig. H.A. Young, an RMC graduate without previous combat experience, seemed confident in his ability to command the brigade, partly because of the quality of his battalion commanders. The South Saskatchewan Regiment was commanded by the highly regarded Freddie Clift, who was on the list for promotion to brigadier.[41] The Queen's Own Cameron Highlanders of Canada were the only battalion in 2nd Corps with a CO, Lt.-Col. J. Runcie, and two company commanders who had been awarded Military Crosses, all for actions at Dieppe. The Fusiliers Mont Royal were, like all the French-Canadian regiments, a bit of a mystery to their unilingual English-speaking commanders, but Lt.-Col. Gauvreau, the CO, was a man of considerable character, and his officers and NCOs seemed exceptionally fit and keen. One company commander, twenty-four-year-old Jimmy Dextrase, had already attracted attention as an experienced leader. Dextrase, 'JDex' to generations of Canadian soldiers, took over command of the battalion in August, days after his twenty-fifth birthday and his first DSO.

Simonds knew a good deal about the strengths and weaknesses of 2nd Division, and he intended to control virtually every aspect of the operation. He ordered 4th Brigade, which was holding the Eterville Ridge, to attack Louvigny on the west side of the river with the assistance of 43rd Wessex Division. If Louvigny fell quickly and 4th Brigade was able to cross the Orne, Brig. Sherwood Lett's battalions were to lead the advance south. Louvigny did not fall quickly. Elements of 272nd Infantry Division arriving from the south of France had taken over positions astride the Orne. The 272nd was a well-equipped and well-trained infantry division[42] but, like 2nd Canadian, it was facing its first battle. The main difference was that the 272nd had been sent in to defend positions that had been carefully built up and camouflaged after the battle for Carpiquet, whereas the Canadians were required to attack and root out the defenders.

The Royals had a difficult time with their first offensive operation since the Dieppe raid. The clearing of the orchards north of the village went well enough, but the advance into the Louvigny grounds of the chateau met mortar fire and strong resistance. Lett, who had been wounded at Dieppe, was one of the victims of enemy mortars, which never seemed to let up. All the lead company's officers were killed or wounded.[43] Sgt. O.C. Tyron of the mortar platoon, who was serving as a mobile fire controller for the battalion's 3-inch mortars, took command and sealed off the chateau[44] while the remainder of the battalion began to clear the village. This task was far from complete when the light began to fade, and Maj. T.F. Whitley decided that neither he nor his scattered platoons knew enough about village night fighting to take this on. He ordered everyone back to a firm base north of the village, 'where we would be able to dig-in quickly and re-organize ready to clear things up the next day.' At 0600 on 19 July, the Royals advanced back into the village to find that the enemy had withdrawn during the night. The troops then enjoyed 'a breakfast of hot coffee from the delighted villagers who insisted on killing a cow, digging up their potatoes and serving a steak dinner.' Whitley's decision not to compound the confusion caused by darkness and the total failure of communications – 'the 18 set was worse than useless' – was a wise if somewhat insubordinate decision.[45] Fortunately, with 7th Brigade established in Vaucelles and the bridges under construction, Simonds was no longer interested in a river crossing at Louvigny. Instead, 5th Brigade was to lead the advance to Fleury-sur-Orne and Pt 67.[46]

The Black Watch had waited on the edge of the Caen racecourse through the day. Lt.-Col. Cantlie called four different O Groups in response to warning orders before H-hour was finally set for 2215. With the army on double daylight time, it was still light when the crossing began. There was no artillery support because of uncertainty about the exact location of 7th Brigade, so one company provided covering fire from the riverbank while another manhandled the assault boats across 800 yards of open ground to the launching points. The left flank platoon got across quickly and installed a kapok footbridge, but on the right, machine gun and mortar fire cost the Watch thirty-six casualties. The night was spent 'patrolling, neutralizing enemy snipers and digging-in.'[47]

Simonds thought about a night advance to Fleury but decided to wait for first light. At 2300 he spoke to Brig. Floyd, O'Connor's Chief of Staff, seeking to coordinate 5th Brigade's advance with the renewal of 8 Corps' offensive.[48] There was little Floyd could tell Simonds because O'Connor had not yet decided how, or if, he wished to continue the battle. Apart from probes toward the ridge, which were quickly stopped by enemy fire, the major event of the morning of 19 July was the clearing of Cormelles by the Highland Light Infantry of Canada working with tanks of 7th Armoured Division.[49]

Late in the morning, the commanders of the three armoured divisions met to work out a combined plan. O'Connor approved their proposals around noon. This was not the way it was supposed to work even in the loosely structured command system employed in the British army. O'Connor believed that little more could be accomplished by the armoured divisions. The joint proposal to stage limited attacks expanding the bridgehead, as opposed to a new attempt to break through the enemy defences, was the most he was prepared to authorize.[50]

Immediately after Goodwood, O'Connor developed an extended critique of the operational doctrine and tactics employed by British armoured divisions. He insisted that unless attacks were made 'on a sufficiently wide front so that all villages or woods ... are either actually attacked, engaged by fire or masked by smoke,' success was unlikely. It was also essential to find some way to ensure that 'infantry is moved in carriers close behind the tanks,' along the lines employed by German armoured divisions in Russia.[51] This comment might help explain O'Connor's reluctance to renew an all-out attack – reluctance that was no doubt strengthened by the loss of 131 more tanks on day two of Goodwood in return for very modest gains.[52] While 8th Corps improved its positions at the eastern end of the Bourquebus–Verrières feature, 2nd Canadian Infantry Division began the advance to secure the western end of the ridge. The attack was timed to coincide with 7th Armoured Division's main effort – the seizure of Borguebus and subsequent exploitation toward Verrières village.[53]

Simonds had issued detailed orders requiring 5th Brigade to capture Fleury-sur-Orne and the high ground south of Ifs (Pt. 67) before seizing St-Andre-sur-Orne and its bridge across the Orne. Simonds and Ritchie, commanding 12th Corps, then planned to coordinate an attack on the high ground on the west bank of the river.[54] Simonds's version of Allied battle doctrine distinguished between attacks on well-prepared enemy positions and those the Germans intended to hold for only a short period of time. In either case, he believed the division must advance on a one-brigade front with full artillery support. He believed that if the enemy decided to 'stand and fight,' an attack 'without adequate reconnaissance and preparation' would 'not succeed.'[55] Presumably, Simonds thought that Verrières Ridge, which his forces attacked on 19 July, was a 'rearguard position' that did not require much reconnaissance, and on the whole he was right.

The Maisoneuves crossed into the Black Watch bridgehead in the morning and moved to their forming up place around 1200. Brigades, like divisions, usually attacked 'one up,' and the Maisies were to make the first bound to the edge of Fleury-sur-Orne three miles south. A platoon of medium machine guns from the Toronto Scottish protected their open left flank, and a squadron of Sherbrooke tanks and a troop of M10s provided support. At first it all went wrong. The lead companies advanced two hundred yards past the start line, and when the artillery program began they were trapped in their own walking barrage. Then the reserve companies took over the advance and moved quickly to their objective, suffering further casualties from enemy mortar fire.[56]

Historians have often drawn attention to this incident, but at the time it seemed just another example of the chaos that envelops battlefields. War, when described by generals and historians, often takes on an organized, coherent pattern that is not at all evident to the men at the sharp end who are asked to carry out the grand design. Lines hastily marked on a talc-covered map board at an Orders Group are not always easy to relate to the actual ground, especially if that ground has been heavily shelled. What was significant was the speed with which the Maisoneuves recovered and pressed on to their objective. The battalion's command structure remained intact, and morale, though shaken, was not shattered.

The enemy's 272nd Infantry Division had withdrawn to positions on the high ground,[57] so when the Calgary Highlanders began to tie in with the Sherbrooke tanks for the next bound they faced a most uninviting prospect. If you stand at the southern edge of Fleury-sur-Orne today you can see clearly the high ground on the western side of the river that the Germans occupied on 19 July. When you look due south, you can easily see the low ridge, marked Pt 67 on the map. The flags that mark the new Canadian battlefield memorial[58] help focus attention on the northern spur of Verrières Ridge. The hill seems to be of little consequence unless you are a foot soldier who has to walk up the road and secure the position under fire in broad daylight. At 1715 a lone piper began to play and the Calgary Highlanders advanced, two companies up. The Sherbrookes sent a troop of tanks forward on either side of the road. They brushed aside enemy outposts, knocking out several machine guns and a number of snipers. One strongpoint was not so easily overcome, and a quick plan was made 'to shell and co-ax' the position from the flank in support of a frontal assault from a Calgary platoon.[59]

Training officers had told sceptical platoon commanders that 'with a common tank–infantry doctrine,' any infantry unit could cooperate with any armoured unit, 'with the minimum of preparation.'[60] The Calgaries, like other 2nd Division battalions, had little experience in working with armour and were surprised to discover that the principles actually worked, though the cost of this small action included two Sherbrooke tanks hit by enemy antitank guns firing from the edge of St-André. The Calgaries dug in just below the crest of Pt 67 and sent a fighting patrol south toward St-Martin-de-Fontenay. The patrol, under Lt. Vern Kilpatrick, was overrun by an armoured battle group from 1st SS Panzer Division. The encounter alerted the Calgaries, who were in contact with the artillery and had their antitank guns in position. When the Panzer Grenadiers and self-propelled assault guns surged forward, attacking individual positions with aimed fire, Baker Company, well to the left of the German thrust, was able to bring fire to bear on the German infantry, and the attack faded away. The Calgaries suffered ninety-two casualties on the 19 July, including Kilpatrick and his men, as well as Maj. Franco Baker, who commanded the company that bore the brunt of the attack. Almost all the casualties were from mortar fire and surprisingly few were fatal. The stretcher bearers and jeep ambulances got the wounded men to safety and immediate surgical treatment with extraordinary speed.[61]

The Calgaries were not left on their own. At 1900 the Black Watch, with two troops of Sherbrooke tanks, followed the barrage, occupying Ifs and the eastern slope of Pt 67 providing protection to the Calgary flank. When 272nd division launched a battalion counterattack, the FOOs of 5th Field Regiment brought down heavy fire forcing the German infantry to ground with heavy casualties.[62] Small groups tried to work their way around the Calgaries, but the Black Watch saw them off with artillery and mortar fire. Neither 1st SS nor the 272nd knew any magic solution to the problem of overcoming an enemy positioned on a reverse slope with good artillery support and antitank guns in position.[63]

By any reasonable standard, 5th Brigade had done very well in its first battle. There had been some mistakes, as is inevitable when green troops commanded by inexperienced officers are committed to action for the first time, but the brigade reached and held its objectives. Infantry–tank cooperation worked well, and 5th Field Regiment demonstrated consummate professionalism with its rapid and accurate responses to requests for defensive fire and SOS tasks.

At 2100 on 19 July, Simonds called an O Group to outline the tasks for the next day. The mood was upbeat as reports of 5th Brigade's success and the capture of Bras and Hubert-Folie by 11th Armoured Division were received. Simonds had met with the army commander at mid-day to discuss plans for the next day. Dempsey wanted to relieve the armoured divisions as quickly as possible, and stated that his 'intentions' for 20 July required 2 Canadian Corps to complete the consolidation of a bridgehead, Pt 67–Ifs–Cormelles.[64] As we have seen, the Canadians had been able to accomplish this on that day. Dempsey also asked Simonds to arrange for 3rd Division to take over Bras and Hubert-Folie from 11th Armoured.

The original plan for Goodwood called for the Canadians to advance south to secure the western flank after the armoured divisions had won control of the high ground all the way to Breteville-sur-Laize. Since this clearly was not going to happen, why did Simonds ignore Dempsey's intentions? And why did the army commander allow him to do so? In his postwar notes on Goodwood, Dempsey insisted that it was not part of the plan to get drawn into a costly infantry battle. His intentions for 20 July were 'to call it off except for trying to get onto the initial objectives.'[65] But Simonds left the meeting convinced that with a fresh infantry division he could get onto the high ground and hold it without O'Connor's armour. He told Foulkes to bring 6th Brigade across the Orne for an advance with 'lots of fire' to capture St-André-sur-Orne and the reverse slope of the main ridge. The 4th Brigade was to leave Louvigny and circle through Caen to provide depth. One of its battalions, the Essex Scottish, was placed under 6th Brigade to serve as a reserve in a three-up attack. Simonds spelled out his 'intention' not as a consolidation but as an effort 'to capture the Verrières feature.'[66]

This decision, which was to result in one of the most costly battles of the campaign, was influenced by Simonds's belief that the 'enemy planned to stand on [the line] May-sur-Orne–Secqueville' and could therefore be pushed off at least parts of the ridge. He was not anticipating a breakthrough, but simply the acquisition of ground favourable for further offensive action.[67] There was, however, more to it than that. Simonds was anxious to prove that he and his corps were worthy successors to Arthur Currie and the Canadians who had captured Vimy Ridge and led the Allied advance in the 'Hundred Days.' If British generals fought cautiously with visions of the Somme as part of their active memory, Canadian generals were more likely to think in terms of bold, successful attacks in a war remembered for its victories. Verrières was to be Simonds's Vimy.

Shortly before midnight, Brig. Bruce Matthews, the corps CRA, began working on the fire plan, arranging to include the medium guns of 8th Corps and air support from 83 Group. It soon became apparent that it would be at least mid-day before all the pieces were in place. Final orders were issued at a conference held at 1000 hours the next morning.[68] By then, 7th Armoured had captured Bourguebus and one of its regiments was mopping up the houses in the vicinity of Beauvoir Farm. An attack on Verrières village carried out by a squadron of tanks and a company of motorized infantry was stopped around noon because 'opposition was too strong.'[69] By then, Brig. Floyd, BGS of 8th Corps, and Brig. Roger, Simonds's BGS, had met to arrange the withdrawal of 7th Armoured Division to the east side of the highway, where the tanks and self-propelled artillery would help shoot the Canadians on to their objectives.[70]

Should Simonds have modified his plans after news of the enemy's successful defence of Verrières village? Was it a good idea to withdraw the British armour from Troteval and Beauvoir farms? Simonds believed that the infantry division was the 'sledgehammer' of the Allied armies and that a properly supported attack with 'lots of fire' would accomplish far more than could be achieved by a couple of armoured squadrons. The attack was to go ahead at 1500.

The 6th Brigade War Diary describes the spectacular sight of the men moving forward through the fields of growing grain over a front of some 4,000 yards. The tanks of the Sherbrooke Fusiliers and the carriers of the infantry battalions could be seen above the grain, which seemed to swallow up the walking soldiers.[71] Les Fusiliers Mont-Royal drew the area abandoned by 7th Armoured as their objective. The lead companies were to move to Beauvoir and Troteval farms; then Dog Company under Maj. Dextrase was to go through to Verrières village. The first objectives were reached without difficulty as the massive barrage forced the enemy underground. As Dog Company prepared to push on, 'a terrific concentration of mortar and gun fire opened up on the whole battalion front' and the German infantry came to life, overwhelming the company at Beauvoir farm.[72]

It now began to rain heavily. In the reduced visibility, command and control was difficult to maintain. Two squadrons of tanks supported the FMR advance.[73] On the right, C Squadron of the Sherbrookes was to assist the FMRs while protecting the flank of the South Sasks. The squadron was down to ten tanks, seven of which were forward with the infantry when the enemy counterattack began. The squadron claimed to have destroyed four enemy tanks and lost four of their own before withdrawing with the infantry. The Sherbrookes followed the practice of having an officer from the infantry battalion ride in the bow gunner's seat of the squadron commander's tank with the radio set netted to the infantry. This system worked well, though visibility problems and inexperience limited full cooperation.[74] One company of the FMRs, with the assistance of a machine gun platoon from the Toronto Scottish, tried to hold Troteval farm, but it was cut off and overrun the next day. The CO, Lt.-Col. Gauvreau, ordered D Company to withdraw down the slope and dig in with the reserve company to prevent a breakthrough.[75]

The South Saskatchewan Regiment entered the battle without its CO. Lt.-Col. Clift had been sent to take command of 4th Brigade after Lett was wounded in the fighting for Louvigny. Maj. George Matthews, the 2IC, took over and held his first O Group shortly after the battalion reached the forming up place at 1130. The attack, originally scheduled for 1200, was postponed, allowing the men to eat and Matthews to describe the battalion objective as 'two map squares' on the north slope of the ridge. Their centre line was the Ifs–Fontenay-le Marmion road.[76]

Little has changed in this landscape, and it is still possible to walk the same fields planted in the same crops. On 20 July 1944 the wheat and oats were waist high, waving in a light breeze that did little to cool the hot and muggy summer's day. The South Sasks advanced in box formation behind a barrage that 'was 300 yards deep, lifted 300 yards and then came down 300 yards more in depth.' Each of the five segments lasted twenty-four minutes before lifting.[77] The battalion moved quickly to the first crossroads. Then, as the barrage lifted, a platoon of infantry from 272nd Division 'widely spread in the wheatfields came to life.' The company was forced into close-quarter combat and took a number of prisoners but lost the barrage. Matthews ordered a reserve company to push through, and at 1600 was informed that they were on the objective. The 6-pounders, mortars, carrier, and pioneer platoon were ordered forward to help prepare a battalion 'fortress.' A troop of 17-pounders from 2nd Anti-Tank Regiment also started to move to previously selected positions. Before the lead companies could dig in, a large number of enemy infantry and tanks appeared over the crest of the hill from the southwest. These were engaged by artillery. Then a strong armoured attack came in from the southeast, 'shooting all hell out of everything in their path.' Baker Company was overrun, and the antitank guns, caught on the move forward, were destroyed.

Maj. L.L. Dickin reported that his men had 'fair concealment thanks to the wheat but we could not fire because we had no fields of fire.' Two armoured battlegroups, one from 2nd Panzer and the other from 1st SS, roamed at will, machine gunning anything that moved. Mortar fire also intensified, and the acting CO was among those killed. It began to rain, first lightly, then in a downpour. A ground fog added to the visibility problems, allowing the enemy battlegroups to operate without fear of air attack. Communications due to battle losses and the rain broke down, so Dickin went back to inform the CO of the Essex that the South Sasks could not survive on the objective and would retire behind the Essex. He then spoke to Brig. Young, who ordered the South Sasks to hold their ground. On returning up the hill, Dickin found that his own men had withdrawn all the way back to their FUP. 'The whole period of the withdrawal was chaos,' Dickin recalled.[78]

That was exactly how it seemed to the forward companies of the Essex Scottish, who saw the South Sask 'withdrawal' as a rout, with men retreating through their position in a state bordering on panic. Both the forward Essex companies also began to withdraw as enemy tanks approached. Lt.-Col. MacDonald tried to maintain control, ordering the lead companies to retire behind the reserve companies and dig in. Once started, the retreat collapsed into a race for safety. Amazingly, the two remaining Essex companies continued to hold their ground and spent the night in wet slit trenches.[79]

The third prong of the brigade attack was the responsibility of the Queen's Own Cameron Highlanders of Canada. Their objectives were the twin villages of St-André-sur-Orne and St-Martin-de-Fontenay. Simonds was hoping to secure the bridge across the Orne at St-André and to assist 12th British Corps in clearing the west bank of the Orne up to Bully, thus ending German observation of the approaches to Verrières Ridge.[80] The Camerons were provided with a squadron of the Sherbrookes to assist them, as well as a company of the Toronto Scottish medium machine guns. There were losses from mortar fire, but the 2nd Battalion, 272nd Division, was forced to surrender the area except for a strong position east of the river at Etavaux. The Camerons had achieved the one notable success of this otherwise disastrous day, but it soon became clear that there were not enough men to hold all of the objective, and the CO, without consulting brigade or division, reorganized his battalion to defend the houses and orchards in the northern part of the built-up area. This left much of St-Martin and all of the 'factory' area to the south in enemy hands.[81]

The role of the Sherbrooke Fusiliers in this successful action requires comment. 'A' Squadron of the Sherbrookes was commanded by Maj. Radley Walters, who emerged from the Normandy battlefields as the best-known and most respected battlefield commander in the Canadian Armoured Corps. Before the Cameron advance, 'Rad' had discussed the operation with the Camerons. Always aggressive, he had moved his tanks ahead of the infantry and engaged 'speculative targets along the forward edge of the town.' As the Camerons began clearing the houses and orchards, the Sherbrooke tanks came under fire from Panthers on the high ground to the southeast. Since 'the range was beyond our effectiveness,' the squadron was withdrawn to an orchard north of the village, where hull-down positions could be obtained. The Sherbrookes were able to help beat off a serious counterattack, killing two Panthers with a Firefly before withdrawing to refuel and rearm.[82] This was the way it was supposed to work.

For Montgomery and Dempsey, Operations Goodwood and Atlantic ended on the night of 20 July. The next day was to be spent completing the relief of the armoured divisions and reorganizing for a new offensive. For the men holding ground, the struggle continued. News of the attempted assassination of Hitler had no effect on 1st SS Panzer Corps, and by the afternoon of 21 July a number of powerful battlegroups from four Panzer divisions were committed to the counterattack role. Under overcast skies and intermittent rain, on a battlefield that could not be deciphered from the air, the Panzers were to have a rare opportunity to operate without looking over their shoulders for Typhoons.

The two Essex companies left in the muddy fields south of Ifs had worked through the night to improve their position and clean their weapons. We must assume that Foulkes and Young believed the battle had ended, for no attempt was made to assist the Essex, not even with warm food. At dawn they came under fire from enemy tanks and were struck by their own artillery. Lt.-Col. McDonald sought permission to withdraw to an intermediate position; this request was denied, and at 1400 the Essex wilted under a well-organized attack and retreated in disorder.[83] This debacle concluded with an adverse report and the dismissal of the battalion CO, who was charged with 'failing to exercise control' and 'being unable to inspire confidence.' McDonald's detailed reply to these charges included the comment that he certainly 'lacked confidence in the Brigadier's plan,'[84] but neither Foulkes nor Simonds, who were equally culpable, was willing to intervene.

The FMRs, just 800 metres to the east, were spared a direct counterattack, but like the Calgaries and the Camerons were under pressure throughout the day. Foulkes decided to use the Black Watch to retake the Essex positions. The battalion leaned into the barrage and quickly filled the gap, restoring the front.[85] The German battlegroups were cautious in approaching Pt 67, where artillery observers could see and antitank guns could inflict serious damage, so the main attacks were directed at St-André. 'A' Squadron of the Sherbrookes, now with fifteen tanks, was back in position at first light in time to greet two groups of Panthers. 'After one hour's exchange of fire, during which we lost one tank, there was no noticeable effect on the enemy,' so using smoke and careful recce, the squadron moved to new firing positions among the infantry. For the next two hours, A Squadron, with help from 3rd Anti-Tank regiment M10s, engaged the enemy 'from three sides,' claiming eight Panthers while losing five Shermans. By the end of the day the squadron was down to six functioning tanks, all of which were again committed to the defence of St-André the next day.[86]

If there was an end to the battle it came on the afternoon of 22 July, when Simonds and Ritchie agreed on a plan to clear the enemy from the west bank of the Orne at least as far as Maltot. Foulkes was told to assist 43rd Division by staging an attack on Etavaux, a hamlet on the east side of the river that the enemy still held.[87] The Régiment de Maisoneuve, in reserve behind Pt 67, was given B Squadron of the Sherbrookes and full artillery support. Etavaux was garrisoned by companies of 1st Battalion, 982nd Regiment, 272nd Infantry Division. Their orders were to hold this position 'at all costs' because the SS would soon recapture St-André.[88]

The Maisies used two companies to attack astride the railway line behind a walking barrage. The armour chose to support the infantry from high ground overlooking the approach. In practice this meant that no aimed fire on precise targets was possible. A large number of machine gun posts had survived the barrage and now brought heavy fire to bear on the infantry. There is an old adage that battles are won by a handful of men who instinctively attack while their comrades equally instinctively hit the ground. First, Sgt. Benoit Lacourse in-spired four of his men to join him on a mad rush that destroyed three machine gun pits; then Maj. Jacques Ostiguy used grenades to single-handedly take out five other positions. More than one hundred prisoners were taken, while others hid until dark and then escaped to rejoin their division.[89] The British were equally successful west of the river, catching the 272nd Division while it was attempting to relieve Maltot. Almost four hundred prisoners from two battalions were captured.[90]

The actions fought by the 2nd British Army in the third week of July can best be compared to the attritional battles that were so typical of the Western Front in the First World War. The most careful estimates of British and Canadian casualties for 18 to 21 July are that 6,168 men were killed, wounded, or missing in this three-day period. Add to this a further 3,000 casualties from 12th Corps operations west of the Orne between 15 and 17 July. Evacuations for battle exhaustion rose steadily through the week; although no exact total is possible, the number could not have been less than 1,500.[91] This terrible drain on the man-power resources of 21 Army Group would soon force Montgomery to disband 59th Division and other units to provide needed reinforce-ments. It was the human cost of Goodwood, not the failure to reach territorial objectives, that mattered, because it greatly reduced the combat power of the Anglo-Canadian armies on the eve of the German collapse.

The same battles had of course contributed to the defeat of the enemy, both by inflicting casualties and by drawing enemy reserves to the most threatened areas. The question is whether this goal could have been achieved at a lower cost. The answer is undoubtedly yes. If Goodwood had been planned as a holding operation designed to draw the German armoured divisions into battle east of the Orne, then O'Connor and Dempsey could have used one or at most two armoured divisions to seize vital ground and defend it until the medium artillery had moved forward to deal with counterattacks and support the unlikely prospect of further exploitation. Such a plan would have con-formed with established doctrine and the recommendations of opera-tional researchers, who best knew the limitations of the available armoured fighting vehicles. Instead, Dempsey's plan called for a breakout, which he later admitted 'was not a very good operation of war tactically.'[92]

Dempsey can be fairly criticized for committing 8th Corps to an operation that it had virtually no chance of carrying out successfully. Simonds, in turn, must be severely criticized for launching an impro-vised infantry attack after 8th Corps had been checked. Simonds seems to have believed that four battalions supported by two understrength armoured squadrons – perhaps forty-five tanks – could occupy and hold positions on the open slope of a ridge. Always an aggressive risk taker, Simonds badly miscalculated the odds on 20 July.

D-Day, Courseulles-sur-Mer. The Regina Rifles landed on Nan Green Beach to the left (east) of the River Seulles, the Royal Winnipeg Rifles, with C. Coy of the Canadian Scottish Regiment, landed on Mike Red west of the river. The advance inland was well underway when this photograph was taken.

The reserve brigade, 9th Canadian Infantry Brigade, began to land at Bernières-sur-Mer around 1200 hours. Bicycles to speed the advance inland were carried by the infantry. The house on the left is today known as Maison Queen's Own Rifles. The railway station and the half-timbered Norman house on the extreme right have survived to the present day.

French children bathing in front of the bunkers at Courseulles-sur-Mer, 1946.

Nan Red Beach, St-Aubin-sur-Mer, 1946. The remains of the resistance nest captured by the North Shore (New Brunswick) Regiment on D-Day can be seen. The antitank gun (centre) has been preserved.

Mortar Crew, Regina Rifle Regiment in June 1944. The 3-inch mortar with a range of 2500 metres played a major role in the defence of Bretteville-Norrey.

A Panther tank of the 12th SS destroyed by fire from a PIAT (Projector Infantry Anti-Tank), Bretteville-l'Orqueilleuse, 9 June 1944.

Infantry at work. The soldier in the centre has a PIAT slung over his shoulder and carries an entrenching tool as well as a Sten gun. The soldier to the right carries the 'No. 4' Lee-Enfield .303 with his bayonet fixed.

Canadian infantry searching the burning ruins of Caen, 10 July 1944.

Field Marshal Montgomery (centre) with Lt.-Gen. Sir Miles Dempsey (left) and Lt.-Gen. Guy Simonds, September 1944.

Maj.-Gen. R.F.L. Keller and Lt.-Gen. Sir John Crocker, 25 June 1944.

Gunners W. Collins (left) and W.R. Gray of 19th Field Regt. Royal Canadian Artillery seated on shell casings. Their M7 'Priest' self-propelled 105 mm gun is in the background.

Support Company, Highland Light Infantry of Canada at rest, August 1944.

Men of the 8th Canadian Infantry Brigade searching one of the bunkers at Carpiquet airport.

German prisoners of war from the 12th SS Hitler Youth Division captured in the battle of Caen, 8 July 1944.

A Sherman tank of the Fort Garry Horse, 8 July 1944.

A German 75 mm antitank gun camouflaged and ready for action.

A Halifax bomber of No. 6 Group RCAF over France, July 1944.

The results of air attacks on railway yards are evident in this photo of Mezidon, south of Caen.

Honorary Capt. Padre Jock Anderson, Highland Light Infantry of Canada, with Pte Lawrence Herbert, 15 July 1944.

Nursing sisters of No. 10 Canadian General Hospital arrive in Normandy, 23 July 1944.

Air Photo (10 July 1944) of the eastern edge of May-sur-Orne and the village of Fontenay-le-Marmion, the Black Watch objective on 25 July 1944. The slope of Verrières Ridge is evident in the shape of the fields. The small dots are haystacks.

Verrières village, foreground, and Rocquancourt. The railway line south to Falaise can be seen upper left. Bretteville-sur-Laize is located in the wooded area at the top of the photo. Verrières village, at 68 metres, is below the crest, of the ridge at 75 metres. Such small differences in elevation were of vital importance to tank crews and infantry but were invisible from the air.

A crossroads on the Caen–Falaise Highway.

The 4th Canadian Infantry Brigade mounted in 'unfrocked priests' for Operation Totalize, 7 August 1944.

Cromwell tanks of the 1st Polish Armoured Division, August 1944.

A Sherman tank of the Canadian Grenadier Guards with Quesnay Woods in the background, 1946.

A German assault gun destroyed in the Falaise gap near Magny. The river Dives, a serious tank obstacle, is visible behind the tank.

A section of infantry from the Fusiliers Mont-Royal follows a tank of the Sherbrooke Fusiliers into Falaise.

German soldiers surrendering in St-Lambert-sur-Dives, 19 August 1944.

7

Operation Spring

Operation Goodwood was a failure both tactically and operationally, but it became a strategic success because of the enemy response. By the end of the first day the Germans had succeeded in containing 8th Corps' advance and destroying scores of British tanks. They had been forced out of the Caen suburbs by the Canadians and pushed back to Troarn by British 3rd Division, but they had lost no really vital ground. Casualties on the night of 18 July included hundreds of men from 16th Luftwaffe Division and some battlegroups from 21st Panzer, but 1st SS Panzer Corps, with its painfully accumulated reserves, was intact. The 272nd Division, occupying the front line west of the Caen–Falaise road, was in position on the high ground. Behind it, work on field positions for a defence in depth, which Rommel had called for on 10 July, was nearing completion. If Field Marshal von Kluge kept his head and fought a purely defensive battle, the British and Canadian troops would be confined to a narrow bridgehead overlooked by the high ground south of Caen. From that ground, the Germans could systematically harass the Allied forces with artillery, mortar, and long-range tank-killing fire without having to expose infantry battalions or Panzer battlegroups to antitank guns or the principal weapon of the Allied armies – 'drumfire,' artillery.

When Hitler's 8 July Directive ordered his commanders to cease major counterattacks until reserves had been created, he was confirming decisions that circumstances had already forced on General Eberbach's Panzer Group. What ought to have been forbidden was the practice of launching immediate local counterattacks to recapture lost ground as a reflex rather than a considered, rational action. Eberbach favoured this alternative, but at 1720 on 18 July, von Kluge's Chief of Staff informed him that von Kluge 'would in no circumstances be in agreement with sealing off the area of penetration, rather, the enemy must be thrown back across the line Caen–Troarn by a concentric attack.'[1]

Given the condition of the German forces, this decision was a far more serious mistake than any made by Dempsey or Simonds. The counterattacks launched by 1st SS Panzer Division on the evening of 18 July were a taste of what was to come. After initial success, the attacking troops were forced back to their startline with significant losses. Over the next twenty-four hours the division gave up Bourgebus, regained it, and lost it again, taking irreplaceable casualties in men and equipment.[2] No one who has walked the ground at Bourguebus can explain this persistence. The village is on the northeastern slope of the ridge and is overlooked, across flat cultivated fields, from Tilly-la-Campagne. After 1st SS conceded Bourguebus, it was able to create a fortress position at Tilly that later withstood four separate attacks; meanwhile, the troops in Bourguebus could not leave their slit trenches in daylight.

The situation elsewhere on the ridge was similar. If it is difficult to understand why Simonds was anxious to place 6th Brigade in the open fields on the northern slope of the ridge; it is equally hard to explain why Dietrich allowed 272nd Division and his Panzer battlegroups to fight so hard, and at such great cost, to regain ground of so little tactical value. The German soldiers were especially ill-served by their commanders; from von Kluge on down, all the senior officers realized that Montgomery's basic strategy of engaging the enemy 'unceasingly' and 'writing off' troops was working far better than Montgomery knew. Panzer Group West's War Diary is only one of many sources that express the growing desperation of the German generals, who were 'deeply shocked' by the situation and by the failure of even the SS to send reinforcements to Normandy.[3]

The crisis confronting the German army had not yet led to a collapse of morale among ordinary soldiers, but Second Army intelligence officers who translated letters recovered from the battlefield noted increasing frustration among them. One veteran told his parents, 'My platoon commander was killed today. Many more will have to give their lives here to achieve victory ... You can scarcely get a wink of sleep as you can always count on an attack by Tommy ... Each time our resistance has beaten him off. You cannot in the least imagine how fierce the fighting is.'[4]

On the same day this letter was written, Eberbach sent a confidential order to all units under his command urging new measures to curb growing 'slackness in the behaviour of our men.' This slackness was worse among units outside the fighting zone. 'There is,' Eberbach wrote, 'an increased number of cases of looting, cattle stealing and so called "purchase" accompanied by a show of weapons.' Motor vehicles are being used to 'get organized or to cultivate some female acquaintance – in spite of the shortage of fuel.' Dress regulations were being ignored, and saluting had 'almost entirely ceased.' Eberbach included his own Waffen SS units among those to be inspected by new discipline patrols. Even officers, he insisted, 'will be checked by special officer-patrols.'[5]

The situation on the front lines meant that discipline patrols were the least of the German soldier's worries. A private in 272nd division, exposed to his first taste of Allied attrition tactics, wrote to his parents on 18 July, the day before he was killed in action:

We hear the whole long day nothing but artillery fire of all calibres. In fact sometimes I don't know whether I am male or female. Whoever succeeds in passing through this hell without being killed can really be thankful to God. This is truly a battle of supplies ... Now I must conclude, Tommy is at it again.[6]

On 20 July, one of his comrades in the same regiment described life at the front in a letter to his mother:

Dear Mother, hell is let loose here. The dirty dog is firing all the time ... The only good thing is that we have a good position which the enemy can't overlook ... I'd like to know how much longer this is going to last. They keep talking such a lot about V2 but I shan't believe it until it actually happens.[7]

A letter from an SS veteran, written on 21 July, echoed these reactions:

One has to endure quite a lot here. I don't know what will happen if we are not relieved soon. So far we have 20 killed and 60 wounded in this company. There is a great difference between Tommy and the Russians. Here one must have good nerves to stand being shelled for hours on end, and whoever manages to get out alive is pretty lucky ... Most of the men begin to lose their hair at 19.[8]

Conditions in the 7th Army's sector were even worse. On 19 July, General Paul Hausser wrote to Field Marshall von Kluge requesting reinforcements. The 'battle potential of the infantry,' he noted, 'is especially undermined by the artillery and mortar fire which the enemy is putting up in hitherto unknown quantity ... In prolonged fighting the potential of the infantry drops from that of a regiment to a company.' Hausser was convinced that the 'enemy are bound to break through' and predicted that the necessary 'defensive actions and counter-attacks ... would quickly use up all the weak reserves in divisions and corps.' His army reserve consisted of just three battalions ready for combat plus the newly arrived 5th Parachute Division and a battalion-sized battlegroup. These reinforcements, Hausser noted, could do little to solve the difficulties of 7th Army, as the troops 'have had absolutely no training in field work or as a unit.' The parachute division, made up of Luftwaffe ground personnel, not trained airborne infantry, lacked experienced leaders and would suffer 'extremely heavy losses' if used in 'danger areas.' The army commander concluded his report with an appeal for immediate help – 'at least 2 infantry battalions' per division as well as mortar brigades, heavy artillery, and 'mobile formation completely ready for battle.' Increased supplies of munitions and fuel were also urgently required.[9] None of these requests were met before Operation Cobra began. The 7th Army did indeed collapse.

The morale of the German commanders in Normandy was further weakened by news of the 20 July plot against Hitler and its failure. The Third Reich seemed to be on shaky ground, and uncertainty about the future must have contributed to the paralysis overtaking the German high command. In fact, at both the tactical and operational levels, the German commanders could have traded space for time in Normandy. So long as the Allies' western flank remained locked onto the coast, the only place where they could extend the length of the front was on the eastern flank. But the flooded valley of the Dives, reaching back to Troarn, provided a barrier that could be defended by a single German infantry division. Beyond the Dives valley, the thickly wooded hills of Pays d'Auge, and the coastal road to Honfleur, which led to the wide estuary of the Seine, were unlikely axes of advance for any Allied force.[10] It seems almost certain that von Kluge, Eberbach, and Hausser could have defended Normandy for much longer than six weeks if they had adopted different tactics. Instead, they interpreted Hitler's orders forbidding a withdrawal in the strictest possible terms. During the week of 17 to 23 July, this policy contributed to record German losses of 362 officers and 16,399 men.[11]

Von Kluge compounded his error of judgment when he ordered 'a concentric attack,' requesting Hitler's permission to release 12th SS from its reserve role and ordering the transfer of battlegroups from 2nd SS Panzer Corps to the east side of the Orne. These actions strengthened Montgomery's claim that Goodwood had succeeded in attracting German armour to the Caen–Falaise sector, thus preventing any possible reinforcement of 7th Army opposite the Americans.

On 21 July, von Kluge wrote his much quoted letter describing the psychological effects of bombs 'raining down with all the force of elemental nature' and the growing shortages of men, weapons, and ammunition. 'The moment,' he told Hitler, 'is fast approaching when this overtaxed front line is bound to break up.' He informed Hitler that his last words at a staff conference south of Caen were, 'We must hold our ground, and if nothing happens to improve conditions, then we must die an honourable death on the battlefield.'[12]

The Allied commanders completely failed to understand the situation they had created. At Eisenhower's headquarters in England, the Deputy Supreme Commander, Air Marshal Tedder, agitated for the removal of Montgomery for his alleged failure to take aggressive action during the opportunity provided by the attempted assassination of Hitler.[13] Eisenhower had no intention of following Tedder's advice, but he did write an extraordinary letter to Montgomery – a letter that suggests just how far out of touch with reality Eisenhower was at that moment. He began by reminding Montgomery of the final paragraph of the 10 July Directive in which Monty had listed the Allied territorial objectives as an expanded bridgehead and the acquisition of Brittany and its ports, while 'engaging the enemy and writing off his troops.' Eisenhower declared his complete agreement with these priorities but expressed the fear that the relative strength of the Allies was at its peak and that time was vital. 'We must not only have the Brittany Peninsula,' he wrote, 'we must have it quickly. So we must hit with everything.' Eisenhower wanted Dempsey to 'maintain the strength of his attack' and intensify it as soon as Operation Cobra, the delayed American attempt at a breakout, was launched.

Eisenhower should have signed off at this point, but Monty's critics at SHAEF were out for blood. The Supreme Commander, who seems to have had no detailed knowledge of what the Second British Army had been doing for the past six days, suggested that Dempsey should follow the example of the First American Army and bring 'the whole front into action to pin down local reserves.' Eisenhower, with uncharacteristic insensitivity, concluded by noting that before long 'American ground strength will necessarily be greater than the British. But while we have equality in size we must go forward shoulder to shoulder, with honours and sacrifice equally shared.'[14] What exactly did Eisenhower think the British and Canadians had been doing?

Montgomery had no better idea of what conditions were like on the other side of the hill. On 21 July he replied to a pessimistic letter from Maj.-Gen. Frank Simpson at the War Office, agreeing that 'we cannot defeat our present opponents decisively in the next fortnight.' The new bridgehead, won at such great cost in Goodwood, would, he told Simpson, allow the forces west of the Orne 'to take quick advantage of anything that may happen,' but the priority now was Brittany and 'the swing' of the American flank.[15] Enclosed with the letter was a copy of a new directive, the first since 10 July. It required the 2nd British Army to operate 'intensively' to gain new ground on both sides of the Orne. After this was achieved, the forces east of the river 'will be kept as active as possible ... the enemy must be led to believe that we contemplate a major advance towards Falaise and Argentan.' This would, Montgomery hoped, induce him 'to build up his main strength east of the Orne so that our affairs on the western flank can proceed with greater speed.' The same directive spelled out a role for the Third U.S. Army, under General George Patton, to operate 'in Brittany,' and described in detail the swing of the American flank to the south and east that would be carried out if Operation Cobra, now scheduled for 24 July, was successful.

The new directive did not completely convince Eisenhower, who replied, 'We are apparently in complete agreement that a vigorous and persistent offensive should be sustained by both First and Second Armies.'[16] Unfortunately, Montgomery – who was now fully aware of the widespread criticism of his leadership – modified the very sensible policy spelled out in the directive and issued new orders to the Second British Army. These called for a series of left-right blows on either side of the Orne, beginning with an attack by 2 Canadian Corps on 25 July.

On 28 July, 12th Corps, west of the Orne, would attack; this would be followed by an 8th Corps advance toward Falaise. These operations, Montgomery informed the Supreme Commander, were 'preliminary to a very large scale operation, by possibly three or four armoured divisions' to Falaise. This 'second' Goodwood was tentatively timed for 3 or 4 August.[17] This letter, written to Eisenhower as news of the delay of Cobra for at least another twenty-four hours was being received, suggests that Montgomery foresaw a continuation of heavy fighting all across the Normandy front as the Allied forces continued to launch attacks designed to tie down and wear down the enemy.

This was certainly the context of the verbal orders that Dempsey gave Simonds on the night of 22 July, when he explained the scope of what would become Operation Spring.[18] 2 Canadian Corps was to employ its two infantry divisions, 2nd Armoured Brigade, and 7th Armoured Division, with Guards Armoured Division available for limited exploitation. The army commander's intention was to capture Verrières Ridge before exploiting to the Cintheaux feature and Bretteville-sur-Laize.[19]

Beyond all this, the plans for Spring were conceived and developed by Simonds. Few options were available to the corps commander during the two days available to him. Simonds knew that 3rd Division, after seven weeks of continuous action, was in need of a rest, but most of its battalions were up to strength and still functioning effectively. The 2nd Division was another matter. Some reinforcements for its shattered battalions were immediately available, but there was no way that 6th Brigade or the Essex Scottish could be rebuilt in time to play a major role in a renewed attack on Verrières Ridge. The Régiment de Maisoneuve had suffered almost one hundred casualties at Etavaux on the 22 July, bringing its three-day total to over two hundred – half the rifle strength of the battalion.[20] This left Maj.-Gen. Foulkes with four infantry battalions – the Black Watch and the Calgary Highlanders in 5th Brigade, and the Royal Hamilton Light Infantry and Royal Regiment in 4th Brigade – fully fit for offensive operations. The situation in 2nd Canadian Armoured Brigade was better. Both the Hussars and the Fort Garry Horse were almost up to strength, and the Sherbrookes could function as a reserve while re-equipping.

Taking these factors into account, Simonds proposed a carefully con-

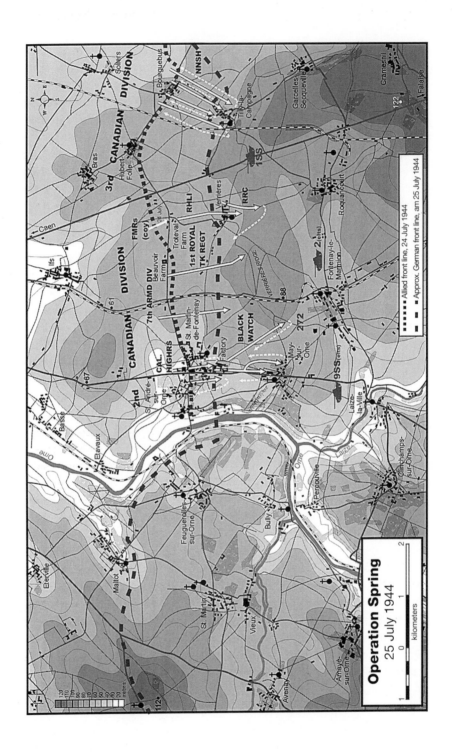

Operation Spring
25 July 1944

kilometers
0   1   2

▪▪▪▪ Allied front line, 24 July 1944
▬ ▬ ▬ Approx. German front line, am 25 July 1944

trolled operation. Three infantry battalions were to attack in Phase I, with H-hour set for full darkness 'two hours before first tank light.' Each battalion's objective was a recognizable village less than a kilometre directly in front. With the assistance of searchlights – 'artificial moonlight' – the infantry should be able to get onto their objectives and dig in before dawn. For Phase II, Simonds proposed to employ three more infantry battalions, each with strong armoured support and a massive artillery barrage. These battalions were to seize the next line of villages while 7th Armoured Division attacked across the centre of Verrières Ridge to reach the high ground, Pt 122, known as the 'Cramesnil spur.' Phase III, to be carried out mainly by the Guards Armoured Division, involved the capture of the wooded area at Garcelles.[21]

Spring was designed to secure the same high ground as had been targeted during Phase II of Goodwood. But this time there was no suggestion that a breakthrough was possible and no talk of 'cracking about' at Falaise. General O'Connor, who expected the British armoured divisions to return to his corps in a few days, sought out Simonds, seeking reassurance on precisely this point. After their meeting, O'Connor wrote to urge General Adair, commanding the Guards Armoured Division, to do his part in Spring as 'a careful operation':

> Now I've seen General Simonds and I know what you are being asked to do. It is a difficult job and will require very careful thinking out ... Go cautiously with your armour, making sure that any areas from which you could be shot up by Panthers and 88s are engaged.
>
> Remember what you are doing is not a rush to Paris – it is the capture of a wood by combined armour and infantry; so it has as an operation, not quite the same background as the last.[22]

O'Connor did not feel he needed to send a similar cautionary letter to Maj.-Gen. Erskine. During and after Goodwood, Erskine and his armoured brigade commander had criticized the pointless sacrifice of armoured regiments, which had been called on to perform tasks that were completely unsuitable for Sherman or Cromwell tanks. So it was highly unlikely that 7th Armoured Division would be tempted to 'make a wild rush of it' on 25 July.[23]

O'Connor's letter, together with the actual operational orders issued by the four divisions, ought to close the debate over the purpose of Spring. The operation was designed as a holding attack, just as Simonds was later to claim, but such an attack would only be rated a success if it secured ground that was truly vital to the enemy and forced von Kluge to commit his operational reserves, including 116th Panzer Division, to the battle. If the enemy responded to Spring with the usual local counterattacks, this would help the wearing down process, but have little strategic value.[24]

The timetable for Spring – an initial advance at 0330, with Phase II just two hours later – required all units involved to move into position during the brief summer hours of darkness. Everyone who had ever been on a night exercise during training thought this was a trifle optimistic. It was also obvious that both the forming up places (FUPs) and the start lines (SLs) would have to be secure or chaos might result. Simonds left these matters to the divisional and brigade commanders, but as always the devil was in such details.

Brig. Bill Megill first heard about Spring on 23 July at a divisional orders group. He listened in astonishment as Foulkes explained the corps plan, complete with exact timings. Megill had seen the ground and did not believe that a frontal attack on the ridge would be any more successful than the German attempts to recapture Pt 67.[25] A night attack was a good theoretical solution, but his brigade had little experience in night operations, which had not been emphasized in training. The plan called for 5th Brigade's lead battalion to advance south, using the road to May-sur-Orne, their objective, as the centre line. The road to Beauvoir Farm was designated as the start line, while the second east-west road to Verrières village was described as a 'check line,' where the artillery barrage was to begin. Megill sent two of his staff officers forward to select a site for his tactical headquarters. They arrived without difficulty, but on opening the door of a likely house heard German voices and withdrew. Megill decided to go and see for himself. He met Maj. John Muncie, the acting CO of the Camerons, who told Megill that his rifle companies made no pretense of controlling St-Martin, which the enemy held in some strength, nor any of the ground immediately south of the proposed start line. The Camerons,

Muncie reported, were under constant observation from the west bank of the Orne and were subject to accurate mortar concentrations at the slightest movement. The enemy kept infiltrating men across the river, making their right flank vulnerable. Megill went immediately to divisional headquarters to explain the situation and to ask to have the Maisoneuves, who were being held in reserve, restored to 5th Brigade to clear St-Martin. According to Megill, Brig. Young insisted that the Camerons controlled the area and would ensure that the start line was free from the enemy. Foulkes refused Megill's request and told him to rely on the Camerons.

Is it possible that neither Young nor Foulkes had been forward to the Cameron positions? Today St-André and St-Martin appear to be a single community, but in 1944 St-André was made up of two clusters of buildings west of the main road, while St-Martin was east of the highway. The Camerons had lost their hold on St-Martin on 21 July and never regained it. No one ever claimed that the *Cité de Mine*, with its prominent tower and cluster of buildings, which the Canadians called the 'factory,' had been captured. Maj. Muncie agreed to try and clear the start line and parts of St-Martin on the night of the 24 July, and Megill had to settle for that commitment.

In theory, the next decision Megill had to make was which of his two battalions to use in the night attack, but he allowed the choice to be dictated by their current locations. The Calgaries at Pt 67 could reach the FUP by following the main road south about 2 kilometres; the Black Watch, still holding ground south of Ifs, were much farther away. They would use the Beauvoir Farm road to reach St-Martin for Phase II and form up in that village, which in theory would be free of the enemy. The Calgaries had done well in the advance to and defence of Pt 67, but it was already evident that their CO, Lt.-Col. MacLaughlan, was not holding up under the stress of combat and had lost the confidence of his company commanders.[26] The Calgaries would fight and fight well, but they functioned as a loose collection of platoons and companies, not as a battalion subject to close command and control. The Black Watch, on the other hand, were the most disciplined battalion in the division and one of the best led. Their claims to elite status in the Canadian army had not always won them friends, but their smooth, effective performance in Atlantic had impressed everyone.

The Black Watch did not have more experience than the Calgaries in night attacks, but there is little doubt they would have executed the task very differently.

Neither Megill nor Muncie was confident that St-Martin could be cleared on time, so the Calgaries were told to sweep east around St-Martin 'as wide as possible,' with three companies up and one in reserve. During the approach march, word was received that no attempt had yet been made to clear the woods along the river south of St-André so MacLaughlan ordered Charlie Company to advance west of the main road, where it could protect the battalion's right flank.[27] Maj. Sherwin Robinson's men had no difficulty in locating the start line, but as soon as they approached it fire erupted from both flanks. The barrage began striking well ahead of their position, and Robinson decided 'it was too dark and difficult to clear the enemy out at night.' The barrage had created so much smoke and dust that 'we could not see anything.' Robinson, a rational citizen-soldier, decided to wait until morning and told his men to dig in. They would advance at first light, fulfilling the intent of their commander's orders.[28]

East of the main road, Maj. John Campbell's A Company discovered that if the area was clear at midnight, when the Camerons reported the start line 'secure,'[29] it certainly wasn't three hours later. In the darkness the MG42s, firing on fixed lines, could be bypassed. Campbell's men pressed ahead, hitting the check line on time and turning farther east to avoid small arms fire from the edge of St-Martin. Campbell, one of the original battle drill enthusiasts, who had served as an instructor at the infantry school in Yorkshire, kept his men moving though it meant leaving 'enemy behind in slit trenches and dug-outs who later fired on us to our cost.' Dawn was breaking when the company reached a spot from which they could see the eastern edge of May. They reported their position at 0550 as 'Gobbo Able' – the code phrase for having reached the forward edge of the objective.[30] The artillery was still targeting the ridge, and the normal number of shells fell short. Campbell's men were spread out across the open fields, exposed to fire from machine guns to their rear and strong forces on the ridge. Campbell waited less than fifteen minutes before ordering a withdrawal to dead ground east of St-Martin. There the company dug in under heavy mortar fire. With no radio left, Campbell was unable to notify battalion HQ of his retreat.[31] His battalion, brigade, division, and corps commanders believed that at least one Calgary company was on its objective.

Baker Company, on Able's right flank, found the start line clear, but well before the check line was reached they came under fire that dispersed the men and killed the company commander. Two of the platoons were forced to the ground in St-Martin. The third platoon, commanded by Lt. John Moffat, continued south to a water hole just north of May-sur-Orne. When the barrage lifted, Moffat set off to recce the crossroads in May. While he was gone, the platoon saw 'three Tiger tanks and two SPs which began firing at them.' Moffat decided that 'the objective was held by too strong a force for twenty men and one PIAT to contest.' The platoon withdrew, taking up positions east of the 'factory.'[32]

The experiences of the reserve company were perhaps the most astonishing example of the confusion that can arise in a night action. Much of Dog Company, including the headquarters group, became disoriented in the fields around Pt 67 and had to return to the hill to figure out where they were. The two platoons that did arrive at the FUP set off around St-Martin and came under fire. The senior platoon commander was wounded. Lt. Michon went forward to take over and led his men to the eastern end of a village, which proved to be St-Martin, not May-sur-Orne. Michon and the men took many prisoners and advanced toward the factory area, but they did not learn where they were until contact was made with the Black Watch at dawn.[33]

Charlie Company, west of the road, began its delayed advance in the first faint morning light. There were snipers in the factory area and 'groups of men who wanted to surrender.' Shortly after 0600 they reached the edge of May-sur-Orne and reported their progress to battalion. So it now seemed that two Calgary companies were attacking the village.[34]

Two miles to the east, the Royal Hamilton Light Infantry, known as the 'Rileys,' faced a very different situation. Lt.-Col. Whitaker had been wounded, and John Rockingham, the former CO, who was in England attending a staff course, had been hastily recalled to take command. The Rileys were the only 2nd Division battalion not committed to action in Atlantic and were at full strength for Spring. Their objective,

Verrières village, nestled below the crest of a ridge less than 1,000 yards away across level ground. Verrières marked the boundary between 1st SS Panzer Division and 272nd Division and was held by elements of a Panzer Grenadier battalion with both tanks and assault guns in reserve.[35] If the Rileys could take the village, the enemy would have to come at them over the top of the ridge, exposed to antitank guns and observed artillery fire.

Rockingham arranged to study the battlefield from an artillery observation aircraft [36] and concluded that the key problem was control of the start line, which was currently in enemy hands. He asked to be given the task of securing it, but his request was refused. The FMRs, who were based at Beauvoir Farm, were to capture Troteval Farm before midnight on 24 July.[37] The FMRs had not yet been reinforced and were using 'cooks and drivers' to help hold the area around Beauvoir Farm. For the night attack on Troteval, Maj. Dextrase 'handpicked a company of 75 all ranks' and used the assigned tank squadron to cover both flanks from positions to the rear. Medium artillery was to fire on the objective and then lift to Verrières and Tilly. Dextrase got his men to advance within seventy-five yards of the farm while it was being shelled, and cleared the buildings in fifteen minutes.[38]

The FMR platoons then tried to clear the road beyond, but enemy firing from close range prevented the scout platoon of the Rileys – which had gone forward with the FMRs – from taping the start line.[39] Rockingham organized two platoons from his reserve company into tank-hunting parties and sent them forward. The PIAT teams reported direct hits on enemy Panthers, which 'if they did not knock them out ... at least scared them off.' The start line was secure.[40]

All of this had taken time, and the attack was postponed to 0400. Rockingham stuck to his plan to advance three companies up to obtain the widest possible frontage. The right flank company was 'pinned by the intense fire,' and only one platoon made it to the first objective, the hedgerow three hundred yards north of the village.[41] Despite the darkness, confusion, and losses, which left the platoon with just nine men, they were able to clear their section of the hedgerow, merge with the reserve platoon, and send two groups, each under the command of a corporal, forward into the village.[42]

Baker Company in the centre had a far easier time. With both flanks protected the men reached the hedgerow, overwhelmed the defenders, and began to clear the houses east of the crossroads. On the left, close to the Caen–Falaise highway, enemy tanks poured fire on Dog Company, killing the CO, Maj. G. Stinson, and all his NCOs. As dawn broke, the attached troop from 2nd Anti-Tank Regiment, which had come forward to positions near Troteval Farm, engaged the German armour silhouetted on the high ground east of Verrières. That armour was well within the killing range of 17-pounders, and four Panzers were destroyed in a matter of minutes. The first counterattacks began before the Rileys could consolidate. Enemy tanks entered the village, destroying two of the battalion's 6-pounder guns, 'but the tanks were beaten off by infantry with PIATS, grenades and smoke.' Rockingham was everywhere, inspiring the defenders. He brought his reserve company and carrier platoon up to the hedgerow to provide all-around defence and a mobile reserve. By 0750, Rockingham was confident the battalion was 'firm,' and he sent, on this day of Shakespearian code words, the message 'Gratiano.'[43]

East of the Caen–Falaise road, 3rd Division's 9th Brigade was carrying out its part in Spring. Neither Brig. Cunningham nor his battalion commanders could change any part of the plan, and Lt.-Col. Charles Petch's plea to be allowed to attack at first light was refused. In a post-war interview, Cunningham insisted that he was not pessimistic before Spring[44] began, but the challenges confronting his brigade might well have made him so. The first task, securing the village of Tilly-la-Campagne, looked difficult enough. Tilly, a small cluster of houses and farms, is located at the 70 metre contour, fully 20 metres higher than Bourguebus, which was the proposed start line. The thousand yards separating the villages consisted of cultivated fields with little cover or dead ground, and the advance would be countered by fire from the left flank, which like the village was strongly held by 1st SS Panzer Division. If the North Nova Scotia Highlanders secured Tilly, Phase II, which required the Highland Light Infantry to push through to Garcelles, would expose the brigade's left flank to the enemy.

Col. Petch knew how difficult command and control would be at night, so he established four 'check lines' and ordered his assault companies to report as they reached each one. At first, Petch and the command group at Bourguebus feared the worst. The half-hour delay in the RHLI attack meant that both flanks were exposed, and when the searchlights flickered on they seemed to silhouette the North Novas. Despite these problems, the lead companies crossed all four check lines in good time. Charlie Company, to the right of the road, moved swiftly to its first objective on the north edge of Tilly. Dog Company, in the centre, stumbled onto the enemy's forward slit trenches, setting off a wild melee that ended with the Canadians in control and able to move on to the village. Baker Company had been assigned the ambitious task of bypassing Tilly to secure a small woods to the southeast. It ran into heavy opposition and went to ground. Between 0430 and 0500, Petch heard Charlie Company report that it was on its objective and learned that Dog Company had fired a success signal with Very lights. Petch immediately ordered his reserve company to move to the west of Tilly to complete the encirclement of the village. Petch then reported 'Hamlet Able' to brigade – code words that indicated his men had reached the objective. Half an hour later, Petch sent 'Hamlet Baker,' meaning the North Novas were on the objective and 'mopping up.'[45] As the eastern sky lightened, the enemy began to counterattack, and gradually it became clear that the situation was less promising than it had first seemed. The battalion was pinned down, and Dog Company had been overrun. Petch called for tank support, and a squadron of the Fort Garrys, waiting to assist the HLI in Phase II, were sent forward to help the North Novas consolidate.[46] It was now 0730. Back at brigade, division, and corps headquarters, decisions about Phase II had to be made.

The corps commander had established his command post next to 3rd Division headquarters in Vaucelles, and remained there until 0630, when he left for 7th Armoured Division. Simonds had acquired and fitted out a Staghound armoured car as a command vehicle, so that he was constantly in touch. The conference with Generals Erskine, Adair, and Keller began at 0700.[47] No record of what was said at this conference exists. What we do know is that on the basis of the information available at 0730, Simonds ordered Erskine to begin Phase II, advancing his leading armoured squadrons between Verrières and St-Martin while the Royal Regiment of Canada and a squadron of First Hussars tanks attacked to the east of Verrières village. Simonds also suggested that Keller employ 9th Brigade's reserve battalion, the Glens, to assist the North Novas in Tilly. He then left for 2nd Division's headquarters in Fleury-sur-Orne to be briefed on the reasons for the delay in beginning 5th Brigade's part in Phase II.

The situation at 0830 was still obscure. A message received by corps at 0715 stated that progress was 'slow but steady' on the 5th Brigade front.[48] This was presumably the result of the advance of the Calgary's Charlie Company, which reported progress in clearing the houses on both sides of the road into May-sur-Orne.[49] There was no news from the Black Watch, who despite orders from division and brigade to 'get on immediately' were still in their assembly area.[50] If Simonds had gone forward to see the situation in St-Martin first-hand, there is little doubt that he would have done precisely what Foulkes and Megill were doing – demanding that the Black Watch get going so that 4th Brigade's attack and the advance of 7th Armoured would be supported. Simonds believed, not unreasonably, that his corps was on the verge of securing Verrières Ridge, and his orders reflect this.

The Black Watch left their positions south of Ifs at 0330 and moved in a long column along the road to St-Martin.[51] When the lead company turned south into the village shortly before 0500, it came under fire from 'weapon slits outside the walls and hedges and dug-outs and scurry holes inside.' The artificial moonlight did nothing to help locate these positions. Just as it appeared that the situation was under control, an undetected enemy machine gun opened fire, killing Col. Cantlie and wounding two of his company commanders.[52]

Command of the battalion passed to the senior surviving officer present, twenty-six-year-old Maj. Phillip Griffin.[53] He faced a daunting task. It was obvious to Griffin that St-Martin was still controlled by the enemy. The battalion was strung out along the roads into the village far from the start-line in May-sur-Orne, where in a matter of minutes the barrage intended to lead them to Fontenay-le-Marmion would begin. Griffin decided to clear up the resistance in St-Martin and make a new plan. He ordered the battalion to reassemble out of the line of observation and fire from the ridge. One of his fellow officers described Griffin as 'a brilliant officer of absolutely outstanding courage and ability ... So complete was his control and so well trained the battalion that this was done at once and in incredibly good order.'[54]

The first priority was to determine the situation in May. Since it was evident that the Calgary CO did not know what was happening Griffin sent his intelligence officer with a three-man patrol to the village around 0630. Lt. Duffield and his men walked up to the cross-roads in May and turned left toward the battalion start line, at which point they came under fire from a lone MG 42. They returned, un-scathed, to battalion headquarters without seeing any of the enemy or the Calgaries.[55] Griffin made contact with the officer commanding what was left of the Calgary's Dog Company, informing them that they were in St-Martin, not May. He asked Lt. Michon to clear out the factory area, but Michon told Griffin that the position was too strong for what was left of his company to clear without artillery support. Griffin then asked Michon to recce the Black Watch start line, the farm track running east from May-sur-Orne, but this task was also rejected.[56]

Time was passing and the brigade and divisional commanders were demanding action, but Griffin was not prepared to lead his men onto the ridge without proper support. He met with Maj. Walter Harris, the officer commanding the Hussar squadron, to explain what he wanted. The original plan had been based on the assumption that the Calgaries would be in control of May, allowing the Black Watch to form up on the edge of the village. Griffin now proposed to bypass both the 'fac-tory' and May, moving on a compass bearing directly over the ridge to the objective. The artillery fire plan would be a repetition of the one fired at 0530, beginning at the start line on the ridge. The Hussars, orig-inally slated to protect the battalion's left flank, were now to cover the right flank and help neutralize May.[57] Lt. Duffield would return to the village with a reinforced patrol to take out the machine gun post. Har-ris had already sent forward one troop of four tanks, and they had located Charlie Company of the Calgaries in the long hollow north of May. The troop then entered the village, but withdrew when one tank was lost at the main crossroads. The two troops in St-André were ordered 'to proceed in a south-easterly direction under the ridge towards the gap between May-sur-Orne and the high ground.'[58]

Brig. Megill learned of the timing of the Black Watch advance from the gunner's radio net and went forward to talk to Griffin. In a postwar interview, Megill recalled that Griffin was on the verandah of a house on the forward edge of St-Martin, looking out toward May. The battlefield was empty and strangely quiet as the young major calmly explained his new plans to the brigadier. Megill's recollection is that he thought it looked like a 'dicey proposition,' and suggested that the battalion should first secure May-sur-Orne. According to Megill, Griffin replied that they 'had patrols into May,' which he doubted was occupied on a continuous basis. Griffin felt sure that once the Black Watch attack went in, the Calgary Highlanders would 'fill in behind.'[59] The enemy had been eliminated from most of St-Martin but the 'factory' was still under German control, so Griffin was proposing to bypass two known centres of enemy resistance. This was the kind of aggressive action that senior commanders were always demanding of the infantry, and whatever doubts Megill had, he did not order Griffin to revise his plan.

The Black Watch began advancing on May-sur-Orne shortly after 0900, in a loose box formation. The Hussars were delayed by the narrow, sunken roads. When the tanks passed the factory area, the infantry was ahead of them moving through the fields onto the first level of the ridge. Both tanks and infantry came under torrents of fire. The village and the ridge were defended strongly by a battalion of 272nd Division, which had been reinforced by a battlegroup from 2nd Panzer Division. Battlegroup 'Sterz,' with a dozen Panthers and a company of Jagdpanzer IVs, hit the Black Watch and Hussars as they appeared over the crest of the ridge.[60] The Hussars lost six tanks before they reached the gap at the edge of the village.[61] The Black Watch lost virtually everyone; many were killed before the start line was reached.

Capt. John Taylor, who was wounded that day, described what happened in a letter he wrote three weeks later: 'From the start we had trouble from very heavy machine-gunning from the flanks as well as mortar and artillery fire. [The men] were as steady as a rock and we kept going ... We overran two strongpoints then I got hit.'[62] Another survivor reported that Capt. John Kemp, commanding D Company, urged Griffin to call off the attack; Griffin had replied that orders were 'to attack and that the battalion would carry on.' Those who made it to the crest of the ridge, including Griffin, ran into a German battlegroup preparing to counterattack and were doomed. Before he was killed, Griffin told the men around him to get back any way they could.[63] Not more than fifteen men from the forward companies were able to do so. Black Watch casualties in this action totaled 307, including 118 killed in action and 83 taken prisoner.[64] As the official historian noted: 'Except for the Dieppe operation there is no other instance in the Second World War when a Canadian battalion had so many casualties in a single day.'[65] It was just like the worst moments on a First World War battlefield.

The tragedy that befell the Black Watch soon became the subject of a bitter controversy that continues to this day. Some of those who survived the action were quick to blame Megill; others focused their anger on Foulkes and Simonds. In 1990 the Canadian Broadcasting Corporation revived the issue when it broadcast a 'docu-drama' that claimed to tell the hidden truth about the battle.[66] The negative reaction of veterans and research historians renewed the debate, but apart from some additional survivor memories, no new information has been uncovered.

With hindsight, everyone agrees that the Black Watch should have concentrated on securing St-Martin and May-sur-Orne. Had they succeeded in gaining and holding these villages, the entire operation would be remembered in a different light and the sacrifices made would seem far more justified. If Megill's recollections are accurate, then his failure to intervene was one of the most unfortunate decisions made during the battle. But are hindsight and recollections offered forty-five years after the events useful historical tools? All we really know from the contemporary sources is that every decision maker, including Griffin, was committed to carrying out the second phase of Spring as soon as possible. At 0830 the operation had been underway for just five hours and still seemed full of possibilities.

After the battle a great deal of attention was paid to the underground tunnels and air shafts of the iron mines in the area. Yet the mine at St-Martin was not connected to the more extensive workings on the ridge. It is possible that elements of the battalion of the 272nd Division that occupied St-Martin used the upper parts of the mine shaft for cover during bombardments, but the plain fact is that neither the Camerons nor the Calgaries ever occupied the area, so no complex explanation of continued resistance from the 'factory' is required.[67]

Immediately to the east of the Black Watch, and almost in sight, the 4th County of London Yeomanry (Sharpshooters) had begun a cautious advance across the St-Martin–Beauvoir road to Pt 72. On their left, the 1st Royal Tank Regiment followed a parallel route just to the west of Verrières village. The division's three infantry battalions of the Queen's Own Royal Regiment followed them into positions south of Ifs.[68] The Sharpshooters claimed five enemy tanks and SPs destroyed 'with the aid of a Typhoon cab rank,' but this success did not persuade them to continue forward on the ridge in the face of accurate enemy fire. The 1st Royal Tank Regiment also claimed some enemy tanks, but its own considerable losses stopped any movement farther onto the ridge.[69] The lead squadrons of 7th Armoured had been told to move cautiously by their division commander, now within days of being replaced because 'he will not fight his division.'[70] General Erksine was convinced that the ground and the enormous superiority of German weapons made armoured attacks futile. He had no wish to emulate the 'Death Ride' of 11th Armoured in Goodwood.[71]

The Rileys, still firm in Verrières, could not see 7th Armoured's hesitant advance, but they watched in amazement as the Royal Regiment of Canada disappeared over the crest of the ridge toward Rocquancourt. Lt.-Col. Anderson tied in the Royals' attack with C Squadron of the Hussars, who were to protect the battalion's left flank. Anderson did not employ a barrage, relying instead on 4th Field Regiment's FOOs to call down fire as required. The Royals attacked two up, but it appears that only one company continued forward after the Hussar squadron was destroyed on the crest of the ridge by the tanks and antitank guns of 1st SS Panzer Regiment.[72] Maj. Marks, who commanded C Squadron of the Hussars, lost fifteen of his eighteen tanks while claiming eight enemy kills.[73] The Royals reported 19 killed, 71 wounded, and 7 taken prisoner in an advance that was checked just five hundred yards beyond Verrières. The battalion then dug in between the village and the Caen–Falaise highway, suffering further heavy casualties. The Royals were almost up to strength on 25 July, but three days later they required 254 replacements.[74]

The situation in Tilly-la-Campagne was even more desperate. By 0800 Petch had radio contact with just one of his four companies and could only use artillery on targets distant from the areas where the companies might be. A number of men crawled like 'snakes on the ground' back through the wheat with reports of dug-in tanks, machine gun posts, and camouflaged strongpoints.[75] Keller waited until mid-morning before deciding to order Brig. Cunningham to use his reserve battalion to assist the North Novas in Tilly. He kept the HLI in place for the planned advance to Garcelles. The warning order reached the Glens at 1125. Lt. Reg Dixon, the intelligence officer, who kept the War Diary, described the news as 'a mental blow felt by all ranks.' Both officers and men were 'looking worn out and very weary.' Dixon noted, 'Even Jerry with his lack of divisions and manpower has withdrawn divisions for rest and refit.' So had the British.[76]

Between 1125 and 1600, an extraordinary drama unfolded at brigade headquarters. The Glens' CO, Lt.-Col. Christiansen, went forward to the North Novas' command post at Bourguebus to see the situation at first hand. Cunningham was already there with Petch, and the three men discussed the situation. Petch was unwilling to send his reserve, made up of men who had made it back from Tilly, into the killing zone, and Christiansen flatly refused to order his battalion to undertake what he considered a hopeless action.[77] Cunningham returned to his tactical headquarters and informed Keller that there was no point in reinforcing failure at Tilly. Keller had just come from a conference with Simonds with instructions to hold Tilly in preparation for a renewed offensive. Relations between the two men had been strained since the dispute over the 'delayed' advance into Caen, and Keller told Cunningham that he would lose his job if he didn't obey. Cunningham replied, 'I understand that, sir,' but he stuck to his position.[78] At 1600 the Glens were told to stand down. There would be no daylight attack on Tilly.

It is not clear exactly when Keller informed Simonds of 9th Brigade's revolt. At 1730, Simonds ordered a renewed assault on Rocquancourt and May-sur-Orne; Tilly-la-Campagne was to be made 'firm' during the night. Simonds also indicated that Fontenay-le-Marmion – the original Black Watch objective – was to be attacked at first light.[79] Foulkes seemed ready to carry out these orders, which he outlined at an O Group at 1800, ordering the only available reserve battalion to capture May-sur-Orne.[80]

The Maisoneuves advanced, two companies up, along the west side of the road to May, with one company assigned to clear out the woods along the river. The barrage and the smoke for the right flank did little good; fire from the ridge and the 'factory' area forced the Maisoneuves to dig in in the small, diagonal wood opposite the 'factory.' Megill, without consulting Foulkes, ordered the Maisoneuves back to St-André to hold the original start line against mounting enemy pressure.[81]

Operation Spring ended in the evening of the 25th as the revolt against Simonds's orders spread. Brig. Young, whose 6th Brigade was supposed to capture Fontenay, concluded that further attacks were futile 'until the west bank of the Orne had been cleared,' due to the intensity of the mortar and artillery fire, 'which the enemy could bring down on the area of the objective.' He returned to divisional headquarters at 2000, 'and especially on learning' that the Maisies had made little progress, informed Foulkes that the proposed attack 'stood little chance of success.'[82] Foulkes agreed with Young and went to see the corps commander 'to tell him that I had no intention to continue the battle as I had nothing left to fight with.'[83]

Simonds in turn saw the army commander that evening and told him 'it was no use to press the attack any further.'[84] The corps had suffered more than 1,500 casualties, about 450 of them fatal. Even the Rileys, who had won the one great victory of the day, recorded 200 casualties, including 53 men killed in action. For the North Novas with 432 casualties and the Black Watch with 307, the second battle for Verrières Ridge meant that the combat elements of both battalions would have to be completely rebuilt.[85]

Dietrich's 1st SS Panzer Corps had dealt a severe blow to the Canadians. By the morning of 26 July the 'former battle line' had been restored except at Verrières village, where the Rileys, the artillery, and 2nd Anti-Tank Regiment were holding firm. Initially Dietrich thought he could recover this position as well, and ordered 9th SS to counterattack with all available strength. This time it was the Rileys and the Canadian anti-tank guns that exploited the advantages of the terrain. Verrières village is tucked under the crest of the ridge, and the enemy armour was easy to target and destroy. The 9th SS battlegroup commander reported that he had run into a 'pak front' and warned that 'whoever crosses this ridge is a dead man.' The division had greater success to the west, where it regained control of St-Martin-de-Fontenay.[86]

While this counterattack was underway, Eberbach proposed launching a much larger operation to destroy the Allied forces south of the

Orne. However, von Kluge, with his eye on Operation Cobra, rejected the proposal. He instead ordered 9th SS to defend its position and allow the badly battered 272nd Division to withdraw to the relative quiet of the sector opposite 1 British Corps. Von Kluge was convinced that Spring was 'not the anticipated major attack ... because the enemy air arm has not yet appeared in sizeable dimension.'[87]

The 2 Canadian Corps Intelligence Summary for 25 July, issued at 2000 hours, reported: 'Our attack was stopped by the enemy disposed along the high ground.' Maj. W.H. Broughall, who signed the report for Brig. Rodger, the Chief of Staff, noted: 'The topography ... along the line of our advance is ideally suited to the defensive tactics adopted by the enemy. With dug-in tanks and antitank guns in positions well sited for a good field of fire he was able to repel our attack with a relatively small amount of infantry in the line.' The report also attempted to explain Simonds's persistence that day: 'It was thought that ... the main German defensive line would have been further back.' Instead, the enemy's shortage of infantry – 'not more than 1000' – across the front forced him to employ some eighty to one hundred tanks in support of 'a strong antitank line formed by dug-in tanks and SP guns.' The enemy, the report concluded, 'has found he can hold the open, gently sloping ground of Normandy with strong forces of armour and comparatively little infantry.'[88]

The battles for Verrières Ridge would soon be rationalized as having greatly assisted the American breakout from St-Lo. But in the immediate aftermath of what looked like a week of disasters, the senior officers of 2 Canadian Corps were forced to think about the events differently. Simonds met with both Montgomery and Dempsey to discuss Spring and then talked with his two divisional commanders.[89] The British generals must have had some reservations about Simonds's conduct of the battle, especially his persistence in continuing daylight attacks – attacks which, like Canadian operations on the last day of Goodwood, had been marked by heavy casualties to infantry battalions. Infantry was a terribly scarce resource in 21 Army Group, and it seems unlikely that Montgomery or Dempsey would have permitted a British general to press such costly operations in the way the Canadians had.[90]

For Simonds, Spring was not a failure of command but a demonstration of the inadequacies of individual Canadian officers and units. Brig. D.G. Cunningham and the commanding officers of two of his battalions were fired for refusing to press the attack against Tilly.[91] Keller was retained in command, perhaps because he had followed orders and demanded that Cunningham mount a new attack. Maj.-Gen. Foulkes was also left in command. Foulkes had functioned as little more than an observer during the first week of battle. He had received an outline plan from corps headquarters and passed it on to his brigadiers without reference to their circumstances. Communications with the assault troops and even with brigade headquarters had been poor throughout the battles, yet Foulkes had not gone forward to learn what was happening. Much can be blamed on the fog of war, but a divisional commander ought to be more than a conduit for orders from higher formations. Foulkes confined his interventions to orders to 'get going.'

The 2nd Division's brigadiers has also failed to play a decisive role in the battles of July. Brig. H.A. Young, commanding 6th Brigade, ignored the problems the Camerons were having in St-André, insisting that the start line for Spring was secure. He did not go forward to determine the situation for himself and does not seem to have grasped how difficult it would be to stage a night attack in these circumstances. Brig. Megill, who has been much criticized for his role in Spring, did go forward repeatedly and did attempt to learn all he could about the actual situation. Megill had been appalled by the plan for Spring, which seemed to have been prepared by someone who could not read a contour map and had never seen the ground.[92] Verrières Ridge, he believed, ought to have been cleared from east to west, not by uphill attacks overlooked from three sides. Megill had discussed this with Foulkes. After a 7th Armoured Division liason officer suggested that his men did not seriously believe their part in Phase II of Spring was possible, Megill returned to Foulkes's headquarters, where he sought assurances that the brigade's left flank would be protected by a vigorous British thrust. Foulkes told him that 7th Armoured would go all-out on the morning of 25 July, and Megill had to accept this assurance.[93]

As the operation began and his worst fears were being confirmed on an hourly basis, Megill could not bring himself to intervene. When Foulkes ordered the Calgaries to press their attack and told the Black

Watch that speed was essential, Megill simply passed the orders on. When he learned over the gunners' net that Griffin had arranged an attack for 0930, he went to see the Black Watch commander but did not overrule his decision.

Later that day, Megill learned that Foulkes was going to renew the attack on May, using the Maisoneuves and leaving them under 6th Brigade command. Foulkes and Young arrived at 5th Brigade headquarters to organize this venture. Foulkes began the discussion by reporting that Simonds was 'furious at the failure which had occurred.'[94] Megill protested the decision to order the Maisonneuves into battle, and a shouting match erupted, with Foulkes demanding to know whether Megill was challenging his orders. The result of all this was not, however, to cancel an ill-conceived plan, but rather to conduct it under the control of 5th Brigade.

In a 1988 interview, Megill offered this explanation of his actions on 25 July:

> It was perfectly clear that the attack should have been called off at a very early stage in the morning. I suggested this not later than perhaps eight or nine o'clock. Instead the corps commander was pressing the divisional commander and he was pressing us to get on with an attack which we knew was almost hopeless. Under these circumstances one does not quit. You do as much as you possibly can and hope that someone will see the light and give you some relief.[95]

If Phillip Griffin had lived, he would no doubt have offered a similar explanation.

Why did Simonds fail to 'see the light'? The message logs suggest that he made the decision to go ahead with the infantry's part in Phase II on the basis of reports that the North Novas and Fort Garry Horse were pressing a new attack on Tilly, the knowledge that the RHLI had captured Verrières, and the information that the Calgaries had troops in or near May. He seems to have used this fragmentary evidence as grounds for launching Phase II. He was wrong, but this was not an unreasonable decision, given what he knew at the time.

It is possible to understand Simonds's decisions in Operation Spring. But it is also clear that his plan was flawed and that he was unable to read the battle correctly once it got underway. It is equally clear that Simonds recognized these problems and got to work on a plan that would break the enemy's hold on Verrières Ridge. Operation Totalize would demonstrate that Simonds could learn and grow as a corps commander.

8

Falaise

Field Marshal von Kluge's fixation on the threat of an Anglo-Canadian offensive toward Falaise was based on the certainty that a breakthrough east of the Orne would trap all of the German forces in Normandy, whereas an offensive in the west might be contained by a staged withdrawal. When on 26 July it became evident that the Americans were on the verge of a breakthrough, Hitler agreed to von Kluge's request to allow 7th Army to withdraw in the sector west of the River Vire. Both von Kluge and Hausser apparently thought this would allow the battered 7th Army to create a new defensive line.[1]

By morning of 27 July the scale of the crisis was becoming evident. Von Kluge ordered 2nd Panzer Division and the headquarters staff of 47th Panzer Corps to move to the support of 7th Army. By midafternoon, 21st Panzer had been ordered to join 2nd SS Panzer Corps west of the Orne, though this move would not be carried out until 28 July, the same day that 116th Panzer Division was transferred to 7th Army.[2] Three vital days had been lost as the American breakthrough turned into a breakout.

While von Kluge hesitated, Montgomery decided on a course of action that was to have profound consequences for the balance of the Normandy campaign. He cancelled 12th Corps' offensive west of the Orne, scheduled for 28 July, as well as the attack by O'Connor's 8th Corps 'down the Falaise road.' Instead, the bulk of the 2nd British Army was shifted to the west to mount Operation Bluecoat on the American flank. Montgomery was convinced that the Germans would respond rationally to the American breakthrough, swinging back to the east while holding the hinge positions on either side of the Orne. In his directive of 27 July he insisted that 'anything we do elsewhere must have the underlying objective of furthering the operations of the American forces to the west of St. Lo and thus speeding up the capture of the whole of the Cherbourg and Brittany peninsulas; it is ports that we require and quickly.'

Operation Bluecoat was to begin 'at the earliest possible moment.' In the meantime the left wing of the Second British Army and all of the First Canadian Army were to press attacks 'to the greatest degree possible with the resources available.' The enemy must, Montgomery insisted, be worried and shot up and attacked and raided, whenever and wherever possible, so that ground could be gained and the Germans prevented 'from transferring forces across to the western flank to oppose the American advance.'[3] Montgomery's directive of 27 July was a major strategic blunder, perhaps the worst of his career. It does not require hindsight, or foreknowledge of Hitler's decision to stage a major counterattack at Mortain, to recognize that Montgomery was shifting resources away from the decisive ground south of Caen at precisely the moment when the enemy was thinning out his defences.

Montgomery's failure to anticipate the German reaction to Cobra was only the beginning of the problems his actions created. The ground south of Caumont, where 'Bluecoat' was to take place, consisted of some of the worst bocage country, as well as a series of ridges, including Mont Pinçon, the highest point in Normandy. Beyond Mont Pinçon the terrain was so hilly and wooded that it is known to this day as la Suisse Normande. There were few roads and even fewer going in the right direction. All of this was well known to staff officers in both the British and German armies, which is why the Caumont front had been inactive since early June.[4]

While the final preparations for Bluecoat were underway, Montgomery met with Harry Crerar to explain his intentions and urge the Canadian army commander to keep up the pressure in the Caen area. Though 'no large scale-effort was required immediately,'[5] Crerar promptly issued orders requiring Simonds to 'draw up plans for an actual attack, axis Caen–Falaise.' Crerar thought such an attack would be ordered if Bluecoat proved successful – that is, if the British reached the line Flers–Conde-sur-Noireau or the Germans began to withdraw on the Caen front. The 3rd British and 51st Highland divisions were drawn into reserve, ready to reinforce Bluecoat or participate in the advance to Falaise. Less than twenty-four hours later, Montgomery ordered 3rd British Division and its armoured brigade to provide O'Connor's 8th Corps with additional infantry.[6] This left the First Canadian Army with three combat-hardened but battle-weary infantry divisions, two armoured brigades, a woefully understrength 6th Airborne Division, and the recently arrived 4th Canadian Armoured Division. Pressure from the senior medical officer of the 3rd Canadian Division, who insisted that 'seven weeks of continuous over the top type fighting' without any break seriously threatened the 'fighting efficiency' of his division, led Crerar to withdraw it for a week's rest,[7] so

4th Division's infantry was needed to hold the ground east of the Caen–Falaise road. The best that Crerar could do in these circumstances was order 1st British Corps, 'by positive attack and deception to persuade the enemy that an advance toward Vimont was in preparation.' Similar efforts to suggest that 2 Canadian Corps was preparing an immediate offensive toward Falaise were ordered.[8]

Simonds met with his divisional and brigade commanders on 30 July, and outlined plans to implement these orders by mounting small-scale operations that would allow the newly arrived 4th Canadian Armoured Division to get 'the feel of things,' and that would also secure vital ground for a future attack toward Falaise. Simonds used this conference to explain his ideas as well as his intentions. He noted that casualties had averaged one hundred men a day since the end of Spring and that if 'we were to sit without further action for 20 days, our casualties would amount to more than would normally be sustained by the Corps in a stiff battle.' He recognized that the battalions were 'wearied by incessant fighting,' but he was 'determined that our existing situation however irksome or discouraging must be exploited no matter how tired the troops might be.'[9] That evening the Essex Scottish captured a farm complex just west of Tilly-la-Campagne, and the next day battalions from the 2nd and 4th divisions launched a costly and fruitless attack on the village. With two Panzer divisions still defending the ridge, such limited attacks were unlikely to succeed,[10] but it is evident that the German commanders were impressed by these probing attacks and by other signs of a 'pronounced build up east of the Orne.'[11] When Bluecoat got underway on 30 July, Panzer Group West waited more than twelve hours before deciding this was a major operation requiring the commitment of 21st Panzer Division, the only available reserve.[12]

That night, 31 July, Hitler presided at a conference to consider an overall strategy for the Western Front. He still believed that a second landing in the Pas de Calais was possible, but the deteriorating situation in Normandy demanded immediate action. The possibility of a staged withdrawal to the Seine was dismissed, as the river line could not be held with the available troops. Hitler ordered the construction of a new defensive line based on the River Somme, but insisted that the commanders at the front were to concentrate on stopping the Allied breakout. Four divisions, including two from 15th Army, were on their way to Normandy, but more would be needed if a new front was to be established.[13]

As the Caumont offensive gained momentum, von Kluge ordered 9th SS Panzer Division west to join the rest of 2nd SS Panzer Corps in blocking the British advance. By 1 August there were four Panzer divisions on the American front, three facing the British, and just two (1st SS and 12th SS) left east of the Orne. This situation cried out for a major attack in the Caen sector to cut off the Germans west of the Orne, but both Montgomery and Eisenhower were still obsessed with Brittany.[14] Fortunately for the Allies, Hitler intervened, ordering von Kluge to cut off Patton's Third Army at Avranches. This decision ended any possibility of re-establishing a new and continuous main line of resistance; it also doomed the German armies in Normandy to destruction no matter what strategy the Allies pursued.

Montgomery's concept of future operations began to change on 4 August, when he issued a new directive that placed less emphasis on Brittany. 'The enemy front,' he declared, 'is now in such a state that it could be made to disintegrate completely.' The First Canadian Army was ordered to join a general offensive 'to gain such ground in the direction of Falaise as will cut off the enemy now facing 2nd Army.' With the Americans advancing to Alençon, British 8th Corps to Argentan, and 30th Corps to Thury-Harcourt, with 12th Corps clearing the west bank of the Orne, the Canadians were to help 'force the enemy back across the Seine' by a carefully staged advance toward Falaise.[15]

Simonds had begun studying the problems of mounting such an operation on 29 July. The lessons learned in Operation Spring were very much on his mind, and in his first 'Appreciation' he outlined new ideas for overcoming the German defences. 'The ground' he noted,

> is ideally suited to the full exploitation by the enemy of the characteristics of his weapons. It is open, giving little cover to either infantry or tanks and the long range of his anti-tank guns and mortars, firing from carefully concealed positions, provides a very strong defence in depth. This defence will be most handicapped in bad visibility, smoke, fog or darkness, when the advantage of long range is minimized.[16]

Simonds decided on a night attack, as in Spring. But this time he proposed to use heavy bombers to neutralize the enemy defences and armour to get through the enemy gun screen in sufficient depth to disrupt the German defences. The tanks were to be accompanied by 'carrier born infantry,' which he proposed to mount in 'stripped Priests,' the self-propelled M7s, which 3rd Division had just traded in for the standard, towed 25-pounder guns.

When Simonds first described his intentions for Operation Totalize, he spoke of a breakthrough with Falaise as the objective.[17] His outline plan was far more cautious. The operation was to take place in three distinct phases. Phase I would be a night 'break-in' supported by heavy bombers, which would bring the 2nd Canadian and 51st Highland divisions through the first German defence line on Verrières Ridge. Phase II, a daylight attack on the next ridge line, Hautmesnil–St-Sylvain, was to be led by 4th Armoured Division with the 3rd in support. Simonds believed that a second massive strike by heavy bombers would be required, even though many of the enemy positions in the fallback zone, created on Rommel's orders, were currently unoccupied. Phase III would require the Polish Armoured Division, which was to join the corps on 5 August, to parallel 4th Division's advance to the high ground north of Falaise.[18]

This outline plan was based on accurate intelligence about enemy dispositions on 31 July. Simonds believed that with both 1st SS and 9th SS holding the forward defences, the main battle would be fought in Phase I, and that Phase II would involve dealing with counterattacks from 12th SS, which was in close reserve. Simonds was careful to integrate his plan with British operations on his flanks. Another attack on Verrières Ridge while the enemy held the high ground west of the Orne would have to be avoided. Totalize, he insisted, would only work if the 2nd British Army had secured or was close to securing a bridgehead across the Orne, 'thus loosening the enemy grip on his Northern pivot.'[19]

On 2 August, Simonds learned that 9th SS Panzer Division had withdrawn 'a sizeable battle group including tanks' from the Canadian front. The next day he received confirmation that Sepp Dietrich's Panzer Corps was now reduced to two Panzer divisions. By the morning of 5 August, evidence of further changes in the enemy order of battle,[20] and reports that 12th British Corps was about to cross the Orne, led

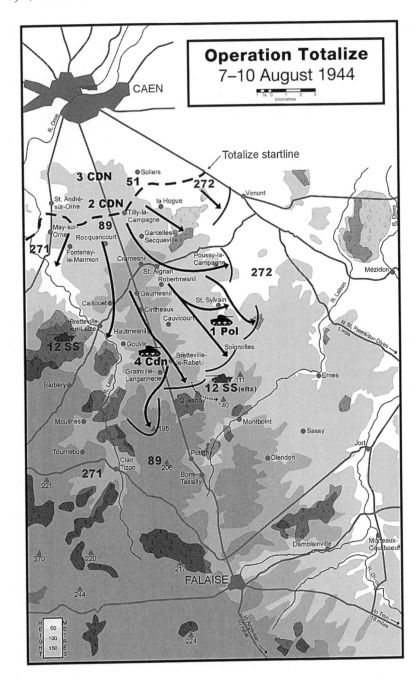

Simonds to order units holding the line to seize the villages on Verrières Ridge. Attacks on la Hogue, Tilly, and May-sur-Orne were repulsed with significant losses, demonstrating that the ridge was still strongly held. Prisoners of war, captured during the night, reported that a new infantry division, the 89th, was relieving 1st SS, which was said to be withdrawing to Bretteville-sur-Laize to form a mobile reserve.[21]

The next morning, Simonds decided to radically revise his plans for Totalize. He seems to have believed that 89th Division would be a much less formidable opponent than an SS Panzer division, and to have concluded that the major battle would occur at 'the Bretteville-sur-Laize position,' where 'tanks and infantry are most likely to be encountered.'[22] He now proposed to attack this area with both armoured divisions, and to require those divisions to continue south to their final objectives without pausing to reorganize.[23] It was this analysis that informed his decision to retain the use of heavy bombers in Phase II.

The significance of these changes would become fully apparent only after the battle had been joined, but Simonds and his commanders certainly knew that the choke point in the initial plan was the narrow gap between Cintheaux and Robertmesnil, a distance of less than 3 kilometres. In the original plan, 4th Division was to deploy on both sides of the Caen-Falaise highway; now it was restricted to the west side of the road, where the 'gap' of less than 1500 metres was dominated by the substantial stone-walled village of Cintheaux. The Poles, to the east, had slightly more room to manoeuvre, but the scattered woods south of Robertmesnil provided perfect cover for antitank guns and armour.

Simonds hoped that the bombing program arranged for Phase II, would neutralize the enemy defences. In a 1947 lecture to British officers studying Totalize on the ground in Normandy, Simonds recalled that he had originally planned to go through the 'very narrow gap' with one armoured division, but 'when it appeared that the layback position [Hautmesnil–St Sylvain] was held in greater strength' he decided 'in order to save time to launch the two divisions together with their tails organized behind them ready to fan out as they came through the gap.'[24]

Saving time seemed especially important on 6 August because the Allied commanders believed, in Montgomery's words, that 'the enemy was falling back, unwillingly, to some new line.' There was no indication yet of where the line might be, but 'he is definitely trying to pivot on the Caen area.' The enemy, Montgomery wrote, 'would be in an awkward situation ... if he lost his positions astride the Falaise road ... and if he lost Falaise itself.' Montgomery, influenced by the news that 12th Corps was across the Orne just north of Thury-Harcourt, assigned the capture of Falaise to the Second British Army and ordered the Canadians to attack toward Falaise. If possible, Falaise was to be secured and held until handed over to the Second Army. The Canadians were then to turn northeast and advance to the Seine on the axis Lisieux–Rouen.[25] That night, reports from Ultra of a major German offensive at Mortain were decrypted,[26] and for the first time Allied commanders began to think about encircling the German armies rather than pushing them back to the Seine. Operation Totalize was to be transformed from an attack designed to assist the Second British Army into the wing of vast pincer movement, but no new resources were allocated to carry out this much more ambitious task.

The changes were explained to divisional commanders at a conference called for 1000 on 6 August.[27] This left little time for proper briefing of subordinate officers. The War Diaries of the 4th Division brigades indicate that their revised role in Totalize was outlined on the morning of 7 August. The 10th Infantry Brigade, less the Algonquins, was told to advance on the right flank of the division, with the Argylls leading, supported by tanks of the South Alberta Regiment.[28] The armoured brigade was to move one regiment up until Cintheaux had been captured and there was room to fan out. Battalion commanders learned of their tasks later in the day, but O Groups for squadron and company commanders could not take place until marked maps were available from brigade. The Lake Superior Regiment – which was to provide the motorized infantry component of 'Halpenny Force' – Halpenny's own regiment, the Canadian Grenadier Guards, held their O Groups after 2200, when the noise of medium 'artillery' made it a trifle difficult for everyone to hear the details of their orders.[29]

For the corps and divisional staff officers, the greatest challenge posed by Totalize was traffic control. The Phase I divisions occupied a wide area north of the Verrières–Tilly line, and the two armoured divisions had to be kept out of the way. Both were, however, supposed to move forward by the morning of 8 August, with 3rd Division following the Poles across the Orne bridges.[30] So long as everything went smoothly, these moves could be made within the rigid timings laid down in the operational orders. But no one could remember the last time things had gone according to plan.

The most complex part of Totalize was the artillery fire plan developed under the supervision of Brig. Bruce Matthews, the Corps Commander Royal Artillery (CCRA). Operational Instruction No. 5, issued at 0900 on 7 August, outlined the tasks to be carried out by the divisional field regiments and the four Artillery Groups Royal Artillery (AGRAs) allotted to Totalize. There was to be no preliminary artillery program, so a great deal of attention was paid to counterbattery tasks scheduled for H+100 minutes, when the assault would be underway, and H+7 hours, when dawn would provide the enemy with visibility. The Service Corps was to ensure that 350 rounds per gun were dumped at medium gun positions and that up to 650 rounds per gun were available to the field regiments.[31]

The biggest challenge facing Matthews was how to support the armoured divisions in Phase II, scheduled to begin at 1400. The first requirement was for a list of targets for medium artillery concentrations, or 'concs on call.' This was the responsibility of each division, but on 7 August, Brig. J.D. Lane, 4th Division's CRA, was scrambling to revise his list while the Polish Armoured Division, with less than twenty-four hours, notice, was still creating its list.[32] Neither division had ever rehearsed a battle using medium artillery as the principal method of breaking enemy resistance,[33] and neither the target list nor the methods of using it received sufficient priority.[34] Another important task was to prepare to move the medium regiments forward if the armoured divisions broke through. Gun recce parties were attached to the headquarters of each division, and arrangements were made to increase the number of air observation flights. This would permit divisional field regiments as well as the AGRAs to have their own air observers.[35]

The soldiers waiting patiently on the east side of the highway were drawn from 51st Highland Division's 154th Brigade and 33rd British Armoured Brigade. Both formations had been fighting in the Normandy bridgehead since early June, but they had never worked

together. The Highland Division's experience had been especially difficult. Brought back to England for Overlord because of their hard-won
reputation in North Africa and Sicily, the Highlanders were committed
to defence of the Orne salient, where the abundant mosquitos were as
annoying – if less deadly – than enemy mortar fire. A static defensive
role, interrupted by ill-conceived orders to stage small-scale attacks on
limited objectives, had demoralized the men, and in late July Montgomery replaced their competent but uninspiring commander with an
authentic Highland hero.[36]

Maj.-Gen. T.G. Rennie had commanded both a battalion and a brigade in the 51st before being appointed to command the 3rd Division
for the invasion. Wounded in Normandy, his convalescence was cut
short, and he arrived at divisional headquarters with his arm still in a
sling. In Highland Division lore, the arrival of Rennie – which coin-
cided with the transfer to 2 Canadian Corps – was the turning point in
the division's experience in northwest Europe. Rennie inspired confidence, and Simonds, 'a man of imagination and ideas,' was a welcome
contrast to Crocker and the staff of 1st British Corps. The Highland
Division was rested, reinvigorated, and ready to roll.[37]

The same could not be said for the Canadians to the west of the highway. The 2nd Division had only been in action for three weeks, but in
that time it had suffered around two thousand casualties, including
more than five hundred men killed in action. Most of these losses had
been suffered by the rifle companies of the nine infantry battalions. On
7 August the division was still more than one thousand men understrength.[38] The 4th Brigade, selected to provide the infantry for the
armoured phalanx, was almost up to strength, but two of its battalions,
the Essex Scottish and Royal Regiment of Canada, had been virtually
rebuilt since late July. Each battalion had a new commanding officer,
and Brig. J.E. Ganong was the fourth officer to lead the brigade since 20
July. If the Canadian infantry performed effectively in Totalize, much
of the credit would have to go to the replacement system and the training of the young captains, lieutenants, and corporals who had been
promoted in the past weeks.

Brig. R.A. Wyman's 2nd Armoured Brigade had been in action
almost continuously since D-Day, but after Spring it was withdrawn
from its forward positions 'to a point about 1000 yards' behind the

infantry. Though the fields were subjected to 'intermittent shelling and mortar fire and to heavy air raids at night,' they were, by the standards of the past weeks, a rest area. There the brigade was visited by the Armoured Fighting Vehicle (Technical) Branch of the First Canadian Army, armed with questionnaires.[39]

The results of this inquiry into tank armour, gunnery, and overall design were summarized in a report completed on 2 August. The investigators were aware of the general criticisms of Allied tanks, which were by then being aired in the press and the British House of Commons, but they were taken aback by the depth of feeling they encountered in Normandy. All the units they visited complained that 'the Sherman is outgunned and out-armoured by the Germans.' Regiments were using the rest period 'to attach lengths of track over the front, back and sides' of their tanks. The technical team noted that this did not provide armour protection in the strict sense; however, when the track was lightly attached, it deflected enemy shot and functioned as 'spaced armour.' The Sherbrookes had experimented with every available type of extra armour, and reported that Maj. Radley-Walters's Sherman, covered in tank tracks, had survived two hits while accounting for twelve enemy armoured vehicles.[40]

Additional armour could be improvised, but little could be done to make the Sherman 75 mm gun an effective antitank weapon. All units had heard about discarding Sabot ammunition and hollow charge, but little had been supplied. The only real hope appeared to be the 17-pounder, though tank crews noted that the flash from the gun made observation at ranges under a 1,000 yards very difficult, and that the high explosive shell was ineffective. Some units saw two 17-pounder Shermans per troop as the best compromise, but there were not enough available to maintain the current ratio of one in four.[41] The armoured regiments would have to make do with what they had.

As darkness fell on the night of 7 August, a strange quiet descended on the battlefield. 'A waning full moon loomed large and red in the eastern sky,' and a ground mist carpeted the flat countryside.[42] Shortly before 2300 the drone of distant aircraft could be heard. Then the first wave of heavy bombers was overhead. Red smoke shells fired by the artillery identified the targets, and flares dropped by the master bombers marked the aiming points. A full-scale artillery barrage began, and the lead troops of the 51st Highlanders and 2nd Canadian Division began their move forward.

Simonds had orchestrated one of the most remarkable operations of the war. On both sides of the Caen–Falaise highway, hundreds of armoured vehicles, marshalled into columns, were advancing over the crest of the ridge. Each column, four vehicles abreast, was led by a gapping force composed of two troops of Shermans, two troops of mine-clearing flail tanks, and a troop of AVREs to mark the route with tapes and lights. Next came the assault force led by Sherman tanks, followed by elements of an infantry battalion riding in 'unfrocked priests' or universal carriers. Mortars, medium machine guns, self-propelled and towed antitank guns, bulldozers, and finally more tanks, known as the 'fortress force,' which were to guard the dispersal area and form a firm base, completed each phalanx.[43]

The enemy's situation on the eve of Totalize was little short of desperate. The long-predicted collapse of 7th Army was at hand, and Panzer Group West – now renamed 5th Panzer Army – could only hope to prolong the agony. Von Kluge's report for the week of 31 July to 7 August noted that a further two hundred officers, including three generals and twenty-one commanding officers, had been lost, while casualties in other ranks exceeded 20,000. Cumulative losses now totalled 148,075, and fewer than 20,000 replacements had reached Normandy.[44] The Mortain offensive was already in doubt. On the left flank of 7th Army's front,

> groups of men, mostly without officers or NCOs with them, are wandering aimlessly through the countryside in a general easterly or southeasterly direction ... They are mostly headed for Bagnoles and le Mans. Most of the struggling group are in a very bad condition ... Many are without headgear and belt and have worn out their boots ... The morale of these struggling forces is badly shaken.[45]

Hausser's Chief of Staff, who forwarded this report with the general's approval, noted that most of the stragglers were trying to find their units and that reception camps were being created to form the men into replacement units.

The situation east of Vire was somewhat better. Despite losses, the terrain of the Suisse Normande permitted small battlegroups to hold ground and even mount local counterattacks. The 2nd British Army's Intelligence Summary for 8 August described overall resistance as stubborn and noted the 'dogged refusal of 9th SS Panzer Division to surrender the village of Estry, or indeed any piece of ground in the whole of this sector.'[46] The bridgehead across the Orne, secured by 59th Staffordshire Division, was being subjected to heavy counterattacks, first by units of the 271st Division and then by one of the three battlegroups that now made up the offensive combat strength of 12th SS Panzer Division. Battlegroup Wünsche was composed of the remains of 26th Panzer Grenadier Regiment and three tank companies. Their counterattack, launched on the evening of 7 August, almost overran the bridgehead until the full power of the artillery of two British divisions broke the momentum of the attack.[47] German losses in this counterattack included twenty-four killed and ninety-one wounded, as well as nine Panthers.[48]

With Battlegroup Wünsche at the Orne and the rest of 12th SS assembling in obedience to Hitler's orders to join in a renewed attack on Avranches, the forces opposing the first phase of Totalize were effectively reduced to the 89th and 272nd Infantry Divisions. The 272nd covered the eastern flank, including la Hogue and the high ground at Secqueville; the 89th was responsible for the 8000 metres stretching west to the Orne. The 272nd was all too familiar with the attritional warfare waged by the Allies, but the 89th, which had trained in Norway before joining 15th Army in the Rouen area, had never been in action as a unit, though most of the officers and NCOs were veterans of the Eastern Front. Once established in France, General Heinrichs, an experienced infantry officer, supervised intensive training with emphasis on support weapons. The 89th was a 'pocket division' composed of two infantry regiments each of three battalions, but it also included a Fusilier battalion as a divisional reserve, a full-strength engineer battalion, an artillery regiment, and three antitank companies including one equipped with 88s.[49]

The 89th relieved 1st SS Panzer Division on the night of 6 August 'without exceptional difficulty.' The troops were told they were facing 'not particularly highly trained' Canadians, who were holding the line with armoured divisions behind them.[50] The 1055th Grenadier Regiment took over the carefully prepared positions at Tilly-la-Campagne and Rocquancourt, with one battalion in reserve at St-Aignan. The 1056th regiment deployed two battalions up around May and Fontenay, with a third battalion at Caillouet. Heinrichs placed his headquarters at a quarry near Bretteville-sur-Laize and established a secondary antitank gun screen 'level with the divisional command post.' The Fusilier battalion was positioned just east of Bretteville. Contact was established with the flanking formations, 1st SS Panzer Corps headquarters, and the mortar brigade stationed to the rear of the divisional sector. The Luftwaffe regiments of the Flak Corps, with their dual-purpose 88s, were much too grand to communicate with a mere division and operated independently throughout the battles of August. The same was true for Kurt Meyer and the 12th SS, which functioned as the corps reserve, with minimal contact with Heinrichs and his officers.[51] Previous accounts of Totalize, relying on Meyer's postwar interviews, have neglected the role of 89th Division and ignored the reality that the defence of the Caen sector was directed by Sepp Dietrich and the headquarters of 1st SS Panzer Corps. Dietrich had two infantry divisions, a mortar brigade, the corps artillery, and the Luftwaffe flak regiments, as well as 12th SS, under command.

Heinrichs and his regimental commanders had been briefed by their 1st SS counterparts to expect a major offensive at any moment. Nevertheless, the timing, weight, and character of the initial attack caught them by surprise, partly because of reports that bombs falling well to the north of their forward defence lines were courtesy of the Luftwaffe, not the RAF.[52] It is not clear why the 641 Lancasters and Halifaxes bombed so inaccurately that night, especially since the artillery must have marked such prominent targets accurately. Presumably, the coloured smoke drifted in the light breeze, misleading the master bombers. Concentrations around mean points of impact were excellent, but only one of the four main targets, the village of La Hogue, was squarely hit. At Sequeville, the mean point of impact was in open fields north of the village. Fontenay-le-Marmion was missed entirely, though the hamlet of Le Val, less than a kilometre away, was wiped out. May-sur-Orne received only a slight attack, with most of the 424 tons striking north of the village or in a good concentration at Bretteville-sur-Laize.[53]

The bombing that preceded the ground attack failed to have any serious impact on the enemy, but the dust raised by the explosions and the craters that pitted the landscape interfered with the progress of the attacking troops. When the armoured columns topped the crest of the ridge, airborne particles and ground mist and the dust thrown up by the vehicles limited visibility to a few feet. Slight detours, taken inadvertently or to avoid craters, led to so much confusion that only one of the four Canadian columns followed the assigned route east of Rocquancourt. All accounts of the first hours of Totalize describe a confused situation that almost, but never quite, collapsed into chaos. In the end, most of the isolated groups and single vehicles worked their way forward, overcoming or avoiding enemy fire.

By first light the RHLI and the Royals were close to their objectives. The Essex Scottish and 8th Recce Regiment column was delayed at Rocquancourt; neither regiment reached its dispersal area until noon. The Royal Regiment missed its dispersal area and at first light found itself northwest of Pt 122, the long-sought high ground that had been a Goodwood objective. According to the War Diary, 'the priests were driven right into an orchard without encountering any opposition.' By 0600 the battalion was dug in and ready to deal with counterattacks. The War Diary continues:

> At approximately 0830 the enemy counterattacked with tanks. Panther tanks moved up the Caen-Falaise highway. We were also fired on by tanks from the far side of Cramesnil. One Panther penetrated our positions and approached to within 70 yards of Bn H.Q. Heavy casualties both in personnel and vehicles were suffered by the platoon of MMGs attached to the battalion. Our 3" mortar platoon also suffered heavily losing four carriers complete with ammunition ... One of our SP A/TK guns was brewed and two of the Shermans supplying us were knocked out ... however the attack was beaten off with the loss of four tanks to the enemy and the capture of their officer who was wounded.[54]

This furious little battle had its counterparts all across the front as the Canadian and Scottish brigade groups encountered scattered 'penny packets' of 12th SS armour obeying their doctrinal imperatives and staging immediate, uncoordinated counterattacks. Such attacks could readily be dealt with. The real problem confronting Simonds was how to deploy his Phase II armoured divisions when their forming up places were under intermittent fire. The 89th Infantry Division was turning out to be a formidable opponent. Tilly-la-Campagne, Fontenay-le-Marmion, and May-sur-Orne were being aggressively defended, and there were other bypassed pockets of resistance. At 0800, when the army commander, General Eberbach, arrived at divisional headquarters, Heinrichs reported that 'the enemy attack had been held and the penetrations sealed off.'[55] His optimism was based on reports from his forward units, which were inflicting heavy casualties on the 6th Canadian and 152nd Highland brigades. The tenacious resistance of the 89th was greatly assisted by the almost complete failure of the heavy bomber attack, but the battalion defending May-sur-Orne, which was an artillery rather than a bomber target, also proved capable of holding its ground.

The 152nd Brigade initially assigned just one battalion to capture Tilly, but in the darkness the 2nd Seaforths were plunged into a nightmarish situation reminiscent of the North Novas' battle of 25 July. Brigade headquarters wanted the 5th Seaforths to join the attack, but their CO insisted that 'the situation was hopelessly confused and he would have to wait until daylight.' He did agree to send one company forward, but that was not enough to prevent the enemy from inflicting casualties and forcing a withdrawal. The next morning, as the Seaforths were teeing up a new assault, with full artillery support, a squadron of tanks borrowed from the forward brigade used the morning mist to enter the village, forcing the surviving enemy to surrender.[56]

The village of Rocquancourt, on the west side of the highway, was also targeted by the gunners rather than the heavy bombers. But here the South Saskatchewan Regiment, which had been completely rebuilt since its devastating losses on 20 July, leaned into the barrage and swept through the village, clearing houses and establishing a defensive perimeter almost as if on exercise. Much credit for the success of the South Sasks must go to Lt.-Col. F.A. Clift, who returned to the battalion to reorganize and retrain it; but it is also evident that the village was not as heavily fortified as Tilly.[57]

On the right flank, the Fusiliers Mont-Royal (FMRs) and the Camerons of Canada, were to advance without medium artillery support to occupy villages that were supposed to have been destroyed by Bomber Command. Instead, they met alert troops in undamaged fire positions. The FMR's first attack on May was quickly repulsed by mortar and artillery fire. A second attempt – this time intended to outflank the village – was equally unsuccessful, and May did not fall until late on the afternoon of 8 August, when four troops of flame-throwing Crocodiles accompanied the FMRs in a third attack that overwhelmed the forward defences and persuaded the rest to abandon the village.[58] This was the first time this weapon, which greatly multiplied the combat effectiveness of every battlegroup employing it, was committed to support 2nd Canadian Division.

The Camerons of Canada attacked Fontenay-le-Marmion with similar hopes that bombing had been effective, and faced similar disappointment. Darkness, mortar fire, minefields, and machine guns firing from the flanks on fixed lines meant that as few as 150 men made it to the edge of the village. With the CO a casualty, the brigade major was sent forward to reorganize the battalion, but he too was wounded in a direct hit on battalion headquarters. The best the Camerons could do was hold off counterattacks[59] and wait for help, which finally came in the form of a squadron of Hussars tanks and two companies of South Sasks sweeping west from Rocquancourt.[60] In these engagements, 6th Brigade suffered 54 killed and 153 wounded.

The prolonged resistance of the enemy's forward battalions delayed the deployment of the field artillery regiments, which found 'their potential positions being systematically shelled.'[61] The medium regiments would have to wait for the two armoured divisions to advance before they could move, and this was unlikely before late afternoon. The situation also had a significant impact on the armoured divisions, which had formed up in an area under intermittent fire. Maj. Ned Amy, who led the vanguard squadron of Halpenny Force, remembered the situation as thoroughly confused: 'The troops were launched into their first battle inadequately briefed and under chaotic circumstances.'[62]

The chaos was compounded by continued uncertainty about the bombing that was to precede the second phase. Simonds had always insisted that this was an essential part of the operation, believing that the enemy would hold the second defensive zone in strength. As late as 1150 on 8 August, Simonds was still trying to determine when the last bombs would fall. He was advised that the first wave would attack at 1226 and the last wave at 1335. Frantic calls produced the information that 'each wave is estimated to last 10 minutes.'[63] The exact H-Hour could now be calculated.

While Simonds was implementing Phase II of his complex plan, the commander of 12th SS Division was preparing a counterattack and organizing an ad hoc defensive position at Cintheaux. Meyer had ordered Battlegroup Wünsche to return to the Caen–Falaise road, and Eberbach agreed to release the Olboeter Group, which was with 9th SS Panzer Division. Until these reinforcements arrived, Meyer's only mobile reserve was Battlegroup Waldmüller, comprising a company of Tigers and forty-nine Mk IVs. As usual, Meyer did not hesitate. The Tigers were ordered to attack north along the highway, and the Panzer IVs to swing east to strike the Scottish battalions, advancing along the broad front between St-Aignan and Secqueville.[64] The appearance of a target-marker B-17, heralding the second phase bombing, encouraged the enemy to move quickly beyond the target area, and this haste may account for the rapid destruction of the lead platoon of Tigers. SS Maj. Michael Wittman, the scourge of 7th Armoured Division at Villers Bocage, led his small force past Cintheaux directly into the field of fire of a troop of Northamptonshire Yeomanry, which included a carefully hidden Firefly. Within seven minutes, Wittman was dead and three tanks were burning. The vaunted power of the Tiger was no proof against a 17-pounder at a range of less than a thousand yards.[65] The other Panzer counterattack force was no more successful at penetrating the Scottish positions, though it too was safe from the two groups of B-17s, which bombed Bretteville-sur-Laize and St-Sylvain 'with accuracy and good concentrations.'[66]

In a postwar interrogation report, Col. Hasso Neitzel, the senior staff officer of 89th Division, recalled the heavy casualties and losses in material caused by the bombing.

Wherever artillery and anti-aircraft positions were hit the guns were destroyed or at least hurled out of place by the pressure of the air. All moving parts were clogged up with sand so that the weapons were no longer usable ... Roads to the front had for the greater part been rendered useless by the deep bomb craters. This made transportation of munitions and the wounded exceptionally difficult ... The psychological effect ... was over-come in a relatively short time. Nevertheless the explosions, the near-hits and also the dust and sand ... dazed units and individual men, even when they were not actually within the effective radius of the falling bombs.[67]

The successful attack on the two villages was about all the U.S. 8th Air Force accomplished on 8 August. The aircraft attacking targets in the Hautmesnil–Gouix area were 'badly disorganized' by flak, and fewer than 250 of the 474 planes assigned to these targets delivered their bomb loads in the correct area.[68] Others bombed near Caen, and inflicted more than 350 casualties on Canadian and Polish troops in the rear areas.[69]

This much-discussed tragedy had no effect on the leading brigades of the armoured divisions, which were slowed by traffic congestion and by a renewal of enemy resistance in the Rocquancourt area.[70] Despite delays, the vanguards of both divisions crossed their start lines shortly after the bombing ended.[71] East of the highway, the Polish 10th Armoured Cavalry Regiment passed through the Scottish positions at St-Aignan, headed for the high ground north of the Laison River. They ran into the tanks of the Waldmüller group, including the remaining Tigers, which had taken up positions in the scattered woods around Robertmesnil. The German armour, as well as antitank guns situated north of St-Sylvain, destroyed forty Polish tanks before brigade head-quarters ordered a withdrawal and called for medium artillery concen-trations on the woods.[72]

The leading troops of 4th Canadian Armoured Division advanced south from Gaumesnil, which the Royals had occupied shortly after the bombing. The original plan called for 5th Brigade to protect their right flank by capturing Bretteville and Quilly, but the divisional artil-lery was still committed to 6th Brigade and no one had sufficient confi-dence in air power to attack without the guns.[73] The situation on the left flank, where the Polish armour was encountering devastating antitank fire, was equally uncertain. Much to the disgust of higher command, the Canadian Grenadier Guards and the Lake Superior Regiment (Halpenny Force) declined to press the frontal attack on Cintheaux after long-range antitank guns knocked out the lead tanks.

Today, visitors to the Canadian Military Cemetery north of Cintheaux find themselves in the middle of a battlefield that has changed little since 1944. Cintheaux and Gaumesnil are just a kilometre apart, and the wooded area to the east, which the Germans held on 8 August, is less than a kilometre from the road – easy killing range for German antitank guns. Lt.-Col. Halpenny wisely decided to outflank the enemy, crossing the railway line and circling around to the west. This manoeuvre took some time, but it allowed the Grenadier Guards to clear the orchard north of Cintheaux, destroying an 88 mm and three 20 mm guns. Lt. Phelan, with the rest of his troop providing covering fire, then accelerated across the open ground toward a hedgerow that 'was plastered with HE and co-ax by his troop sergeant and it was found to contain three 88s and one 20mm all of which were knocked out.' Phelan saw three self-propelled guns withdrawing, and hit one, which went up 'on impact with a tremendous flash.'[74]

While this brave action was underway, the Argyll and Sutherland Highlanders, working with a South Alberta squadron and the field artillery, teed up an attack on Cintheaux from the north and secured the village, meeting little resistance. Two Argyll companies then moved south toward the quarry at Hautmesnil, but with the sun low in the western sky, the lead company commander decided to wait until first light to clear the quarry.[75] This was the deepest penetration made by any formation on 8 August, and it marked the end of the first day of Totalize.

Simonds, who had been hoping for a breakthrough, was very unhappy with his armoured divisions, but from the enemy's perspective Totalize had ripped open prepared defences and forced Dietrich to try and organize a new position to block the advance to Falaise. The 271st Infantry Division was ordered to disengage with the British troops in the Orne bridgehead and take over positions from north of Thury-Harcourt to the River Laize.[76] The 89th Division, which had lost about half its combat troops, was to establish contact with the 271st at the Laize and hold the Urville–Bretteville-le-Rabet area. Heinrichs created an ad hoc unit out of his supply troops to reinforce the right flank, and co-ordinated his plans with elements of 12th SS.[77] To the east, the 272nd Division was responsible for the area St-Sylvain–Vimont.

Dietrich and Eberbach wanted these positions held until 85th Division, due to arrive in the next thirty-six hours, had dug in on a new defensive line to be created north of the Laison. Eberbach persuaded von Kluge to transfer two Panzer battlegroups, one of which deployed twelve Tigers, to reinforce Dietrich's corps.[78] While von Kluge juggled his forces, Simonds ordered his armoured divisions 'to press on by night aided by searchlights.'[79] The 3rd Rifle Brigade of the Polish Armoured Division began preparations for a night attack but did not continue forward after the hamlet of Robertmesnil and the nearby woods were cleared.[80] Halpenny Force, which was to seize Bretteville-le-Rabet, moved off at 0400, bypassed Hautmesnil, and was in position north of the objective at first light. The battle for the Bretteville-le-Rabet, which was the first sustained action carried out by the Lake Superior Regiment, lasted all morning and yielded over two hundred prisoners.[81] During the last phase of the action the Grenadier Guard tanks killed scores of the enemy by speculative shooting on houses and hedges, which flushed the enemy, who were then co-axed.[82]

The third night advance was carried out by a fresh battlegroup comprising the British Columbia and Algonquin Regiments under the command of Lt.-Col. Don Worthington of the BCRs. They were ordered to seize Pt 195, a hill just west of the main highway and north of Potigny. The plan, outlined to the officers at a brief O Group, called for the battlegroup to circle east around Bretteville-le-Rabet and cross the highway to reach Pt 195. The column 'moved slowly through waist-high wheat.' After breaking through enemy outposts between Bretteville and Cauvicourt it 'began to move more rapidly getting pretty well spread out and travelling generally south.'[83] By first light, 0530, Worthington and his command group were lost. They had become completely disoriented and mistook the east-west road from Estrees-la-Campagne for the north-south Caen–Falaise highway. At 0630 they moved to occupy the high ground near Pt 140, 5 kilometres east of Pt 195. There they reported that they were on their objective and would hold 'until our friends come forward to consolidate the position.'[84] Worthington deployed his force of tanks and two infantry companies in a rectangle with woods on two sides. By 0800 the enemy, fully aroused by this unexpected breakthrough onto ground that 85th Division was slated to occupy, had begun converging attacks, which in the course of the day overwhelmed the battlegroup, inflicting casualties estimated at 240 officers and men, including 79 taken prisoner.[85]

The battle on Hill 140, which the official historian described as 'a tragic mixture of gallantry and ineptitude,' raises a number of questions that have little to do with faulty navigation. The most obvious concerns the inability of the Polish Armoured Division to advance the 2 kilometres beyond the Bretteville-le-Rabet–St-Sylvain road to join the Canadians. Their advance, which did not begin until 1100, reached Cauvicourt at 1225. There, the leading tank regiment reported encounters with Tigers and a battle for Pt 84. According to the division's Operation Report, the regiment attacked Hill 111, several hundred metres north of the BCR–Algonquin position, at 1300 and rescued 'about 100 Cdn soldiers'[86] before withdrawing. What remains to be understood is why the Poles did not carry out the night advance ordered by Simonds, why it took until almost noon the next day to mount a new attack, and why the armoured brigade withdrew from Hill 111.

A second question relates to the role played by the tactical air force in this and other battles during August. Early on the morning of 9 August, Worthington and his men watched as two Typhoons 'circled overhead and then let fly ... with their rockets and machine guns.' When recognition panels were displayed and yellow smoke was burned, 'the planes rocked their wings in acknowledgement [and] returned at half hour intervals all day long rocketing and strafing the enemy.'[87] There was, however, no method of communicating with the men on the ground; nor was there any procedure for informing brigade, divisional, or corps headquarters about the situation.

The American 9th Tactical Air Force had begun the battle for Normandy employing a doctrine closely modelled on the one developed by the RAF, but was far more willing to learn from experience than 2TAF. By late July its commander, Maj.-Gen. Pete Quesada, had implemented a system known as Armoured Column Cover, which enabled for direct communication between aircraft assigned to an armoured command and an air officer with the tanks.[88] This system was employed to good effect after the Cobra breakout, yet it was unacceptable to the RAF, which resisted all attempts to tie air resources to specific army formations or to establish direct communication between tactical ground commanders and the tactical air force. Much is made of the RAF system of 'cab rank,' which allowed air officers attached to army units to call down air strikes on specific targets, but this was a poor substitute for intimate cooperation of the kind that was developed between American ground forces and their tactical air groups. If the BCR–Algonquin battlegroup had been an American formation, it would have had no difficulty identifying its location or relaying information to the divisional commander.

What of the rest of 4th Division on 9 August? The Argylls, supported by a squadron of the South Alberta Regiment, cleared the Hautmesnil quarry; then the Lincoln and Welland Regiment passed through to attack the defences of Langanerie, which were strongly contested by 89th Division.[89] The remaining uncommitted armoured regiment, the Governor General's Foot Guards, had been held back as divisional reserve. At 0700 it was just south of Rocquancourt, waiting to tie up with the remaining company of the Algonquin Regiment before going to the support of the battlegroup thought to be on Hill 195. Despite constant demands to get going, Lt.-Col. Scott waited until the Algonquins, along with a New Brunswick Rangers machine gun platoon, an antitank battery, and a troop of AVREs, were available. The advance began at 1430. The battlegroup turned off the highway to circle around the fighting that was still raging in Langanerie, and came within five hundred yards of Quesnay Woods before 'very accurate 88 and machine gun fire' began. Fourteen Shermans were lost in the next hour as the Foot Guards tried fire and movement to close with the enemy. The defenders were not content with long-range destruction, and they counterattacked, forcing the Canadians to withdraw and establish a defensive position in dead ground.[90]

Simonds, still unhappy with what he saw as excessive caution on the part of the armoured divisions, ordered the Poles to seize Pt 140, cross the Laison, and clear the south bank of the river. The Canadians were told to secure the high ground west of the highway as far south as Pt 206 and exploit to Falaise.[91] Simonds did not, however, offer any advice on how this was to be accomplished given the strength of the enemy defences.

Lt.-Col. Dave Stewart, the CO of the Argylls, was quite prepared to try and fulfil the general intent of his orders, but not at the sacrifice of his battalion. When told that the Argylls were to seize Pt 195, he and his scout platoon recced a circuitous route around the enemy defences and posted scouts along the way to ensure that no one got lost. Company locations on the objective were selected from the map, as were antitank gun positions. The men muffled their equipment and moved in single file as silently as possible. At 0430, just before first light, the Argylls were digging in in preparation for counterattacks. The Lincs occupied Pt 180 protecting the right flank.[92]

East of the highway, the Polish Armoured Division, unable to deal with the tanks of the Waldmüller battlegroup, had spent the day fighting for St-Sylvain and Soignolles. Shortly after midnight the liaison officer at General Maczek's headquarters reported that an attempt to capture the Pt 140 feature had been repulsed by an enemy counterattack of 'an estimated 40 tanks.' The woods to the south were thought to be strongly held.[93] The Poles were attempting to advance into positions that 12th SS was holding while 85th Division completed its deployment.

Simonds was determined to continue the offensive on 4th Division's front, so he issued orders to push the armour through the Argylls to Pt 206. The Grenadier Guards were in the process of carrying out a cautious, phased move to Pt 195 when they were told to prepare a co-ordinated daylight attack with artillery. However, they got no farther than the 'cornfield to the north of Point 195' before 88 fire from the left flank and a counterattack, which included robot tanks, ended any thought of further advance.[94] The Argylls and Lincs had been dealing with counterattacks since dawn, but with the men dug in, antitank guns in place, artillery DF tasks arranged, and Typhoons available, the enemy suffered heavy losses trying to retake Hill 195.[95]

A similar fate awaited the Queen's Own Rifles and North Shores. Simonds knew that 85th Division had begun to arrive in strength, so he gambled that a hastily arranged attack on Quesnay Woods might gain control of the area before the enemy was ready. His CCRA arranged to employ the guns of four field regiments and two AGRAs, but in the absence of any detailed knowledge of enemy positions, the fire plan could not produce sufficient density in any one area to do more than temporarily suppress enemy fire. Acting brigadier Jock Spragge received his orders less than four hours before the attack. The divisional recce regiment reported that the woods were strongly held, and Spragge had few illusions about the difficulty of the assignment he had been given. The battalions were told to 'sweep the woods' south-east from the village of Quesnay, but this proved utterly impossible.[96] According to German sources, Quesnay's guns and mortars were defended by two hundred Panzer Grenadiers and as many as twenty-three tanks, with the infantry dug in along the forward edge of the woods.[97] Both the QORs and the North Shores suffered significant casualties in a gruesome battle that lasted well into the night.

Operation Totalize came to an end in Quesnay Woods as Simonds decided to pause and re-organize. Early on the morning of 11 August he issued new orders, which included an outline of a 'break-in attack ... to be made under cover of a smoke screen with infantry carried forward in Priests.' This was to take place in seventy-two hours; the 4th Canadian and 1st Polish Divisions were to be withdrawn while the infantry divisions took over the defence of the deep salient that had been created in the past three days.[98] The human cost of Totalize included more than 600 Canadian dead – the inevitable price of a large-scale offensive. It was estimated that the enemy lost over 3,000 men, including 1,270 taken prisoner and a similar number killed in action.[99]

By any reasonable standard, Totalize was a very successful operation. The corps had broken through a strong defensive position manned by a fresh, full-strength infantry division and advanced 14 kilometres toward Falaise. The breakthrough did not become a breakout because 89th Division fought with considerable skill, as did the battlegroups of 12th SS. The arrival of the lead elements of 85th Division on 10 August added significantly to the enemy's strength and convinced commanders on both sides that the new defensive position north of the Laison could be held against improvised attacks. It was time to pause and reorganize.

Guy Simonds was never willing to accept such a realistic assessment of Totalize. On 13 August he organized a 'private talk' with commanders down to and including regimental COs.[100] According to Maj.-Gen. Kitching, Simonds gave a 'very tough and unpleasant briefing' in which he 'blasted armoured regiments for their lack of support for infantry ... He demanded much greater initiative from armd regts – drive on – get amongst the enemy etc. Forget about harbouring at night – keep driving on. Arrange your supply accordingly. Don't rely on the infantry to do everything for you.'[101]

This rant, which 'shook up everyone,' was intended to encourage the assembled officers to go all out in the next operation, but it made little sense to those who had actually been in battle. The BCRs could scarcely be accused of harbouring at night. And what exactly did Simonds mean when he said 'drive on – get amongst the enemy'? Did he really believe Sherman-equipped tank squadrons could prevail against the enemy's antitank guns? Simonds developed his critique of the armoured divisions in an interview with Chester Wilmot and a postwar lecture to British officers. When Wilmot asked for an explanation of the 'partial failure' of Totalize, Simonds referred to 'inexperience and lack of drive and control in commanders.'[102] His subsequent address to the British officers added a criticism of what he called 'road-boundedness' to the list of errors. 'There were,' he claimed, 'cases where there was all the room in the world to deploy across country but nevertheless armour kept to the road and in due course met the anti-tank gun sited to cover it.'[103] This was a strange remark to make to men who were setting out on a tour of a battlefield, which apart from the main highway was, and still is, singularly lacking in north-south roads. Did Simonds have any idea of what happened at the squadron level, or was he content with a level of abstraction suitable for planning at the corps level?

The same kinds of questions can be asked of most contemporary critics of the Canadian performance in Totalize, who treat the battles as a contest between Simonds and 12th SS. The exception to this is the work of John A. English, who has offered an insightful analysis of the operation. English concludes that the 'failure' of Totalize was less a product of troop inexperience than the result of a flawed concept. The Canadians, he writes, had performed well when correctly employed.[104] Unfortunately, his counterfactual solution – an all-out drive to Falaise without 'phases' or heavy bomber support – relies on the perspective of Kurt Meyer, who ignored the existence of 89th Division, the implication being that only his Panzers stood in the way of a breakthrough to Falaise.

The debate over Totalize always comes back to the view put forward by C.P. Stacey – that the capture of Falaise was long delayed due to various 'shortcomings' among the Canadians.[105] Stacey has little to say about the slow progress of British forces west of the Orne or the inability of 59th British Division to advance out of its bridgehead north of Thury-Harcourt. Perhaps it is time to recognize that there was no easy solution to the problems posed by an enemy that continued to wage a determined defensive battle even as its combat forces withered away.

9

Victory in
Normandy?

While the First Canadian Army was fighting its way toward Falaise through a well-organized defence-in-depth, General George Patton was, in his own words, 'touring France with an army.' Patton's lead corps advanced from Avranches to Laval, a distance of 80 kilometres, in five days. They met only scattered resistance and were slowed by command indecision rather than by the enemy. Once the German counterattack at Mortain, which began on the night of 6 August, was contained, Patton ordered Lt.-Gen. Wade Haslip's 15 Corps to continue the advance to Le Mans, 70 kilometres to the east. Le Mans fell on 8 August. When General Omar Bradley proposed turning 15 Corps north in the direction of Argentan to attack the enemy's 'flank and rear,' Montgomery agreed. Patton's reading of the situation led him to issue far more ambitious orders. Haslip was to cut through the enemy's rear areas on a narrow front and complete an encirclement of the enemy by making contact with the Canadians.[1]

General Felix Leclerc's 2nd French Armoured Division was added to 15 Corps. Early on 10 August, just as Simonds was issuing orders for the attack on Quesnay Woods, the Corps started north, brushing aside scattered resistance. Montgomery, still in command of the overall land battle, now made another serious error of judgment. The British and Canadians faced a well-organized enemy; in the American sector the German forces were weak and disorganized and the situation was changing almost hourly. Montgomery's new directive, issued on 11 August, attempted to impose order on this chaos by setting out boundaries within which the armies were to operate. He assigned both Falaise and Argentan to the First Canadian Army while restricting the entire U.S. 12th Army Group to a containment role on the southern flank of the rapidly forming Falaise–Argentan pocket.[2]

Montgomery believed that the enemy's Panzer Group Eberbach would be forced to break out eastwards and concentrate in the area south of Argentan, where it would have the benefit of the difficult bocage country. This estimate made a good deal of sense, though the enemy was in fact planning a new attack toward Avranches. This attack was only cancelled on 11 August, when the American thrust to Argentan forced von Kluge to order his Panzer Group to counterattack in the opposite direction. Ultra reported this change in German intentions late on 11 August, and confirmed it with details the next day.[3]

This information reinforced Montgomery's commitment to the ideas outlined in a new directive. His nightly message to London focused on orders, given verbally to Crerar and Dempsey, which called for the 2nd Canadian and 53rd Welsh divisions to cooperate 'in order to get Falaise in the next 48 hours.' At the same time, Bradley was told 'to collect a fresh army corps of three divisions at Le Mans, ready to rush quickly through to Chartres if and when we decide to drop an airborne division into this area.'[4]

Why did Montgomery reject the obvious solution to the problem of achieving total victory in Normandy? A decision to reinforce 15 Corps and close the rapidly forming pocket with six to eight American divisions was a practical option, and Montgomery's failure to seize this opportunity was a monumental strategic error. It is, of course, possible to argue that Montgomery sincerely believed that the British and Canadians could close the pocket from the north, and that the enemy would behave rationally and withdraw before the pocket could be closed, but the plain fact is that between 8 and 21 August, Montgomery's direction of the battle and Bradley's passive acceptance of Montgomery's policy combined to allow large elements of the German armies in Normandy to escape.

German resistance south of Argentan was quickly overcome despite Leclerc's disregard for divisional boundaries. This snafu delayed 5th U.S. Armoured Division for six hours; even so, its leading elements were on the edge of Argentan by nightfall. Haslip asked for additional troops to protect his extended left flank and sought permission to continue north to meet the Canadians.[5] The Americans were already more than 16 kilometres beyond their army group boundary, and no one had ordered Patton to pull back. Shortly after midnight, Patton, without consulting Bradley or Montgomery, ordered Haslip to 'push on slowly in the direction of Falaise.' When that objective was reached the corps 'was to continue on slowly until contact with our allies was made.'[6]

Montgomery's nightly message to London, timed at 2220, 12 August, noted that 'leading elements of 15 U.S. Corps were now reported in the Argentan area. ... This means that the ring is very nearly closed round the Germans except we have not yet got Falaise in the north and Germans are resisting very desperately in that area.' Montgomery also reported that though it was 'not possible to say what German forces were still inside the ring ... there is no doubt that there is a great mass of the more immobile formations still west of the line Falaise-Argentan ... but there has been an obvious withdrawal eastwards of enemy forces all day.'[7]

The situation on the night of 12 August called for the kind of decisive action proposed by Haslip and Patton. Leclerc's men had put patrols into Argentan, and early the next morning, 5th U.S. Division's recce units probed north to within six miles of Falaise. The details of what followed are clear – Bradley overruled Patton and ordered him not to go beyond Argentan. It is the reasons for the decision that are in dispute because of gaps in the primary evidence and Bradley's postwar claim that he alone made the decision because of the threat signaled by Ultra of an impending attack on 15 Corps' exposed flank. 'Better,' Bradley later recalled, 'a solid shoulder at Argentan [than] a broken neck at Falaise.'[8]

If this was the basis of the decision made by Bradley, then a good case can be made for the orders he issued on 13 August. The problem is that Bradley offered another, quite contradictory explanation for his caution. Falaise, he said, was 'a long sought British objective and for them a matter of immense prestige. If Patton's patrols grabbed Falaise it would be an arrogant slap in the face at a time when we clearly needed to build confidence in the Canadian Army.'[9] So which was it? Fear that Haslip's 'thinly strung out forces' would be overwhelmed, or fear that they would reach Falaise before the Canadians?

The best contemporary evidence does little to clear up the confusion. On the afternoon of 13 August, Montgomery met with Bradley and Dempsey to discuss further plans. An entry in Dempsey's diary, dated that day, notes:

> We discussed future operations – particularly as regards Army Group and Army boundaries, and the bringing up by Third Army of another corps directed on Laigle. So long as the northward move of Third Army meets little opposition, the two leading corps will disregard inter-army boundaries, the whole aim is to establish forces across the enemy's lines of communication so as to impede – if not to prevent entirely – his withdrawal.[10]

Bradley reported the outcome of the same meeting rather differently. An entry in the Allied Expeditionary Air Force Headquarters War Diary, dated 0950 hours 14 August, reads:

> The American forces had little opposition between Alencon and Argentan and had started towards Falaise but had been instructed by the C-in-C 21 Army Group to halt on the inter-army boundary. There had been few German troops in the area when the Army forward elements arrived there and he was confident that the Third Army now held a firm front on the Arc to the [south] of Falaise.[11]

The only way these two accounts can be reconciled is by assuming that Bradley, on his own authority, issued the first 'Stop' order on the night of 12 August because of the threat to 15 Corps' flank. After listening to a description of the new Canadian offensive planned for 14 August, he concluded that the resistance met by 15 Corps that morning in their attempt to encircle Argentan from the east[12] constituted serious opposition and that the gap must therefore be closed from the north. This explanation accords with Montgomery's 13 August report to London indicating that 15 U.S. Corps 'is now firmly established at Argentan' and that the Canadians were preparing to launch 'a strong attack with powerful air support towards Falaise.' In the same message Montgomery noted that his intelligence staff estimated that 'the fighting portion of five German Army Corps are still west of the road Falaise–Argentan,' so in theory an encirclement was still possible.[13] The decision to leave 15 Corps at Argentan while 21 Army Group closed the pocket from the north was explained in terms of Montgomery's belief that the British and Canadian armies were advancing quickly enough to deal with an embattled enemy that was short of petrol and harassed by the tactical air forces.[14]

Montgomery had issued verbal instructions to the 2nd British Army on 10 August telling Dempsey to transfer his 'main weight to the left flank and to operate strongly towards Falaise.'[15] Had Dempsey selected a code name for this operation, which involved one Canadian and two British divisions, historians might now be giving this five-day period of intense combat the attention it deserves. Success depended on overcoming the resistance of 271st Division, which was continuing to prevent 59th Division from expanding its Orne bridgehead and gaining access to Thury-Harcourt and its road network.[16]

Perhaps the challenge did not seem so great at Army Group Headquarters, especially when viewed on a large-scale map, but on the ground the ridge between the Forêt de Cinglais and the Orne was a major obstacle.[17] An advance along the narrow river valley to Thury-Harcourt was equally uninviting, and an attempt to reach the town along the even more rugged west bank of the river was unsuccessful. When Lt.-Gen. Neil Ritchie, the corps commander, received orders to break out of this constricted bridgehead and go for Falaise, he must have wondered whether Montgomery and Dempsey had taken leave of their senses. The approaches to Thury-Harcourt were difficult enough, but south of the town lay the *Suisse Normande* and the gorges of the Orne. There was one narrow paved road, the D6, leading to Falaise, but it wound through easily defended wooded hills and was lined with hedgerows. Today, with careful navigation, motorists can find other routes south and east, but in 1944 these local roads were – as the Welsh divisions would discover – little more than forest tracks.[18]

When 12th Corps renewed the offensive on 12 August, the plan was to employ 53rd Division, one brigade up, on 59th Division's left flank and use the corps artillery to break enemy resistance on the ridge. If this was successful, the enemy holding Thury-Harcourt would be outflanked. The 'Welch' battalions of the lead brigade spent all of 12 August in close combat with enemy troops holding the high ground, and achieved only local penetrations.[19] Ritchie had been promised Canadian support, and late on 11 August, Crerar ordered Simonds 'to put a brigade around the right flank' as part of this effort to reach Falaise from the west. If the move was successful,[20] Simonds was to ignore the boundary with 12th Corps.

Foulkes selected 4th Brigade for the task. Just before midnight on 11 August, well before the Welsh Division's attack began, the Royal Hamilton Light Infantry, with a squadron of Sherbrooke tanks, started down the D23. The brigade plan called for the Rileys to capture Barbery and the high ground beyond the village. The Royals were to take the second bound to Moulines; after this the Essex Scottish were to seize and hold Pt 184. The Rileys were slowed by machine gun fire from outposts north of Barbery, but by first light they had cleared the village and were ready to continue 1 kilometre south to occupy the Phase I objective.[21]

The low ridge beyond the village is barely noticeable from the north. The steeper reverse slope is covered in apple orchards, which surround the hamlet of Cingal. The 271st Division, responsible for the sector between the Laize and the Orne, was still trying to maintain a continuous front and had selected a series of good positions on dominating ground. The divisional artillery, mortars, and Nebelwerfers had been registered on the obvious approach routes, and a screen of antitank guns – including 88s – had been deployed in depth. The division also employed a small number of self-propelled assault guns to support local counterattacks, and could draw upon further armoured support from 12th SS.[22]

When the Rileys moved out of the village onto open ground, they discovered just how well prepared the Germans were. They came under heavy machine gun fire, followed by 'the most intensive mortar fire and shelling the unit ever witnessed.' The Germans then attacked, using self-propelled assault guns. The battalion, which lost 120 men in this encounter, including 20 killed, could do little more than dig in.[23] The Royals took advantage of this intense battle to move through the woods toward Moulines, but they too were held by enemy fire, which knocked out the lead Sherbrooke tank and sent the rest of the troop back for cover. After a new artillery fire plan was worked out, Moulines fell quickly, but a night attack by the Essex Scottish failed to capture Pt 184.[24] The Rileys found that the enemy had withdrawn from Cingal, and were able to advance to Fontaine-Halbout that night, but Pt 184 was not occupied until the following evening, after the enemy had withdrawn.[25]

The attacks carried out by 4th Brigade provided considerable assistance to 53rd Division, which was able to capture Bois-Halbout on the morning of 13 August, taking more than one hundred prisoners.[26] Not surprisingly, word of this success and the news of the capture of the smoking ruins of Thury-Harcourt greatly encouraged senior British commanders. Since Operation Tractable would begin within twenty-four hours, Montgomery was encouraged to believe that the gap might indeed be closed from the north. More good news arrived from 5th Canadian Brigade, which had begun to move south at 0145, 13 August. The Calgary Highlanders, with the Maisonneuves close behind, advanced along the west bank of the Laize 'over territory not recce'd before through country where ... the trails were no wider than a carrier with high banks on either side.' By morning they were just 2 kilometres north of Clair Tizon, with its bridge across the Laize, on the direct route to Falaise. The Calgaries were ordered to dig in while 4th Brigade captured Pt 184. When they resumed the advance at 1400, they kept to the river valley, 'leap-frogging companies' and holding firm after each 'bite.' By 1800 they had reached Clair Tizon and established a small bridgehead across the narrow, shallow river. The Maisonneuves, functioning with just two rifle companies, tried to secure the high ground, Pt 176, above the village, but ran into a well-prepared position that could not be taken on the run.[27]

As darkness fell, the 271st Division was told to withdraw 'to the line Martainville–Combray,' south of the D6, and to establish 'firm contact' with the 89th and 277th divisions on either flank.[28] Both British and Canadian commanders were determined to press the attack. In the Canadian sector, Foulkes committed 6th Brigade to a night attack on Pt 176. By dawn the South Sasks and Camerons were on the objective 'with every tank' of the Sherbrookes available to withstand the inevitable counterattacks.[29] Battlegroup Krause arrived to lead this effort,[30] but 6th Brigade easily repelled the attacks until ordered to withdraw its forward companies: Tractable was about to begin, and the village of Ussy, less than a kilometre away, was an aiming point for heavy bombers. Ironically, it was these companies that suffered the most casualties from the bombs, which fell short of the target area.

Preparations for Operation Tractable, the second great armoured assault on the German defences north of Falaise, began on 12 August, when Simonds outlined his concept to the divisional commanders. No formal operational order was issued; instead, staff officers produced their own 'Outlines of Instructions' to assist in the planning. The primary object of Tractable was 'to gain command of the enemy's communications through Falaise' by seizing the high ground northeast of the town. There was some uncertainty about subsequent objectives because Montgomery kept changing his mind. When Simonds met with his officers on the morning of 13 August, he noted that 'Falaise is only a name'[31] – it was the east-west roads through the town that mattered. Unfortunately, Falaise was more than a name to Montgomery, and Simonds was forced to include the capture of the town in his initial plan. By the time Montgomery changed his mind and assigned Falaise to the 2nd British Army, it was too late to consider reorienting a complex attack, so the object of Tractable became to 'exploit south-eastwards and capture or dominate Trun,'[32] *after* the high ground north and east of Falaise was secure.

If Trun rather than Falaise had been the primary objective of Tractable, Simonds would surely have shifted the corps' axis of advance to the east to take advantage of the open country and good north-south roads between Jort and St-Pierre-sur-Dives.[33] Simonds was well aware of the opportunities on his left flank. He ordered the Polish Armoured Division to form a 'special group' for reconnaissance in the area, and he moved the balance of that division into corps reserve, but the Phase II objectives for Tractable were unchanged.[34] This meant that 4th Division was to turn west toward Falaise, into the heart of the German defences, instead of continuing south to Trun and closing much of the gap.

On the morning of 13 August, Simonds explained his plan to the divisional and brigade commanders. The problem, he noted, was exactly the same as in Totalize – to obtain a breakthrough in sufficient depth to push past the enemy's gun screen and to set the armour behind his positions so as 'to deny him freedom of manoeuverability.' The solution was to have the two Canadian armoured brigades formed up on a wide, two-regiment front, with the tanks 'about 15 yards apart.' A smoke screen would prevent the German antitank guns from aiming their fire. If the tanks maintained a pace of 12 miles an hour they would be through the enemy defences very quickly.[35] The armoured brigades were to cross the Laison River, 'bypassing all opposition,' and reach the high ground south of the river. The 8th and 9th infantry brigades, mounted in Priests, half-tracks, and carriers, were to follow behind the armour and mop up resistance in the valley. Two other 'lorry-borne' infantry brigades were to pass through the mopping-up troops and join the armour on their first objective. The armoured brigades would then advance to their objective near Falaise before turning around to exploit toward Trun.[36]

Despite very short notice, Bomber Command had agreed to assist the operation. The heavies were to strike targets close to the Caen–Falaise highway on the flank of the advance, so the air plan did not affect the timing of the ground attack. Only medium and fighter bombers were to be employed in front of the troops.[37] The artillery fire plan focused on laying down a smoke screen and on suppressing the enemy's artillery and antitank guns. However, each armoured brigade was assigned an AGRA for the later stages of the advance. Brig. Todd, 3rd Division's CRA, directed the artillery from the air.[38]

Tractable was much more than a replay of Totalize; it incorporated lessons learned and proposed new and innovative ideas. There was, however, one serious flaw – the failure to appreciate that the Laison River, little more than a small creek by Canadian standards, was in fact a serious tank obstacle. An after-action report issued by 2nd Armoured Brigade suggested that in future, tank commanders rather than engineers ought to be consulted when deciding what was likely to be a tank obstacle.[39]

The Canadian attack struck directly at 85th Infantry Division, which was positioned on the reverse slope of the high ground north of the Laison River. The 85th was as good an infantry division as the Germans possessed at this stage of the war. Raised in February 1944, with cadres drawn from veterans of the Eastern Front, it had ample time to train while serving with 15th Army in the Somme sector.[40] The division was responsible for an 8 kilometre sector from Quesnay Woods to Mazières, and it deployed both its infantry regiments north of the Laison. The divisional artillery, some of the antitank guns, and the Fusilier battalion were south of the river. So was each regiment's reserve battalion. But the decision to concentrate most of the division's combat troops and many of the Flak Corps' 88s north of the river played into Simonds' hands. The enemy's inability to mount any kind of serious counterattack when the Canadians were at their most vulnerable (i.e., while waiting to cross the Laison) indicated just how successful Tractable was at penetrating a heavily defended reverse-slope position.

It is again important to note that the defence of the Laison was conducted by 1st SS Panzer Corps, not by Kurt Meyer and 12th SS, which played only a marginal role in Tractable. Battlegroup Krause was fighting northwest of Falaise against the 2nd Canadian and 53rd Welsh

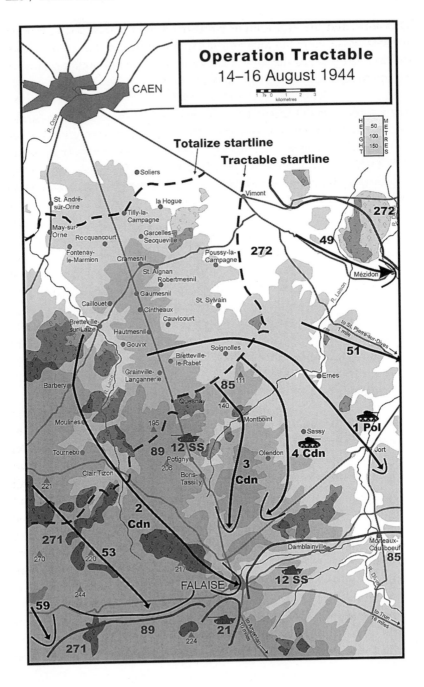

Divisions, and the Waldmüller battlegroup was committed in 'penny packets' to support the forward battalions of the 85th. A third battle-group functioned as the corps reserve, and strong antitank forces were placed to cover the Jort–Trun routes.[41]

The approach to the Laison began precisely at 1140, when the message 'Move now' was relayed. The artillery and waves of medium bombers had been at work for thirty minutes before the lead tanks crossed the start line. On the right flank, the Fort Garry Horse advanced in the approved fashion, two squadrons abreast. They burst through the for-ward defences, enjoying 'a great run over open country with the tank gunners taking on all likely targets by speculative shooting.' On reach-ing the river near Montboint, they encountered antitank guns, includ-ing 88s 'cutting down good sized trees.' A crossing was improvised, and then a usable bridge was discovered. Most of the regiment got across the river, and by 1700 the advance was resumed. The Garrys were pretty well on their own, and even though the area was 'stiff' with antitank guns and 'pockets of infantry,' they fought their way through, reaching their first objective at 2230. The Garrys lost almost one-third of their tanks and suffered a number of crew casualties (including Captain Eddie Goodman, who was wounded), but the extraordinary determi-nation of the regiment led to a considerable success.[42]

The First Hussars struck more determined resistance north of the river. As one squadron commander reported, it was essential 'to main-tain speed for any hesitation was rewarded by determined attacks from enemy infantry.' The Hussars also ran into German tanks, and reported destroying two Tigers. The lead squadrons lost direction and ended up well to the east in 4th Armoured Brigade's zone. The enemy continued to contest every move, and Lt.-Col. Colwell described the fighting on the river bottom as the most hectic of the operation. Never, he remarked, had the regiment killed so many of the enemy or thrown so many hand grenades. In addition, hundreds of prisoners were taken. The Hussars reached their initial objective to the east of the Gar-rys during the night, but by then the regiment was at half-strength.[43]

The 4th Armoured Brigade advanced with the two Guards regi-ments leading, followed closely by the BCRs and Lake Superior Regi-ment. There was ample room, and each regiment deployed all three squadrons up, over an 800 metre front. By now many of the tanks were festooned with extra armour made out of loosely attached tank tracks. The neat formations quickly collapsed as smoke, dust, uneven ground, and enemy resistance were encountered. In the woods south of Pt 140, the Foot Guards ran into an enemy strongpoint that had escaped the medium bombers. The approaches were mined, and both MK IV tanks and antitank guns had to be dealt with while the rest of the regiment pressed on. In the river valley a series of miniature close engagements took place that resulted in losses on both sides and many enemy prisoners.[44] The confusion on this part of the front was compounded by the greater width of the Laison, which turned improvised crossings into tank traps.

The main crossing point at Rouvres had to be shared with the Hussars and the BCRs, but small groups edging east found intact bridges at Maizières, Ernes (which was 'vaguely in our hands'),[45] and Ifs-sur-Laison, well to the east of the divisional boundary. The road to Trun was wide open but the assigned objectives were still at Falaise. Attempts to reorganize the scattered squadrons were complicated by the loss of Brig. Booth, who was wounded in action, and by the need to transfer command to Lt.-Col. Scott of the Foot Guards.[46] However, the squadron and troop commanders knew their jobs, and the immediate objectives at Olendon-Sassy were secured despite continued resistance and losses from antitank guns. Fortunately, the BCRs and Lake Sups moved forward to help. Just outside Sassy the Lake Sups encountered a large enemy force and captured 250 prisoners.[47]

While the armoured brigades were fighting their way onto the high ground south of the Laison, the two mounted infantry brigades cleared the valley behind. This was 3rd Division's first experience riding into battle, and apart from bruises from the rough ride, the troops were exhilarated by their part in the 'charge of the light brigade.'[48] Resistance in the eastern, 8th Brigade sector was scattered; the biggest problem was enemy artillery and mortar fire.[49] To the west, 9th Brigade found the area where the Garrys had broken through alive with enemy infantry and at least two Tiger tanks. Three of the four Crocodiles supporting the Glens were quickly knocked out, and rather than wait for M10s, the infantry dealt with the Tigers as best they could. The Glens' antitank platoon got one by placing a 6-pounder behind a disabled

Fort Garry tank. Two rounds at close range killed the Tiger. The enemy infantry were dealt with using Wasp flame throwers, 'which utterly consumed both men and weapons ... and chased the seared and screaming survivors off into the sun.'[50]

While the battles of the Laison raged, Bomber Command struck accurately at Quesnay Woods and the targets around Potigny, but 77 of the 811 bombers misidentified their targets and wreaked havoc among Canadian and Polish troops in the rear areas. The errant crews, many from No. 6 Group, RCAF, interpreted instructions from the Master Bomber incorrectly and bombed 'many seconds' before the end of their timed run from the coast. Confusion over the army's use of yellow smoke – a signal to tactical air force pilots of friendly troops, but a target marker to Bomber Command, contributed to the tragedy.[51] More than 150 Allied soldiers were killed and 241 wounded in four separate incidents.[52] There were signs of mass panic in many units, and 'unauthorized self-evacuation' from bombed areas made reorganization difficult.[53] The 'short bombing' had no direct effect on the forces committed to Tractable, most of whom only learned of the tragedy the next day. The vast majority of the bomber crews identified their targets correctly, and accurate bombing devastated the enemy anchor position in Quesnay Woods as well as areas held by 89th Division east of the highway.[54]

By the evening of 14 August it was apparent that though both armoured brigades were firm on their intermediate objectives, a continued advance to the high ground overlooking Falaise would have to wait until morning. On the British–Canadian front west of Falaise, leading troops were 8 to 10 kilometres from the town. But the main Falaise–St-Pierre-sur-Dives road was still available to the enemy, as were the two other east-west routes through the town. Montgomery's report to London, timed at 2200, noted this reality and offered the 'opinion' that though a 'good many enemy' had escaped eastwards, a 'good many' were still inside the ring. His solution was to order Bradley 'to stop the enemy from turning southeast [as] we want those who escaped us here to be pushed up against the Seine.'[55] Bradley received no orders or suggestions pertaining to 15 Corps, and Montgomery made no move to reinforce the First Canadian Army or to change the orders directing 2 Canadian Corps to Falaise. His decision to stop Patton at Argentan on 12–13 August might be defended as prudent in view of reports of an impending counterattack, but thirty-six hours later no such attack had occurred. Why was Montgomery unwilling to order the Americans to resume their advance north? Even if the Canadians reached Falaise the next day, the enemy could still use a number of secondary roads north of Argentan to leave the pocket. The most likely answer is that Montgomery no longer believed the enemy could be encircled at Argentan–Falaise and was intent on trapping those who had escaped the air forces at the Seine. This left the Canadians with the unenviable task of trying to block the exodus of tens of thousands of German troops determined to avoid entrapment. On the morning of 15 August they discovered just how difficult this was going to be. The 12th SS Division had been ordered to employ its surviving units to provide antitank support to the four infantry divisions holding positions north of Falaise. The combat strength of the 85th, 89th, 271st, and 272nd Divisions had been reduced by at least 50 per cent, but all four divisional headquarters still exercised good control and cooperated in creating a continuous line of strongpoints north of the Condé–Falaise–St-Pierre-sur-Dives highway.[56]

Montgomery's orders required the Canadians to press their advance toward Falaise, and Simonds reluctantly followed orders. The 3rd Division was told to renew its attempt to break through along the highway while 4th Division moved forward 'with all possible speed' to 'Idaho,' the code name for Pt 159 northeast of the town.[57] To reach Idaho, 4th Armoured Brigade would have to overcome enemy positions – including a powerful antitank gun screen – at Epancy and Pt 175. The Lake Superior Regiment and a squadron of Foot Guard tanks were assigned to help the Algonquin Regiment clear Epancy; the rest of the armoured brigade began a tentative advance to Pt 159. The enemy had deployed its artillery and mortars in the extensive woods of the Mont d'Eraines, so when the tanks advanced beyond Epancy they were moving parallel to the enemy guns in open country. Any movement forward brought fire from the flank as well as from the antitank screen to their front.[58] Repeated attacks from Spitfires and Typhoons[59] added to the confusion, and the two leading armoured regiments were soon isolated and out of touch.

By mid-afternoon, little progress had been made. The Grenadier Guards and BCRs met with officers of the leading elements of 10th Brigade, and it was decided that an attack across 'open and flat ground without cover [and] without infantry and proper artillery support would prove disastrous.' A plan was drawn up that utilized infantry from the Lincs and the Lake Sups as well as tanks, but the artillery concentrations 'failed to come down' and no real attack on Pt 159 took place. The Foot Guards reported at 1500 that they were on the objective; in fact they were nowhere near it. The Grenadier Guards war diarist summed up the events on 4th Division's front accurately: 'The whole day proved very much wasted.'[60]

The 3rd Division was also ordered to reach Pt 159, but when 7th Brigade began the advance it quickly became apparent that they were attacking directly into the enemy's strength. Soulangy and the high ground to the east were held by infantry of 89th Division and elements of Battlegroup Krause, including Tiger tanks. To the east, in the woods above Epancy, antitank guns covered the northern as well as the eastern approaches to Falaise.[61] The acting divisional commander, Brig. Blackader, and his CRA were able to exercise much better command and control than their 4th Division counterparts, but the objectives were close to the extreme range of the medium guns.[62]

The lead battalions of 7th Brigade were at first able to move forward, but when the Royal Winnipeg Rifles tried to capture Soulangy the enemy's response was overwhelming. The lead company suffered 50 per cent casualties from intense mortar and machine gun fire, and the attack was called off.[63] Soulangy was occupied the next day, when the enemy withdrew to avoid encirclement from the west. The Canscots, with the First Hussars, bypassed the village to reach Pt 168, but after the antitank guns at Epancy put an end to their armoured support, the Canscots were on their own. The Canadian Scottish Regiment had a well-deserved reputation as an exceptionally effective and highly successful battalion, and on 15 August they displayed all their skill and determination. The men used their battle drill training to get onto the objective and hold it against enemy counterattacks. This experience, which the War Diary described as a 'molten fire ball,' cost the Canscots thirty-seven men killed and ninety-five wounded – their worst single-day casualties of the war.[64]

Tractable is usually described as an 'operational failure' because it failed to meet Simonds's expectations.[65] It should be noted, however, that if 4th Division had captured the high ground northeast of Falaise and then entered the city, the stated objective – the advance to Trun – would have been further delayed. Tractable ought to have been a great success. The Canadians broke through the best-organized defensive position left to the Germans in Normandy and on 14 August achieved the long-sought freedom to manoeuvre armoured divisions at the operational level. Montgomery's orders to take Falaise before exploiting to Trun sidetracked 4th Division.

On the morning of 15 August, Simonds ordered the Polish Armoured Division to move around the enemy defences and seize the crossings over the River Dives at Jort and Vendouvre.[66] If successful, this would open the way to Trun and outmanoeuvre the enemy dug in around Falaise.

The Poles started east at 1100, moving in two columns over the Caen–Falaise highway and cutting through the rear areas of 3rd and 4th divisions. The Poles operated with their divisional recce regiment, 10th Mounted Rifles, out in front, and it was the 10th that 'reconnoitred the crossings and after their daring capture went on to Courcy.' The armoured brigade secured the area, which the enemy 'defended furiously.' During the night, 3rd Rifle Brigade took over the bridgehead, forming a firm base. The Poles captured 120 prisoners from the 272nd and 85th divisions, and claimed the destruction of three Panthers as well as antitank guns and an artillery battery. That night the recce regiment moved farther south toward Louvangy.[67] The Polish advance was facilitated by an order requiring the Luftwaffe flak regiments to withdraw out of the pocket. This removed the 88 mm guns covering the area[68] – which is not to diminish the brilliance of the Polish achievement in a classic armoured manoeuvre role.

What did Montgomery make of the situation as it developed on 15 August? He met with Bradley and Dempsey, once again ignoring Crerar, and indicated that after the capture of Falaise the Canadians would advance to Trun to meet the Americans and close the gap. Ultra was reporting yet another plan for a large-scale attack by German Panzer divisions in the Argentan area, as well as an attempt to prevent an advance to Trun. Montgomery learned for the first time that Patton was furious with his interference and had persuaded Bradley to allow him to send 15 Corps headquarters and its two best divisions on their way to the Seine.[69] The Argentan shoulder was now held by just two divisions, 2nd French Armoured and 90th U.S. Infantry. That night, Montgomery told Brooke that '15 U.S. Corps is up against determined resistance astride Argentan and a full scale withdrawal by the enemy is underway.' There was no mention of closing the pocket; the only new orders were those sent to the First Canadian Army, informing Crerar that 7th Armoured Division, which had been in a rest area since 4 August, was to be transferred to his command, not to reinforce the advance to Trun but rather 'to develop a thrust eastwards to Lisieux.'[70] As far as Montgomery was concerned, closing the gap was not a priority – it was now a race to the Seine.

While Montgomery and Bradley concentrated on the long envelopment at the Seine, the German commanders were preparing to evacuate the remaining troops – around 100,000 – who were still in the pocket. The Allied landings in the south of France on 15 August had convinced Hitler that Normandy – perhaps all of France – was lost, and he authorized an immediate withdrawal behind the Dives. To accomplish this, both Argentan and Falaise were, he insisted, to be held as 'corner pillars.'[71]

By the morning of 16 August it was clear that 2nd Division would enter Falaise that day. Simonds ordered Kitching to cancel plans for an attack from the east. Instead, the division was to turn 180 degrees and assemble north of Olendon to join the Polish Armoured Division in the advance to Trun. Unfortunately, both divisional and brigade O Groups for the attack on Pt 159 had been held earlier that morning, and battalion commanders were briefing their officers when the new order arrived. Since it would take some time for the division to disengage and reassemble, the corps commander decided to use the day for rest, reinforcement, and refitting. The advance would begin early on 17 August.[72] The Grenadier Guards, whose tank strength had been reduced to twenty-three Shermans, were grateful for the chance to obtain replacements, but only ten were available. The Foot Guards could obtain only enough tanks and crews to operate with two squadrons, each of twelve tanks.[73]

While 4th Division redeployed, 6th Canadian Infantry Brigade

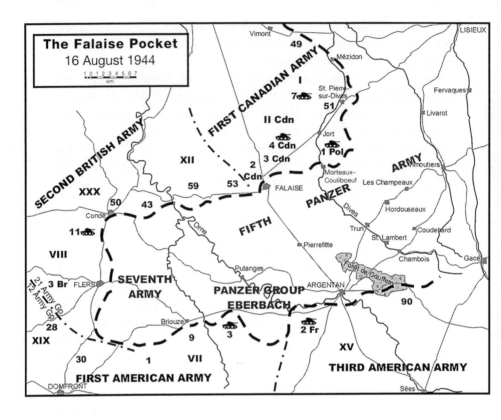

The Falaise Pocket
16 August 1944

fought its way into Falaise. Its orders were to ensure that all the roads through the town were closed off – a task complicated by bomb craters and by rubble from hundreds of destroyed buildings. The South Sasks and Sherbrookes, held up by an antitank gun covering a bridge over the River Ante, watched in amazement as Lt.-Col. Freddie Clift and his intelligence officer borrowed rifles from men in the leading section and dashed forward, overcoming the defenders. By 1730 the South Sasks were across the bridge and into the town, but another day of brutal street fighting was required to win control of the ruins.[74] The order to evacuate the town was apparently issued by 12th SS around noon on 17 August but a large number of Panzer Grenadiers did not receive word, so the Fusiliers Mont-Royal were compelled to fight a difficult, costly, and pointless battle that ended in death of yet more young men, including all but two of the Hitler Youth.[75]

The enemy had made enormous sacrifices in the struggle to hold Falaise and the northern shoulder of the pocket. Since 8 August the First Canadian Army had destroyed the combat power of two fresh, full-strength infantry divisions and further weakened three others, including 12th SS. According to the headquarters of 1st SS Panzer Corps, by noon on 15 August, 85th Division could muster only one-and-a-half battalions of infantry and a battery of 88 mm guns. The 89th, 271st, and 272nd were only slightly better off, and the Hitler Youth were said to have only fifteen tanks left.[76] The German army had maintained a cohesive front in the British and Canadian sectors, but at a price no army could afford to pay.

While the battle for Falaise raged, the Polish Armoured Division continued to advance toward Trun. They closed an important east-west road (the D39 to Livarot) and pushed on to Baron, a village astride the next escape route. By the evening of 16 August the leading Polish regiments were less than 12 kilometres from Trun. But since 4th Division had not yet started south, there were no friendly troops on either flank. With strong enemy forces reported in Morteaux, the Poles paused to secure their gains.[77]

Montgomery's nightly message reflected his continuing commitment to pushing the enemy up against the Seine. His major initiative was to send 7th Armoured Division across the river at St-Pierre-sur-Dives and then turn it 'in a northeasterly direction' to Lisieux. Closing the gap was still not a priority, and Ultra reported that five of the six Panzer and SS divisions, still inside the pocket, were planning to break out to the south between Argentan and Sees. The Americans, Montgomery believed, would have to concentrate on holding this attack. He did mention the Canadians: 'If we can get 2nd British Army tomorrow to Putanges and the left wing of 2 Canadian Corps to Trun we shall be pretty well placed.' The balance of his report dealt with plans for swinging detachments from 20 U.S. Corps 'up onto the Seine.'[78]

One of the great weaknesses of Ultra intelligence was that it provided strong evidence of enemy intentions but only indirect evidence of capabilities. Hitler had orderd a breakout south of Argentan, but von Kluge insisted it was impossible, so as we have seen, Hitler agreed to a withdrawal behind the Dives on the afternoon of 16 August.[79] This was to take place along the highways through Trun, Chambois, and Gacé, and along the secondary roads paralleling the main escape routes.[80]

Most accounts of Montgomery's actions on 16 August suggest that he ordered Bradley to 'push on from Argentan towards Trun and Chambois,'[81] but there is no direct evidence for this. What we do know is that the confused command situation at Argentan, involving the transfer of authority from the Third to the First U.S. Army, prevented any such attack from taking place for the next forty-eight hours.[82] This meant that the burden of blocking the enemy's desperate drive to escape encirclement would be borne by two understrength armoured divisions and the tactical air forces. This situation was a result of a series of misjudgments made by Montgomery and Bradley. Though it is possible to understand the choices they made, it is clear that they were responsible for command decisions that offered the enemy ample opportunity to escape encirclement.

Assigning major responsibility for the events of 17–21 August to the senior commanders does not explain or excuse the command failures that marred the record of 4th Armoured Division during this crucial period. Maj.-Gen. George Kitching had functioned as little more than a spectator in Totalize and Tractable, which had been orchestrated by Simonds. Now, on 16 August, he was on his own with instructions to advance to Trun. Kitching issued two orders that day. He decided 'to abandon hard scale living from slit trenches' and to restore the 'caravans, messes and other administrative vehicles' to division headquarters, and he outlined Operation Smash, an advance by the entire division on a single axis to the main Falaise–Trun road. The infantry brigade was to seize the crossing over the River Ante at Damblainville, after which the armoured brigade would pass through.[83]

The enemy could also read a map. After Falaise was lost it abandoned the hills east of the town and established new blocking positions to cover the main crossings of the Ante. The high ground south of the river was held by elements of 12th SS, including antitank guns to cover the narrow stone bridges and Panzer Grenadiers with mortars and machine guns to stop an infantry attack.[84] All of this was familiar stuff to both sides, but Kitching's decision to send his entire division forward in an extended column transformed a routine if difficult operation into a chaotic, costly encounter that delayed the advance for most of the day. Maj. G.L. Cassidy of the Algonquins, who was present, recalled the scene in a history of the regiment.

> The brigade column had been oozing over and down the hill north of Damblainville, coming into perfect view of the German force only 1800 yards away. Plastered against the side of the forward slope of the hill, and jammed together in a nose-to-tail column, they made a dream target for enemy artillery. For three hours there was a scene of complete confusion as elements of the column tried to deploy off the roads and disperse.[85]

Fortunately, the armoured brigade was not caught up in the nightmare. When Simonds arrived at divisional headquarters he told Kitching to divert it to Couliboeuf, where a platoon from the Algonquin Regiment had seized bridges over the Ante.[86] By the time the leading armoured regiment, the Grenadier Guards, got there it was early afternoon. There was more delay when a Polish liaison officer insisted that the main road south was the Polish centre line and that the Canadians must stay off it. A new route was worked out, and after a brief skirmish with some SS supply troops the regiment captured Louvières-en-Auges. The most difficult moment in its 10 kilometre advance was 'a short severe bombing' by Allied aircraft.[87] The Foot Guards encountered antitank guns and by nightfall were still 5 kilometres north of Louvières. The BCRs and the infantry, including the Lake Superior Regiment, were even farther back,[88] so on the night of 17 August the Canadian force, 2 kilometres north of Trun, consisted of fewer than thirty tanks.

The Polish armoured recce regiment had moved forward more quickly. At 0930 hours it reported that it could see enemy columns moving east along the Falaise–Trun highway. The Polish armoured brigade attacked south from Barou and captured Norrey-en-Auge, which was defended by a battlegroup from 21st Panzer Division. It then fought its way east to Hill 259, close to Trun–Vimoutiers highway, taking eighty-four prisoners from a composite battlegroup made up of men from 12th SS, 85th, and 271st divisions.[89]

Though no one would argue that 2 Canadian Corps was functioning with smooth efficiency, its armoured divisions had narrowed the gap and were on the verge of closing one of the two main escape routes. This achievement contrasted sharply with the confusion on the American side of the pocket, where plans to attack north toward Chambois on the morning of 17 August were postponed due to uncertainty about command arrangements and orders. Montgomery made no attempt to pressure the Americans; instead he flew to Bradley's headquarters to discuss how to trap the Germans at the Seine, and also to broach his idea of a single thrust to the Ruhr.[90] After the meeting he contacted Crerar and told him it was 'absolutely essential that both the Armed Divs of 2 Cdn Corps ... close the gap ... 1 Pol Armed Div must thrust on past Trun to Chambois at all costs and as quickly as possible.'[91] Crerar transmitted these orders to Simonds who went forward to meet his divisional commanders. Kitching was understandably confident that Trun would fall the next morning, but the Poles were more than 10 kilometres from Chambois and would have to move along unmarked forest tracks across the grain of the country. Maczek decided to send the Koszutski battlegroup (2nd Tank Regiment, 8th Rifle Regiment, and 1st Anti-Tank Battery) to Chambois while the balance of the division occupied the high ground Coudehard – Mount Ormel, where the ring contours enclosing Pt 262 north, Pt 252, and Pt 262 south suggested the shape of a mace – *maczuga* in Polish.[92] If all went well and the Americans finally got moving, the gap would be closed early on 18 August.

Montgomery's nightly report to London stated that 'the gap has now been closed,' although there were clear signs 'that the Germans are going to attempt a major breakout tonight.' He estimated that five Panzer divisions and 'a good mess of immobile infantry were still west of the Argentan–Falaise road' and thought it 'quite possible elements will get through.' Montgomery added that 'we now sit astride the main roads leading east but have not had time to organize definite blocks of every exit.'[93] There were, of course, no blocks on the Chambois–Vimoutiers highway or the roads through Trun. Montgomery, his thoughts focussed on the Seine and beyond, was mistaken or deliberately exaggerating progress.

During the night of 17–18 August, the surviving fragments of

Hausser's 7th Army withdrew across the Orne and through the narrowing gap between Argentan and Falaise. Their goal was to reach the densely wooded areas northeast of Argentan before daylight, a distance of some 18 kilometres. On the northern flank, the shrinking battlegroups of 12th SS withdrew to positions along the Falaise–Trun road, hoping to keep parts of the highway open. The next morning, Field Marshal Walter Model arrived to take over from von Kluge, who after writing an obsequious letter to his Führer, committed suicide. Model's first order, for all his brave words about 'a new front before or behind the Seine,' confirmed von Kluge's decision to withdraw the 1st and 10th SS Panzer divisions immediately and to defend the shoulders of the pocket with the remaining Panzer divisions. The 2nd and 9th SS were to join the 116th in the defence of the Trun area[94] – if the Allied air forces would let them get there.

Simonds arrived at Kitching's headquarters south of Morteaux-Couliboeuf at about the same time Model was issuing instructions for the withdrawal. There were no new orders. The Poles were to reach Chambois to link up with the Americans, and 4th Division was to secure the east bank of the Dives down to and including Trun. Once the infantry brigade arrived, the armoured regiments were to occupy the high ground covering the roads through Trun and serve as a counterattack force.[95] But that day belonged to the tactical air forces, which flew a record 3,057 sorties on 18 August. The 2nd TAF alone claimed 124 tanks destroyed and 96 damaged, as well as close to 3,000 transport vehicles. The action was especially hectic west of Trun, but targets were found throughout the pocket, and inevitably many Allied units were attacked. The Polish Armoured Division suffered many casualties from 2TAF fire during its advance toward Chambois, which paralleled the German escape routes. The 51st Highland Division, which was also heading east, reported forty incidents of friendly fire on 18 August, resulting in forty-one casualties and the destruction of twenty-five vehicles.[96] The Canadians, moving south to Trun, were less likely targets. However, they did not attempt to occupy the town until air attacks – in this case by Thunderbolts of the 9th U.S. Tactical Air Force – ceased.[97]

The rich array of targets in the pocket proved irresistible to the fighter pilots of both air forces, and attempts to divide up the territory between rival and highly competitive groups had little effect. The 2nd TAF demanded that 9th Air Force stay away from the immediate battle area, which Coningham insisted was reserved for 83 Group, as well as the roads to Vimoutiers, which were the responsibility of 84 Group. The proposed boundary left 9th Air Force with the area between Bernay and the Seine, but neither Quesada nor Bradley was willing to accept such restrictions, which limited the ability of U.S. fighter-bombers to support American ground forces.[98]

By mid-afternoon of 18 August, Trun was secure and 4th Division was on or approaching all its objectives, but the Poles had not yet captured Chambois. When Simonds met his divisional commanders at 1500,[99] Maczek reported that the Koszutski battlegroup had gone astray and ended up at Les Champeaux, 10 kilometres north of Chambois. It was short of ammunition and fuel, and Maczek had sent one of his infantry battalions to assist it. The divisional recce regiment had reached the edge of Chambois but could not enter the town, which was under constant Allied air attack.[100]

Simonds urged Maczek to redouble efforts to reinforce the recce regiment at Chambois, but he also ordered 4th Division to advance from Trun to Chambois. The 3rd Division was to take over its positions on the east bank of the Dives. This would take some time, and according to 4th Division's War Diary would only be 'put into effect' on 19 August, 'as soon as the division had cleared the enemy from the area north and NW of Trun.'[101] Brigadier Jefferson decided not to wait. Shortly after the Lincs took control of Trun he ordered the South Alberta Regiment (SAR), with a company of Argylls under command, 'to seize and hold Chambois before last light.'[102] Lt.-Col. Wotherspoon got Maj. David Currie's C Squadron, fifteen tanks strong, with a half-strength company of Argylls, underway by 1800. Despite long-range fire from Polish tanks and a strafing attack by two Spitfires, the battle-group reached St-Lambert-sur-Dives at dusk. The village was occupied by enemy troops, and Currie was told to wait until first light before clearing it. Later that day, Wotherspoon 'took his RHQ Troop of four tanks, Recce Troop, B squadron and four M-10s of K Troop 5th Anti-Tank Regiment down the road to Currie's position ... on the top of Hill 117.'[103] The rest of the division occupied high ground in an area running northeast from Trun, all the way to Pt 236 north of Hordouseaux, where contact with the Polish Armoured Division was established.[104]

The decision to place 4th Armoured Brigade in defensive positions along the Trun-Vimoutiers highway instead of committing it to the closing of the gap between Trun and Chambois may have been the result of Ultra intelligence. At 0916, 18 August, Ultra recipients were informed that 2nd SS Panzer Corps had been ordered 'to clear up the situation resulting from the Allied penetration north-west of Trun which had created a gap in the German front.' This was to be accomplished by 'a concentric attack' carried out by 2nd SS Panzer Corps and two other Panzer divisions directed on Trun from both inside and outside the pocket.[105] Removing the armoured brigade, which by then included the Lake Superior and Algonquin Regiments, from the struggle to close the Trun-Chambois gap created an impossible situation for Brig. Jefferson. His two understrength infantry battalions had to cover the approaches to Trun and provide infantry to support the South Alberta thrust toward Chambois. Until 9th Brigade arrived to take over the defence of Trun, Jefferson had to juggle scarce resources as best he could.

The Polish Armoured Division was no closer to closing the gap. The 10th Mounted Rifles were hunkered down a kilometre from Chambois, and the rest of the division was scattered well to the north. A situation report sent to 2 Canadian Corps at 2040, 18 August, stated that one battlegroup was trying to reach Bourdon but 'were temporarily immobilised due to lack of petrol.' A second group was close behind but was being held up by enemy forces. The third battlegroup had occupied Pt 258 south of Les Champeaux. The report continued: 'Units and armed bde HQ have been continually bombed by own forces, half the petrol sent to 2nd Armoured Regiment was destroyed through bombing just after 1200 hrs. Movement in this country is very difficult and slow for tanks ... One squadron recce regiment have been observing Chambois for some time but could not get in owing to bombing, this town is not believed strongly held.'[106]

Complaints about the accidental bombing and strafing of Allied and especially Polish troops led 2TAF to propose that the Poles be withdrawn to allow 84 Group complete freedom to deal with the area north of Chambois, which was 'packed with German transport.' By the time a meeting with the Chief of Staff of 21 Army Group was held, the Poles were at Coudehard and Pt 262 North, cut off from their supplies and directly in the path of the enemy retreat. It was now impossible to withdraw the Poles, even if Montgomery had agreed.[107]

On the morning of 18 August, on the south side of the pocket, U.S. 5 Corps had finally begun operations to close the gap. Lt.-Gen. L.T. Gerow had three divisions available, but the commander of his only armoured division, General Leclerc, was determined to avoid involvement in a battle that might prevent his division from participating in the liberation of Paris. Gerow agreed that the French division's role would be limited to artillery support and flank protection for the Americans. This left 80th Division with the task of bypassing Argentan and moving north toward Trun while 90th advanced from le Bourg-St-Léonard to Chambois. The 80th, attacking one regiment up across rising ground, was unable to make any progress, and the attack was called off. The 90th was more successful. The leading infantry 'outflanked resistance' and closed to within 2 kilometres of Chambois before a Werfer brigade and elements of 116th Panzer Division checked the attack.[108] Gerow was content with this modest advance because his fifteen artillery battalions were finding and hitting targets all across the gap.[109] That night, Allied artillery continued to pound the enemy, but the roads north of Chambois remained open and in use.

Montgomery's nightly message on 18 August referred to 'intense fighting ... in many places in the pocket' and the 'immense destruction to enemy personnel and equipment' achieved by the air force. He was satisfied that 'any German formations or units that escape eastwards over the Seine will be quite unfit to fight for months to come.'[110] In a separate report to the prime minister he described the pocket as a 'scene of great destruction ... With such air power as we possess the Germans cannot escape us.'[111] Clearly, Montgomery was content with actions designed to squeeze the pocket while the air force dealt the final blows to the enemy. Those who made it past Chambois faced the squadrons of 84 Group waiting for morning to pounce on the thousands of vehicles strung out along the roads around Vimoutiers. Tactical air force claims may have been exaggerated, but panic, chaos, and destruction was everywhere visible.

The decision to employ air power rather than a sufficient number of ground troops made a good deal of sense. It was cost effective, and when combined with great quantities of artillery fire, it was capable of destroying the combat power of the remaining enemy forces. Air power could not occupy ground and complete the encirclement, so Allied commanders did not cancel orders to close the remaining exits from the pocket. There was, however, no sense of urgency. The senior commanders focused on future plans. Both Simonds and Gerow, the two corps commanders, hesitated to commit additional resources to a difficult and costly task that was better left to the air force.

Simonds spent the morning of 19 August 'tidying up official correspondence.' At noon he met with his divisional commanders and heads of arms to outline plans for the advance to the Seine.[112] Maczek reported that his division was advancing slowly in difficult country to Chambois and Coudehard – Mt Ormel but was not there yet. Kitching reported that the progress of 10th Brigade's advance to Chambois had stalled at St-Lambert-sur-Dives. Simonds decided that 4th Division 'was to concentrate attention' on the area from Trun through St-Lambert-sur-Dives to the western edge of Moissy. The Poles were to occupy Moissy after securing Chambois.[113]

Maczek left the conference determined to press his weary men on to their objectives. Advancing in three separate battlegroups, the Poles reached Coudehard at 1539 and, after a battle with Panthers, occupied Pt 262 North. In the centre, 'a great number of prisoners' were taken in the capture of Pt 137; the subsequent advance toward Coudehard and Chambois through difficult country was 'very slow.' The 10th Dragoons linked up with the recce regiment outside Chambois and by 1930 were involved in 'heavy hand to hand battles' on the edge of the village.[114] American troops reached the southern edge of Chambois at about the same time. The soldiers of both nations were stunned by the scenes of death and destruction. German armour, trucks, and horse-drawn wagons and the corpses of men and horses jammed the roads to and from the village. The Poles turned their prisoners over to the Americans and joined them in organizing the defence of the area. There was no possibility of fulfilling orders to meet the Canadians at Moissy, and no one had instructed 90th Division to go beyond Chambois.[115]

That night Crerar sent a message to Simonds that read:

Desire you transmit to GOC Polish Armoured Division my congratulations concerning the important and gallant part all under his command have played in the recent fighting. The First Canadian Army is very proud to count the Polish Armoured Division amongst its formations. If we all work as determinedly and as well together in the future as in the past our mutual celebration of final victory cannot be long delayed.[116]

There was good reason to congratulate the Poles, who had finally closed the pocket, but were there enough troops on the ground to *keep* it closed?

The contrast between the Polish efforts to reach their objectives and the limited role played by 4th Armoured Brigade on 19 August requires explanation. Simonds had instructed 4th Armoured Division 'to concentrate attention' on the Trun–Chambois gap, but he had also decided that the armoured brigade – commanded as of noon 19 August by Robert Moncel, a staff officer at his headquarters – was to be used to lead the Canadian advance to the Seine. Additional troops to close the gap would have to come from 3rd Division. At his first O Group, held at 2130 on 19 August, Moncel outlined plans 'to advance to a position on high ground overlooking Vimoutiers.' No mention was made of the situation at St-Lambert.[117]

These decisions must have been influenced by reports that the allied air forces were again in action, especially around Chambois and the roads to the north, and by optimistic reports from the SARs. Wotherspoon had placed one of his squadrons along the road from Trun 'to guard the line of the Dives and to secure communications.' Regimental HQ Troop and the four 17-pounders of 5th Anti-Tank Regiment were stationed on Pt 117 above the village, and B Squadron was available in reserve.[118] Maj. Currie's battlegroup had entered the village at 0630 and was able to report 'Rooster' – the occupation of St-Lambert – at 1037. Wotherspoon decided to commit his reserve squadron; at 1230 he signalled that it was 'pushing on to Cock,' the code word for Chambois. At 1500, after hearing that American troops had been sighted southeast of Chambois, Wotherspoon ordered his men 'to liaise with friends and have friends take care of Cock. Remain firm at Rooster.'[119] These reports, and subsequent ones throughout the day, suggested that everything was under control. The arrival of an second infantry

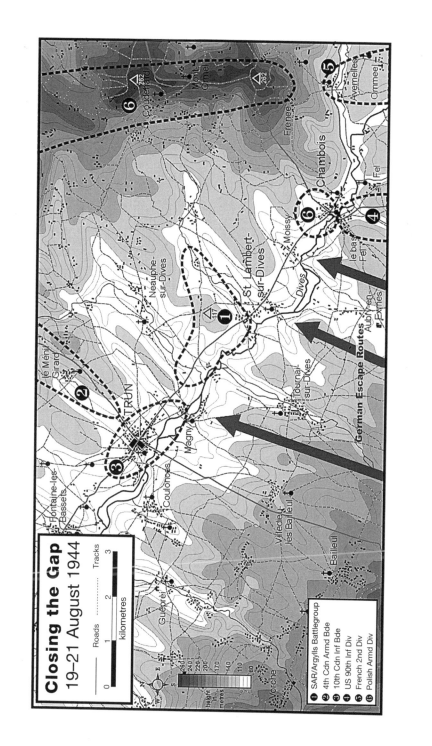

Closing the Gap
19–21 August 1944

Roads ———
Tracks ·········

0   1   2   3
kilometres

Height
in.
metres
260
240
220
200
170
140
110
80

N
W ——— E
S

● SAR/Argylls Battlegroup
❷ 4th Cdn Armd Bde
❸ 10th Cdn Inf Bde
❹ US 90th Inf Div
❺ French 2nd Div
❻ Polish Armd Div

le Ménil-
Girard

Fontaine-les-
Bassets

TRUN

Guéprei

Vorche

Coulonces

Magny

Villedieu-
les-Bailleul

Bailleul

Neauphe-
sur-Dives

St Lambert-
sur-Dives

Tournai-
sur-Dives

Dives

Moissy

Chambois

Fel

le ba...
Fel

Aubry-en-
Exmes

German Escape Routes

Couderard

Mont
Ormel

262

262

Frenée

Avernelles

Ormel

117

company from the Argylls and a composite company from the Lincs added to the sense of security, as did the arrival of a FOO from 15th Field Regiment, who reported that both field and medium artillery were in range.[120]

This optimism was evident when C Company of the Argylls reached St-Lambert. They 'went right through the village and out the other side heading towards Chambois,' and reached Moissy as it was growing dark. Here they encountered the enemy; after a brief, confusing firefight in which the company commander was wounded, they returned to St-Lambert.[121] While the Argylls headed for Moissy, Wotherspoon sought further reinforcements. Shortly before 1900 on 19 August he sent a message to brigade: 'Still in Rooster – tired and must have relief in the form of infantry. Slight enemy resistance. PW still surrendering. Unless relief comes Germans will move back in.' Jefferson informed division about the situation, reporting that the SARs were under attack and 'had been attacked all afternoon by company after company of infantry.' Each 'must be fought for a few minutes before surrendering.'[122] There was little that Kitching could do. Further Ultra decrypts suggested that the enemy was now preparing a major attack in the Trun–Vimoutiers area for first light on 20 August.[123] There could be no question of sending reinforcements to St-Lambert until battalions from 3rd Division arrived.

Late on the afternoon of 19 August, Maj.-Gen. Dan Spry, now commanding 3rd Division, ordered 9th Brigade to take over the line Trun–Chambois. The lead battalion reached Trun at 0200 on 20 August. The town was in chaos, teeming with prisoners of war – including many who were wounded – and hundreds of civilian refugees. The Stormont Dundas and Glengarry Highlanders organized the defence of Trun and the nearby village of Magny while the Highland Light Infantry waited to tie up with the First Hussars in preparation for an advance to the high ground north of St-Lambert. The North Novas were to relieve the SAR/Argyll battlegroup, but well before these arrangements could be carried out, the final enemy breakout began.[124]

General Hauser had made the decision to try to break through the loose encirclement that night even though he now knew that the counterattack by 2nd SS Panzer Corps could not begin until the morning. The breakout was to begin shortly before midnight, with two columns of paratroopers crossing the Dives at Magny and St-Lambert. Remaining elements of the Hitler Youth were to follow the paratroopers while the 1st SS and 116th Panzer divisions broke through near Chambois. The rest of the German forces – 10th SS, 2nd Panzer, and elements of three infantry divisions – were to form a third wave, securing the flanks and the rear as they withdrew. If all went well, the concentric attack would open the Chambois–Vimoutiers road so that both vehicles and men could escape.[125]

While the German paratroopers were moving into position to begin the breakout, Montgomery informed London that 'all exits from the pocket are completely blocked and no further enemy will escape ... I have issued a fresh directive' outlining future plans.[126] The directive, M519, dated 20 August, stated that 'the destruction or capture of large bodies of enemy still fighting hard inside the Normandy "bottle" [was a] first priority.' It was up to the First Canadian Army, with the support of the American troops in place, to keep 'the cork in position' while the First U.S. Army advanced along the south bank of the Seine 'to cut off the retreat of enemy forces.' The rest of the directive dealt with plans for the advance into Germany, which was becoming his real preoccupation.[127]

As commander of the ground forces, Montgomery's primary responsibility was for long-term strategy, and by 19 August it was far too late to reinforce either 5 American or 2 Canadian Corps. But what of the 2nd British Army? On 16 August, 53rd Division had been south of Falaise, 'delayed by small pockets of enemy and mines.' The next day the advance, against 'slight opposition,' brought the lead brigade to within 10 kilometres of Trun. Then, on 18 August, this cautious approach slowed to a stop as 12th Corps reorganized to prepare for the advance to the Seine.[128] On 19 August the reliefs continued, and troops in place were ordered to 'mop up' and to stop if 'serious enemy opposition' was met.[129] The decision to order British troops to follow up rather than actively engage enemy troops was an intrinsic part of Montgomery's plan for the advance to and beyond the Seine. This decision, however, bought vital time for the enemy to organize for the final breakout.

The small groups of American, Canadian, and Polish soldiers actually in position to hold the cork on the bottle knew nothing of these strategic visions. For them, 20 August was a day of intense combat as the enemy fought with growing desperation. St-Lambert was inevitably a focal point because two roads led to its bridges over the Dives. The Argylls, lacking explosives, had left the bridges intact when they were forced to withdraw in the face of enemy infiltration across the entire front. At 0500, Wotherspoon informed brigade that his troops were 'much too thin on the ground' to stop the enemy advance. He asked for 'all artillery support possible' but was told that there was to be 'no shooting south west of River Dives unless definitely recognized enemy,' as '12 British Corps moving from wood toward river.'[130] Since the leading British unit, 53rd Division's recce regiment, was still well to the east of Trun,[131] this restriction could only aid the enemy.

By mid-morning the Germans had forced the SARs and Argylls to withdraw to the western edge of St-Lambert; this allowed them full use of the bridges. The enemy also crossed at Moissy and at the edge of Chambois, joining a flood of men and vehicles, including tanks, moving toward Vimoutiers. Jefferson ordered the Lincs and the Argylls, who had just been relieved by 9th Brigade in Trun, to 'get astride as many roads northeast out of Trun as possible.' He then asked 4th Armoured Brigade to try to stop the breakout by occupying Pt 240 east of Ecorches.[132] Moncel's brigade had already begun its planned move north, but the regiments halted, turned, and took up positions that denied the enemy the use of three minor roads as well as the Trun–Vimoutiers highway. The Grenadier Guards were sent to Pt 240, 2 kilometres east of the Poles at Pt 262, but they did not secure it until 1400.[133] These moves had no impact on the situation in St-Lambert, where Maj. David Currie was tirelessly encouraging his shrinking band of men to hold on and continue firing at the enemy. The SAR positions on Pt 117 and Pt 124 were also under attack, and Pt 124, overlooking one of the main escape routes, had to be abandoned.[134] The SARs sent a stream of messages asking for the promised reinforcements, but Jefferson and Kitching were unwilling to commit the Lincs or the last two companies of Argylls to a battle hours before a handover to 9th Brigade. The Lincs (less the one company in St-Lambert) spent the day north of Trun getting 'as much rest as possible,' and at 1900 moved north to join in the advance to the Seine.[135]

The North Nova Scotia Highlanders, assigned to take over St-Lambert, left their position near Morteaux-Couliboeuf at 0920 on

20 August and reached Trun at 1100, but were then ordered to Neau-phe-sur-Dives, 2 kilometres north of St-Lambert. They did not attempt to relieve the SARs until the fighting had died down that evening.[136] The Highland Light Infantry, who were waiting for the First Hussars, were equally hesitant to get involved in this confused situation. The next morning, 21 August, under a steady rain, the HLI dealt with hundreds of prisoners who emerged from the woods without weapons or the will to escape.[137] Despite direct orders to move immediately, the Hussar/HLI force did not reach the outskirts of Chambois until mid-afternoon.[138] By then the enemy who had crossed the Dives were dead, on their way north, or in prisoner of war cages.

Polish accounts of the fighting on 20 August describe a battle with the 1st and 2nd tank regiments that raged the entire day at Pt 262 North, which was under attack from all directions. The Poles could count on the support of the medium and field artillery. The FOO from 4th Canadian Medium Regiment, Capt. Pierre Sévigny, called for repeated 'Mike and Uncle' targets as well as a 'Victor' target employing more than two hundred guns.[139] The artillery, and the determination of the Polish soldiers, prevented the Germans from overrunning the fortress position, but at least one escape route was kept open throughout the afternoon and into the night.[140] It is impossible to say how many German soldiers escaped the net after midnight of 19 August, but the number was certainly in the thousands.[141]

Polish losses in the struggle to close the gap, calculated at 1,441 – including 466 killed in action – offer some indication of the intensity of the battle.[142] General Maczek and his officers were openly critical of 4th Armoured Division's failure to cooperate with them, especially on 20 August, when the fighting was at its peak. According to Maczek, repeated requests for assistance were ignored until Simonds arrived at the divisional headquarters and 'hearing of the situation in Chambois and north ordered an immediate counterattack by 4th Armoured Brigade to relieve the situation.'[143] Simonds then went to 4th Division headquarters to make sure the orders were obeyed promptly. Kitching protested the order and told the corps commander, 'To hell with them. They have run out of food and ammunition because of the inefficiency of their organization; our people have been fighting just as hard but we have managed to keep up our supply system.'[144]

Simonds silenced Kitching and ordered immediate action. He knew perfectly well that 4th Armoured Brigade had been virtually out of the action for forty-eight hours. Simonds had himself given the order to prepare for the advance to Vimoutiers. The next day Kitching was relieved of his command.[145] The armoured brigade advanced that evening and made visual contact with the Poles before midnight. The next morning the three armoured regiments encountered groups of the enemy, including tanks. It was mid-afternoon of 21 August before direct contact was established with the Poles and a supply route established. The War Diary of the Grenadier Guards reported the loss of four tanks in the advance to Pt 262 and offered a vivid description of the scene:

> No. 1 Squadron led off at 0800 hours in the pouring rain. The road, as were all the roads in the area, was lined and in places practically blocked by destroyed German vehicles of every description. Horses and men lay rotting in every ditch and hedge and the air was rank with the odour of putrification. Most of the destruction was caused by the air force, but the Poles had done their share ... No. 1 Squadron's co-axes fired almost continually ... until arriving at Pt 262 and the results were devastating ... The picture at 262 was the grimmest the Regiment had so far come up against. The Poles had had no supplies for three days; they had several hundred wounded who had not been evacuated, about 700 prisoners-of-war lay loosely guarded in a field ... unburied dead and parts of them were strewn about by the score ... The Poles cried with joy when we arrived ...[146]

The gap was now closed, both at Pt 262 and at the Dives. By the evening of 21 August all that remained was to round up stragglers. Evidence of the enemy's crushing defeat astounded all those who arrived in the pocket. Among the observers were representatives from 21 Army Group's Operational Research Section on a mission to determine the extent and causes of German vehicle losses. Their report divided the battlefield into four sectors: 'the Pocket' west of the Argentan-Falaise highway; 'the Shambles' between the highway and Vimoutiers; 'the Chase' from Vimoutiers to the Seine; and the 'Seine Crossing.' The investigators counted more than 8,000 damaged, destroyed, or abandoned vehicles, including 456 tanks and self-propelled guns and 367

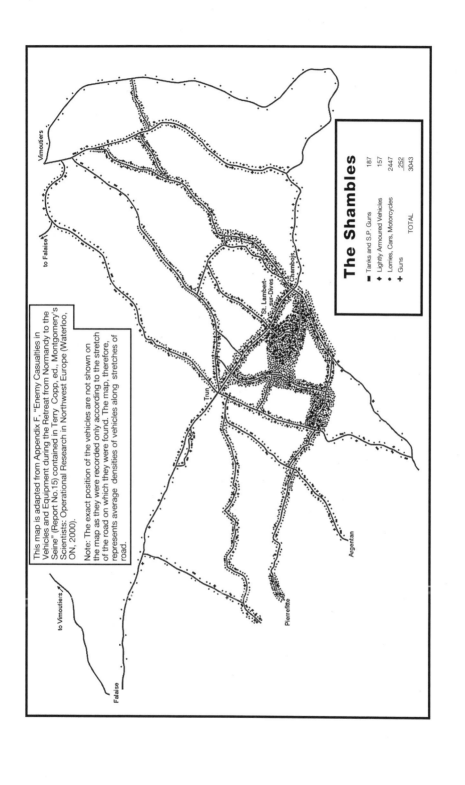

The Shambles

- Tanks and S.P. Guns   187
- Lightly Armoured Vehicles   157
- Lorries, Cars, Motorcycles   2447
- Guns   <u>252</u>

TOTAL   3043

This map is adapted from Appendix F, "Enemy Casualties in Vehicles and Equipment during the Retreat from Normandy to the Seine" (Report No.15) contained in Terry Copp. ed., Montgomery's Scientists: Operational Research in Northwest Europe (Waterloo, ON, 2000).

Note: The exact position of the vehicles are not shown on the map as they were recorded only according to the stretch of the road on which they were found. The map, therefore, represents average densities of vehicles along stretches of road.

Vimoutiers

to Falaise

Chambois

"St. Lambert-sur-Dives

Trun

Argentan

Pierrefitte

to Vimoutiers

Falaise

lightly armoured vehicles. Their estimate of uncounted vehicles raised the total to 10,000, and a subsequent survey raised the figure to over 12,000. Their report was highly controversial because it attributed less than one-third of the losses to air action and contradicted the air force's claims of the destruction of enemy armour. The OR team also reported that as many as 20,000 motor vehicles and 250 tanks and self-propelled guns had escaped across the Seine, though many of these never made it back to defend Germany.[147] Because of a lack of evidence, no attempt was made to calculate how many troops made it across the river.

As the Allied armies moved toward Germany, the controversy over the delay in closing the gaps at Falaise–Argentan and Trun–Chambois was forgotten in the euphoria of victory – a victory that Montgomery described as 'definite, complete and decisive.' The Canadians and Poles who had, by strategic default, become the main instrument of the encirclement, took pride in their achievement and turned toward the Seine confident that they had done their duty and that the end of the war was in sight.

10

Normandy:
A New Balance
Sheet

The Allied campaign in Normandy resulted in one of the great military victories in modern history. After a successful assault on a defended coast, General Eisenhower's naval, air, and ground forces destroyed two powerful German armies in just seventy-six days. Enemy losses of close to half a million men included the combat elements of thirty-seven divisions deployed in Normandy as well as another six left behind to delay Allied access to ports. Other large fragments of Army Group B – about 25,000 men from twenty different divisions – were encircled at Mons on 4 September.[1]

This extraordinary achievement has failed to impress military historians, who have developed an interpretation of the campaign that emphasizes operational and tactical failure. The Allied armies – and especially the British and Canadian armies – have repeatedly been measured against the German army 'and have been found wanting in almost every respect.'[2] The British historian John Ellis – an admittedly extreme proponent of this view – has described the Normandy campaign 'in a nutshell' as 'acute German shortages of munitions [and replacements] on the one hand, and on the other an Allied cornucopia which could provide an overwhelming level of firepower and a remorseless stream of replacements that could compensate for all but the grossest tactical bêtise.'[3]

No part of the Allied achievement is less well understood than the D-Day landings. Ellis concedes that on paper the odds perhaps would have favoured the enemy on 6 June were it not for overwhelming naval and air power, which provided 'decisive assistance in the land battle.' This image of massive fire support from the sea and the air has persisted despite conclusive evidence that the weather and the technical limitations of naval and air support meant that few enemy positions were destroyed or even neutralized by the preliminary bombing or bombardment. At Juno, as elsewhere, no serious damage was done to the defences before the infantry, tanks, and combat engineers overcame the enemy in close combat. Eighty per cent of the 359 Canadians killed in action and the 715 wounded on D-Day fell during the struggle to get off the beach and overcome an enemy occupying fortified positions.[4] The battles for Courseulles, Bernières, and St-Aubin were won by men of outstanding courage and considerable skill. No one who seriously examines the evidence can argue that overwhelming force won the battle for the beaches.

Other critics of the British and Canadian performance focus on the failure to advance inland quickly and capture the final D-Day objectives. This framework of analysis was first advanced by Chester Wilmot, who blamed the failure to reach Caen on the 'defensive complex' of 3rd British Division and the 'unduly cautious' advance of its lead battalions.[5] Canada's official historian, C.P. Stacey, joined in the chorus, arguing that a more 'sustained effort' by the Canadians would have produced a 'deeper penetration [and] saved many weeks of bloody fighting.'[6] Neither historian explained how tired troops on thinly held ground closer to Caen would have better withstood the powerful German counterattacks mounted on 6–7 June, or how this would have avoided weeks of bloody fighting. Gen. Dempsey's decision to hold a solid position on the intermediate objective made a good deal more sense than pushing small battlegroups forward to Caen and Carpiquet.

Stacey outlined his criticism of the Canadian effort in a chapter titled 'Normandy: The Balance Sheet,' which questioned the training and combat effectiveness of the Canadian (and other Allied) armies relative to the German forces they encountered in Normandy. Stacey was especially impressed with 12th SS, but noted that 'other German divisions which had not fought before gave a very good account of themselves [because] they contrived to get more out of their training than we did.'[7]

The events of the first five days on the bridgehead do not lend themselves to such sweeping generalizations. The 12th SS were imbued with the belief that 'decisive action remains the prerequisite for success in war,' and with the idea that everybody 'from the highest commander to the youngest soldier must be conscious of the fact that inactivity and lost opportunities weigh heavier than the choice of means,'[8] and so they leapt to the attack. Against the North Nova–Sherbrooke battlegroup, this doctrine produced a tactical victory with negative operational consequences. Against the 7th Brigade fortress, repeated attacks by battlegroups which had 'often been practised and proven in Russia' produced one temporary local success (Putot) and a series of costly defeats. Anglo-Canadian doctrine, with its emphasis on dug-in troops supported by artillery, proved to be highly effective as long as the enemy stuck to its doctrine and pressed forward into calculated zones of fire. By the end of the first week in Normandy, the senior officers of 1st SS Panzer Corps knew they would have to modify their doctrine and seal off the Allied penetration by creating a defence-in-depth. From now on, counterattacks would be ordered selectively, in response to Allied advances, and used to regain vital ground at least until infantry divisions arrived to release the Panzer divisions from their static role. When 2nd SS Panzer Corps arrived from the Eastern Front, these lessons had to be learned all over again.

Dempsey's decision to use 7th Armoured Division in a deep penetration role, while sending the Canadian Armoured Brigade to seize open high ground near Le-Mesnil-Patry, resulted in losses comparable to those suffered in the attacks by 12th SS. No further attempts to lead with armour were made until Operation Goodwood, and Montgomery concentrated on building up resources for a series of set piece, bite-and-hold battles.

The performance of Canadian units in these actions varied enormously, but was this due to character or circumstance? The Royal Winnipeg Rifles fought with determination and success on D-Day but were overrun and virtually destroyed on D+2. The Regina Rifles were equally successful in the assault and absolutely outstanding in the defence of Bretteville-Norrey. If such things as unit citations existed in the Canadian Army, one would surely have been awarded to Lt.-Col. Matheson and his men. How much of this was due to the leadership and cohesiveness of the battalion, and how much to Matheson's dispositions and the skill of the gunners of 13th Field Regiment? The Reginas also benefited from the arrogance and inexperience of the 12th SS commanders, who seemed incapable of coordinating attacks between battalions, never mind regiments.

The Canadian Scottish Regiment, like the Reginas, emerged from the bridgehead battle with a high reputation. The CSR's success in retaking Putot has been all but ignored despite – or perhaps because of – the evidence of close infantry–tank cooperation, superb use of a lifting barrage, incredible courage in closing with the enemy, and an intelligent understanding of how best to ensure the ground would not be lost again. The First Hussars worked well with all three of 7th Brigade's battalions, providing close support from the D-Day beaches to the destruction of the Panthers at Norrey. The Hussars and the Fort

Garry Horse fought as separate squadrons in exactly the way that infantry-support armour was trained to do. The Sherbrooke Fusiliers alone fought as a regiment during the bridgehead battle of D+1. Sherbrooke veterans recall their first encounter with 12th SS as the greatest day in the regiment's history. They reacted to the sudden German counterattack with both fire and movement, inflicting losses that the Germans could ill afford. Even one of the sternest critics of the Canadian performance in Normandy agrees that their 'basic training was validated; troops manouevred, "Fireflies" provided overwatch and panzers were destroyed.' They 'left the battlefield weary, bruised but tested.'[9] The North Nova Scotia Highlanders were the only other battalion-sized unit involved in intense combat in the four-day period. Their losses at Buron and Authie do not reflect adversely on the courage or leadership of the battalion. The resolute defence of Authie and the counterattack on Buron are indications of just how good a unit the North Novas were.[10]

The battles for Caen, which began on 25 June and ended with the liberation of the city on 9 July, revealed the strengths and weaknesses of the operational and tactical doctrines employed by British and Canadian divisions. With the enemy committed to holding carefully selected and skilfully camouflaged positions, the Second British Army had little choice except to wage a series of attritional battles employing set piece techniques. Operations Martlet, Epsom, Windsor, Charnwood, and Jupiter succeeded in wearing down the enemy, but neither the British nor the Canadians had prepared for actions so costly in human lives, and both lacked an adequate supply of replacements.[11]

The set piece battles of late June and early July demonstrated that well dug-in troops, deployed in depth could survive massive artillery concentrations and continue to fight effectively. The soldiers of the 2nd British Army, required to emerge from their slit trenches and cross open ground to close with the enemy, discovered that the success of the air forces in slowing the resupply of Panzer Group West had no apparent effect on the firepower employed on the battlefield. German mortars, Nebelwerfers, and artillery were used mainly against observed targets or to place rounds immediately behind the forward edge of a moving barrage. When the Germans mounted an organized counterattack, they used indirect fire in much the same way as the

Allies did, but there were few such operations in the 'dogfight' stage of the battle. Immediate counterattacks employing direct fire from tanks or assault guns were the favoured method of preventing the Allies from consolidating on an objective, and such attacks required limited quantities of aimed fire.

The Allied attacks also suffered from the inaccuracy of their predicted artillery fire and from the inability of medium, heavy, and fighter bombers to find and hit small targets dispersed over a battlefield. Well before D-Day, operational research scientists had tried to persuade the Royal Artillery that serious problems existed and had advocated the use of radar both for target identification and for wind forecasting.[12] Experiments demonstrated that 'Meteor' forecasts, which provided estimates of wind speed and direction in the airspace through which artillery shells would pass, could be dramatically improved by radar observation of weather balloons, but the authorities did not respond to this finding until the need to do so was demonstrated in Normandy.[13] As well, the employment of radar in a counter-battery and counter-mortar role was undertaken only after evidence of the devastating effect of enemy mortar fire was analysed in Normandy.[14]

A constant problem was that artillery concentrations were off for line and range or too thin to neutralize the enemy. The only available solution was to increase the number of guns and rounds per gun in the hope of achieving 'a density of 650 field and medium shells per hour per kilometre square, or one or two shells every minute within 200 yards' of an enemy position. Operational researchers reported that this was needed 'to keep officers and everyone else in their shelters.'[15] When such weights of bombardment were used, the enemy still survived, but the attackers were able to secure their objectives with dramatically reduced casualties.[16] The artillery-based battle doctrine employed by the Allies was theoretically sound, but without improvements in both accuracy and the volume of fire, the guns of Normandy could be only a partial solution to the challenges posed by the enemy.

Unfortunately, Allied air power could not compensate for the artillery's limitations. Throughout the Normandy campaign, 2nd Tactical Air Force waged a separate war against the enemy's air force, lines of communication and targets of opportunity. The tactical air squadrons were overwhelmingly successful at winning the campaign they chose to fight, but this was not the same campaign the army was waging. The technical limitations of the Spitfires and Typhoons were a major factor in their ability to provide close support or to attack precision targets, but it is also clear that Air Marshal Coningham and his staff officers had little interest in learning how to carry out missions of the sort the army was requesting. Tactical air power weakened the enemy by slowing and then reducing the logistical support available to it, but it was far from the decisive factor in the Normandy victory.[17]

Hitler's decision to demand a resolute defence of the Orne and Hill 112, and his subsequent orders to hold the high ground immediately south of Caen, set the stage for a second round of attritional battles on both sides of the Orne. By mid-July, Panzer Group West had concentrated seven Panzer divisions, six infantry divisions, all three Tiger battalions, the 3rd Flak Corps, and three Nebelwerfer brigades against the Second British Army. This deployment provided the enemy with near-total security in the Caen sector, as Dempsey could not possibly commit sufficient troops to achieve the kind of force ratio required to defeat such a powerful, well-entrenched enemy.

Montgomery understood this but let himself be persuaded to attempt an ill-conceived armoured blitzkrieg. Operationally and tactically, Goodwood was a disaster which demonstrated that Allied armour was too vulnerable to be employed against well-established defences. Critics of Allied armour doctrine insist that much of the problem arose from poor infantry–tank cooperation, but they fail to explain exactly what infantry was supposed to do about a distant anti-tank gun screen or enemy tanks firing from ranges in excess of 1000 metres.

Goodwood was the occasion of 2 Canadian Corps' first battle; it was also Guy Simonds's introduction to the realities of Normandy. Simonds's outline plan for Operation Atlantic was well conceived, and the veteran 3rd Canadian Infantry Division again demonstrated the commitment and flexibility that consistently distinguished its operations. Simonds was strongly aware of the need to introduce green troops into battle under the right conditions, and managed the first two phases of 2nd Division's attack with considerable skill. The initial plan, which called for 4th Brigade to cross the Orne at Louvigny, was abandoned when it became apparent that the enemy could not be moved from the high ground west of the river. He then ordered Maj.-Gen. Foulkes to wait until 3rd Division had established a firm bridgehead before committing 5th Brigade to an assault crossing of the Orne at Caen. The brigade then captured Pt 67, the northern spur of Verrières Ridge, in a carefully controlled action. Simonds should have been content with this marked success; instead, he ordered Foulkes to commit his reserve brigade to an attack on Verrières Ridge that could only have succeeded if the enemy had been caught in the midst of a withdrawal.

Simonds's actions on 20 July raise serious questions about his judgment and temperament – questions that are reinforced by a careful review of decision-making during Operation Spring. Again, full credit should be given to Simonds for the careful and innovative plans developed for the operation. A night attack on limited, reachable objectives, followed by an early morning advance supported by armoured squadrons and an armoured division, was a reasonable approach to a difficult task designed as a holding operation to assist the Americans. It is also clear that Simonds's orders to begin Phase II, including the attack by the Black Watch, were based on the best available information and were entirely reasonable. But within hours of launching Phase II, the enemy demonstrated its commitment to holding the ridge by mounting powerful armoured counterattacks. Simonds's actions from mid-morning on 25 July until Spring was finally called off suggest that he was completely out of touch with reality. According to Foulkes, Simonds wanted to continue the battle through the night of 25 July and was in an absolute rage when told this was impossible as no more troops were available.[18]

The 2nd Division's first two weeks in combat included both victories and defeats. The achievements of the Royal Regiment at Louvigny, the Calgaries at Pt 67, the Black Watch at Ifs, the Camerons and Sherbrookes at St-André-sur-Orne, the Maisonneuves at Etavaux, and the Royal Hamilton Light Infantry at Verrières deserve to be considered along with the actions that failed to secure their objectives. It is also important to note that the shortage of infantry replacements had an especially adverse effect on 2nd Division. By 28 July it was short 1,060 riflemen; and by 20 August it was reporting a deficiency of 1,840 infantry other ranks.[19] German divisions were not the only ones to suffer from attritional warfare.

On 8 August 1944, 2 Canadian Corps launched the first of two operations that were to establish Simonds's reputation as one of the best corps commanders in the Allied armies. Sir Richard O'Connor, arguably the outstanding Allied armoured commander of the war, regarded the Canadian achievements in August as something approaching a revolution in the conduct of armoured warfare. On 23 August he informed his divisional commanders that his Brigadier General Staff (BGS) had visited 2 Canadian Corps to learn the details of the 'two most successful operations' carried out by the Canadians. 'I felt,' he wrote, 'that they were so important that my BGS is lecturing to the COs of the Guards Armoured Division this evening and would do the same for other divisions.'[20] Writing to Montgomery the same day, O'Connor reported that he had 'studied with great interest and admiration the Canadian operations including a night attack with tanks and a day operation involving smoke.' He admired Simonds's 'courage in employing such tactics,' and he urged Montgomery to include armoured personnel carriers in the establishment of the armoured division: 'Nothing can happen, of course, unless it has your support. I hope you will agree.'[21] O'Connor's campaign helped ensure that armoured personnel carrier regiments operating Ram-based 'Kangaroos' were created, but he gave Simonds full credit for a revolution in British armoured warfare.

Simonds's 'wonderful operations' did not achieve the goals he and Montgomery had set, and the Canadians are usually criticized for taking eight days to capture Falaise and five more to close the Trun–Chambois gap. The evidence presented in this account requires a reconsideration of this critique. Operation Totalize required 2 Canadian Corps to break through an established defence-in-depth manned by 89th Infantry Division (eight battalions), and three battalions of the 272nd Division. These well dug-in troops were supported by battlegroups of 12th SS Panzer Division, divisional and corps artillery, 7th Werfer Brigade, and a number of other antitank and artillery units. Dietrich's 1st SS Panzer Corps had been preparing to deal with an advance toward Falaise for several weeks and had established two defensive zones with well-constructed field positions.[22] During the first two days of Totalize, 2 Canadian Corps broke through both lines, achieving a 15 kilometre penetration before 1st SS Panzer Corps was able to establish a temporary blocking position north of the Laison River.

The Canadian and Scottish units that carried out Phase I of Totalize won a series of hard-fought actions that owed little to overwhelming force. Operational research reports prepared a few days after the battle informed senior commanders that the RAF had failed to hit most of its targets, leaving 89th Division unscathed. Consequently, the battles for Tilly-la-Campagne, Fontenay-le-Marmion, and May-sur-Orne were day-long struggles of great intensity. The armoured battlegroups that broke through on either side of the Caen-Falaise highway might have been able to continue toward the second defensive line, but there is no basis for believing that such an advance – by units that had just carried out a challenging and exhausting night attack – would have succeeded. The much-criticized pause was made necessary by the timing of the second heavy-bomber attack and by the requirement to allow the armoured divisions to reach their start lines.[23] It is by no means clear that Phase II of Totalize could have begun much earlier even if the bombing had been cancelled.

The second phase of Totalize featured a mixture of tactical success and failure. The achievements of Halpenny Force at Cintheaux and the Argylls at Pt 195 have been overshadowed by the destruction of the BCR/Algonquin battlegroup at Pt 140. This action – which achieved the desired breakthrough and threatened the security of the new Laison River defences – demonstrated problems in command and control, within and between divisions and between the army and air force, that were to adversely effect the operations of 21 Army Group throughout the campaign. The decision to stop and reorganize so that a new, corps-level operation could be mounted was necessitated by the arrival of 85th Infantry Division, which occupied positions north of the Laison on 10–11 August. The addition of a new division with eight infantry battalions and the normal compliment of artillery, mortar, and antitank guns to the defences north of Falaise was bound to have a strong effect on the pace of operations. 1st SS Panzer Corps was stronger on 13 August than it had been on 8 August, with the equivalent of sixteen infantry battalions under command as well as the 12th SS battlegroups. The corps was responsible for holding a 32 kilometre section of the front, but most of the available force was positioned to defend the 8 kilometres of open country east of the Caen–Falaise highway, which was the obvious area for a large-scale armoured operation.

By 14 August, 1st SS Panzer Corps was stronger than it had been at the beginning of Totalize, while 2 Canadian Corps was much weaker. The 51st Highland Division and 33rd British Armoured Brigade had reverted to 1st British Corps to assist in holding the long eastern flank. The 2nd Canadian Infantry Division, though still nominally under Simonds's command, had been committed to support 12th British Corps' advance from the Orne bridgehead. This left Simonds with one infantry and two armoured divisions as well as two armoured regiments for a total of seventeen infantry battalions and ten armoured regiments. For Operation Tractable, Simonds employed ten infantry battalions and six armoured regiments, providing at most a 2:1 superiority over an entrenched enemy.

Before Tractable, Montgomery ought to have shifted substantial resources to the First Canadian Army, including a corps headquarters and several divisions capable of carrying out offensive operations against the thinly defended sector from Vimont to Jort.[24] His belated decision to transfer 7th Armoured Division to the First Canadian Army on 16 August was accompanied by instructions to direct the division northeast to Lisieux, not south to help close the pocket. Despite these limitations, Phase I of Tractable was a brilliant success, and Simonds's decision to send the Polish Armoured Division on a wide left hook around the enemy's main defences ought to be recognized as an outstanding example of manouevre warfare. However, the main offensive did bog down, and two days were lost in a confused and unnecessary attempt to overcome the enemy defences north of Falaise. Simonds recognized that Falaise was just a name – it was the road net that mattered. Montgomery, however, with his mind on other matters, had set Falaise as the objective, and Crerar simply passed on the orders.

The last four days of the battle of Normandy, 17 to 21 August, involved attempts to close the Trun–Chambois gap, the only escape route for tens of thousands of German soldiers. The 1st Polish and 4th Canadian Armoured Divisions were ordered to reach Trun and Chambois in the expectation that American divisions would close on these centres from the south. Instead, the burden of closing the gap, and holding it closed, was largely borne by elements of the Polish and Canadian armoured divisions. Simonds's failure to reinforce the Poles or the South Alberta battlegroup at St-Lambert was the result of a combination of optimistic reports from the front and his focus on the next stage of the campaign. Simonds was especially reluctant to send 4th Armoured Brigade to reinforce the Poles because he wanted it to be ready to lead the advance to the Seine, which Crerar had ordered on 19 August. Simonds's solution was to send Rockingham's 9th Brigade to take over the Trun–Chambois sector, but his orders, issued later the same day, conveyed no sense of urgency. By the time 9th Brigade was ready to carry out the takeover, the German breakout was underway and Rockingham was understandably cautious about plunging his battalions into the chaotic situation.

2 Canadian Corps' conduct of the struggle to close the gap can fairly be criticized. What, then, should we make of the confusion in the American command structure, the utter failure of 80th U.S. Division to advance at Argentan, and the role of the French Armoured Division, which watched the German exodus from a safe distance? The 2nd British Army was equally reluctant to become involved in the difficult business of engaging large numbers of enemy troops determined to escape. On 18 August, three British divisions – 11th Armoured and the 59th and 53rd infantry – were within striking distance of the enemy concentrations north of Argentan. With 30th Corps slated to lead the pursuit north, 11th Armoured was ordered to avoid becoming entangled in combat, and 59th was told to halt in place, as it was to be broken up to a provide a pool of infantry replacements.[25] The 53rd Division, already east of the Argentan–Falaise road, was told to advance only if no serious opposition was met. Montgomery, who had never believed the enemy could be encircled near Falaise, concentrated on the long envelopment at the Seine, which he then abandoned in the pursuit of his single-thrust strategy.

When C.P. Stacey prepared his 'Normandy Balance Sheet,' he emphasized Montgomery's 'firm and effective' grip on operations and awarded him much of the credit for the Allied victory. The evidence presented in this account requires a different conclusion. While Montgomery was certainly an effective commander in the set piece battles of June and July, his decision to commit large resources to the Caumont offensive, Operation Bluecoat, and his failure to orchestrate the total destruction of the German armies in Normandy, suggest that once operations became fluid, Montgomery failed to meet the standards he set for other commanders.

Stacey also insisted that 'Canadian generalship in Normandy [did] not suffer by comparison with that of the other allies engaged,' though a proportion of regimental officers 'were not fully competent for their appointments.' Though some would agree with Stacey that Crerar was an adequate army commander and Simonds the equal of any corps commander in the Allied or German armies, it does not seem possible to argue that any of the three Canadian divisional commanders passed the test of battle. It is not however clear how much this failure of leadership at the divisional level mattered. The major responsibility of the divisional commander and his staff was to ensure that the formation was prepared for battle, and from a logistical and administrative perspective, the Canadian armies were well served.

Stacey's comments on incompetent regimental officers require more detailed review. The only brigade commander 'considered unsuitable' and removed in Normandy was Cunningham, whom many would argue was fired for making the correct decision during Operation Spring. The two battalion commanders who were replaced at the same time made equally sensible choices, and their removal does not reflect on their competence. No other battalion commanders in 3rd Division were removed unless wounded or promoted.

The situation in 2nd Division was more complicated. Two commanding officers, Lt.-Col. B.F. Macdonald of the Essex Scottish and Lt.-Col. A.M. Young of the Royal Regiment of Canada, were removed from command soon after arriving in Normandy. Macdonald protested his dismissal and made a credible case for himself.[26] Young proved unsuited for the stress of front line command and was replaced by his very able 2IC before the battalion's first offensive operation. The other CO removed for cause in Normandy, Lt.-Col. J.G. McQueen of the Lincoln and Welland Regiment, served as CO for two weeks before he was replaced by an accomplished veteran of the Italian campaign, who proved to be an outstanding leader.[27] Given that there were nine brigades, twenty-six battalions, and nine armoured regiments in the First Canadian Army, it seems reasonable to argue that the overwhelming majority of commanding officers were fully competent for their appointments. It would be tedious to review the experience of each battalion and regiment in Normandy, but anyone familiar with the details of the campaign can list dozens of young officers who rose to the challenge when required to command a company, squadron, or battalion.

The Canadian citizen army that fought in the Battle of Normandy played a role all out of proportion to its relative strength among the Allied armies. This was especially true within 21 Army Group, where due to a mixture of Canadian pride and the British desire to limit their own casualties, Canadian divisions were required to fight more often than their British counterparts. The oft-quoted statistics which show that the Canadians suffered considerably heavier casualties than other divisions in 21 Army Group[28] are the product of a greater number of days in close combat with the enemy, not evidence of operational or tactical failure. Perhaps it is time to recognize the extraordinary achievements that marked the progress of the Canadians across Normandy's fields of fire.

Appendix A

To All Formation Commanders   17 Feb 44

2nd Canadian Corps

OPERATIONAL POLICY – 2 CDN CORPS

1. A corps operates in a 'territorial corridor,' covering the communications along which it moves and is maintained. The number and types of divisions, independent brigades and artillery groups included in it will depend upon the nature and width of the allotted frontage and the task of the corps. It is impracticable to lay down a clear-cut doctrine for the employment of a corps when its composition is, and must be, variable. It is practicable to define the probable roles and methods of employing the different types of divisions operating within the corps under specific conditions.

2. The probable role of 2 Cdn Corps will be to pass through a beach-head which has been secured by assaulting forces and attack, wear down and destroy German troops which oppose it, within the corps 'corridor' defined by the army commander.

3. Once a firm lodgement has been secured on the continent and we are able to build up reserve formations within a beach-head, the German armies will probably try to sap the strength of the Allied armies in a series of defensive battles. The main battles will be fought on succes-

sive positions chosen by the Germans. When driven from one position the Germans may give ground, gaining time to re-organize on the next rearward position on which they have elected to fight again. 2 Cdn Corps will be prepared:

(a) to follow up and harass whenever the Germans give ground
(b) attack when the Germans make a stand to fight a defensive battle

4. The sequence in which these types of operations may occur cannot be foreseen. Once a firm beach-head has been established, the Germans may decide that the ground on which they find themselves is unsuitable for a main battle and they may step back to a position some distance in the rear. Alternatively, they may stabilize the initial beach-head operations in front of a position on which they are prepared to fight. In the first case the immediate operation of 2 Cdn Corps would be to follow up; in the second case the first operation would be an attack against a defensive position.

FOLLOWING UP A GERMAN RETIREMENT

5. When the Germans decide to give ground to some depth they may endeavour to gain time by extensive demolitions in conjunction with the liberal use of mines and booby traps. Demolitions may be covered by small rear parties, including machine guns, multiple light flak and anti-tank guns. The purpose of these detachments will be to inflict casualties and impose caution on the advancing troops. Such rear parties operate on the 'hit and run' principle, and they will seldom make a prolonged stand. *Determined* infiltration, with quick artillery support controlled by forward observing officers will usually dislodge these rear parties. Such detachments are most likely to be found covering demolition of the crossings of a continuous obstacle or narrow 'bottle necks.'

6. Where the ground favours it, the Germans may occupy a rearguard position on principles similar to our own. They may intend to hold such a position to gain a specific period of time – from midday until it is dark, 24 hours, 2 days, 3 days. Such positions will be strong in

machine guns, anti-tank guns, and will be backed by reserves of tanks, self-propelled guns and small bodies of infantry. They are unlikely to be wired or protected by extensive minefields. The Germans so disposed will 'see-off' attempts at infiltration by our leading troops. A well prepared and co-ordinated brigade attack organized by leading divisions will usually succeed in overrunning these rearguard positions.

7. Either infantry or armoured divisions may lead in a follow-up. Divisions will be directed on centres of front-to-rear and lateral communication as their objectives. The securing of these restricts the enemy power of manouevre and lateral switching of formations, whilst the opening of front-to-rear communications for all types of traffic is essential to maintain the momentum of our own advance, and the opening of lateral communications, as they are secured, gives us the power to switch formations and concentrate against any part of the enemy defensive positions when the Germans make a stand.

8. Either infantry or armoured division should advance on a single thrust line, disposed in depth on a one-brigade front, opening a two-way maintenance route as they advance. Leading brigades should be preceded by strong reconnaissance across the whole front of the division. In the case of the infantry division, infantry brigades may be passed through one another, the leading brigade being directed on to ground of tactical importance and there forming a firm base through which the next brigade can be passed. Thus, the division will be disposed in depth with successive brigades established on firm bases covering centres of communication. In the case of the armoured division, the infantry of armoured brigade will lead, depending on the suitability of the country for the employment of infantry or armour. When the infantry brigade leads the armoured brigade forms the firm base from which it operates, and when the armoured brigade leads the infantry brigade forms the firm base from which the armour operates.

9. When the enemy detect the thrust line on which the division is operating they tend to concentrate their strength astride it. It is then advantageous to move a reserve brigade wide to a flank to force the enemy to

dissipate his strength on a wider frontage. When a second brigade is thrown wide of the leading brigade in this manner, it may be possible to site the divisional artillery so that the whole of it may support either brigade. But the weight of artillery support must *not* be divided.

10. Advancing on a single thrust line with brigades disposed in depth has the following advantages:

(a) The divisional artillery, even if reinforced by a proportion of medium and field artillery from the corps, is only sufficient to support attack by one brigade.
(b) If the Germans are using demolitions extensively, the divisional engineers are only sufficient to open and maintain one all-weather two-way traffic route.
(c) With the division in depth, with rearward established on firm bases, the leading brigade may be pushed along its thrust line without worrying about flanks. Any move of the enemy against a flank can be dealt with by a counter-thrust from one of the brigades held in depth.
(d) The leading brigade, operating from a firm base, can act with great boldness, for these is always a solid anchor on which recovery can be made if the Germans make a sudden, strong counter-thrust.
(e) By passing one brigade through another the staying power of the division is preserved, so that on coming up to the main position on which the Germans intend to fight, the division is fit for a main attack.
(f) The depth in which the division is disposed gives great flexibility for manouevre.

11. The divisional artillery and engineers should be centralized under the control of the CRA and CRE, respectively, and operate in support if the leading brigade. The necessity for strong reconnaissance across the whole divisional front has already been indicated. This must include engineer examination of alternative crossings of obstacles proceeds simultaneously and an early decision as the place of crossing may be made without premature commitment of engineer resources to what may later prove to be a difficult and slow crossing.

12. When an infantry division leads in the advance an armoured regiment will be placed under its command, and one medium regiment will always be either in support or under command of a forward division, whether infantry or armoured.

ATTACK

13. *When the Germans decide to stand and fight a defensive battle, attack without adequate reconnaissance will not succeed.* The attack must be carefully organized and strongly supported by all available artillery. The frontage of attack must be limited to that in which really heavy support may be given. The essence of the German system of defense is the counter-attack. His forward defenses are not thickly held in terms of men, but are strong in automatic weapons and well supported mortars, sited up to three or four thousand yards in rear of forward defended localities. These mortars are capable of bringing in very heavy fire to bear in front of, or within, the German defensive position. A well planned infantry attack, with ample fire support, will penetrate such a position with comparative ease, but the first penetration will stir up a hornet's nest. As long as fresh reserves are available the Germans will counter-attack heavily and continuously, supported by self-propelled guns brought up to close range and by any mortars which have not been over-run in the initial assault. *The success of the offensive battle hinges on the defeat of the German counter-attacks, with sufficient of our reserves in hand to launch a new phase as soon as the enemy strength has spent itself. The defeat of these counter-attacks must form part of the original plan of attack which must include arrangements for artillery support and the forward moves of infantry supporting weapons – including tanks – on the objective.* Further, in selecting the objectives, the suitability from the point of view of fighting this 'battle of the counter-attacks' must receive important consideration. The following points must be considered in the initial planning:

(a) The depth of the initial objectives. To over-run the German mortar positions requires penetration of his forward defenses to a depth of some four thousand yards. Unless these mortars are dislodged, or dealt with by a pre-arranged counter-battery programme (this is often very difficult, owing to the siting of the mortars behind very steep cover) the effect of mortar fire makes mopping up and reorganization on the objective a most difficult task for the infantry. The Germans do not hesitate to engage a position in which their own troops are still holding out.

(b) The phase of the attack at which the bulk of the artillery is to be moved forward must receive early consideration. There is bound to ne a pause during this phase when the leading troops on the objectives are going to be without the full support of the artillery. This is the period at which the employment of all available air support is most useful to tide over the gap. When the Germans really stand to fight, it is seldom that the full depth of their defenses can be penetrated without a forward displacement of the bulk of the artillery.

(c) The way in which the Germans support their infantry in the counter-attack must be clearly understood. They move tanks or self-propelled guns to within close range of the objective they are trying to retake. These do not support by neutralizing fire, in the ordinary sense, but with aimed shell fire directed through telescopic sights at a range at which individual infantry dispositions can be picked out. The moral and material effect on our own troops of this type of fire is considerable.

14. Any one of the following have proved effective in making the German tanks or self-propelled guns stand off at a range which greatly reduces their effect:

(a) Anti-tank guns well up with the leading infantry
(b) Tanks following close behind the leading infantry
(c) Medium artillery concentrations directed onto the enemy tanks or self-propelled guns by a forward observing officer with the leading troops

The initial plan of attack should legislate for at least two of these forms of support being available to leading infantry in arrival on their objective.

15. For a defensive battle the Germans generally dispose of their main

position behind an anti-tank obstacle or thick mine-fields. The initial attack, therefore, must be made by infantry to secure gaps through minefields of a bridgehead across an obstacle.

16. The infantry division is the 'sledge-hammer' in the attack against an organized defensive position, for it is strong in infantry and has the staying power to carry an attack through in depth. The armoured division is a 'weapon of opportunity,' for it has not strength enough in infantry to carry through an attack in depth through an organized defence and still retain fresh infantry to co-operate with the armour in more fluid operations for which it is specially designed. The armoured division, however, must be prepared to deal with a rearguard position, for after we have made a successful break through a defensive position the Germans will try to cover their withdrawal and re-organize behind a rearguard formed some distance in rear of their main position. The armoured division, on passing through to exploit, may find their task that of clearing a way through such a rearguard position, before they can disorganize the enemy's further withdrawal by thrusting deeper.

17. In the planning of an attack, as in all military operations, the correct allocation of troops and simplicity of command arrangements are of great importance. The correct allocation of troops is best assured if each commander thinks in terms of formations or units 'two below his own command.' Thus the divisional commander should think in terms of unit tasks and the brigade commander in terms of squadron or company tasks. By 'grouping tasks' so that each 'group of tasks' comes within the power of achievement of each of his immediately subordinate formations or units, each commander will arrive at a correct allocation of troops without breaking up existing organization – the latter always a bad practice in battle where team work counts for so much. Each commander should explain to his immediate subordinates how he visualized the tasks 'two below his own command' when he allots them their tasks and issues his orders. It simplifies command arrangements if each distinct phase of an operation can be carried out through to completion without changes of responsibility in respect to command and changes of commanders of supporting arms working with the infantry or armoured commander concerned. Operations should

be 'phased' accordingly. A new phase – the transfer of responsibility between units and formations and their commanders for continuance of operations in a given area of the battlefield – necessitates a pause and pauses always give valuable time to the enemy. The higher the level at which transfer takes place the longer the pause necessary (a company can be quickly passed through another company – to pass one battalion through another takes longer – to pass a brigade through a brigade is a matter of hours). It is therefore advantageous to operate formations and units in depth on narrow frontages, giving them 'staying power,' rather than on wide frontages necessitating early relief by passing through new formations or units. If on examination, a plan of attack shows complications in command arrangements or a number of apparently unnecessary phases or pauses, it is a good indication that the allocation of troops has been badly done and the whole plan should be reconsidered.

18. A sound, simple plan based upon:

(a) The ground
(b) Enemy dispositions and probable intentions
(c) The support available
(d) The characteristics and capabilities of our own arms and troops

and pressed home with resolution, will usually succeed. Complicated, involved plans seldom succeed.

(GG Simonds)
Lt Gen Comd 2 Cdn Corps

Appendix B

Canadian Army Fatal Casualties, Northwest Europe, 6 June 1944 to 21 August 1944

Date	Total fatal casualties, all ranks	Date	Total fatal casualties, all ranks
June 1944		July 1944	
6	359	1	14
7	156	2	3
8	174	3	2
9	132	4	127
10	43	5	58
11	153	6	18
12	16	7	15
13	13	8	262
14	7	9	70
15	5	10	19
16	8	11	19
17	18	12	23
18	18	13	40
19	7	14	17
20	3	15	21
21	4	16	25
22	10	17	29
23	2	18	142
24	10	19	53
25	4	20	121
26	12	21	125
27	7	22	75
28	7	23	57
29	10	24	49
30	–	25	344

Canadian Army Fatal Casualties, continued

Date	Total fatal casualties, all ranks	Date	Total fatal casualties, all ranks
July 1944		August 1944	
26	91	8	290
27	49	9	122
28	60	10	148
29	46	11	40
30	38	12	118
31	20	13	92
August 1944		14	261
1	79	15	153
2	30	16	67
3	15	17	65
4	42	18	27
5	49	19	22
6	30	20	26
7	15	21	48

Source: National Archives of Canada (NAC), RG 24, vol. 18825

Appendix C

Unit Deficiencies Canadian Infantry Other Ranks, 9 June 1944 to 21 August 1944

Date	2nd Cdn. Inf. Div.	3rd Cdn. Inf. Div.	4th Cdn. Armd. Div.
June			
9	–	490	–
17	–	290	–
24	–	188	–
30	–	150	–
July			
8	–	168	–
14	212	495	–
21	542	339	–
28	1,060	622	–
August			
1	1,335	316	–
3	1,471	237	132
4	1,511	224	146
5	1,385	231	151
6	1,622	246	206
7	1,407	249	212
8	1,528	124	212
9	1,216	200	236
10	1,355	173	263
11	1,298	352	506
12	1,280	400	445
13	1,481	318	421
14	1,702	497	438
15	1,641	458	432
16	1,675	491	482
17	1,664	624	502
18	1,749	859	530
19	1,828	939	546
20	1,840	974	564
21	1,830	1,040	578

Source: NAC, RG 24, Vol. 10669

Appendix D
Prisoners of War

Between 18 July and 8 August 1944, 2 Canadian Corps handled 1,114 prisoners of war. After the commencement of Operation Tractable, that number jumped to 15,077 handled between 14 and 23 August. The table below gives the number of prisoners of war who passed through 2 Canadian Corps' prisoner of war cage from the commencement of Operation Totalize, on 8 August, to 23 August 1944.

Division	Total prisoners	Division	Total prisoners
1 SS Panzer Division	169	272 Infantry Division	282
2 SS Panzer Division	21	275 Infantry Division	165
2 Panzer Division	765	276 Infantry Division	793
9 SS Panzer Division	92	277 Infantry Division	1,616
9 Panzer Division	140	326 Infantry Division	670
10 SS Panzer Division	196	331 Infantry Division	106
12 SS Panzer Division	206	352 Infantry Division	131
17 SS Panzer Grenadiers		353 Infantry Division	418
Division	21	363 Infantry Division	879
21 Panzer Division	579	708 Infantry Division	32
116 Panzer Division	86	2 Parachute Division	9
Panzer Lehr	27	3 Parachute Division	994
48 Infantry Division	1	Army, Corps, GHQ	
84 Infantry Division	581	Troops	815
85 Infantry Division	1,527	Artillery Units	322
89 Infantry Division	1,566	Flak Units	843
243 Infantry Division	7	Werfer Units	234
245 Infantry Division	1	Russians, Poles, etc.	1,111
266 Infantry Division	3	Miscellaneous	1,291
271 Infantry Division	499	Total prisoners	17,198

Source: 2 Canadian Corps Intelligence Summaries

Notes

1. INTRODUCTION: MILITARY HISTORY WITHOUT CLAUSEWITZ

1 *Globe and Mail*, 7 August 1998.
2 B.H. Liddel Hart, 'Lessons of Normandy' (1952), in Canadian Land Forces Staff Course (CLFSC), *Normandy Battlefield Study* (1988). Liddel Hart Centre for Military Archives MSS 11/1944–45.
3 C.P. Stacey, *The Victory Campaign* (Ottawa, 1962). The quotations are from chapter 11, 'Normandy: The Balance Sheet,' 271–7.
4 John A. English, *The Canadian Army and the Normandy Campaign: A Study of Failure in High Command* (New York, 1991).
5 The proceedings of the conference have been published as Paul Addison and Jeremy Crang (eds), *A Time to Kill* (London, 1998).
6 English, 2–6.
7 Lt.-Col. Field, 'The Use of Atomic Weapons in Support of Operations in N.W. Europe during the Second World War,' Ronnie Shephard Archives, Laurier Centre for Military Strategic and Disarmament Studies, (LCMSDS).
8 Maj.-Gen. Kurt Meyer, 'Interview 6 September 1950, Dorchester, N.B.,' in CLFSC, *Normandy Battlefield Study* (1988).
9 Karl von Clausewitz, *On War*, trans. Michael Howard and Peter Paret (Princeton, 1976) 119.
10 Martin Van Creveld, *Fighting Power: German and U.S. Army Performance, 1939–1945* (London, 1983), 163–6.
11 Ibid., 6.
12 Interested readers should review the debate between Dupuy and John Sloan Brown in the pages of *Military Affairs*. John Sloan Brown, 'Col. Trevor N. Dupuy and the Mythos of the Wehrmacht Superiority: A Reconsideration,' in *Military Affairs* 50 (1986), 16–20. See also the debate

between Dupuy and Brown in the next four issues. Dupuy makes assumptions about Allied firepower – especially the effects of air power and artillery – which are not borne out by the evidence from operational research.

13 John Keegan, 'Towards a Theory of Combat Motivation,' in Addison and Crang, 3–11.

14 Russel Weigley, *Eisenhower's Lieutenants* (Bloomington, 1981), 15.

15 Ibid., 26.

16 Ibid., 28–9.

17 Carlo D'Este, *Decision in Normandy: The Unwritten Story of Montgomery and the Allied Campaign* (New York, 1983), 279–83.

18 Brigadier James Hargest's 'Notes,' Public Record Office (PRO) CAB 106/ 1060, present a complex picture of actions carried out by the 50th and 49th divisions. Many of his observations, such as his D+10 summary, '50 Div fights well and has gained a lot of ground. Its casualties have been heavy, 2 Brig Comdrs, 8 COs and over 3000 men,' have been overlooked.

19 D'Este, *Decision*, 298.

20 Max Hastings, *Overlord: D-Day and the Battle for Normandy* (London, 1984), 11.

21 Ibid., 179.

22 Roger Spiller, 'S.L.A. Marshall and the Ratio of Fire,' in *RUSI Journal* 133/4 (winter 1988).

23 John Gooch, preface to Timothy Harrison Place, *Military Training in the British Army, 1940–1944: From Dunkirk to D-Day* (London, 2000).

24 Russell A. Hart, *Clash of Arms: How the Allies Won the War* (Boulder, 2001), 92.

25 David French, *Raising Churchill's Army* (Oxford, 2000), 4.

26 Stephen A. Hart, *Montgomery and 'Colossal Cracks': 21st Army Group in Normandy, 1944–45* (Westport, CT, 2000).

27 Leonard V. Smith, *Between Mutiny and Obedience* (Princeton, 1994), 17.

28 C.P. Stacey, *Six Years of War* (Ottawa, 1955) appendix A.

29 The observations about the makeup of the Canadian army are based on the study of more than 1,000 individual personnel records for Terry Copp, *The Brigade: The Fifth Canadian Infantry Brigade, 1939–1945* (Stoney Creek, ON, 1992), and a further 300 records examined for Gordon Brown and Terry Copp, *Look to Your Front ... Regina Rifles: A Regiment at War, 1944–45* (Waterloo, ON, 2001).

30 Geoffrey W. Hayes, 'The Development of the Canadian Army Officer Corps, 1939–1945' (PhD thesis, University of Western Ontario, 1992).

31 Robert England, 'Statistical Analysis of Discharges from Armed Forces of

Canada, 1939–1942,' National Archives of Canada (NAC), MG 27, vol. 61. Courtesy of the late Dr Shaun Brown.

32 Sample of Personnel Records. See note 29.

33 Terry Copp and Bill McAndrew, *Battle Exhaustion: Soldiers and Psychiatrists in the Canadian Army, 1939–1945* (Montreal, 1990), 37–43.

34 Jonathan Vance, *Death So Noble* (Vancouver, 1997).

35 C.P. Stacey and Barbara Wilson, *The Half-Million: The Canadians in Britain, 1939–1945* (Toronto, 1987), 160–1.

36 Copp, *The Brigade*, 25–6.

37 Great Britain, War Office, *Infantry Training*, Part VI, *The Anti-Tank Platoon* (1943).

38 M. Swann, 'A Comparison of the British and German 3-inch Mortars,' 1943, Ronnie Shephard Archives, LCMSDS.

39 L.F. Ellis, *Victory in the West*, vol. 1 (London, 1962), appendix 4.

40 See French, 244–9, for a discussion of the 'shrinking size of the army.'

41 I Corps Instructions, 28 May 1944, NAC, RG 24, vol. 10790.

42 The outline plan is fully described in Ellis, *Victory*, chapter 4; and Gordon A. Harrison, *Cross-Channel Attack* (Washington, 1951), chapter 5.

43 Ellis, *Victory*, 536.

44 G.W.L. Nicholson, *The Gunners of Canada*, vol. 2. See also George G. Blackburn, *The Guns of Normandy* (Ottawa, 1995).

45 Quarterly Report, Advisor in Psychiatry 21 Army Group, 31 March 1945, NAC, RG 24, vol. 12631.

46 G.W.L. Nicholson, *The Canadians in Italy* (Ottawa, 1956), 22–3.

47 The War Diaries of 3rd Division units present a uniformly bleak picture of life at Sussex and Debert. All units of the Canadian army were required to maintain a War Diary from the first day of mobilization. The quality and length of the daily entries vary greatly. The War Diaries can be found in NAC, RG 24.

48 H.D.G. Crerar Papers, NAC, MG 30 E157, vol. 3 – Correspondence with B.L. Montgomery.

49 The reference is to the Toronto financial district. The division's staff included militia officers with established civilian careers in business, law, and engineering. See J.L. Granatstein, *The Generals* (Toronto, 1993), 165–8, for an analysis of Keller's problems as a commander in Normandy.

50 Crerar Papers, vol. 3.

51 The comments on the character of the units and their commanding officers are based on personal interviews and the interviews conducted by Jean Portugal for her seven-volume series, *We Were There* (Toronto, 1998). Col.

E.A. Coté kindly responded to questions about the training and administration of the division.

52 Quoted in Copp and McAndrew, 111.

53 'Operational Policy – 2nd Canadian Corps 17 February 1944,' in NAC, RG 24, vol. 10797. Edward Luttwak is the best known of the many military theorists who insist that 'it is a peculiarity of English-language military terminology that it long had no word of its own to describe the middle level of thought and action between the tactical and the strategic' and suggests that he 'introduced the operational-level concept.' Edward Luttwak, *Strategy: The Logic of War and Peace* (Cambridge, 2001), 112.

54 The letters are attached to a copy of 'Operational Policy – 2nd Canadian Corps 17 February 1944' in NAC, RG 24, vol. 10797.

55 Shelford Bidwell, *Gunners at War* (London, 1972), 145–8.

56 'Infantry Training Conference, Record of Discussions 15 May 1944,' 30 pp., NAC, RG 24, vol. 13241; and PRO WO 204/1895.

57 'Infantry Training Conference,' 4–6, 27–8.

58 In February 1944, Major Michael Swann, the army operational research analyst assigned to the Infantry School, prepared a summary of current information on attacking reverse slope positions, which he defined as one of the biggest problems now engaging the attention of the school. Reverse slopes had rarely been encountered in the desert, but in Tunisia, Sicily, and Italy, 'the problem became urgent.' The author had the opportunity to discuss this issue with Lord Swann in 1989. He suggested that no satisfactory solution to the problem of reverse slope defences was developed until Operation Totalize in August 1944.

59 'Infantry Training Conference,' 28.

60 Ibid., 27.

61 Place, 169. Place notes that this view has been strongly argued by Williamson Murray in his very influential essay, 'British Military Effectiveness,' in A.R. Millet and W. Murray (eds), *Military Effectiveness*, Vol. 3, *The Second World War* (London, 1988).

62 Great Britain, War Office, *The Co-operation of Tanks with Infantry Divisions* (May 1944), 5.

63 Ibid., 7–8.

64 Great Britain, War Office, *The Tactical Handling of Armoured Divisions* (July 1943).

65 Place, 126.

66 L.O. Lyne, *History of the 7th Armoured Division, June 1943–July 1945* (Germany, 1945), 29.

67 Stanislaw Maczek, *Avec mes blindés* (Paris, 1967).

68 The Poles used British liaison officers to overcome some of the language difficulties, but British and Canadian War Diaries and memoirs are full of complaints about the problems of communications with the armoured division.

69 Larry Worthington, *Worthy* (Toronto, 1961).

70 George Kitching, *Mud and Green Fields* (St Catharines, 1993).

71 War Diary, 2nd Canadian Corps, 'Weekly Progress Reports to Canada,' 6 February–21 May 1944.

72 War Diary, 4th Canadian Armoured Brigade, 'Exercise Iroquois,' 1 July 1944.

2. D-DAY

1 Gordon A. Harrison, *Cross Channel Attack* (Washington, 1951), 71.

2 COHQ, 'Naval Fire Support in Operation Overlord,' Bulletin Y/37 NAC, RG 24, vol. 10673. Eleven destroyers and the cruisers *Belfast* and *Diadem* were assigned to the Juno area alone.

3 Lt.-Gen. Andrew McNaughton initiated the development of specialized armour with the First Canadian Army, but his designs did not reach the development stage. Instead, the 79th British Armoured Division was formed to centralize testing of specialized armour and the training of crews. Nigel Duncan, *79th Armoured Division* (Windsor, 1972), 4–9.

4 Stacey, *Six Years of War*, 405.

5 Ibid., 405.

6 A.G. Steiger, 'The Campaign in North West Europe, Information from German Sources,' (Ottawa, 1951). Report No. 40, Historical Section (GS) Directorate of History and Heritage, Dept. of National Defence (DHH).

7 The German defences in the Anglo-Canadian areas are described in L.F. Ellis, *Victory in the West* (London, 1962), 116–17. Stacey, *The Victory Campaign* 64–9. For a detailed report on gun, MG, and mortar positions, see AORG Report, 'Fire Support on the British Beaches in Normandy,' April 1945, PRO WO 291/243. See also 'Comparison of British and American Areas in Normandy in terms of Fire Support and Its Effects,' PRO WO 291/270.

8 Stacey, *The Victory Campaign*, 67.

9 F.H. Hinsley, *British Intelligence in the Second World War* (London, 1988), vol. 3, Pt. 2, discusses what was known, about these divisions, when it was known and by whom.

10 Ellis, *Victory*, 145–7.

11 Carlo D'Este, *Bitter Victory: The Battle for Sicily* (New York, 1988), chapter 13.

12 Ellis, *Victory*, 138–9.

13 Napier Crookenden, *Dropzone Normandy* (Shepperton, 1976), 162–4.

14 The official history of 1st Canadian Parachute Battalion is John A. Willes, *Out of the Clouds* (Kingston, ON, 1995). In the following paragraphs I have relied on the unit War Diary, Lt. F.R. McGuire, *The 1st Canadian Parachute Battalion in France* Historical Section Report No. 26, 1949, DHH; Dan Hartigan, *A Rising of Courage: Canada's Paratroopers in the Liberation of Normandy* (Calgary, 2000), and my interviews and correspondence with Brig. James Hill.

15 Brian Nolan, *Airborne: The Heroic Story of 1st Canadian Parachute Battalion* (Toronto, 1995), 35.

16 Robert W. Love and John Major (eds.), *The Year of D-Day: The Diary of Admiral Sir Bertram Ramsay* (Hull, 1994), 82.

17 Interview, Terry Copp with Richard Hillborn, Elora, ON, 1998.

18 A great deal of effort had gone into the development of a radar beacon that pathfinder troops could use to mark drop zones. By 1944 the systems known as 'Rebecca' (airborne receiver) and 'Eureka' (ground radar beacon) were operational, but the weather prevented even the pathfinder from reaching the DZs in time to mark them. See J.W. Pringle, 'The Work of TRE in the Invasion of Europe,' *IEE Proceedings*, 132, no. 6 (October 1985), p. 351. The limited value of Rebecca–Eureka on D-Day was a source of great disappointment to the operational research scientists who had tested the equipment under field conditions. Interview, Terry Copp with David Bayly Pike, 1990.

19 War Diary, 1st Canadian Parachute Battalion. Most of C company was dropped west of the Dives, although some sticks were dropped a considerable distance away, including one that landed west of the Orne.

20 Interview, Terry Copp with James Hill, Chichester, 1996.

21 Ellis, *Victory*, 161.

22 United States Strategic Air Forces in Europe, *Survey of Effectiveness of Bombing of the Invasion Coast*, July 1944, U.S. Army Military History Institute (USAMHI). A field party of seven airforce officers spent seven days examining targets on the ground immediately after D-Day.

23 No. 2 ORS, 'Self Propelled Artillery in the Assault on the Beaches 3rd Canadian Infantry Division Sector,' Report No. 1, 1944. The reports of No. 2 ORS are now available in Terry Copp (ed.), *Montgomery's Scientists: Operational Research in Northwest Europe* (Waterloo, ON, 2000). An AORG postwar report offers a slightly more optimistic estimate of the overall effects of fire support and credits air attacks with putting out of action 13 per cent of the 10 per cent of enemy posts knocked out by all forms of fire support. PRO, WO 291/243.

24 Copp, *Montgomery's Scientists*, 385.

25 COHQ, 'Naval Fire Support.'

26 Copp, *Montgomery's Scientists*, 381–4.

27 Charlie Martin, *Battle Diary* (Toronto, 1994), 5.

28 It is impossible to reconcile the 'touchdown' times reported in the various Message Logs and War Diaries. The question of when the DD tanks landed and how quickly they were brought into action is more important than reported touchdown times, and it is possible to reconstruct what happened at each of the four Canadian beaches.

29 War Diary, Queen's Own Rifles, 6 June 1944.

30 G. Blight, *The History of the Royal Berkshire Regiment, 1910–1947* (n.p., 1948), 327.

31 W.T. Barnard, *The Queen's Own Rifles of Canada* (Toronto, 1960), 194.

32 'Interview with Major J.N. Gordon 12 July 1944' (DHH). Gordon was interviewed in hospital in England after being wounded on D+6 at le Mesnil Patry.

33 War Diary, Queen's Own Rifles, 6 June 1944.

34 Stacey, *Victory Campaign*, appendix B, 650.

35 Will R. Bird, *North Shore (New Brunswick) Regiment* (Fredericton, 1963), 200. See also the battalion War Diary, 'Memorandum of an Interview with Major R.B. Forbes OC "B" Coy,' 13 June 1944, DHH.

36 Maj. Fairlie provides a detailed description of the 'massive reinforced concrete fortification' at St-Aubin-sur-Mer. He concludes: 'No damage was done to any of the defensive system though 90% of the buildings in the front row were destroyed.' Copp, *Montgomery's Scientists*, 384–5.

37 Bird, 202–4.

38 Jean E. Portugal, *We Were There*, 7 vols. (Toronto, 1998), 3:1431.

39 J.R. Moulton, personal account, Portugal, 4:1661–4.

40 The 3rd Division Message Log records a signal from the 8th Brigade at 1610 reporting that 'Coy NSR mopping St. Aubin cannot be released yet.' War Diary, the 3rd Canadian Infantry Division, 6 June 1944, afterwards WD, 3CID.

41 Bird, 205.

42 Message Log, 8th Canadian Infantry Brigade, Appendix to War Diary, 6 June 1944.

43 Stacey, *Victory Campaign*, 68–9. Stacey is quoting from Maj. Fairlie's report. See note 36.

44 War Diary, Royal Winnipeg Rifles, 6 June 1944.

45 Stacey, *Victory Campaign*, 104.

46 War Diary, Royal Winnipeg Rifles, 6 June 1944.

47 Interview, Maj. R.F. Crofton with Reg Roy, 8 July 1956. DHH.

48 Interview, Lt.-Col. F.W. Matheson, June 1944. DHH.

49 At 1035 the 7th Canadian Infantry Brigade reported 'Yew,' the codeword for the capture of the first objectives by the Winnipegs and Canscots. However, no firm report was available from the Reginas. Their message 'Courseulles cleared beyond Market Place' was timed at 1010, but 'Yew' included control of the first lateral road (the D514). The Reginas finally reported 'Yew' at 1200, sometime after they had begun the move inland. Message Log War Diary, the 3rd Canadian Infantry Division, 6 June 1944.

50 Stacey, *Victory Campaign*, 118.

51 Message Log, War Diary, 3rd Canadian Infantry Division.

52 Stacey, *Victory Campaign*, 79.

53 Message Log, War Diary, 3rd Canadian Infantry Division, 6 June 1944.

54 Interview, Terry Copp with Ross Munro, 1983.

55 Interview, D.G. Cunningham with Terry Copp and Mark Dykeman, 1982.

56 The Chaudières landed at 0850. One LCA hit a mined obstacle, and most of the platoon was killed or wounded. The balance of the four companies waited behind the sea wall while the RCRs cleared the town. A. Ross and M. Gauvin, *La Geste du Régiment de la Chaudière* (Rotterdam, 1945), 28.

57 Letter, Gunner Fred Miller, F Troop 14th Field Regiment, to Terry Copp, 22 March 1984.

58 The battery was engaged by HMS *Diadem*, which reported that its fire had straddled the battery at 0700 hours. The cruiser's spotter aircraft reported 'no movement' at 0923 and 'six direct hits' at 1033. There is ample evidence of the existence of the 88; see, for example, 'Summary of Events 27 Canadian Armoured Regiment,' War Diary, Sherbrooke Fusiliers, 6 June 1944.

59 Ibid.

60 Ross and Gauvin, 29.

61 Bird, 272–4.

62 Ibid.

63 'Memorandum of Account by Lieutenant H.L. Day, IO, North Shore Regiment, 27 July 1944,' DHH.

64 'That night however we distinctly heard talking from the town. A commando captain, a North Shore corporal and 3 ORs of 7 Platoon discovered more dug-outs. About 40 PWs were taken that night. The completeness of the German underground defences had almost the character of a movie setting. In the officers mess hall we found a trap door leading to an underground passage.' Ibid.

65 Bird, 223.

66 War Diary, Canadian Scottish Regiment, 6 June 1944.

67 See Gordon Brown and Terry Copp, *Look to Your Front ... Regina Rifles* (Waterloo, ON, 2001), for a detailed account of the Regina 'Johns' D-Day.

68 Stacey, *Victory Campaign*, 112.
69 Don Learment, 'Soldier, POW, Partisan: My Experiences during the Battle of France, June–September 1944,' *Canadian Military History* 9, no. 2 (2000), 91–104.
70 Dempsey's orders must have been given orally, for there is no record, but since all units of 2nd British Army were ordered to consolidate at the intermediate objective at about the same time, the necessary inference can be made with confidence.
71 Ellis, *Victory*, 204.
72 Ibid., 205.
73 Chester Wilmott, *The Struggle for Europe* (London, 1952), 278–9.
74 Stacey, *Victory Campaign*, 118.
75 Brown and Copp, 47–8.
76 'Interview, Lieutenant-Colonel F.N. Cabeldu, June 1944,' DHH.
77 Interview, Terry Copp with W.F. McCormick, 2000.

3. THE BRIDGEHEAD

1 Stacey, *Victory Campaign*, 122.
2 M. Howard, *British Intelligence in the Second World War*, Vol. 5 *Strategic Deception* (London 1998), 185.
3 Roger Hesketh, *Fortitude: The D-Day Deception Campaign* (London, 1999).
4 The command arrangements and orders are summarized in Stacey, *Victory Campaign*, 121–2, and Hubert Meyer, *The History of the 12SS Panzer Division Hitlerjugend* (Winnipeg, 1994), 39.
5 Meyer, *History*, 40.
6 Ellis, *Victory*, 225.
7 Ibid., 228–9. For a more detailed account, see Norman Scarfe, *Assault Division* (London, 1947).
8 Interview, Terry Copp with Brig. D.G.B. Cunningham, Kingston, 1983. Brig. Cunningham was especially adamant when asked if it might have been better to have moved more cautiously.
9 Interview, Maj. Don Learment, Guelph, Ontario, 2000.
10 Learment, 'Soldier, POW, Partisan,' 95.
11 War Diary, North Nova Scotia Highlanders, 7 June 1944.
12 The 27th Canadian Armoured Regiment (Sherbrooke Fusiliers), 'Diary of Events,' by Maj. V.O. Walsh, OC C Sqn, Appendix to War Diary, June 1944.
13 Meyer, *History*, 41.
14 War Diary, 3rd Canadian Infantry Division, 7 June 1944.

15 Lt. E. Spafford, C Squadron, 'Notes,' War Diary, Sherbrooke Fusiliers, 7 June 1944.
16 Meyer, *History*, 42. Meyer lists the names of the commanders of the three German tanks knocked out in this encounter.
17 Spafford, 'Notes.'
18 Meyer, *History*, 42.
19 Learment interview.
20 War Diary, North Nova Scotia Regiment, 7 June 1944.
21 Stacey, *Victory Campaign*, 128.
22 War Diary, 14th Field Regiment, June 1944, RG 24, vol. 14471.
23 Learment, 'Soldier,' 93.
24 War Diary, 9th Canadian Infantry Brigade, and Historical Officer, 'Interview with Brig. D.G. Cunningham, June 1944,' DHH.
25 Stacey, *Victory Campaign*, 132.
26 Howard Margolian, *Conduct Unbecoming: The Story of the Murder of Canadian Prisoners of War in Normandy* (Toronto, 1998). Maj. Learment witnessed some of the murders, but he was one of those marched to a POW cage.
27 War Diary, Royal Ulster Rifles, 7 June 1944, PRO, WO 171/321.
28 Meyer, *History*, 45. The 12th SS casualty estimate does not include significant losses incurred in combat with the British at Cambes.
29 Gen. Pz Geyr von Schweppenburg, *Pz Gp West*, MS B 466.
30 There are a number of conflicting accounts of the losses and delays suffered by Panzer Lehr. The timings in this account are from Meyer, 48–9. The comment on 'minor damage' is from a letter from Helmet Ritgen to Terry Copp 13 September 1988, who wrote that 'our marching column, it was the centre of the division, had to suffer the worst attacks. I lost 2 or 3 tanks, temporarily because they could be repaired. We had a few soldiers killed or wounded. Worse was the loss of a few of our precious gasoline trucks ... The other two marching columns of our division and our Recce battalion in front of my battalion reached the front without serious air attacks.' See Helmut Ritgen, *The Western Front in 1944* (Winnipeg, 1995), for another, earlier version of events.
31 Ritgen letter.
32 Ibid.
33 War Diary, Regina Rifle Regiment, 8 June 1944.
34 War Diary, Royal Winnipeg Rifles, 8 June 1944.
35 Tony Foulds, 'In Support of the Canadians: A British Anti-Tank Regiment's First Five Weeks in Normandy,' *Canadian Military History* 7, no. 2 (spring 1998), 23–4.
36 Ellis, *Victory*, 230.

37 This statement is based on a careful examination of the air photos, the actual ground, and a number of Tactical Exercises Without Troops (TEWTs) carried out in Normandy. On the ground, it is impossible to see how the Winnipegs could have held the straggling village. The Canadian Scottish Regiment came to the same conclusion after recapturing the area, and defended it from positions that allowed better fields of fire.

38 War Diary, Regina Rifles, May 1944, 'Operational Order No. I.'

39 Brown and Copp, *Look to Your Front*, 61.

40 Meyer, *History*, 49–50.

41 War Diary, Royal Winnipeg Rifles, 8 June 44.

42 Foulds, 74. See also 'Memorandum of an Interview with CSM Belton, 14 June 1944,' DHH.

43 War Diary, Royal Winnipeg Rifles, 8 June 1944.

44 Meyer, *History*, 51.

45 Brig. F.N Cabeldu, 'Battle Narrative of the Normandy Assault and First Counterattack,' 15 May 1956, DHH.

46 Ibid. See also R.H. Roy, *Ready for the Fray* (Vancouver, 1958).

47 War Diary, Canadian Scottish Regiment, June 1944.

48 Cabeldu.

49 Stacey, *Victory Campaign*, 136, and Meyer, *History*, 51.

50 Margolian, 63.

51 Hubert Meyer relates a story of the deliberate killing of prisoners by British troops on 8 June and claims 'because of this three Canadian prisoners of war were ordered shot near the command post of II/26 on the following day.' Meyer, *History*, 53. His account glosses over the organized mass murders carried out by the 12th SS.

52 Ibid., 54.

53 Lt.-Col. F.W. Matheson, 'Account of Operations of Regina Rifles, 6–8 June,' War Diary, Regina Rifles, June 1944, p. 291.

54 Brown and Copp, 80.

55 Meyer, *History*, 57.

56 Ibid., 58.

57 A.B. Conron, *A History of the First Hussars Regiment* (London, 1981), 66.

58 Meyer, *History*, 61. Losses in the last attempt to seize Norrey were twenty-five killed, forty-seven wounded, and eight missing.

59 Montgomery's plan is referred to in all of the standard sources. The best discussion is D'Este, *Decision*, 164–6.

60 Ralph Bennet, *Ultra in the West* (London, 1979), 74.

61 Ellis, *Victory*, 251–3.

62 Stacey, *Victory Campaign*, 139.

63 'Interview with Maj. J.N. Gordon 12 July 1944,' DHH.
64 Barnard, 201.
65 Brown and Copp, 76.
66 Meyer, *History*, 68. For a full account of this battle and its aftermath, see Michael R. McNorgan, 'Black Sabbath for the First Hussars: Action at le Mesnil-Patry,' in Donald E. Graves (ed.), *Fighting for Canada: Seven Battles, 1768–1945* (Toronto, 2000), 279–316.
67 Stacey, *Victory Campaign*, 140.
68 Ellis, *Victory*, 253.
69 Ibid., 254–7, and D'Este, *Decision*, 174–98.

4. THE BATTLES FOR CAEN

1 Stacey, *Victory Campaign*, 143. The most detailed descriptions of Montgomery's strategy are in Carlo D'Este, *Decision in Normandy*, and Nigel Hamilton, *Monty, Master of the Battlefield, 1942–44*.
2 Ellis, *Victory*, 272.
3 Hinsley, 192. Second British Army Intelligence provided a detailed breakdown of the order of battle of 1SS and a report that it would operate west of the Orne on 22 June. Second British Army Intelligence Summary No. 18. RG24, vol. 10557. Three infantry divisions, 16 GAF, 276, and 277, were en route to Normandy. Attempts to speed up their arrival by providing additional transport were ordered on 23 June, but none had arrived when Epsom began. Steiger Report No. 50, 52.
4 Hamilton, 677.
5 Ellis, *Victory*, 275; and Terry Copp, 'The 51st Highland Division in Normandy,' unpublished paper, 1996.
6 Ritgen, 52.
7 According to the 2nd British Army, 'prisoners confirm the view that Panzer Lehr has had more than a bloody nose and is in no shape to resist any really strong attack. Nevertheless they have shown themselves fighters unwilling to give ground without a good fight.' Second British Army Intelligence Summary, No. 18.
8 Meyer, *History*, 93–4.
9 Second British Army Intelligence Summary, No. 13. Translation of a captured enemy document.
10 For accounts of Operation Martlet, see Ellis, *Victory*, 277, and Patrick Delaforce, *The Polar Bears* (Stroud, UK, 1995), 58ff. I had the opportunity to meet and correspond with Brig. Trevor Hart Dyke, DSO, whose privately printed memoir *Normandy to Arnhem: History of the Hallamshires* (Sheffield, 1966), provides a detailed account of his battalion experience at Fontenay

and Tessel woods and one of the best commentaries on the role of a CO in print. Brig. James Hargest, whose criticisms of the British soldier are so often quoted, reported that the 49th Division 'soundly defeated the enemy' in Martlet. Hargest, 18–29.

11 Kurt Meyer, *Grenadiers* (Winnipeg, 1994), 135–6.

12 This account of the first day of Epsom is based on a reading of the War Diaries of the 15th Scottish Division, PRO, WO 171. H.G. Martin, *The History of the Fifteenth Scottish Division* (Edinburgh, 1948), Ellis, *Victory*, and Meyer, *History*. For a first-person account, see Robert Woollcombe, *Lion Rampant* (London, 1955). J.J. How, *Hill 112* (London, 1979) is the best overview of Epsom. It was written by a participant who was also a careful historian.

13 Meyer, *History*, 112.

14 Woollcombe, 65.

15 Appendix H to Steiger, *Report No. 50*.

16 D'Este, *Decision*, 245.

17 Montgomery used these exact words in his signal to the Chief of the Imperial General Staff, timed 1300, 29 June. M33, Montgomery Papers, Imperial War Museum. See Hamilton, 678–82, for a statement of the view that Montgomery did have a master plan and that the aim of Epsom was to draw in Panzer divisions so that they not reach the Orne.

18 Steiger, *Report No. 50*, 56.

19 Hinsley, 197–8.

20 War Diary, Panzer Group West, 30 June 1944, LCMSDS.

21 Report No. 50, 58.

22 Delaforce, 88–102. The War Diaries of the 70th Infantry Brigade and its battalions the 10th and 11th Durham Light Infantry and 1st Battalion Tyneside Scottish provide a rich source for the events of 1 July 44.

23 Hastings, 150–1.

24 Ritgen, 85–6.

25 Steiger, *Report No. 50*, Appendix J.

26 War Diary, Panzer Group West, 3 July 1944.

27 The 8 Corps War Diary records 4,200 killed, wounded, and missing for the five-day battle, 2,331 for 15th Scottish and 1,256 for 11th Armoured and 43 Wessex. D'Este, 244. To these must be added the losses sustained by the 49th Division, estimated at more than 1,000. War Diary ADMS 49 Div, PRO, WO 177/396.

28 Copp and McAndrew, 130–3.

29 The *Joint Air Plan and Executive Order for Operation 'Neptune,'* 25 May 44, is one of many documents (including the 'Initial Joint Plan,' 1 Feb. 1944) to stress the objective 'of securing as a base for further operations a lodgement

area which will include airfield sites.' The Air Marshals believed that Montgomery had committed the army to securing Caen for this purpose.

30 See D'Este, *Decision*, chapter 13, 'The Air Chiefs,' for the summary of the traditional view.

31 Ian Gooderson, *Air Power at the Battlefront* (London, 1998), offers an overview of the role of tactical air power in the Italian and Northwest European campaigns.

32 Ellis, *Victory*, 488.

33 The debate over the Transportation Plan may be reviewed in Solly Zukerman, *From Apes to Warlords* (London, 1978), chapter 12, and W.W. Rostow, *Pre-Invasion Bombing Strategy* (Austin, 1981).

34 Fighter Command Tactical Memorandum No. 30, 14 March 1943, DHH 79/32.

35 ORS AEAF, 'The Accuracy of Attacks on Small Targets by Fighter-Bombers and R.P. Fighters,' PRO, Air 37/653.

36 Ibid.

37 AEAF, 'The Liberation of Northwest Europe,' vol. 1, PRO, Air 41/66.

38 Ibid.

39 Christopher Evans, 'The Fighter-Bomber in the Normandy Campaign: The Role of 83 Group,' *Canadian Military History* 8, no. 1 (1999), p. 24

40 Fighter Command, Memorandum No. 30.

41 'Neptune Initial Joint Plan,' 6 NAC, RG 24, vol. 10415.

42 Ellis, *Victory*, 62. There were in addition four squadrons of Seafires of the Fleet Air Arm, and seven squadrons of Spitfires and Mustangs employed to observe the fall of shells from the naval bombardment.

43 AEAF, 'The Liberation,' 1.

44 Ben Greenhous et al., *The Crucible of War, 1939–45* (Ottawa, 1994), 294.

45 Robert Vogel, 'Tactical Air Power in Normandy: Some Thoughts on the Interdiction Plan,' *Canadian Military History* 2, no. 1 (1994), 37–7.

46 Photo reconnaissance was of enormous assistance to the ground forces, who planned all of their operations from patrols to Corps-level attacks using air photos. In June alone, 83 Group flew 446 photo reconnaissance sorties, producing 34,000 negatives, from which 287,000 prints were made. AORG Memo A8, Appendix D, WO 291/1178. Cited in Christopher Evans, 'Tactical Air Power in the Normandy Campaign: The Role of 83 Group' (M.A. thesis, Wilfrid Laurier University, 1998), 88.

47 Vogel, 45–7.

48 Zukerman, 268.

49 Ibid., 269.

50 B. Michael Bechthold, 'The Development of an Unbeatable Combination:

US Close Air Support in Normandy,' *Canadian Military History* 8, no. 1 (1999), 7–20.

51 Evans, 93.

52 Evans, 91–2.

53 Evans, 131.

54 *German Views on Allied Combat Efficiency*, Appendix D, II Canadian Corps Intelligence Summary No. 90. RG 24, vol. 13714.

55 M. Swann, *The Infantry Battle*, 29 April 43, and M. Swann, *Reverse Slope Positions*, February 1944, AORS 6 (Infantry School Memos), Swann Papers, Ronnie Shephard Archives, LCMSDS.

56 These paragraphs are based on 'Notes for Corps Commander on Air Support Ref Visit of AOC 83 Group,' 24 June 1944. Appendix 'O,' War Diary, 51st Highland Division, WO 171/758.

57 2TAF ORS Report No. 16, May 1944, DHH.

58 2TAF ORS Report No. 37, June 1944, DHH.

59 Air Historical Branch, 'Tactics Used by Spitfire Day Fighter-Bomber Squadron of the Second Tactical Air Force during the Campaign in Western Europe,' Tactical Paper No. 4, PRO, Air 20/6857 92550.

60 This paragraph is based on interviews with D.K. Hill and D.F. Pike, the two members of No. 2 ORS most concerned with air matters. See the introduction to Copp, *Montgomery Scientists*.

61 2nd British Army, Intelligence Summary No. 18.

62 Terry Copp, *A Canadian's Guide to the Battlefields of Normandy* (Waterloo, ON, 1994), 77.

63 A translation of this talk appeared in 2nd British Army, Intelligence Summary No. 36.

64 Ellis, *Victory*, 309; Stacey, *Victory Campaign*, 153–4.

65 Report on Operation Windsor, War Diary, 8th Canadian Infantry Brigade, July 1944, 5 pages.

66 Report on Operation Windsor, 3.

67 War Diary, North Shore (New Brunswick) Regiment, 4 July 1944.

68 War Diary, Regiment de la Chaudière, 4–5 July 1944.

69 War Diary, Royal Winnipeg Rifles, 4 July 1944.

70 *Vanguard–Fort Garry Horse* (Winnipeg, 1945), 31.

71 The Queen's Own Rifles dealt with a by-passed strongpoint at the edge of the village. Neither tanks firing AP nor Crocodile flame throwers had any effect on the bunker, nor did demolition charges. Grenades and petrol poured down a ventilator shaft finally produced the surrender of 11 Hitler Youth who explained that they had been told the Canadians took no prisoners. Interview Maj. S.M. Lett, 15 July 1944, DHH.

72 *Vanguard*, 33.

73 To the east of Verson, woods obscure the view, while to the north, there is a roll in the landscape. Whatever the reason, there was no interference with the German armour counterattacking the Garries. The author has walked the ground on battlefield tours and checked 1944 air photos.

74 Meyer, *History*, 139.

75 Meyer, *History*, 140.

76 Stacey, *Victory Campaign*, 155.

77 Meyer, *History*, 140.

78 'Enemy Tactics (lessons of war No. 1),' HQ, 8th Canadian Infantry Brigade, 12 July 1944, NAC, RG 24, vol. 10673.

79 The Charnwood plan is outlined in Ellis, 312–14, and Stacey, 157–60.

80 Stacey, *Victory Campaign*, 157. There is a good deal of confusion about the role played by the raid of 7 July in the destruction of Caen. Caen had been bombed and shelled repeatedly before 7 July and would be shelled again by German forces after 9 July. Air photos of Caen taken before Charnwood indicate widespread damage in central of Caen. The raid of 7 July had two aiming points, one of which included the northern suburbs of the city. There was, however, 'some spill into the heavily built-up areas to the south, where particularly heavy destruction was caused.' Copp, *Montgomery's Scientists*, 73.

81 The original plan prepared by staff officers at Leigh-Mallory's AEAF Headquarters proposed to use both Bomber Command and the U.S. 8th Air Force to deliver tons of bombs on a ten-square-mile area known to be occupied by enemy troops. The final plan was a compromise between those who advocated the independent use of heavy bombers against 'areas known to be occupied by the enemy' and bombing as part of a major offensive. T.C. Trail to Air Vice Marshall H.E.P. Wigglesworth, 7 July 1944, PRO, WO 232/51.

82 Ellis, *Victory*, 316. He suggests that I Corps casualties were 'about 3,500' but gives no source. Canadian casualties (Stacey, 163) were 1,194, of which 230 were fatal. The 59th Division suffered 1,070 killed, wounded, and missing. War Diary, 59th Division, 9 July 1944. PRO, WO 171/571. 3rd British Division casualties appear to have been considerably less.

83 War Diary, 3rd (British) Infantry Division 8 July 1944.

84 Meyer, *History*, 141.

85 War Diary, 1/7 Royal Warwickshire Regiment, 8 July 1944.

86 Allan Snowie, *Bloody Buron* (Erin, ON, 1984) 54–76.

87 Tony Foulds, 'In Support of Canadians,' 78. Foulds, then a troop commander, walked the battlefield the next day and counted the thirteen

destroyed tanks. The British troop lost six of its 8 M10s in the battle, but four were repairable. Letter, T. Foulds to Terry Copp, April 1999.
88 Reginald Dixon, *Autobiography* (Ottawa, 1998), 17. War Diary, Stormont Dundas and Glengarry Highlanders, 8 July 1944.
89 War Diary, Canadian Scottish Regiment, 8 July 1944.
90 Roy, *Canadians*, 258.
91 Brown and Copp, 96–108.
92 Meyer, *History*, 147.
93 War Diary, Royal Winnipeg Rifles, 8 July 1944.
94 Ellis, *Victory*, 318
95 Ibid., 319.

5. STALEMATE?

1 Situation Reports, 33.
2 Quoted in Ellis, *Victory*, 322. Rommel as well as the other senior leaders in the west shared the view that a second landing was imminent.
3 German divisions scheduled to arrive in mid-July included the 271st and 272nd, both from the south of France, and the 326th from 15th Army. This left nine static coastal divisions, two field infantry divisions, and 116th Panzer Division north of the Seine. Ellis, *Victory*, 333, and Niklas Zetterling, *Normandy 1944* (Winnipeg, 2000), 396ff.
4 In his postwar interview for the U.S. Army, Eberbach elaborated on the necessity of a defence in depth to buy time for a political solution to the war. MS B840, 13.
5 Situation Reports, 44.
6 Ibid., 45.
7 Hinsley, 200–1.
8 Martin Blumenson, *Breakout and Pursuit* (Washington, 1961), 36–43.
9 Alfred D. Chandler (ed.), *The Papers of Dwight D. Eisenhower* (Baltimore, 1970), 3:1797.
10 Ibid., 3:1982.
11 Ibid., 3:2081.
12 One estimate suggests that British infantry battalions were short 4,600 men on 1 July 1944. Russel Hart, 'Learning Lessons: Military Adaptation and Innovation in the American, British, Canadian and German Armies during the 1944 Normandy Campaign' (PhD thesis, Ohio State University, 1997), 431.
13 Canadian casualties as of 22 July were 8,512 of whom 2,433 were killed in action or died of wounds. NAC, RG 24, vol. 10669.

14 Cited in Copp and McAndrew, 130.

15 D'Este, *Decision*, 282, 283.

16 The 49th (West Riding) Division joined I British Corps and thus the First Canadian Army on 23 July. The reasons for the transfer from XXX Corps were the subject of much discussion among the senior officers of the division, who were puzzled by the decision. Interview, Brig. Trevor Hart Dyke with Terry Copp. The 49th Division was one of the formations reporting a high battle exhaustion ratio, and this may have been a factor.

17 Letter, Crocker to Dempsey, 5 July 1944, Crerar Papers.

18 Letter, Dempsey to Montgomery, 7 July 1944, Crerar Papers.

19 Minutes, 7th Canadian Infantry Brigade Conference, War Diary, 7 Canadian Infantry Brigade, 23 June 1944.

20 Cunningham interview.

21 War Diary, 1 East Suffolk Regiment, PRO, WO 171/381, and War Diary, 2 East Yorkshire Regiment, PRO, WO 171/397.

22 This view was freely offered by officers of 51st Highland Division, who attended a lecture given by the author at the University of Edinburgh, October 1996.

23 Montgomery to Allan Brooke, 15 July 1944, quoted in full in D'Este, 274.

24 English, 189.

25 Typescript, 31 pages, no title, no date. NAC, MG 27 III B II, vol. 54 (Ralston Papers). The document can readily be identified as the work of Lt.-Gen. Ken Stuart, and the date as late-1943.

26 Letter, Col. E.A. Coté, to Terry Copp, 30 March 2001. Col. Coté wrote an account of his impressions of Keller and the staff of 3rd Division in response to my request. Coté was the divisional assistant adjutant and quartermaster general.

27 J.L. Granatstein, *The Generals* (Toronto, 1993), 167.

28 Ibid.

29 English, 127.

30 Ibid., 208.

31 For a full discussion of the Crerar–Montgomery relationship, see Paul D. Dickson, 'The Hand That Wields the Dagger: First Canadian Army Command and National Autonomy,' *War and Society* 13, no. 2 (1995), 113–41.

32 Granatstein, 166.

33 Interview, Gordon Brown, 1998.

34 Granatstein, 167.

35 Ibid.

36 Montgomery to CIGS, 14 July 1944, BLM 126/12.

37 Interviews, Terry Copp with senior officers serving at the First Canadian

Army Headquarters (Lt.-Gen. W. Anderson, Brig.-Gen. George Pangman, Lt.-Col. Leslie Chater). Relatively few British officers were in fact appointed.

38 Brian Horrocks, *Corps Commander* (London, 1977), 157.

39 Stephen Hart comes to a similar conclusion in his chapter 'Crerar and First Canadian Army,' S. Hart, *Montgomery*, 155–83.

40 Diary of Elliot Rodger, NAC, RG 24, vol. 10797.

41 The text of the address was recorded by Maj. T.A. Sesia, OC, 2nd Field Historical Section. It is reproduced in 'General Simonds Speaks,' *Canadian Military History* 8, no. 12, 64–76.

42 War Diary, Fort Garry Horse, 12 July 1944.

43 'Censorship Reports 21 Army Group,' NAC, RG 24, vol. 10784. The following quotations are from the 'Canadian Mail' sections of these reports.

44 Chandler, 1964.

45 War Diary, Queen's Own Rifles, June 1944, Appendix 3.

46 Copp and McAndrew, 113.

47 Copp and McAndrew, 126. The DDMS, Second British Army, recorded 1,835 battle exhaustion casualties in the period 6 June to 1 July, with divisional rates varying from very low (6th Airborne and 15th Divisions) to very high 3rd (Br), 43rd, 49th, 51st. War Diary, DDMS, Second British Army, June–July 1944, PRO, WO 177/321; Copp and McAndrew, 131–2.

48 Terry Copp, 'Counter Mortar Operational Research in 21 Army Group,' *Canadian Military History* 3, no. 2 (1994), 45–51. The report is reproduced in Copp, *Montgomery's Scientists*. An earlier version was circulated as an attachment to the minutes of the First Meeting of Second Army Counter Mortar Committee, 8 August 1944, NAC, RG 24, vol. 10464. The First Canadian Army committee met to consider these recommendations on 26 July 1944, PRO WO 171/263

49 Copp, *Montgomery's Scientists*, 437.

50 HQ RCA, 'First Canadian Army Notes No. 1,' NAC RG 24, vol. 14306, 23–6.

51 Ibid., 26.

52 Copp, *Montgomery's Scientists*, 435.

53 Copp, 'Counter Mortar,' 50–1.

54 Copp, *Montgomery's Scientists*, 435.

55 The questionnaire and the 'combat lessons' submitted by brigades, battalions, and regiments are in NAC, RG 24, vol. 10925.

56 8th Canadian Infantry Brigade, 'The Barrage in the Attack,' NAC, RG 24, vol. 10925.

57 7th Canadian Infantry Brigade, 'Combat lessons.'

58 Ibid.

59 Ibid.
60 2nd Canadian Armoured Brigade, 'Combat Lessons.'
61 Ibid.
62 AORG Report No. 196, 'The Accuracy of Anti-Tank Gunners,' July 1944. PRO, WO 291/196.
63 Copp, *Montgomery's Scientists*, 395–8.
64 Ibid., 399–408
65 Interview, Terry Copp with Tony Sargeaunt, May 1989, and Tony Sargeaunt 'The Evolution of Tank Tactics in the Second World War,' 1990. This brief, four-page paper was written for the author from memory to reflect a note Sargeaunt had prepared on this topic in 1944.
66 Letter Tony Sargeaunt to Terry Copp, 22 June 1990. Elements of Sargeaunt's suppressed forecast are evident in the post-action report he wrote on 'Goodwood.' Copp, *Montgomery's Scientists*, 81–2.

6. OPERATION GOODWOOD – ATLANTIC

1 21 Army Group Intelligence Summary, 9 July 1944, and Stacey, *The Victory Campaign*, 165.
2 Montgomery's directive M-510 is discussed by Ellis, *Victory*, 327, and Stacey, *Victory Campaign*, 165.
3 Ibid.
4 O'Connor Papers, 11 July 1944, LHCMA, 5/3/16.
5 PRO, WO 205/644, quoted in D'Este, 331.
6 D'Este, *Decision*, 333.
7 John Baynes, *The Forgotten Victor: General Sir Richard O'Connor* (London, 1989), 183.
8 The debate can be followed in Ellis, *Victory*, 327–32.
9 Martin Blumenson, *Breakout and Pursuit* (Washington, 1961), 187–9.
10 British Army of the Rhine (BAOR), *Battlefield Tour, Operation 'Goodwood,'* 9 DHH.
11 H.G. Martin, *The History of the 15th Scottish Division* (Edinburgh, 1948), 66. The plans for Greenline and Pomegranate did not reflect the advice offered by General O'Connor.
12 Ellis, *Victory*, 334.
13 Stacey, *Victory Campaign*, 165.
14 BAOR, 'Goodwood,' 23–9.
15 The enemy was deceived as to the timing and scale of Goodwood and was in fact more concerned about the area west of the city, but a general offensive was expected and there were no additional reserves available to deploy. Meyer, *History*, 157.

16 According to Meyer, 158, the 88 mm battery was also responsible for the destruction of two Tigers, which were erroneously targeted at long range.

17 Military Operational Research Unit (MORU), *Report No. 23 Operation 'Goodwood'* (1946), 24, Shepherd Archives, LCMSDS.

18 BAOR, 'Goodwood,' 41–4. General O'Connor was critical of 7th Armoured for its failure to move forward more quickly. It seems likely that the GOC General Erskine and his Armoured Brigade commander Brig. Hynde, who regarded the entire plan as a pointless sacrifice of the armoured regiments were content to proceed cautiously. See R.N. O'Connor, 'Notes on "Goodwood" Meeting,' 26 July 1944, NAC, RG 24, vol. 10554.

19 MORU, 'Report ...,' 24.

20 War Diary, Queen's Own Rifles, July 1944, Appx 18, 'Attack on Factory Area ...' and War Diary, 1st Hussars, July 1944.

21 MORU, 'Report ...,' 18.

22 The QORs took more than two hundred prisoners from the two formations. War Diary Queen's Own Rifles, 18 July 44. See also 'Memorandum of Interview with Lt. J.C. Auld 22 July 44,' DHH.

23 The Divisions Operations log times this at 2130, the Corps log at 2230. The quote is from the 2nd Canadian Corps Ops Log 'Op. Atlantic,' 18 July 1944, NAC, RG 24, vol. 10797.

24 MORU, 'Report ...,' 18.

25 The 1st Hussars War Diary says that C Squadron was assigned to the Chaudières. War Diary, 1st Hussars, 18 July 1944.

26 War Diary, Stormont Dundas and Glengarry Highlanders, 18 July 1944.

27 War Dairy, 1st Hussars, July 1944, Appx 9, 'Account of Action by "C" Sqn 18 July 44.'

28 War Diary, Stormont Dundas and Glengarry Highlanders, 18 July 1944.

29 The alternative plan and timings are noted in II Canadian Corps Ops Log, 18 July 1944. For a fuller version of the action of the Reginas, see Brown and Copp, 117–18.

30 MORU, 'Report ...,' 19.

31 'Interview Lt.Col. D.B. Buell, 27 July 44,' DHH. Buell reported that the area had been 'well bombed,' with many German dead, but that some survivors 'resisted fiercely' and the area was not clear of snipers until 0600 the next morning.

32 Stacey, *Victory Campaign*, 176.

33 Granatstein, 173–5.

34 Interview with Brig. George Pangman, Cambridge, Ontario, 1990.

35 Paul Dickson, 'Harry Crerar' (PhD thesis, University of Guelph, 1993), 584.

36 Before the division went into action, Rockingham was sent on a staff course

and Whitaker promoted to command the battalion. Whitaker was wounded on 14 July, and Rockingham returned to command the battalion in Operation Spring. Interview, Brig.-Gen. Denis Whitaker, Oakville, Ontario, 1999.

37 The appointments are noted in Stacey, *Victory Campaign*, Appx G.

38 D.G. Goodspeed, *Battle Royal* (Toronto, 1962), 418.

39 Terry Copp, *The Brigade: The Fifth Canadian Infantry Brigade, 1939–1945* (Stoney Creek, ON, 1992), 39–40, and interview with Maj.-Gen. W.J. Megill, Kingston, 1990. Megill provided written permission to review his personnel file at the National Personnel Records Centre, NAC.

40 Copp, *The Brigade*.

41 Crerar Papers, vol. 3.

42 Friedrich Schack, *272nd Infantry Division (15 December 1943–26 July 1944)*, United States Army Military History Institute, MS B 540.

43 Total casualties at Louvigny on 18 July were thirty-four killed and seventy-seven wounded. See George Blackburn, *The Guns of Normandy* (Toronto 1993), 161–5 for a description of the battle.

44 'Account of the Attack on Louvigny Night 18–19 July,' Sgt. O.C. Tyron, 21 July 44, and 'Account ...,' Lt. Tomas Wilcox, 21 Jul 44, DHH.

45 '"Account ..." Maj. T.F. Whitley,' 20 July 44, DHH.

46 At 1630, Simonds still hoped to 'take out Louvigny' but ordered 5th Brigade to cross the Orne and prepare for a possible advance to Fleury-sur-Orne that night. II Canadian Corps Ops Log, 18 July 1944.

47 War Diary, Royal Highland Regiment of Canada, July 1944. The operation is described in Copp, *The Brigade*, 52–5.

48 II Canadian Corps Ops Log, 19 July 1944.

49 War Diary, Highland Light Infantry of Canada, 19 July 1944.

50 BAOR, 'Goodwood,' 49.

51 O'Connor, 'Notes' 26 July 1944.

52 MORU, 'Report,' 19.

53 BAOR, 'Goodwood,' 52.

54 II Canadian Corps Ops Log, 19 July 1944.

55 Simonds, 'Operational Policy.'

56 War Diary, Régiment de Maisonneuve, 19 July 1944. This account of 5th Brigade's actions on 19 July is adapted from Copp, *The Brigade*, 55–9.

57 Schack, 7.

58 The Pt. 67 memorial was created through the co-operative efforts of the Toronto Scottish Regiment, the village of St-Martin-de-Fontenay, and the Canadian Battle of Normandy Foundation. It was officially opened in July 2000.

59 War Diary, Sherbrooke Fusiliers, 19 July 1944.

60 War Office, *The Co-operation of Tanks with an Infantry Division* (May 1944), 5.

61 Copp, *The Brigade*, 57.

62 War Diary, Queen's Own Cameron Highlanders of Canada, 19 July 1944. See also Lt. Gunther Schmidt, 'My Experiences During the Invasion: A Memoir' (5 pages), author's collection, courtesy of Colonel Jacques Ostiguy.

63 Copp, *The Brigade*, 60.

64 Historical Section (GS), *Report No. 58.* 95, DHH.

65 Lt.-Gen. Sir Miles Dempsey, 'Operation "Goodwood" Notes 1952,' NAC, RG 24, vol. 10554.

66 All quotations in the paragraph are from II Canadian Corps Ops Log, 19 July 1944.

67 Simonds noted that it would be necessary to 'pause' on 21 July to 'get all guns forward including 8 AGRA,' Canadian Ops Log, 19 July 1944.

68 Ibid., 20 July 1944

69 BAOR, 'Goodwood,' 59.

70 Report No. 58, 98.

71 War Diary, 6th Canadian Infantry Brigade, 20 July 1944.

72 The best information on the day's events are in Lt.-Col. Gauvreau, 'Account of the Actions of the FMRs 19–25 Jul,' 28 July 1944, and Capt. Maurice Gravel, 'Attack on Beauvoir and Troteval Farms 20 Jul 44,' 28 July 1944, DHH. See also War Diary, Toronto Scottish Regiment, 20 July 1944.

73 'A' Squadron of the First Hussars also supported the FMR attack. War Diary, 1st Hussars, 20 July 1944.

74 The 27th Canadian Armoured Regiment, Operation Atlantic, 31 July 1944, 17. War Diary, Sherbrooke Fusiliers, July 1944.

75 Gauvreau, 'Account ...'

76 War Diary, South Saskatchewan Regiment, 20 July 1944.

77 The divisional historical officer interviewed six South Saskatchewan Regiment officers on 23 July 1944. Each produced 'an Account of the attack by S. Sask R. on the High Ground 0459 in the Afternoon of 20 July 44.' Together with the War Diary, these accounts permit a fairly detailed reconstruction of events. DHH.

78 War Diary, South Saskatchewan Regiment, 20 July 1944.

79 The most detailed account of the Essex action is contained in the letter Lt.-Col. MacDonald wrote to Maj.-Gen. Foulkes to protest his removal from command of the battalion. NAC, MG 30 E480.

80 II Canadian Corps Ops Log, 19 July. Simonds seems to have envisaged his corps boundary as including the high ground west of the Orne, with the village of Bully 'exclusive to XII Corps.'

81 War Diary, Queen's Own Cameron Highlanders of Canada, 20 July 1944.
82 These events are outlined in 27 CAR, 'Op Atlantic.'
83 This account is based on the War Diaries of 6th Canadian Infantry Brigade and the Essex Scottish as well as the letter McDonald to Foulkes. See note 79.
84 McDonald to Foulkes, see note 79.
85 Copp, *The Brigade*, 59.
86 The 27th Canadian Armoured Regiment, 'Operation Atlantic.'
87 II Canadian Corps Ops Log, 21 July 1944.
88 Schmidt, 3.
89 Copp, *The Brigade*, 60–2.
90 Ibid., 62.
91 Figures are from D'Este, *Decision*, 385, Ellis, *Victory*, 334, Stacey, *Victory Campaign*, 176, and MORU, 27–31. Battle exhaustion estimates are based on War Diary, DMS, the Second British Army, and War Diary, No. 2 Canadian Exhaustion Unit.
92 Dempsey, interview with Chester Wilmot, quoted in D'Este, *Decision*, 387.

7. OPERATION SPRING

1 War Diary, Panzer Group West, 18 July 1944, LCMSDS.
2 Ibid., 19 July 1944.
3 Ibid., and *Situation Report*, 46–7.
4 2nd British Army Intelligence Summary, 24 July 1944.
5 Ibid., 4 August 1944
6 Ibid., 29 July 1944
7 First Canadian Army Intelligence Summary, 23 July 1944.
8 Second British Army Intelligence Summary, 29 July 1944.
9 Letter, Hausser to Kluge, 21 July 1944, *Situation Report* 47–8.
10 To those familiar with the ground in Normandy, Montgomery's failure to mount offensive operations on the axis Vimont–St-Pierre-sur-Dives is puzzling. I British Corps was never strong enough to carry out a major operation, but why wasn't it strengthened?
11 *Situation Report*, 48.
12 Ibid., 46.
13 Systematic interrogation of German prisoners captured in the week after the attempted assassination revealed that few had heard of the events. When informed, very few indicated support for the army officers involved in the plot. Second British Army Intelligence Report, 29 July 1944, Appx A, 'PW Reactions to the Attempt on Hitler's Life.'

14 Eisenhower to Montgomery, 21 July 44, Chandler, 2018.
15 Montgomery to 'Simbo,' 21 July 1944 (Maj.-Gen. Frank Simpson, Military Secretary to the War Office), Montgomery Papers.
16 Eisenhower to Montgomery, 23 July 1944. Stacey, *Victory Campaign*, 183.
17 Montgomery to Eisenhower, 24 July 1944. Stacey, *Victory Campaign*, 183.
18 GOC's Activities, War Diary, II Canadian Corps, 20 July 1944.
19 2 Canadian Corps, Ops Log, 22 July 1944.
20 Copp, *The Brigade*, 62.
21 2nd Canadian Corps, Operational Instruction No. 3, 23 July 1944, and the Operational Orders of the four divisions involved in 'Spring' are in the Corps War Diary. See also, Stacey, 186–7. The most detailed description of Simonds's intentions is found in the War Diary of 2nd Canadian Field Historical Section. Maj. A.T. Sesia attended the 23 July conference and recorded Simonds's remarks.
22 O'Connor to Adair, 24 July 1944, O'Connor Papers, 5/3/22.
23 Bayne, 208–9.
24 I am indebted to Lt.-Col. Roman Jarymowycz, who has helped clarify this and other matters related to the operations south of Caen.
25 This and the following paragraphs on 5th Brigade in 'Spring' are based on chapter 4 of Copp, *The Brigade*.
26 Interviews with Calgary Highlander veterans are cited in Copp, *The Brigade*, 39. For a somewhat different interpretation and a more favourable view of MacLaughlan, see David J. Bercuson, *Battalion of Heroes* (Calgary, 1994), 80.
27 Lt.-Col. Maclaughlan, 'Account of the Attack by the Calg Highrs on Maysur-Orne,' 6 pages, 28 July 1944, DHH.
28 Lt. Mageli, 'Account ...,' 29 July 1944, DHH.
29 Message Log 24 July 1944, War Diary, 5th Canadian Infantry Brigade.
30 Maclaughlan, 'Account ...'
31 Lt. Morgandeem, 'Account ...,' 29 July 1944, DHH.
32 Lt. John Moffat, 'Account ...,' 29 July 1944, DHH.
33 Lt. Michon, 'Account ...,' 29 July 1944, DHH.
34 Lt. Mageli, 'Account ...'
35 Michael Reynolds, *Steel Inferno* (London, 1997), 191.
36 War Diary, Royal Hamilton Light Infantry, 25 July 1944.
37 Lt. Col. J. Rockingham, 'Account ...,' n.d. DHH.
38 Maj. J. Dextrase, 'Account of a Coy Attack on Troteval Farm,' 30 July 1944, DHH.
39 Rockingham, 'Account ...'
40 Capt. J. Williamson, 'Account ...,' 5 August 1944, DHH.
41 Rockingham, 'Account ...'

42 Maj. Halliday, 'Account ...,' 4 August 1944, DHH.

43 Rockingham 'Account ...'

44 In an interview Brig. Cunningham, replying to a direct question as to whether he was pessimistic about Spring replied, 'No, I don't think if you are a commander that you would ever put your troops into action in a pessimistic frame of mind.' Later in the interview he commented with some emotion: 'The thing I always felt was that it would have been a hell of sight better if they just left Tilly alone.' Cunningham, interview transcript, 13, 18.

45 Lt.-Col. C. Petch, 'Report on the Attack on Tilly-la-Campagne,' 28 July 44.

46 Ibid.

47 2 Canadian Corps War Diary, 'GOC's Activities,' 25 July 1944.

48 2 Canadian Corps 'Ops Log,' 25 July 1944.

49 Ibid.

50 Ibid.

51 The following paragraphs are based on pages 77–86 of Copp, *The Brigade*, and on conversations with individuals involved in the events since the publications of that book. The timings and exact sequences of some of the events cannot be demonstrated with certainty.

52 Maj. E. Bennett, 'Account ...,' 1 August 1944, DHH.

53 Personnel file, Maj. Phillip Griffin, NAC, Personnel Records Centre.

54 Bennett, 'Account ...'

55 Sgt. Benson, 'Account ...,' 1 August 1944, DHH.

56 Michon, 'Account ...'

57 'Memorandum of an Interview with Maj. W.E. Harris, M.P. 24 Jan 1946,' DHH.

58 Ibid.

59 Interviews, Terry Copp with Maj.-Gen. W.J. Megill, 1989 and 1992.

60 Jarymowycz, 'Canadian Armour,' 169.

61 Harris, 'Memorandum ...'

62 Capt. John Taylor to Lt.-Col. D.H. Taylor, 15 August 44. Taylor Personnel File, Archives Black Watch (Royal Highland Regiment) of Canada, Montreal.

63 Pte. M. Montreuil, 'Account ...' 1 August 1944, DHH. Sgt. M. Roulston, who was with Griffin on the ridge, recalls Griffin saying, 'Let's get the hell out of here ... We turned left. I got a few steps and was shot through the thigh, he continued a short distance and was killed.' Letter, MacGregor Ralston to Terry Copp, 16 February 2000.

64 Stacey, *Victory Campaign*, 192.

65 Ibid.

66 For a review of the controversy see David Bercuson and S.F. Wise (eds), *The Valour and the Horror Revisited* (Montreal, 1994).

67 'Intelligence Report on the Rocquancourt–St-Martin-de-Fontenay Iron Mines,' II Canadian Corps Intelligence Summary, 29 July 1944.

68 Patrick Delaforce, *Churchill's Desert Rats* (Stroud, UK, 1994), 57–8.

69 Ibid., 58–9.

70 Hamilton, 758–90.

71 Brig. Megill recalled a conversation with the OC of a squadron of the County of London Yeomanry who said quite flatly that he did not believe the operation was on. Megill interview. Erskine's views seem quite reasonable in light of the Second British Army intelligence report issued at the end of Goodwood (2359, 19 July, 1944). It estimated that the flak corps alone had seventy to one hundred 88 mm guns in position, while 1st SS Panzer Division was thought to muster 60 MK IVs, 20 MK Vs, 35 assault guns, and 70 antitank guns 'over 50 mm' in their 4000-metre-wide defensive zone. It was less than 4000 metres from their left flank at Verrières to the Orne, where 272nd Division with 9 assault guns and 27 antitank guns was supported by battlegroups of the 2nd and 9th SS Panzer Divisions, with the potential to bring another hundred armoured fighting vehicles into action.

72 Goodspeed, 429.

73 Blackburn, 254–6.

74 Stacey, *Victory Campaign*, 193. On 28 July the Royals received 254 replacements in addition to the 80 they had obtained after the battle for Louvigny. Blackburn, 256.

75 Bird, 175

76 War Diary, Stormont, Dundas and Glengarry Highlanders, 25 July 1944.

77 Cunningham interview, notes. Brig. Cunningham talked about these events freely when the tape-recorder was turned off. I have also consulted tape-recorded conversations between Christiansen and Petch provided by Reg Dixon.

78 See note 77.

79 CMHQ, *Report No. 150*, 138.

80 War Diary, 6th Canadian Infantry Brigade, 25 July 1944.

81 Copp, *The Brigade*, 83, and interviews with Col. Jacques Ostiguy, Brig. W.J. Megill.

82 War Diary, 6th Canadian Infantry Brigade, 25 July 1944.

83 Maj.-Gen. Foulkes recalled: 'General Simonds had already issued orders to continue that evening and was in such a rage when I arrived at his H.Q. to tell him that I had no intention to continue the battle as I had nothing left to fight with.' DHH 83/269.

84 'Memorandum of an Interview with Lt.-Gen. G.G. Simonds, 1946,' DHH.
85 Stacey, *Victory Campaign*, 194. The North Nova casualties are for 24–6 July.
86 Jarymowycz, 'Canadian Armour,' 137–8.
87 Stacey, *Victory Campaign*, 194–5.
88 2 Canadian Corps Intelligence Summary, 25 July 1944.
89 War Diary, 2 Canadian Corps, 26 July 1944.
90 Dempsey Papers. The entry for 25 July 1944 states that Dempsey met with Simonds at 2130. Dempsey told Simonds 'to halt where he is, hold all ground gained, no further attacks without reference to me.'
91 Cunningham interview.
92 Megill interview.
93 Ibid.
94 Ibid.
95 Ibid.

8. FALAISE

1 Martin Blumenson, *Breakout and Pursuit* (Washington, 1960), 247–53.
2 Operations Log, Panzer Group West, 28 July 1944.
3 Montgomery's Directive M515, 27 July 1944.
4 The author has examined the ground over which Bluecoat was fought and consulted the War Diaries and regimental histories for the period of the offensive. J.J. How, *Normandy: The British Breakout* (London, 1981), is currently the best published account of this operation, which requires further study.
5 Stacey, *Victory Campaign*, 201.
6 Ibid.
7 Copp and McAndrew, 120. As veterans of 3rd Division have often recalled, the army's idea of rest involved 'inspections every day' and training with brief periods off duty.
8 Stacey, 204.
9 The full text of Simonds's address is printed in *Canadian Military History* 8, no. 2 (1999), 69–80.
10 For accounts of the second battle for Tilly see Copp, *The Brigade*, 92–4, and Ken Tout, *The Bloody Battle for Tilly* (Stroud, UK, 2000), 103–7. The best account is David Pattterson, 'The Battles for Tilly-la-Campagne,' unpublished paper, Laurier Military History Conference, 2001.
11 CMHQ Report No. 50, 31 July 1944.
12 Operations Log, Panzer Group West, 30 July 1944.
13 Ellis, *Victory*, 396–8.

14 Montgomery letters of 1 and 2 August, BLM 94/7, 94/8. Eisenhower wrote to Marshall on 2 August emphasizing the need to secure Brittany, Chandler, 2048.

15 Directive M516, BLM 126/17.

16 The original 'Notes' Appreciation and Outline Plan for Totalize are grouped in File 225C2.012 (D10), RG 24, vol. 10799. Afterwards, Totalize File.

17 Notes, Corps Commanders Conference, 30 July 1944. Ibid.

18 Ibid.

19 Ibid.

20 II Canadian Corps Intelligence Summary, 2 August 1944.

21 Ibid., 5 August 1944.

22 Ibid., 6 August 1944.

23 Letter, G.G. Simonds to H.D.G. Crerar, 6 August 1944, Totalize File.

24 British Army of the Rhine (BAOR) *Battlefield Tour Operation Totalize* (Germany, 1947).

25 Directive M517, 6 August 1944, BLM 126/18.

26 Ralph Bennet, *Ultra in Normandy* (London, 1979), 115.

27 In his memoirs Maj.-Gen. George Kitching (GOC 4th Canadian Armoured Division) claimed that at a second meeting with Simonds on 7 August he and Maj.-Gen. Maczek protested against the narrow frontages allotted to their divisions but failed to convince Simonds. Once the decision to employ both armoured divisions was made, there was no realistic way of increasing the frontages even if Simonds had wished to. George Kitching, *Mud and Green Fields* (Langley, 1986), 210. It should be noted that in a 1981 interview with Dr Reginald Roy, Kitching did not refer to this problem and instead emphasized traffic control problems and the rigidity imposed by the timing of the Phase II bombing. DHH 81/150.

28 War Diary, 10th Canadian Infantry Brigade, 2 August 1944.

29 War Diary, Lake Superior Regiment (M), 7 August 1944; and War Diary, Canadian Grenadier Guards, 7 August 1944. 'Halpenny Force,' named for Lt.-Col. W.W. Halpenny, CO of the Canadian Grenadier Guards, also contained an antitank battery and a squadron of engineers.

30 War Diary, 2nd Canadian Field Historical Section, 6 August 1944.

31 Royal Canadian Artillery, II Canadian Corps, Operational Instruction No. 5, 7 August 1944, NAC, RG 24, vol. 10799.

32 Ibid.

33 NDHQ Historical Section, *Training of the 4th and 5th Canadian Armoured Divisions, October 1941–July 1944*, Report No. 43 (Ottawa, 1951).

34 'Simonds Lecture,' BAOR, *Totalize*.

35 Royal Canadian Artillery, Operational Instruction No. 5.
36 Based on conversations with veterans of 51st Highland Division who served in Normandy, Edinburgh, October 1996.
37 Salmond, 150–3.
38 On 7 August, 2nd Canadian Infantry Division was short 1,407 other ranks, almost all riflemen. This was the equivalent of the combat soldiers of three battalions. The 3rd Division reported a deficiency of 249 ORs, 4th Division 212. 'Deficiencies and Holding of Canadian Infantry Other Ranks, North-West Europe, 9 June 1944 to 28 April 1945,' NAC, RG 24, vol. 10669.
39 Report by AFV(T), First Canadian Army, 2 August 1944, NAC, RG 24, vol. 10460.
40 Answers to Tank Gunnery Questionnaire in ibid. See also the interview with Brig. S.V. Radley-Walters in Portugal, vol. 5, 2488.
41 Report by AFV(T).
42 War Diary, 2nd Canadian Field Historical Section, Appendix 1; A.T. Sesia, 'All in a Day's Work.'
43 CMHQ Historical Section, *Canadian Operations 1–23 August* (London, 1948), paragraph 43.
44 Situation Reports, 54.
45 Ibid., 55.
46 Second British Army Intelligence Summary, 8 August 1944.
47 Knight, 66–8.
48 Meyer, *History*, 169.
49 Colonel H. Neitzel, 'Activity of the 89th Infantry Division,' July 1946, MS B-012.
50 Colonel H. Neitzel, '89th Infantry Division in Battles on the Invasion Front,' MS B425, Grenadier Regiment 1056, Regimental Order 4 August 1944, II Canadian Corps Intelligence Summary, 8 August 1944.
51 Ibid., 3.
52 Ibid., 3.
53 No. 2 ORS Report No. 8, printed in Copp, *Montgomery's Scientists*, 95–8.
54 War Diary, Royal Regiment of Canada, 8 August 1944.
55 Neitzel, '89th Infantry Division in Battles,' 3.
56 Alistair Borthwick, *Battalion* (London, 1994), 143. See also Tout, *Bloody Battle for Tilly*, 196–7.
57 Maj. Courtenay, Account of the Attack by South Saskatchewan Regiment on Rocquancourt, 10 August 1944, DHH.
58 Maj. Brochu, Account of the Attack and Capture of May-sur-Orne, 12 August 1944, DHH.
59 John Graham, Account of the Attack by the Camerons of Canada on Fontenay-le-Marmion, 11 August 1944, DHH.

60 Lt.-Col. A.D. Marks, Account of C Squadron 6CAR, Action at Fontenay-le-Marmion, 17 June 1946, DHH.
61 Nicholson, 317.
62 Quoted in Jody Perrun, 'Missed Opportunities: First Canadian Army and the Air Plan for Operation Totalize' (MA thesis, Carleton University, 1999) 129.
63 Telephone Notes Totalize – 7 August 1944. NAC, RG 24, vol. 10797.
64 Meyer, *History*, 172.
65 K. Tout, *A Fine Night for Tanks* (Stroud, 1998), 89; Stacey, *Victory Campaign*, 223–4; Perrun, 133–9.
66 Air Aspects of Totalize and Tractable Extracts from RAF Narrative, 3; NAC, RG 24, vol. 10794.
67 Neitzel, '89th Infantry Division in Battle,' 5.
68 Air Aspects of 'Totalize' and 'Tractable' 3.
69 Stacey, *Victory Campaign*, 223.
70 War Diary, Canadian Grenadier Guards, 8 August 1944.
71 Ops Log HQ, II Canadian Corps, Serial 69, 'leading troops crossed line ... at 1335–1400 hours.'
72 Operational Report, 1st Polish Armoured Division, 3.
73 2nd Canadian Infantry Division Operational Order No. 2, 7 August 1944, and 'Ops log,' 8 August 1944, NAC, RG 24, vol. 13751.
74 War Diary, Canadian Grenadier Guards, 8 August 1944.
75 War Diary, Argyll and Sutherland Highlanders, 8 August 1944.
76 Meyer, *History*, 124.
77 Neitzel, '89th Infantry Division in Battles,' 7.
78 Meyer, *History*, 126.
79 Stacey, *Victory Campaign*, 225.
80 Operational Report, 1st Polish Armoured Division, 3.
81 War Diary, Lake Superior Regiment, 9 August 1944.
82 War Diary, Canadian Grenadier Guards, 8 August 1944.
83 Maj. L.C. Monk, 'An Account of the Battle Participation of the Algonquin Regiment Between 6 and 11 August 1944,' 11 pages, DHH 4.
84 War Diary, 4th Canadian Armoured Brigade, Log Ops/Int., 9 August 1944.
85 Stacey, 228.
86 Operational Report, 4.
87 Monk, 5.
88 General Brereton reported the success of column cover to his RAF colleagues on 27 July 1944. Notes of CinC Meetings, Stanmore, May 1944 to August 1944, PRO, Air 37/1126.
89 G. Hayes, *The Lincs* (Alma, 1986), 100–3.

90 *The Regimental History of the Governor General's Foot Guards* (Ottawa, 1948), 100–3.
91 War Diary, 1st Canadian Army, Ops log, 9 August 1944.
92 Robert L. Fraser, *Black Yesterdays, The Argylls War* (Hamilton, 1996), 226–7. Hayes, 31–2.
93 Ops log, II Canadian Corps, 10 August 1944.
94 War Diary, Canadian Grenadier Guards, 9 August 1944.
95 Fraser, 227–9.
96 War Diary, 8th Canadian Infantry Brigade, August 1944, Appendix 3, 'The Attack on Quesnay Woods.' Brig. Blackader, the acting divisional commander, outlined a plan for another three-phase operation, with 8th Brigade launching the first phase. War Diary, Historical Officer, 3rd Canadian Infantry Division, 10 August 1944.
97 Meyer, *History*, 180.
98 Outline Plan, Future Operations, 11 August 1944. 2 pp. Totalize File.
99 Prisoner of war figures are from II Canadian Corps intelligence summaries. 12SS casualties, Meyer, *History*, 182. *Canadian Fatalities: Canadian Army Statistics – War 1939–1945*, Fatal Casualties North West Europe, NAC, RG 24, vol. 18825.
100 GOC's Activities, 1–30 August, Totalize File.
101 Quoted in Graham, 154.
102 Chester Wilmot, Queries for General Simonds, ND, Liddel Hart Archives LH/S/IS/130.
103 BAOR, *Totalize*, 33.
104 English, 291.
105 Stacey, *Victory Campaign*, 276.

9. VICTORY IN NORMANDY?

1 Blumenson, *Breakout and Pursuit*, 494, Eisenhower, who was at Bradley's headquarters when the decision was made, told Marshall that Patton's 'marching wing . . . will turn towards Alençon and Falaise.' This suggests that Patton was not the only one thinking in terms of an encirclement. Eisenhower to Marshall, 9 August 1944, Chandler, 2062.
2 Directive M518, 11 August 1944, BLM 126/19.
3 Hinsley, 260.
4 M87, Personal For CIGS from General Montgomery, 2245, 11 August 1944, BLM 110/38.
5 Blumenson, *Breakout and Pursuit*, 502–3.
6 Ibid., 504. The message was timed at 0040, 13 August 1944.

7 M89, 2200, 12 August 1944.
8 Bradley, 298.
9 Ibid.
10 War Diary, Lt.-Gen. M.C. Dempsey, PRO, WO 285/9.
11 The entry, which is fully quoted in D'Este, *Decision*, 440–1, is from PRO, Air 37/574. D'Este reproduces the words exactly, but it is evident that the diarist is mistaken in placing the Third Army north of Falaise.
12 Blumenson, *Breakout and Pursuit*, 504.
13 M90, 2235, 13 August 1944.
14 Ibid.
15 M86, 2220, 10 August 1944.
16 The official British history of the campaign devotes one paragraph to this operation, Ellis, *Victory*, 427. The best published account is in Knight, 66–8. I have consulted the War Diaries of Second British Army and the War Diaries of the divisions and brigades involved. PRO, WO 171/201. As with so many other actions involving elements of 2nd British Army, little published material of any value is available.
17 The ground on which this battle was fought is virtually unchanged and can easily be examined. The distance from the start line at la Moissonniere to Pt 182 above Bois-Halbout is 6 kilometres and includes two distinct ridges.
18 This statement is based on examination of the map, Potigny, France, 1:25000 Edition, of 6 August 1944, LCMSDS map collection.
19 Paul Danhauser, '271st Infantry Division (August 12–28, 1944),' MS B529, provides a good description of the fighting from the German perspective. All Welch battalions used this spelling, though the division was known as the 53rd (Welsh).
20 War Diary, II Canadian Corps, GOC's Activities, 11 August 1944.
21 War Diary, RHLI, 12 August 1944.
22 Danhauser, 3–4.
23 Denis and Shelagh Whittaker, *Victory at Falaise: The Soldier's Story* (Toronto, 2000), 150–2. The Riley's terrible experience at Barbery contrasts sharply with the previous successful actions carried out by the battalion, which suggests the importance of chance and circumstance in the history of even the most consistently effective units.
24 Goodspeed, 447–8.
25 The Royals were especially bitter that the attacks of 13 August were planned without adequate tank or artillery support. Both the divisional and brigade commanders came forward to Lt.-Col. Anderson's headquarters to press for action, even though artillery support was not available. The

'General's Cake-Walk' cost the battalion twenty killed in action and seventy-four wounded. See Goodspeed; also see W.R. Bennett, 'Moulines,' 12–13 August, 1 page, N.D., LCMSDS Archives.

26 War Diary, 53rd Division, 13 August 1944.

27 Copp, *The Brigade*, 103–4.

28 Danhauser, 4. The Second British Army Intelligence Report for 16 August includes a captured document detailing the orders issued to 271st Division to withdraw 'to the prepared second line' on the night of 12–13 August. Battle Group Brehmer, which had defended Thury-Harcourt, was to maintain contact with 277th Infantry Division on its left.

29 War Diary, 2nd Canadian Infantry Division, Ops Log, 13–14 August. The War Diaries of the regiments concerned and the account of the night action by the Camerons' intelligence officer, Lt. Bruce Marshall, provide details of the well-executed night attack. Lt. Bruce Marshall, Account of the Attack on La Cressonniere ..., DHH.

30 Meyer, *History*, 184.

31 See Notes on Corps Commanders Outline Talk, 1000, 13 August, RG24, vol. 13,751, and Outline of Instructions, 4th Canadian Armoured Division, 1200, 13 August, War Diary, 4th Canadian Armoured Division.

32 '"O" Group Conference by GOC 2 Canadian Corps 13 August 1944,' 3 pages. War Diary, 2nd Field Historical Section, August 1944.

33 Stacey, 237. The new orders were presented to Simonds after his final review of 'Tractable' on the morning of 13 August.

34 The 51st Highland Division, restored to I British Corps, and 49th West Riding Division were responsible for the long eastern flank, stretching back to Caen and beyond. The Highlanders were to protect the Canadian flank, following up enemy withdrawals.

35 Outline of Instructions, II Canadian Corps.

36 Outline of Instructions, 4th Canadian Armoured Division.

37 The air plan is outlined in Stacey, *Victory Campaign*, 238–45.

38 2 Corps Operations Log, 14 August 1944.

39 The 2nd Canadian Armoured Brigade, Operation Tractable, NAC, RG 24, vol. 10992.

40 Meyer, *History*, 184. Despite heavy losses in Tractable, enough of the division survived Normandy to become the core of Battle Group Chill, the force that the Fifteenth Army used as its 'fire brigade' in holding the line north of Antwerp in October 1944. The division was reported to consist of 3,000 men on 1 September 1944. Zetterling, 236.

41 Meyer, *History*, 184.

42 The War Diary of the Fort Garry Horse lacks details. This account is based

on the regimental history, *Vanguard*, 55–7. See also Eddie Goodman, *The Life of the Party*, and the interview with Goodman in Portugal, vol. 3, 1476.

43 Both the War Diary and regimental history lack detail. The quotations are from 'Memorandum of an Interview with Lt.-Col. R.S. Colwell and Maj. J.E. White,' 20 August '44, DHH. This interview, with 'Lessons Learned,' was widely distributed within the Royal Armoured Corps. 21 Army Group RAC Liaison Letter No. 3. NAC, RG 24, vol. 10554.

44 War Diary, Governor General's Foot Guards, 14 August 1944.

45 War Diary, Canadian Grenadier Guards, 14 August 1944.

46 Lt.-Col. M.J. Scott commanded the brigade for the next twenty-four hours despite a broken ankle.

47 War Diary , Lake Superior Regiment, 14 August 1944.

48 War Diary, Stormont Dundas and Glengarry Highlanders, 14 August 1944.

49 War Diary, Régiment de la Chaudière, 14 August 1944.

50 Boss and Patterson, 161.

51 A.T. Harris, 'Report on the Bombing of Our Own Troops during Operation "Tractable,"' 25 August 1944, 12 pp., LCMSDS Archives.

52 Stacey, *Victory Campaign*, 243.

53 Copp and McAndrew, 141.

54 Unfortunately, No. 2 ORS did not investigate the accuracy of the bombing in Tractable or examine evidence of German losses. The very detailed investigation carried out by the RAF only looked at the ground where the short bombing occurred. PRO, Air 14/861.

55 M 93, 2240 hours 14 August.

56 Meyer, *History*, 185.

57 War Diary, 4th Armoured Brigade, 15 August 1944.

58 This account is based on the diaries of the units involved.

59 A number of such incidents are reported in the War Diaries. See War Diary, Lake Superior Regiment, 15 August 1944.

60 All quotations are from the War Diary, Canadian Grenadier Guards, 15 August 1944.

61 Meyer, *History*, 185.

62 War Diary, Canadian Scottish Regiment, 15 August 1944.

63 War Diary, Royal Winnipeg Rifles, 15 August 1944.

64 War Diary, Canadian Scottish Regiment, 15 August 1944. See also the account in Roy, 287. Roy's interviews with Canscot veterans, including Lt.-Col. Meldrum, who commanded the battalion on 15 August, are in DHH and the University of Victoria archives.

65 English, 298–9.

66 Montgomery first assigned Falaise to the Canadian Army, then to the British, and finally, on 14 August, back to the Canadians. Stacey, 249–50.

67 1st Polish Armoured Division, Operational Report, 10.

68 Meyer, *History*, 185.

69 Blumenson, *Battle of the Generals*, 222.

70 M94, 2230, 15 August 1944.

71 Blumenson, *Battle of the Generals*, 225–9.

72 War Diary, 10th Canadian Infantry Brigade, 16 August 1944. Also, War Diary, 4th Canadian Armoured Division, 16 August 1944. It is apparent that XII Corps also used the day to reorganize, launching new attacks on the evening of 16 August. MS B529 and War Diary, 53rd Welsh Division, 16 August 1944.

73 War Diary, Canadian Grenadier Guards, 16 August 1944. War Diary, Governor General's Foot Guards, 17 August 1944.

74 War Diary, 6th Canadian Infantry Brigade, 16 August 1944.

75 War Diary, Fusiliers Mont-Royal, 17 August 1944. See also Maj. Brochu, 'Account of the Capture of the Monastery in Falaise,' DHH, and Meyer, *History*, 189–91.

76 Meyer, *History*, 187.

77 1st Polish Armoured Division, Operational Report, 11.

78 M97, 2245, 16 August 1944.

79 Hinsley, 262n and 264–6.

80 Little attention has been paid to the enemy's use of the roads to and from Gacé, including the N138 to Bernay. The Chambois–Gacé road was closed on 19 August by 2nd French Armoured Division.

81 Stacey suggests that Bradley was given such orders by phone about the same time (1530 hours) that Crerar was told to accelerate the capture of Trun. Montgomery made no reference to such orders in his nightly summary. Stacey, *Victory Campaign*, 251.

82 Blumenson, *Breakout and Pursuit*, 527.

83 War Diary, 4th Canadian Armoured Division, 16–17 August 1944.

84 Meyer, *History*, 192.

85 Cassidy, 105.

86 War Diary, 4th Canadian Armoured Division, 17 August 1944.

87 War Diary, Canadian Grenadier Guards, 17 August 1944.

88 War Diary, 10th Canadian Infantry Brigade, 17 August 1944.

89 Operational Report, 1st Polish Armoured Division, 11.

90 Blumenson, *Battle*, 235.

91 Stacey, *Victory Campaign*, 252.

92 Operational Report, 1st Polish Armoured Division, 11.

93 M98, 2230, 17 August 1944.

94 Ellis, *Victory*, 444.

95 War Diary, 4th Canadian Armoured Division, 18 August 1944.

96 Stacey, *Victory Campaign*, 257–8.

97 Air Marshal Coningham asked the U.S. 9th Tactical Air Force to keep its aircraft out of the 2nd TAF area, as American pilots were making 'sustained attacks on Canadians.' So too were the pilots of 83 Group. War Diary, AEAF Operations and Plans, 18 August 1944, PRO, Air 37/594.

98 Ibid.

99 2 Canadian Corps, 'GOC's Activities, 18 August 1944. The Grenadier Guards began to advance into Trun at 1423 but did not occupy it until 1848. Operators Log, 4th Canadian Armoured Division.

100 Operational Report, 1st Polish Armoured Division, 11–12.

101 War Diary, 4th Canadian Armoured Division, 18 August 1944.

102 War Diary, 10th Canadian Infantry Brigade, 18 August 1944.

103 Donald Graves, *South Albertas: A Canadian Regiment at War* (Toronto, 1998), 140.

104 War Diary, 4th Canadian Armoured Brigade, 18 August 1944 'Operators Log.'

105 Hinsley, 267–8.

106 Operations Log, II Canadian Corps, 18 August 1944.

107 War Diary, AEAF Operation and Plans, 19 Aug. 1944.

108 Heinz Guderian, *From Normandy to the Ruhr with the 116th Panzer Division* (Bedford, 2001), 85.

109 Blumenson, *Breakout and Pursuit*, 534–5. Only two of the 80th Division's three regiments were present, and only one was used in the attack.

110 M100, 2255, 18 August 1944.

111 M101, 2300, 18 August 1944.

112 2 Canadian Corps 'GOC's' Activities, '19 August 1944.

113 War Diary, 4th Canadian Armoured Division, 19 August 1944.

114 Operational Report, 1st Polish Armoured Division, 13.

115 Whitaker, 243–6. Blumenson, *Breakout*, 541.

116 Ops Log, II Canadian Corps, 19 August 1944.

117 War Diary, 4th Canadian Armoured Division, 19 August 1944; War Diary, 4th Canadian Armoured Brigade, 19 August 1944.

118 Graves, 143.

119 Ops Log, 10th Canadian Infantry Brigade, 19 August 1944.

120 Graves, 149.

121 Fraser, 238–9.

122 Ops Log, 10th Canadian Infantry Brigade, 19 August 1944.

123 Hinsley, 268.
124 War Diary, Stormont Dundas and Glengarry Highlanders, 20 August 1944.
125 Meyer, *History*, 197.
126 M103, 2210, 19 August 1944.
127 M519, 20 August 1944.
128 War Diary, Second British Army, 18 August 1944.
129 War Diary, 53rd Welsh Division, 19 August 1944.
130 Operator's Log, 10th Canadian Infantry Brigade, 20 August 1944.
131 War Diary, 53rd Recce Regiment, 20 August 1944, PRO, WO 171/565.
132 Operator's Log, 10th Canadian Infantry Brigade, 20 August 1944.
133 Operator's Log, 4th Canadian Armoured Brigade, 20 August 1944.
134 Graves, 160–70, provides a full account. The citation for Maj. Currie's Victoria Cross is reproduced in Copp and Vogel, *Maple Leaf Route: Falaise*, 132.
135 War Diary, Lincoln and Welland Regiment, 20 August 1944
136 War Diary, North Nova Scotia Highlanders, 20 August 1944.
137 Graves, 170.
138 Ops Log, 10th Canadian Infantry Brigade, 21 August 1944.
139 Whitaker and Whitaker, 277.
140 Meyer, *History*, 199.
141 One study by an author determined to show that very large numbers of the enemy escaped gives an estimate of 44,800 for the period midnight 19 August to 1600 21 August. In the absence of evidence, one may suppose whatever one wishes. Michel Dufresne, 'Normandie, heurs et mal heurs d'un fin de campagne,' *Revue Historique des Armées* 168 (Sept. 1989), 48–60. See also Michel Dufresne, 'La succes Allemand sur la Seine (Aout 1944), 'Revue Historique des Armées' 176 (Sept. 1989). 48–60.
142 Operational Report, 1st Polish Armoured Division, 15.
143 II Canadian Corps, 'GOC's Activities,' 20 August 1944.
144 Kitching, 204–5.
145 According to Simonds, Kitching 'has not shown in operations that grip of the situation and that power of definite command so requisite in divisional commander.' J.L. Granatstein Papers, York University Archives, Kitching File.
146 War Diary, Canadian Grenadier Guards, 21 August 1944.
147 Copp, *Montgomery's Scientists*, 181–205.

10. NORMANDY: A NEW BALANCE SHEET

1 On 29 September the German Commander-in-Chief West reported losses

of 371,400 soldiers and total losses of 460,900 when naval and air elements were included. Stacey, *Victory Campaign*, 270. The surrender in the Mons Pocket is described in Blumenson, *Breakout*, 684–5. Niklaus Zetterling, *Normandy 1944*, (Winnipeg, 2000), argues that losses in Normandy were just over 200,000 to 22 August. He does not calculate further losses. Army Group B placed its losses at 158,930 up to 14 August and 75,000 1 to 25 September, but did not report losses for 15 to 31 August.

2 The quotation is from John Gooch's Preface to *Place*, vii.

3 John Ellis, *Brute Force* (London, 1990), 361.

4 Stacey, *Victory Campaign*, 650.

5 Wilmot, 278–9.

6 Stacey, *Victory Campaign*, 118.

7 Ibid., 277.

8 The quotations are from *Command of Troops*, the basic statement of the German Army's doctrine, quoted in Van Creveld, 28–9.

9 Roman Jarymowycz, 'The Quest for Operational Manouevre' (PhD thesis, McGill University 1998), 89–90

10 As usual, little has been said about the contributions of the Camerons of Ottawa, the machine gun and mortar battalion, 7th Recce Regiment, 17th Duke of Yorks Hussars, and 3rd Anti-Tank Regiment, RCA. Their story is so thoroughly integrated into the experience of the infantry battalions that it is impossible to separate it, but they too shared in the achievement of a solid bridgehead.

11 The manpower problem in 21 Army Group is discussed in D'Este, *Decision*, chapter 15, and in Stephen Hart, 'Montgomery, Morale, Casualty Conservation and Colossal Cracks: 21st Army Group Operational Technique in North-West Europe 1944–45' *Journal of Strategic Studies* 19, no. 4 (December 1996): 141–50. The specifically Canadian situation is described in E.L.M. Burns, *Manpower in the Canadian Army, 1939–45* (Toronto, 1956).

12 A.O.R.G. Report No. 181, 'Accuracy and Dispersion of Fire from a 25 Pounder Troop,' September 1943. The use of radar was first discussed in 1943. See the summary of radar development for army purposes in PRO, WO 291/1288. The inaccuracy of the 1:25,000 maps, based on the existing French survey, added to the problems of accuracy in predicted fire. Minutes of Staff Conference, 21 Army Group, 9 June 1944. NAC, RG 24, vol. 10564.

13 Copp, *Montgomery's Scientists*, 325.

14 Copp, 'Counter Mortar ...,' 49–51.

15 Copp, *Montgomery's Scientists*, 359–71.

16 Ibid., 373.

17 For a similar assessment of the impact of air power, see Zetterling, 37–53.
18 Foulkes, DHH 83/69.
19 On 27 June the First Canadian Army held 8,326 men in its replacement pool. It is not clear why there were not enough trained infantry available to meet a deficiency of less than 1,500 men a month later. Letter, Stuart to Crerar, 27 June 1944, Crerar Papers, vol. 3.
20 O'Connor to Maj.-Gen. G.L. Whistler, 23 August 1944, O'Connor Papers.
21 O'Connor to Montgomery, 24 August 1944, O'Connor Papers.
22 The positions were plotted and marked as 'Defense Overprints' on maps distributed before 8 August. LCMSDS Map Collection.
23 The lead elements of the Polish Armoured Division, which was located close to Bayeux, reached the bridges at Caen at 0630 on 8 August, but the infantry brigade did not cross until 1300. Operational Report, Polish Armoured Division 2.
24 Visitors to the Normandy battlefield should explore this area and the wide valley of the Dives, south of St-Pierre-sur-Dives with its considerable road networks. Conversations with Lt.-Col. Roman Jarymowycz on the differences between a corps and an army-level approach to these operations have helped clarify my ideas on this and other matters.
25 These statements are based on the respective divisional War Diaries.
26 Bruce Macdonald deposited a copy of the Officer's Confidential Report, calling for his dismissal as well as his protest against the action, in the National Archives of Canada, MG 30 E480.
27 Hayes, 32.
28 B.L.M. Montgomery, *Memoirs* (London, 1958), 277.

Bibliography

Archival Sources

Canada

National Archives of Canada, Record Group 24
  War Diaries
  Army, Corps, Divisional and Brigade Files, '200' Series.
  Crerar Papers, MG 30 E157
Directorate of History and Heritage, Department of National Defence
  Biographical Files
  Historical Officer Interviews

United Kingdom

Public Record Office
  WO171 21st Army Group War Diaries
  WO 291 Operational Research Reports
  Air 24, Air 41
Liddell Hart Centre for Military Archives, King's College London
  Allanbrooke Papers
  Chester Wilmott Papers
  O'Connor Papers
Imperial War Museum
  Montgomery Papers

United States

United States Army Military History Institute
  Bradley Papers
  World War II German Military Studies

Secondary Sources

Addison, Paul, and Jeremy Crang (eds). *Time to Kill: The Soldier's Experience of War in the West, 1939–1945.* London: Pimlico, 1997.
Ambrose, Stephen E. *Citizen Soldiers: The U.S. Army from the Normandy Beaches to the Bulge to the Surrender of Germany.* New York: Simon & Shuster, 1997.
– *The Victors: Eisenhower and His Boys: The Men of World War II.* New York: Simon & Shuster, 1998.
Barbé, Dominique. *Charnwood: La Battaile de Buron-Saint Contest.* Condé-sur-Noireau: Charles Corlet, 1994.
Barclay, C.N. *The History of the 53rd (Welsh) Division in the Second World War.* London: William Clowes, 1956.
Barnhill, David A. 'RAF Bomber Command and Tactical Air Support: Normandy 1944.' MA thesis, Wilfrid Laurier University, 1988.
Bates, Thomas J. *Normandy: The Search for Sydney.* Berkeley, CA: Bayes, 1999.
Bechthold, B. Michael. 'The Development of an Unbeatable Combination: U.S. Close Air Support in Normandy,' *Canadian Military History* 8, no. 1 (1999): 7–20.
Belfield, Eversley, and H. Essame. *The Battle for Normandy.* London: Pan, 1967.
Benamou, Jean-Pierre. *Battaille de Caen.* Bayeux: Editions Heimdal, 1988.
Bennett, Ralph. *Ultra in the West: The Normandy Campaign, 1944–45.* London: Hutchinson, 1979.
Bercuson, David. *Battalion of Heros: History of the Calgary Highlanders.* Calgary: Calgary Highlanders Regimental Funds Foundation, 1994.
Berger, Sid. *Breaching Fortress Europe.* Dubuque, IO: Kendall/Hunt, 1994.
Bidwell, Shelford. *Gunners at War.* London: Arms and Armour Press, 1970.
Blackburn, George. *The Guns of Normandy: A Soldier's Eye View, France, 1994.* Toronto: McClelland & Stewart, 1995.
Blumenson, Martin. *The Battle of the Generals.* New York: Morrow, 1993.
– *Breakout and Pursuit.* Washington: Center of Military History, 1961.
– *Patton: The Man behind the Legend.* New York: Morrow, 1985.
– (ed.). *The Patton Papers.* Boston: Houghton Mifflin, 1972.
Borthwick, Alastair. *Battalion.* London: Bâton Wicks Publications, 1994.

Boss, W., and W.J. Patterson. *Up the Glens: Stormont Dundas and Glengarry Highlanders, 1783–1994*. Cornwall, ON: Old Book Store, 1995.

Bradley, Omar. *A Soldier's Story*. New York: Henry Holt, 1952.

Bradley, Omar, and Blair Clay. *A General's Life: An Autobiography by General of the Army Omar N. Bradley*. New York: Simon & Shuster, 1983.

Brode, Patrick. *Casual Slaughters and Accidental Judgments*. Toronto: University of Toronto Press, 1997.

Brown, Gordon. 'The Attack on the Abbaye d'Ardenne,' *Canadian Military History* 4, no. 1 (spring 1995).

Brown, Gordon, and Terry Copp. *Look to Your Front ... Regina Rifles: A Regiment at War, 1935–45*. Waterloo: LCMSDS, 2001.

Brown, John Sloan. 'Col. Trevor N. Dupuy and the Mythos of Wehrmacht Superiority: A Reconsideration.' *Military Affairs* 50 (January 1986): 16–20.

Cameron, J. Robert. 'Two Days of My Six Year War.' *Canadian Military History* 4, no. 2 (1995): 82–4.

Carell, Paul. *Invasion: They're Coming*. New York: Bantam, 1964.

Carrington, Charles. *Soldier at Bomber Command*. London: Leo Cooper, 1987.

Cassidy, G.L. *Warpath*. Cobalt, ON: Highway Book Shop, 1990.

Chandler, Alfred D. (ed.). *The Papers of Dwight D. Eisenhower*. Vol. 3. *The War Years*. Baltimore: Johns Hopkins University Press, 1970.

Clay, E.W. *The Path of the 50th*. Aldershot: Galen and Pole, 1950.

Colby, John. *War from the Ground Up: The 90th Division in WWII*. Austin, TX: Nortex, 1991.

Cooper, Belton Y. *Death Traps*. Novato, CA: Presidio, 1998.

Copp, Terry. *The Brigade: The Fifth Canadian Infantry Brigade, 1939–1945*. Stoney Creek, ON: Fortress, 1992.

– *A Canadian's Guide to the Battlefields of Normandy*. Waterloo: Laurier Centre for Military Strategic and Disarmament Studies, 1994.

– 'Counter Mortar Operational Research in 21 Army Group.' *Canadian Military History* 3, no. 2 (1994): 6–21.

– 'Scientists and the Art of War: Operational Research in 21 Army Group.' *RUSI Journal* 136, no. 4 (1991): 65–70.

– (ed.). *Montgomery's Scientists: Operational Research in Northwest Europe, 1944–1945*. Waterloo: Laurier Centre for Military, Strategic and Disarmament Studies, 2000.

Copp, Terry, and Bill McAndrew. *Battle Exhaustion: Soldiers and Psychiatrists in the Canadian Army, 1939–1945*. Montreal: McGill-Queen's University Press, 1990.

Copp, Terry, and Robert Vogel. *Maple Leaf Route: Caen*. Alma: Maple Leaf Route, 1983.

– *Maple Leaf Route: Falaise*. Alma: Maple Leaf Route, 1983.

Cotey, Robert. 'The Battle for Verrières Ridge.' MA thesis, Wilfrid Laurier University, 2000.

Crookendon, Napier. *Dropzone Normandy*. London: Ian Allan, 1976.

Currie, Major David D. 'Story in His Own Words,' in *After the Battle: The Battle of the Falaise Pocket, Number 8*. Ed. Winston G. Ramsey. London: Britain Prints International, 1982.

Danchev, Alex, and Daniel Todman. *War Diaries, 1939–1945: Field Marshall Lord Alanbrooke*. London: Weidenfeld and Nicolson, 2001.

De Guingand, Major-General Sir Francis, KBE, CB, DSO. *Operation Victory*. London: Hodder & Stoughton, 1947.

Delaforce, Patrick. *Churchill's Desert Rats: From Normandy to Berlin with the 7th Armoured Division*. London: Alan Sutton, 1994.

D'Este, Carlo. *Decision in Normandy*. New York: Dutton, 1983.

– *Eisenhower: A Soldier's Life*. New York: Henry Holt, 2002.

– *Patton: A Genius for War*. New York: HarperCollins, 1995.

Dickson, Paul. 'The Hand That Wields the Dagger: Harry Crerar, First Canadian Army Command and National Autonomy.' *War and Society* 13, no. 2 (1995): 113–41.

– 'Harry Crerar.' Unpublished manuscript, 1996.

Dupuy, Trevor N. 'Mythos or Verity? The Quantified Judgement Model and German Combat Effectiveness.' *Military Affairs* 50, October 1986.

– *Numbers, Predictions and War*. Fairfax, VA: Hero Books, 1979.

Ellis, John. *Brute Force*. London: Viking, 1990.

– *Sharp End of War: The Fighting Men in World War II*. Newton Abbot, Devon: David & Charles, 1980.

Ellis, L.F. *Victory in the West*. Volume 1. London: HMSO, 1962.

English, John A. *The Canadian Army and the Normandy Campaign: A Study of Failure in High Command*. New York: Praeger, 1991.

Evans, Christopher. 'The Fighter Bomber in the Normandy Campaign: The Role of 83 Group.' *Canadian Military History* 8, no. 1 (1999): 21–36.

– *Tactical Air Power in the Normandy Campaign: The Role of 83 Group*. MA thesis, Wilfrid Laurier University, 1998.

Florentine, Eddy. *Battle of the Falaise Gap*. London: Elek, 1965.

Forbes, Charly. *Fantassin*. Quebec: Septentrion, 1994.

Foulds, Tony. 'In Support of the Canadians: A British Anti-Tank Regiment's First Five Weeks in Normandy.' *Canadian Military History* 7, no. 2 (1998): 71–8.

Fraser, Robert. *Black Yesterdays: The Argylls' War*. Hamilton: Argyll Regimental Foundation, 1996.

French, David. *Raising Churchill's Army*. Oxford: Oxford University Press, 2000.

Fritz, Stephen G. *Frontsoldaten: The German Soldier in World War II*. Lexington: University of Kentucky Press, 1995.

Graham, Dominick. *The Price of Command: A Biography of General Guy Simonds*. Toronto: Stoddart, 1993.

Graves, Donald E. *South Albertas: A Canadian Regiment at War*. Toronto: Robin Brass Studio, 1998.

– (ed.). *Fighting for Canada: Seven Canadian Battles, 1758–1945*. Toronto: Robin Brass Studio, 2000.

Gooderson, Ian. *Air Power at the Battlefront*. London: Cass, 1998.

Goodman, Eddie. *Life of the Party*. Toronto: Key Porter, 1998.

Goodspeed, D.J. *Battle Royal: A History of the Royal Regiment of Canada*. Toronto: Royal Regiment of Canada Association, 1962.

Greenfield, Kent Roberts, (ed.). *Command Decisions*. Washington, DC: Office of the Chief of Military History, United States Army, 1960.

Grodzinski, John. 'Kangaroos at War.' *Canadian Military History* 4, no. 3 (1995): 43–50.

Guderian, Heinz G. *From Normandy to the Ruhr with the 116th Panzer Division*. Bedford: Aberfona Press, 2001.

Hain, Alistair. 'The Calgary Highlanders: A Profile Based on Personnel Records.' MA thesis, Wilfrid Laurier University, 1990.

Hamilton, Nigel. *Monty: Master of the Battlefield, 1942–1944*. London: Hodder & Stoughton, 1983.

Harrison, Gordon A. *Cross Channel Attack*. Washington: Center of Military History, 1951.

Hart, Russell A. *Clash of Arms: How the Allies Won in Normandy*. Boulder: Lynne Rienner, 2001.

Hart, Stephen A. 'Field Marshall Montgomery, 21st Army Group and North West Europe, 1944–1945.' PhD thesis, University of London, 1995.

– *Montgomery and 'Colossal Cracks': 21st Army Group in Northwest Europe, 1944–45*. Westport, CT: Praeger, 2000.

Hart-Dyke, Trevor. *Normandy to Arnhem: A Story of Infantry*. Sheffield: Greemup and Thompson, 1966.

Hastings, Max. *Overlord: D-Day and the Battle of Normandy*. London: Pan, 1985.

Hayes, Geoffrey. *The Lincs: A History of the Lincoln and Welland Regiment at War*. Alma, ON: Maple Leaf Route, 1986.

Hesketh, Roger. *Fortitude: The D-Day Deception Campaign*. London: St Ermins Press, 1999.

Hinsley, F.H. *British Intelligence in the Second World War*. Vol. 3, Pt. 2. London: HMSO, 1981.

Hogg, Ian V. *The Guns, 1939–1945*. New York: Ballantyne, 1970.

Horn, Bern, and Stephen Harris. *Warrior Chiefs*. Toronto: Dundurn, 2001.

– *Generalship and the Art of the Admiral*. St Catharines: Vanwell, 2001.

Horrocks, Sir Brian, with Eversley Belfield. *Corps Commander*. London: Magnum Books, 1979.

How, J.J. *Hill 112*. London: William Kimber, 1984.

– *Normandy: The British Breakout*. London: William Kimber, 1981.

Ince, Jack. *Gunners of the 61st*. Stirling: self-published, 1997.

Isby, David C. (ed.). *Fighting the Invasion: The German Army at D-Day*. London: Greenhill Books, 2000.

Jamar, K. *With the Tanks of the 1st Polish*. Hengelo: H.L. Smith & Son, 1946.

Jarymowycz, Roman. 'Canadian Armour in Normandy: Operation Totalize and the Quest for Operational Manouevre.' *Canadian Military History* 7, no. 2 (1998): 19–40.

– 'Der Gegenangriff vor Verrières: German Counterattacks during Operation Spring, 25–6 July 1944.' *Canadian Military History* 2, no. 1 (1993): 75–89.

– *Tank Tactics from Normandy to Lorraine*. Boulder: Lynne Rienner, 2001.

Kitching, George. *Mud and Green Fields*. Langley: Battleline, 1986.

Knight, Peter. *The 59th Division*. London: Frederic Muller, 1954.

Lamb, Richard. *Montgomery in Europe*. London: Buchan and Enright, 1983.

Leinbaugh, Harold P., and John D. Campbell. *The Men of Company K*. New York: William Morrow, 1985.

Lindsay, Martin. *So Few Got Through: The Personal Diary of Lt. Col. Martin Lindsay*. London: Collins, 1946.

Lindsay, Martin, and M.E. Johnston. *History of the 7th Armoured Division*. Germany, 1945.

Lindsay, O. (ed.). *A Guards General: The Memoirs of Major-General Sir Alan Adair*. London: Hamish Hamilton, 1986.

Love, Robert W., Jr., and John Major (eds). *The Year of D-Day: The 1944 Diary of Admiral Sir Bertram Ramsay*. Hull, UK: University of Hull Press, 1994.

Luck, H. von. *Panzer Commander: The Memoirs of Colonel Hans von Luck*. New York: Praeger, 1989.

Luther, Craig W.H. *Blood and Honor: The History of the 12th SS Panzer Division 'Hitler Youth,' 1943–1945*. San Jose, CA: Bender, 1987.

Luttwak, Edward N. *Strategy: The Logic of War and Peace*. Cambridge: Harvard University Press, 2001.

Malone, Colonel Richard Sankey, OBE. *Missing from the Record*. Toronto: Collins, 1946.

Mansor, Peter R. *The GI Offensive in Europe, 1941–1945*. Lawrence: University of Kansas Press, 1999.

Margolian, Howard. *Conduct Unbecoming: The Story of the Murder of Canadian Prisoners of War in Normandy.* Toronto: University of Toronto Press, 1998.

Marshall, S.L.A. *Men against Fire.* New York: William Morrow, 1947.

Martin, Charles, with Roy Whitestead. *Battle Diary.* Toronto: Dundurn Press, 1994.

McAndrew, Bill, Donald E. Graves, and Michael Whitby. *Normandy 1944.* Montreal: Art Global, 1994.

Meyer, Hubert. *The History of the 12SS Panzer Division Hitlerjugend.* Winnipeg: J.J. Fedorowicz, 1992.

Meyer, Kurt. *Grenadiers.* Winnipeg: J.J. Fedorowicz, 1994.

Millett, Allan R., and Williamson Murray (eds). *Military Effectiveness.* Boston: Allen and Unwin, 1988, 3 Vols.

Milner, Marc. 'Reflections on the Bocage and the Gap: A Naval Historian's Critique of the Normandy Campaign.' *Canadian Military History* 7, no. 2 (1998): 7–18.

Montgomery, Field Marshal, the Viscount Montgomery of Alamein. *Normandy to the Baltic.* London: Hutchinson, 1946.

Morgan, Frederick E. *Overture to Overlord.* London: Hodder and Stoughton, 1950.

Morton, R.E.A. (ed.). *Vanguard: The Fort Garry Horse in the Second World War.* Winnipeg: Fort Garry Horse, 1945.

Nicholson, G.W.L. *The Gunners of Canada.* Vol. 2. Toronto: McClelland & Stewart, 1972.

Orange, Vincent. *Coningham.* London: Methen 1990.

Perrun, Jody. 'Missed Opportunities: First Canadian Army and the Air Plan for Operation "Totalize."' MA thesis, Carleton University, 1994.

Place, Timothy Harrison'. *Military Training in the British Army, 1940–1944.* London: Cass, 2000.

Portugal, Jean E. *We Were There.* 7 vols. Toronto: The Royal Canadian Military Institute, 1998.

Rawding, Brian G. 'To Close with and Destroy: The Experience of Canloan Officers.' MA thesis, Wilfrid Laurier University, 1998.

Reynolds, Michael. *Steel Inferno: 1st SS Panzer.* New York: Spellmount, 1997.

Ritgen, Helmut. *The Western Front 1944.* Winnipeg: Fedorowicz, 1995.

Roberts, G.P.B. *From the Desert to the Baltic.* London: William Kimber, 1987.

Rockingham, J.M. 'The Royal Hamilton Light Infantry at Verrières Ridge.' *Canadian Military History* 2, no. 1 (1993): 90–2.

Roy, Reginald H. *1944: The Canadians in Normandy.* Toronto: Macmillan and the Canadian War Museum, 1984.

– *Ready for the Fray.* Victoria: Canadian Scottish Regiment, 1958.

Salmond, J.B. *History of the 51st Highland Division, 1939–1953,* Edinburgh: privately published, 1953.

Shephard, Ben. *A War of Nerves: Soldiers and Psychiatrists, 1914–1994.* London: Pimlico, 2002.

Shephard, Ronnie. *Readings on Early Military Operational Research.* Shrivenham: Royal Military College of Science, 1984.

Shulman, Milton. *Defeat in the West.* London: Secker and Warburg, 1947.

Sirluck, Ernest. *First Generation.* Toronto: University of Toronto Press, 1996.

Smith, Wilfred L. *Code Word Canloan.* Toronto: Dundurn Press, 1992.

Snowie, Allan. *Bloody Buron.* Erin, ON: Boston Mills Press, 1984.

Spiller, Roger S. 'S.L.A. Marshall and the Ratio of Fire 1, no. 4.' *RUSI Journal* (1988).

Stewart, Neil S. *Steel My Soldiers Hearts.* Victoria: Trafford, 2000.

Stacey, Colonel Charles C.P. *Six Years of War.* Ottawa: Queen's Printer, 1955.

– *The Victory Campaign: North West Europe, 1944–1945.* Ottawa: Queen's Printer, 1962.

Stacey, Colonel Charles C.P., and Barbara Wilson. *The Half-Million: The Canadians in Britain, 1939–1946.* Toronto: University of Toronto Press, 1987.

Szygowski, Ludwick J. *Seven Days and Seven Nights in Normandy.* London: self-published, 1976.

Tout, Ken. *A Fine Night for Tanks: The Road to Falaise.* Stroud, UK: Sutton, 1998.

– *Tanks, Advance! Normandy to the Netherlands 1944.* London: Grafton Books, 1987.

– *The Bloody Battle for Tilly.* Thrupp, UK: Sutton, 2000.

Vance, Jonathan. *Death So Noble.* Vancouver: UBC Press, 1997.

Van Creveld, Martin. *Fighting Power: German and U.S. Army Performance, 1939–1943.* Westport, CT: Greenwood Press, 1982.

Vogel, Robert. 'Tactical Air Power in Normandy: Some Thoughts on the Interdiction Plan.' *Canadian Military History* 3, no. 1 (1994): 37–47.

Weigley, Russel. *Eisenhower's Lieutenants.* Bloomington: Indiana University Press, 1981.

Whitaker, Denis, and Shelagh Whitaker, with Terry Copp. *Victory at Falaise.* Toronto: HarperCollins, 2000.

Wilmot, Chester. *The Struggle for Europe.* London: Collins, 1952.

Zetterling, Niklaus. *Normandy, 1944.* Winnipeg: J.J. Fedorowicz, 2000.

Illustration Credits

Canadian Forces Photo Unit: A Halifax bomber, PL3028.

Department of National Defence: French children bathing, PMR 82-068; Nan Red Beach, St-Aubin-sur-Mer, PMR 82-072; A Sherman tank of the Canadian Grenadier Guards, PMR 82 387

Imperial War Museum: British infantry at work, BU 1335

Laurier Centre for Military Strategic and Disarmament Studies: A German 75 mm antitank gun; The results of air attacks; Air Photo (10 July 1944); Verrières village; Cromwell tanks; A German assault gun

National Archives of Canada: 9th Canadian Infantry Brigade began to land at Bernieres-sur Mer, NAC 131506; Mortar Crew, Regina Rifle Regiment, NAC 128 794; A Panzer tank, NAC 130 149; Canadian infantry searching, NAC 115 029; Field Marshall Montgomery, NAC 416 20: Maj.-Gen. R.F.L. Keller, NAC 129 170; Gunners W. Collins, NAC 169 319; Support Company, Highland Light, NAC 129 141; Men of the 8th Canadian Infantry, NAC 116 513; German prisoners of war, NAC 131 397; A Sherman tank of the Fort Garry Horse, NAC 133 977; Nursing sisters, NAC 108 174; Honourary Capt. Padre Jock Anderson, NAC 136 961; A crossroads on the Caen–Falaise Highway, NAC 129 137; The 4th Canadian Infantry Brigade, NAC 129 172; A section of infantry from the Fusiliers Mont-Royal, NAC 115 568; German soldiers surrendering, NAC 116 586

United States Airforce Archive: D-Day, Courseulles-sur-Mer, USAA7 Photo 52168

Index

THE JOANNE GOODMAN LECTURES

1976
C.P. Stacey, *Mackenzie King and the Atlantic Triangle* (Toronto: Macmillan of Canada 1976)

1977
Robin W. Winks, *The Relevance of Canadian History: U.S. and Imperial Perspectives* (Toronto: Macmillan 1979)

1978
Robert Rhodes James, 'Britain in Transition'

1979
Charles Ritchie, 'Diplomacy: The Changing Scene'

1980
Kenneth A. Lockridge, *Settlement and Unsettlement in Early America: The Crisis of Political Legitimacy before the Revolution* (New York: Cambridge University Press 1981)

1981
Geoffrey Best, *Honour among Men and Nations: Transformations of an Idea* (Toronto: University of Toronto Press 1982)

1982
Carl Berger, *Science, God, and Nature in Victorian Canada* (Toronto: University of Toronto Press 1983)

1983
Alistair Horne, *The French Army and Politics, 1870–1970* (London: Macmillan 1984)

1984
William Freehling, 'Crisis United States Style: A Comparison of the American Revolutionary and Civil Wars'

1985
Desmond Morton, *Winning the Second Battle: Canadian Veterans and the Return to Civilian Life, 1915–1930* (published with Glenn Wright as joint author, Toronto: University of Toronto Press 1987)

1986
J.R. Lander, *The Limitations of the English Monarchy in the Later Middle Ages* (Toronto: University of Toronto Press 1989)

1987
Elizabeth Fox-Genovese, 'The Female Self in the Age of Bourgeois Individualism'

1988
J.L. Granatstein, *How Britain's Weakness Forced Canada into the Arms of the United States* (Toronto: University of Toronto Press 1989)

1989
Rosalind Mitchison, *Coping with Destination: Poverty and Relief in Western Europe* (Toronto: University of Toronto Press 1991)

1990
Jill Ker Conway, 'The Woman Citizen: Translatlantic Variations on a Nineteenth-Century Feminist Theme'

1991
P.B. Waite, *The Loner: Three Sketches of the Personal Life and Ideas of R.B. Bennett, 1870–1947* (Toronto: University of Toronto Press 1992)

1992
Christopher Andrew, 'The Secret Cold War: Intelligence Communities and the East-West Conflict'

1993
Daniel Kevles, 'Nature and Civilization: Environmentalism in the Frame of Time'

1994
Flora MacDonald, 'An Insider's Look at Canadian Foreign Policy Initiatives since 1957'

1995
Rodney Davenport, *Birth of the 'New' South Africa* (Toronto: University of Toronto Press 1997)

1996
Ged Martin, 'Past Futures: Locating Ourselves in Time'

1997
Donald Akenson, *If The Irish Ran the World: Montserrat, from Slavery Onwards* (Montreal: McGill-Queen's University Press 1997)

1998
Terry Copp, *Fields of Fire: The Canadians in Normandy* (Toronto: University of Toronto Press 1993)

1999
T.C. Smout, 'The Scots at Home and Abroad 1600–1750'

2000
Jack P. Greene, 'Speaking of Empire: Celebration and Disquiet in Metropolitan Analyses of the Eighteenth-Century British Empire'

2001
Jane E. Lewis, 'Should We Worry about Family Change?'

2002
Jacklyn Duffin, 'Lovers and Livers: Disease Concepts in History'